American Realities

VOLUME II

Historical Episodes from Reconstruction to the Present

SEVENTH EDITION

J. WILLIAM T. YOUNGS

Eastern Washington University

Text illustrations by Cecily Moon

PEARSON
Longman

New York • San Francisco • Boston
London • Toronto • Sydney • Tokyo • Singapore • Madrid
Mexico City • Munich • Paris • Cape Town • Hong Kong • Montreal

Executive Editor: Michael Boezi
Executive Marketing Manager: Sue Westmoreland
Production Manager: Savoula Amanatidis
Project Coordination, Text Design, and Electronic Page Makeup: GGS Book
   Services, Inc.
Cover Design Manager: John Callahan
Cover Designer: Maria Ilardi
Cover Photo: Dale Kennington/Superstock
Manufacturing Buyer: Roy Pickering
Printer and Binder: R.R. Donnelley and Sons Company—Crawfordsville
Cover Printer: Phoenix Color Corporation

For permission to use copyright material, grateful aknowledgment is made
to the copyright holders on page 353, which are hereby made part of this
copyright page.

Library of Congress Cataloging-in-Publication Data

Youngs, J. William T. (John William Theodore), 1941–
    American realities : historical episodes / J. William T. Youngs ; text
illustrations by Cecily Moon. — 7th ed.
        v. cm.
    Includes bibliographical references and index.
    Contents: v. 1. From the first settlements to the Civil War — v. 2. From
Reconstruction to the present.
    ISBN 0-321-43345-9 (v. 1)—ISBN 0-321-43344-0 (v. 2)
    1. United States—History. I. Title.
    E178.6.Y68 2007
    973—dc22

                                                    2006031388

Please visit our website at http://www.ablongman.com.

ISBN 0-321-43344-0

5 6 7 8 9 10—DOC—11 10 09

To the memory of my mother and my father

Contents

Preface   vii

1. Beyond Emancipation

Booker T. Washington and the Atlanta Compromise   *1*

2. The New Industrial Era

The Rise of Andrew Carnegie   23

3. The Birth of Environmentalism

John Muir and the American Wilderness   45

4. Imperial America

Dewey and Aguinaldo at Manila Bay   65

5. New Immigrants

Russian Jews in the United States   85

6. Expanding American Democracy

The Woman Suffrage Victory   105

7. American Volunteers in World War I

The Lafayette Escadrille   123

8. Modernity Versus Tradition

The Scopes Trial and the American Character   151

9. The New Deal

Eleanor Roosevelt and the Politics of Compassion   181

10. Total War

The Bombing of Hiroshima   203

11. The Cold War at Home

Joseph McCarthy and Anticommunism   229

12. The Civil Rights Movement

Martin Luther King Jr. and the Road to Birmingham   257

13. Turmoil on the Campuses

Berkeley in the Sixties   281

14. America and the Cold War

*Colin Powell's Military Career from Vietnam
to the Persian Gulf*   303

15. The New Age of Technology

Steve Jobs and Apple Computer   327

Credits   353

Index   355

Preface

American history is an epic composed of many events: colonists made their homes in a new world; soldiers fought for independence; capitalists built giant industries; civil rights activists struggled for equality. In such episodes we encounter the emotions, thoughts, and experiences that made up the distinct worlds of the past. In the two volumes of *American Realities*, my goal has been to recreate some of those worlds, to capture the immediacy—the reality—of life as lived in other eras. I have not tried to reduce all these events to a single pattern, but in the aggregate, the chapters trace the course of American history from the distant past to the present.

Each chapter is designed to lead the reader to a better understanding of major themes in United States history. Each volume can be read by itself or in tandem with a conventional American history textbook. The standard surveys present the general patterns of the past; this book reveals in greater depth the life beneath those patterns.

These stories reveal the broad contours of American history as well as the illustrative particulars. The death of Thomasine Winthrop leads us to know Puritanism better, and the flight of the *Enola Gay* to Hiroshima exhibits the harsh outlines of total war. The Lewis and Clark Expedition reveals the marvelous land on which the nation developed, and Joseph McCarthy's career illuminates the turmoil of cold war politics.

While writing *American Realities*, I have often wished I had the novelist's poetic license to fill gaps not covered by the sources. But fortunately, facts can be as engaging as fiction. Documents are often colorful and evocative, allowing us to listen to the deathbed conversation of John and Thomasine Winthrop, to see the light of the South Pacific from a B-29, to enter imaginatively into the realities of other men and women.

Like ourselves, the people of the past were immersed in their times. But even while living fully in their own worlds, they bequeathed us ours. We can find historical kinship in the ordinary circumstances of daily life. George Washington is comprehensible because he was stunned when his army in Manhattan collapsed. John Muir is like most of us because he was troubled once about choosing a career. My touchstone in choosing topics for *American Realities* was that each should suggest our common humanity, even while revealing worlds distinct from our own. More simply, I had to care about the subjects and believe others could care about them as well. Through such sympathy, we come actually to live in history and feel our involvement with the past: his story and her story become our story.

The seventh edition of *American Realities* includes two new chapters, revisions in others, revised bibliographies, and study guides. These guides are intended to help readers understand the chapters better and to consider ways of exploring these historical materials in greater depth. They consist of brief summaries of the chapters, identification topics, study questions, and research topics. In Volume I, I have added a new chapter on John Woolman—the Quarker reformer—describing his efforts on behalf of justice for slaves, Indians, and the poor in pre-revolutionary America. In Volume II, I have described the role of Steve Jobs in the ongoing story of technological innovation in modern America.

The effort in *American Realities* to recreate history in words is supplemented by the imaginative drawings of Cecily Moon. Ms. Moon based her illustrations on careful reading of each chapter and on personal research in historical paintings and photographs. Each drawing highlights a major theme in the chapters.

Supplements

An Instructor's Manual is available to accompany *American Realities*. Written by Melinda Barr of Oklahoma City Community College in consultation with the author, this tool is designed to aid both the novice and experienced instructor in teaching American history. Each chapter includes a concise chapter overview, multiple choice questions, identification questions, and a list of topics for online research.

Acknowledgments

American Realities arrived at its present form with the help of many other scholars, writers, and editors. I am particularly grateful to Marian Ferguson, Dave Lynch, and Katie Carlone for their help on the first edition. A writer could not ask for more congenial and intelligent assistance in nurturing his ideas than these editors provided. The book also owes a great deal to the assistance of Clair Seng-Niemoeller, Frank Kirk, Lois Banner, Ron Benson, Peter Carroll, Joseph H. Cartwright, David Coon, Doris Daniels, Emmett M. Essin, Don Glenn, James Hunt, Donald M. Jacobs, Maury Klein, Ralph Shaffer, Julius Weinberg, Charles Baumann, Joseph Corn, James Gale, Richard Johnson, William Kidd, Nancy Millard, Sue Murphy, Robert Toll, Albert Tully, and my students in American History. For their help on previous revisions I am particularly grateful to Linda Stowe, Jay Hart, Russ Tremayne, Madeleine Freidel, August W. Giebelhaus, Emmett M. Essin, Paul W. Wehr, James L. Gormly, Guy R. Breshears, Larry Cebula, Matthew A. Redinger, Jason

Steele, Brenda Cooper, David Danbom, Paul Mertz, Carole Shelton, Bruce Borland, Michele DiBenedetto, Carol Einhorn, David Nickol, Matthew Kachur, Lily Eng, Jessica Bayne, Peter S. Field, Jim Hunt, Timothy Koerner, Jeffrey Roberts, Tom Russell, Laura White, Laura Loran, Jim Keenan, Jay O'Callaghan, Jennifer Ahrend, Victoria Fullard. Terri O'Prey, Eileen O'Sullivan, Kerrie Ann Pearson, Seán Reagan, Erin C. Stetler, V. Keven Shipman, Anna S. Meigs, Robert Dean, Ashley Dodge, Jacob Drill. Everett W. Kindig, Bruce Cohen, Catherine Tobin, James Hedtke, Scott Barton, Jolane Culhane, Wilson J. Warren, Dixie Haggard, and David Price.

For the Seventh Edition, I would especially like to thank William Furdell, University of Great Falls; Virginia Bellows, Tulsa Community College; Ted Kallman, San Joaquin Delta College; Robert Vitz, Northern Kentucky University; Archie McDonald, Austin State University; Harold Aurand Jr., Pennsylvania State University Schuylkill; Michael Boezi, Executive Editor at Longman Publishers, and his assistant, Vanessa Gennarelli; as well as Doug Bell at GGS Book Services and Stephanie Magean, who copyedited this edition.

Linda Youngs gave me many valuable suggestions when I began writing the book while she was busy pursuing her own schedule as a mother and an attorney. Finally, in dedicating *American Realities* to the memory of my mother, Marguerite Youngs, and my father, J. W. T. Youngs, I wish to recognize their part in helping me find my own place in history.

J. William T. Youngs
Eastern Washington University
jyoungs@ewu.edu

CHAPTER 1

Beyond Emancipation

Booker T. Washington and the

Atlanta Compromise

The long ordeal of slavery came to an end in 1865 for four million African Americans. Suddenly the freedom they had longed for during two centuries of bondage was theirs. The world opened before them: they could freely visit loved ones, attend schools, or run for public office. Blacks soon realized, however, that chains other than slavery still held them. Penniless, they could not afford to buy farms; untrained, they could not move into better jobs. In the 1870s and 1880s, they lost many of the privileges they had gained when freed, including the right to vote. Booker T. Washington grew to maturity in years when blacks experienced both the exhilaration of freedom and the humiliation of segregation. He proved in his early life that an ex-slave could prosper by hard work. When in his later years he saw the cords of prejudice tightening around his people, he responded in the best way he knew, advocating self-help in the face of prejudice and segregation.

As the parade moved through the streets of Atlanta on its way to the opening of the Cotton States Exposition, Booker T. Washington, riding in a carriage near the end of the procession, was deeply troubled. He was a black man who would soon address a white audience, and in the South of 1895 he could not be certain of a friendly reception. Washington's fears contrasted strangely with the jubilation around him. Here in a city that Sherman had laid in ruins only thirty years before, the buildings were decorated with American flags, and the citizens stood cheering a parade that symbolized the birth of a "new South." The procession ahead of Washington moved proudly along: white dignitaries in fine carriages, military officers glittering with gold trim and white helmets, rows of soldiers marching with bayonets gleaming in the sun, and a cannon rumbling jauntily over rough cobblestones.

Sitting in the hot sun at the back of this long parade with a cluster of African American soldiers and dignitaries, Washington felt the courage drain from his body. Thousands of blacks lining the road cheered when they saw him. But while their hands reached out to encourage him, they seemed to burden him with a heavy responsibility. How could he speak in a manner that would please whites while doing justice to his own race?

The Atlanta Exposition had been designed to celebrate the achievements of both races. But blacks had been accepted grudgingly. The committee that had invited Washington to speak had done so reluctantly, anticipating at first that he would take part only in the opening of a separate "Negro Building." Although Washington was belatedly included in the opening day ceremonies, his people would be segregated into a "jim crow" section of the auditorium, just as their exhibits were segregated in a separate hall. Booker T. Washington knew that he could easily alienate the whites and damage his people if he spoke carelessly. If he simply flattered the whites, however, he would let down his black supporters.

Washington's carriage entered the fairgrounds, a magical place with 189 acres of grounds set off by a white fence three miles long. Hillsides at its edge sloped down to a flat green plain dotted with pine trees. He saw a broad lake, speckled with gondolas, rowboats, and steam launches; buildings covered with domes, minarets, and angels; and a midway crowded with Germans, Mexicans, plantation blacks, and Native Americans dressed in traditional costumes.

The parade wound through this festive scene to the auditorium, a large building packed with noisy spectators who had waited an hour or more for the speakers to arrive. They yelled as the dignitaries entered and took their seats on a broad platform, cheering boisterously for Rufus Brown Bullock, a popular former governor of the state, and for Charles A. Collier, who had inspired the exhibition. When Booker T. Washington entered the hall, the jim crow section of the audience applauded wildly, but there was only scattered applause among the whites: "What's that nigger doing on the stage?" several asked.

Washington felt faint as he took his seat and glanced over the large audience. A bishop in a colorful robe gave an invocation. A man read a poem celebrating the opening of the fair. These rather conventional performances made Washington feel all the more uneasy about the unusual speech he would soon present. When Charles Collier spoke, he must have given Washington heart. He discussed the genesis of the fair and praised various groups of people who had helped. Women had proved by their part in the exposition that they deserved wider horizons for their work. Blacks had given proof "of the progress they have made as freemen." The audience listened politely.

Washington continued to wait for his turn to speak. The setting sun filled the windows of the auditorium, casting its beams on the speaker's platform. Another speaker, Mrs. Joseph Thompson, talked about the women's part in the fair. Her hands trembled as she spoke in a low, timid voice. Washington knew how she felt.

When she finished there was a musical interlude. A band played "The Star-Spangled Banner," and the audience cheered happily. Then the band played "Dixie," and the auditorium was filled with rebel yells. As his time to speak neared, Washington reflected: in a moment he would seek to compress a lifetime of experience into a ten-minute oration. Perhaps he thought about his own journey—his odyssey of hardship and triumph—to this place.

Booker T. Washington was born the property of James Borroughs on a plantation near Hale's Ford, Virginia, on April 5, 1856. His mother, Jane Ferguson, had "high ambitions for her children." Washington did not know who his father was, assuming merely that he lived on a neighboring plantation. He knew even less about his ancestors but remembered "whispered conversations among the colored people" about the hardships endured by their forebears on slaveships in the Middle Passage to America.

His world was the daily life on a small plantation in Virginia. His mother was cook for the estate, preparing meals for the big house in the fireplace in her own small cabin. From childhood Washington was put to work, cleaning the yard, carrying water to the men in the fields, and taking corn to the mill. In later years he could not recall any period of his life that had been devoted to play.

His home was a log cabin with a dirt floor. The wind blew freely through cracks in the walls and doorway, making it bitterly cold in the winter. At night the children lay on the dirt floor with only a pile of rags as bedding. They ate no regular meals as a family—snatching a bite here and there, eating from the skillet or from a pan balanced on their knees. Even the young slave's clothes were a burden: his wood-soled shoes hurt

Booker T. Washington's childhood home. This drafty one-room slave cabin had a dirt floor and cracks large enough for a cat to pass through.

his feet, and his rough flax shirts pricked his skin like "a hundred small pin-points."

Despite such hardships, Washington recalled that the slaves felt affection toward their owners. Slaves guarded the big house when the whites went off to fight in the Civil War, and Washington believed that they would have died to protect their masters. Slaves mourned almost as much as the whites when young "Mars Billy," eldest son of the owner, was killed in the war, and they competed with each other for the opportunity to watch over two other wounded sons. With the end of the conflict in sight, the slaves could be trusted to help their masters hide their valuables from marauding soldiers.

Memories of plantation hardships blended in Washington's mind with memories of a sentimental kinship between slave and owner. But such mutual affection did not dispel the blacks' desire for freedom—a desire that had grown year by year over the previous decades. Even before the war the slaves had heard about abolitionist activities in the North through a grapevine that reached even the most isolated blacks. They had learned about the election of Abraham Lincoln and followed the progress of the Civil War.

Out of deference to their southern masters, and perhaps from fear of punishment, they did not openly express their northern sympathies. But their excitement grew with each year of the war. Washington remembered awakening one night in his bed of rags and seeing his mother kneeling over her three children praying for the success of Lincoln's armies. The yearning for freedom pulsed through the slave quarters. Night after night blacks stayed up late to sing their plantation songs, which contained words about freedom. The slaves had once associated these words—for their master's benefit—with the next world, but now the songs took on a new, bolder tone; the slaves "were not afraid to let it be known that the 'freedoms' in these songs meant freedom of the body in this world."

At the end of the war the blacks were told to assemble outside the great house for an announcement. The master's family stood on the veranda while a visitor representing the U.S. government read the Emancipation Proclamation and told the slaves they were free. The blacks were ecstatic. Jane Ferguson kissed Booker and his brother and sister as tears ran down her face. All the newly freed blacks shouted and hugged one another, wild with joy.

Then a strange thing happened. Within a few hours the people became serious, even gloomy. Previously they had always thought of freedom merely as the removing of shackles. Without chains, it had seemed, life would be glorious. But now that the fetters had been removed, the people began to wonder what they would do with their lives. They realized that new trials would follow the blessing of freedom. Now they must plan for themselves. "It was very much like suddenly turning a youth of ten or twelve years out into the world to provide for himself," recalled Washington. "In a few hours the great questions with which the Anglo-Saxon race had been grappling for centuries had been thrown upon these people to be solved. These were the questions of a home, a living, the rearing of children, education, citizenship, and the establishment and support of churches."

Not all of these questions, of course, had to be settled at once. But the slaves did have to consider what they would do with their freedom. For the older people it was especially hard to contemplate moving. They had spent their lives on the plantation, and "deep down in their hearts," said Washington, "there was a strange and peculiar attachment to 'Old Marster' and 'Old Missus.'" Moreover, when the proclamation was read the owners themselves had seemed sad at the approaching loss of their people, at the departure of friends as well as workers. One by one the older slaves went up to the big house and carried on "whispered conversations" with their former masters. On the James Borroughs plantation and on other estates throughout the South some slaves chose to stay in their old homes, contracting with the owners to work on the lands with which they were so familiar.

But most ex-slaves wanted to do something to celebrate and observe their new freedom. Washington remarked that some blacks were content to leave the plantation for only a few days or weeks, simply "that they might really feel sure that they were free." Others reminded themselves of their new estate by changing their names. Throughout the South thousands of African Americans took on names of their Civil War heroes, including Sherman and Lincoln. Washington had been named Booker Taliaferro by his mother but chose the additional surname by which he became famous.

Many slaves tested their new independence by going west as pioneers in Oregon, Washington, and other distant places, or riding the range as cowboys. Others went north to join relatives in the old free states; still others simply migrated within the South looking for free land or city jobs.

Booker T. Washington and his family left the Borroughs lands. His mother had married a man on a neighboring plantation who had already fled from slavery on the heels of the Union army. Now this man, named Washington Ferguson, sent word from the Kanawah Valley in West Virginia that the family should join him. They set out across the mountains, traveling on foot and carrying their few possessions in a cart.

The family settled in Malden, West Virginia, in circumstances that showed little improvement over the years in slavery. They lived in a small cabin in an impoverished neighborhood where sanitary facilities were primitive and drunkenness was common. The boys worked long hours in the local salt furnaces and coal mines with their stepfather. Washington might easily have been overcome by poverty and hard work, but for the vision of a better life that drove him to improve himself.

Ever since he was a child on the plantation he had yearned for an education. When carrying books for the master's children, he had sometimes looked into the school and felt that "to get into a schoolhouse and study in this way would be about the same as getting into paradise." In his new home he used every opportunity to learn to read, first memorizing the number 18 marked on his stepfather's salt barrels, then pestering his mother until she bought him a copy of Webster's "blue-black" spelling book. When a young black man from Ohio opened a new school, he was one of its most enthusiastic students.

There was no uniform pattern of free education for blacks in the South, but the federal government's Freedman's Bureau supported many educational programs for the ex-slaves, and in time the bureau would contribute to the support of the Malden school. The school's funding came mostly from black families, who pledged cash support and took turns boarding the teacher. Washington felt that the desire to learn was not unusual among the newly freed blacks. Most had been denied an education under slavery, and now that they were free, literacy seemed one of the precious opportunities of their new condition. Not only did the children attend the new schools, but many older people went, hoping to read the Bible before they died. "It was," said Washington, "a whole race trying to go to school."

Booker T. Washington learned to read and write in the simple, crowded school that his people set up in Malden, West Virginia. In these years he worked as houseboy for Mrs. Viola Ruffner, a Vermont Yankee and the wife of Gen. Lewis Ruffner, one of the mining aristocracy of the Kanawah Valley. She demanded that everything around her be clean and orderly, and she would not tolerate slovenly behavior. These standards became part of the poor ex-slave's vision of civilized life.

In 1872, when Booker Washington was sixteen years old, his horizons widened once more, and he set off on the most daring enterprise of his young life. He had heard that a college for blacks, called the Hampton Institute, had been set up in Virginia. He was not even clear where it was, but he was determined to attend. His parents were skeptical, even his normally supportive mother fearing his departure from home would be "a wild goose chase." But he saved a small amount of money and set out one fall day to find the school. Most of his black neighbors could not go to college, but the old people sought to help him along: some gave him a quarter, others a nickel or a handkerchief. Booker Washington carried with him the hopes of all the blacks in the Kanawah Valley.

His journey to the Hampton Institute has an epic quality, like Benjamin Franklin's flight from Boston to Philadelphia a century and a half before. Both men left home with little money in their pockets and endured hardships along the way; both arrived impoverished in a new home but triumphed over their circumstances.

When Washington left home, he was not certain exactly where he was going; he simply headed east across the mountains and learned quickly how difficult it was for a black man to travel in the white South. He was allowed to ride on a stagecoach across the Allegheny Mountains, but when the coach stopped at a small inn for the night and he sought to follow the white passengers in obtaining a room, he was told that the inn did not serve blacks. He spent the night huddled outside in the cold. He arrived penniless some days later in Richmond, Virginia, about eighty miles from Hampton. After walking around the city—the biggest he had ever seen—until midnight, he chose a place to sleep beneath a board sidewalk. The next day he found a job on the docks and earned enough money for breakfast, which he long remembered as one of the best meals of his life.

Washington stayed in Richmond for a few days, unloading ships and sleeping under the sidewalk. After saving a little money, he set out again for Hampton. As the school appeared before him, he was struck with wonder. The academic building was an imposing three-story edifice. Undoubtedly he had seen larger buildings in Richmond, but none dedicated to the education of his people. "It seemed to me," he later recalled, "to be the largest and most beautiful building I had ever seen."

Although the fall term was under way at Hampton, Washington was admitted to the institute and assigned a room in the boys' dorm in the schoolhouse attic. The school was coeducational, and the girls lived in nearby buildings that had once served as Union army barracks. Most of the students were older than Washington. Some had grown to adulthood as slaves and were in their late thirties. Even among these humble peers Washington stood out as a peculiarly rural and unsophisticated youth.

The students generally paid half of their room and board fee with labor and the other half with cash, but because of his acute poverty—he had arrived with only fifty cents in his pocket—Booker Washington was allowed to earn all his living expenses by working as a janitor. Like other students, he received his tuition from a northern benefactor, a man in New Bedford, Massachusetts. Even his clothes came from northern donors, who shipped barrels of discards to Hampton.

Washington's three years at the Hampton Institute were spent in rigorous physical and intellectual labor. The students arose at 5:00 A.M. and were inspected for dress and grooming forty-five minutes later. At 6:00 A.M. they had breakfast, then prayers and room inspection. Classes and study hall occupied most of the remainder of the day. The curriculum included reading, geography, history, algebra, government, natural science, and moral philosophy. Hampton was a trade school as well as an academy, and the students worked as waiters, farmers, janitors, carpenters, painters, printers, and shoemakers. Education at Hampton did not proceed beyond secondary school level, largely because even the philanthropic northern educators who ran the school harbored racial stereotypes of the black intellect. One of the instructors was asked why the school did not teach more advanced courses and replied, "Oh, the colored people are not prepared for those studies yet. They are too ignorant. It will be time enough to talk about that, years from this time."

In later years African American leaders would object to such condescension. But to ex-slaves like Washington who attended Hampton in the 1870s, the school was remarkable for the wonderful opportunities it did afford rather than for its limitations. Booker Washington seems to have spent his years at Hampton in a state of perpetual euphoria. As much as he enjoyed his classes and even his janitorial work, he was especially impressed by the opportunity to come into contact with "great men and women." There was, for example, Miss Mary F. Mackie, the female principal of the institute, a northern woman who was not above working side by side with Washington in cleaning the school before a new term. Above all, there was the head of the school, Gen. Samuel Chapman Armstrong, of whom Washington said, "I never saw a man who so completely lost sight of himself." Armstrong was a slender, soldierly man who had risen to command as a youth in his twenties during the Civil War. A northern idealist, he had resigned from the army after the war in order to devote his life to the education of the former slaves. As the school's head he seemed to embody its emphasis on hard work, liberal intelligence, and moral rectitude. The students were so devoted to him that one winter when the men's dormitory became overcrowded, almost everyone in one class volunteered to sleep outside in tents. Each morning during that cold season the general came by the tents to see how the men were doing, and out of loyalty to him they never admitted their acute discomfort in the canvas dwellings. Armstrong became like a father to Washington, helping the young man with his career and providing a role model for his work as an educator.

The promise and achievement of the Hampton Institute was symbolized by the commencement exercises in June 1875, an impressive event attended by both black and white observers, including journalists from several northern newspapers and magazines. Several students recited poetry, and a chorus sang "Farewell My Own True Love" and "Nobody Knows the Trouble I've Seen." Seniors read their essays on "Beauty," "Compulsory Education," and "The Black Man as a Voter and Citizen." Washington and another student debated "The Annexation of Cuba," Washington taking the negative side and impressing several reporters with his forceful oratory and keen logic.

The most engaging performance of all was a lecture on slave music by a student, Joseph B. Towe. A reporter from the *Springfield Daily Republican* was spellbound by the presentation. "The writer," he said, "himself brimful of song, a powerful soloist, with a voice of wonderful sweetness, took us back into the past of slavery, and even further back, into Africa itself, for the original sources of this strange music." Towe described the work songs of his own plantation days "when the fields were full of music." Slave soloists were especially important, leading the field hands in song. They drew a large price from plantation owners, "for it paid well in the increased amount of work when the air was alive with work songs." Towe remembered one soloist, John Jones, who could speak an African language.

He recalled the cadences and variations of the work songs. "I will give you an instance," he said, and a chorus of students began to sing. The music, born in Africa, nourished through generations of slavery, uttered now by a chorus of young emancipated black students, swelled through the auditorium. Towe continued his lecture, pausing again and again while the students illustrated his points with song. The audience was entranced, and even former secessionists congratulated the school for its fine program.

Booker T. Washington's career at Hampton ended in a celebration of his people's past achievements, current attainments, and future hopes. But dark clouds hung over that promising future. Already many of the opportunities that had opened ten years before with emancipation were threatened by racial animosity. Many whites did not want to see the ex-slaves advance politically, economically, or intellectually. Among Washington's classmates was a man who had lost two friends and nearly been killed himself when bigots attacked the school where he taught. Through violence and legislation southern whites had begun to take away the basic rights blacks had seemingly won through emancipation.

During the years of Reconstruction following the Civil War, southern blacks had made advances by their own initiative and with the help of governmental and private agencies. The very fact of freedom radically altered many lives. It allowed Washington and his family to move to West Virginia, enabling Booker T. Washington to attend Hampton and become a teacher—options that could be taken for granted in 1875 but had been unthinkable fifteen years before.

Many northerners believed that ending slavery should be only the first step in an extensive program to assist blacks in achieving equality with whites. One could not simply remove the chains of bondage and expect that blacks would immediately and automatically acquire the intellectual and material resources of their former masters. Washington had been assisted by the Freedman's Bureau, when it helped establish the Malden school, and by northern philanthropists who helped him pay his way at the Hampton Institute. In addition to founding black schools, federal authorities supervised the operation of new state governments, encouraging blacks to vote and to seek public office. Because many whites were disfranchised for participating in the rebellion, ex-slaves temporarily controlled several southern governments. The United States also considered measures to assist blacks economically. In the early years of Reconstruction, experiments had been conducted on the Sea Islands of South Carolina; at Davis Bend, Louisiana; and elsewhere in the South, proving that if blacks were given land they could prosper.

For a time it had seemed that Reconstruction might revolutionize the political, economic, and intellectual lives of African Americans as surely as emancipation had altered their legal status. But the reforms often proved fragile and incomplete. On the morning of emancipation a rumor had circulated widely among the freedmen that they would receive "forty acres and a mule," but the hope for economic assistance proved illusory. In an age that emphasized self-help, the government was unwilling to confiscate plantations or provide other lands for ex-slaves. Political reform, too, had its limits. In the 1870s the North became disenchanted with Reconstruction. The issue of black freedom and progress had agitated the nation for many decades, and many northerners now thought that other issues were more important. Perhaps it would be best, they reasoned, if the ex-slaves were now required to make their own way. The federal government ended its supervision of state politics and ex-Confederates were allowed to vote again.

Once local control returned to southern whites, blacks quickly lost one of Reconstruction's greatest benefits, the opportunity to vote and hold office. In the last quarter of the nineteenth century blacks who sought to vote were often beaten and sometimes killed. State laws formalized their political exile by requiring that voters be descendants of grandfathers who had voted or that they pass literacy tests that were crookedly administered, accepting even the most backward whites while excluding the best-educated blacks.

Black men and women were further disadvantaged by the growth of jim crow laws creating two spheres of life in the South: one the privileged existence of the white, the other the inferior place of the black. A third burden—poverty—combined with disfranchisement and segregation to limit black growth. Without property of their own, many African Americans had been forced to enter contracts with white landlords whereby they farmed the land and paid a share of their crops as rent. They often fell into virtual serfdom by borrowing from owners against future profits.

At age twenty Booker T. Washington left Hampton to enter a world where prejudice and poverty threatened to take away the promise of freedom. He faced this world with a program for black advancement modeled on his own experience. Having transcended the squalor of his youth by working hard, he would teach others how to succeed. Quite simply, he believed that good character could overcome any hardship. He would build men and women of good character.

Booker T. Washington's teaching career began at home in Malden, West Virginia. He had contemplated entering politics but decided he could do more for his people as an educator than as a statesman. And surely the residents of the Kanawah Valley needed help as much as any people in the South. Work in the salt furnaces and the coal mines broke men's bodies and spirits, and tensions seethed between poor whites and poor blacks throughout the region. Interracial animosities often erupted into violence and lynchings. Washington brought to Malden his commitment to "assisting in laying the foundation of the race through a generous education of hand, head and heart." He established a day school, a night school, a reading room, and a debating society. He took a personal interest in his students and prepared the best of them for admission to the Hampton Institute.

In 1879 he received an invitation to teach at Hampton. General Armstrong had probably identified him as a prospective faculty member while Washington was at the school but wanted him to experience at first hand the hardships of primary school teaching before enabling him to prepare others to teach. At Hampton, Washington taught classes, directed a program for Indians, and headed the new night school. He particularly enjoyed the latter role. The men and women in this program were impoverished and had to work during the day. Washington grew fond of these students, who worked late into the night on their studies; he issued them honorary certificates over his signature designating them members of "The Plucky Class." The name stuck and the class grew. Washington's doctrine of hard work and self-help apparently touched many responsive souls.

After two years at Hampton, Washington received an invitation to assume a still greater responsibility. A group of citizens in Tuskegee, Alabama, had decided to establish a school for black students and needed a president; they wrote to General Armstrong asking him to recommend a candidate. They had expected him to name a white man, but Armstrong suggested Washington. The committee in Tuskegee agreed after a brief delay.

When he arrived in Tuskegee in 1881, Booker T. Washington was pleased with his new surroundings. The town's two thousand residents were half white and half black, and relations between the races appeared good. The letter asking for a school president had been signed by a black and a white. The only hardware store in town was owned by members of each race.

Before beginning the school year, Washington decided to spend a month traveling by mule through the region in order to gauge his prospective students. He visited dozens of impoverished farms, sleeping often on the floor in one-room shacks and sharing simple meals of corn bread, black-eyed peas, and pork. He believed the people were poor mainly because they did not have the energy and the knowledge to improve themselves. They did not make the best use of their land, spent too much time loitering in town, and used their money unwisely—one family, so poor that they shared a single fork, possessed a $60 organ bought on time.

When Washington reflected on the troubles of his race, he usually thought of exactly this type of people—men and women who, in his estimation, did not know how to make the most of life. He felt that many African Americans had taken the wrong road during Reconstruction, seeking a life of ease and luxury instead of building a firm foundation by useful labor. In Washington, D.C., for example, men would earn $4 in a week and spend $2 on a buggy ride down Pennsylvania Avenue. Or they lived in idleness, waiting for the federal government to provide jobs. Here and elsewhere too many blacks had devoted their energies to learning Latin and Greek when they should have studied agriculture or mechanics. They had snobbishly assumed that education meant freedom from manual labor. But their education, in many cases, was of no practical value. Or so Washington believed.

He assumed that his people needed to concentrate on the fundamentals: they should become better farmers, blacksmiths, carpenters, and teachers rather than lust after such gewgaws as $60 organs, $2 buggy rides, or superfluous learning. People who could do some useful work would advance themselves, even in the face of racial prejudice. He wrote: "My experience is that there is something in human nature which always makes an individual recognize and reward merit, no matter under what color of skin merit is found."

Washington hoped to mold the Tuskegee Institute into a school that would fill Alabama and the whole South with young men and women who followed his creed of self-help and who could, in turn, inspire other blacks to uplift themselves. But in 1881 his dream required its own foundation-building. There was not even a campus for the new university. At first Tuskegee occupied an old shanty and a black Methodist church, both of which leaked profusely. Then with borrowed money Washington purchased a run-down plantation and began to build Tuskegee by "a slow and natural process of growth."

His first students were shocked when they learned that he intended them to construct and maintain the school. Most had expected that the golden road of education would take them far away from such labor. But Washington intended "to teach them to study actual things instead of mere books alone." Besides, there was almost no money for the new school, and if the students did not build it, no one else would. Washington carried the students along by precept and example, and in time they erected buildings, dug cellars, baked bricks, and crafted bedsteads and mattresses.

Washington gained the funds for these enterprises by seeking donations from every conceivable source. He traveled to the North where, with the help of General Armstrong, he learned how to open the purses of wealthy philanthropists. He appealed to the region's poor blacks, who sensed that their lives were caught up in some way in the growth of the school and gave generously of their own possessions—a pig, a quilt, sugar cane, or other farm products. Local whites helped the school, too, with loans, donations, or materials. With the aid of these contributions, large and small, and the labor of Tuskegee's students, Washington was able to bring "order out of chaos" and establish the school.

Tuskegee offered a regular schedule of traditional courses as well as inculcating in students a "love of work for its own sake." Tuskegee's achievements even appeared to cement relations between blacks and whites in the region. Tuskegee's brickyard was a good example. After several unsuccessful efforts Washington finally built a kiln that could make good bricks. Since there was no other local brickyard, white people soon came to Tuskegee to shop. "As the people of the neighborhood came to us to buy bricks," says Washington, "we got acquainted with them. Our business interests became intermingled. We had something which they wanted; they had something which we wanted. This, in a large measure, helped to lay the foundation for the pleasant relations that have continued to exist between us and the white people."

When Tuskegee opened in 1881, only sixteen years had passed since it had been illegal to educate a black in Alabama. Within a decade Washington built Tuskegee into one of the best-known African American colleges in the nation. By speaking at philanthropic gatherings and educational association meetings he acquired a modest national reputation as an effective orator with an interesting background. Thus, it was natural when in 1895 he was selected as a "responsible" representative of the black South at the opening of the Atlanta Exposition.

When Washington received the invitation to speak, he immediately recognized the importance of the occasion. The Atlanta Exposition was the first major trade fair held in the South since the Civil War, and so symbolized the resources and growth of the region. Washington had been called upon to address the largest white audience ever to hear a black speaker in the South, and he would never have a better chance to present his program for black progress and interracial cooperation.

In preparing his Atlanta address Washington combed through former lectures, selecting an image here, an idea there. After completing a draft of the talk, he read it to the Tuskegee faculty and won their approval. Despite this encouragement, however, he became increasingly apprehensive as the day for the speech drew near. Many southern newspapers had already published articles criticizing the fair committee for inviting a black man to speak. Washington recalled that when he left Tuskegee by train for Atlanta on September 17 he felt like a man "on his way to the gallows."

Everyone seemed to know he was going to deliver a major address. At stops along the way people pointed him out and discussed his forthcoming speech. In the station at Atlanta he heard an old black man say, "Dat's de man of my race what's gwine to make a speech at de Exposition to-morrow. I'se sho' gwine to hear him."

He was exceedingly uncomfortable in the spotlight. That night he hardly slept. In the morning he prayed for God's assistance. Then he took the long ride to the convention. Now, in a moment, he would speak.

When the band completed its musical interlude, Governor Bullock announced: "We have with us today a representative of Negro enterprise and Negro civilization." Washington rose to his feet and approached the platform. The sun's rays were flooding through the west windows, bathing the platform in light. Washington moved about, awkwardly trying to escape the brightness, but could not. He looked out at the silent crowd and the thousands of eyes upon him. He paused and then, his face aglow with the light of the setting sun, began his address.

The speech was fashioned around one essential point—that southern whites and blacks needed one another. "One-third of the population of the South," he began, "is of the Negro race. No enterprise seeking the material, civil, or moral welfare of this section can disregard this element of our population and reach the highest success." Washington advised each race to assist the other. He counseled whites to look to blacks rather than to foreign immigrants to cultivate the surplus land and to labor in the factories. He urged them to recognize the ability of the ex-slaves who after only thirty years of freedom were engaged in the "production

Tuskegee Institute, 1881–1895. Booker T. Washington began his school with a few crude buildings. With the help of local supporters, northern philanthropists, and cooperative students, he built Tuskegee into a substantial academy.

of agricultural implements, buggies, steam-engines, newspapers, books, statuary, carving, paintings, the management of drug stores and banks." They had made this progress with the help of both southern and northern philanthropists, and with continued encouragement in the "education of head, hand, and heart" they would contribute further to southern prosperity. He reminded the whites that blacks had proved themselves constructive members of southern society. They had "tilled your fields, cleared your forests, builded your railroads and cities and brought forth treasures from the bowels of the earth." They had even been faithful to their slave masters, rearing their children, watching at their sickbeds, and following their dead "with tear-dimmed eyes to their graves." Over the years blacks had proved "the most patient, faithful, law-abiding, and unresentful people that the world has seen."

While reminding the whites of the importance of African Americans, Washington warned against abusing them. Injustice to blacks, he said, would damage the whole society: "The laws of changeless justice bind oppressor and oppressed." If the blacks were treated fairly, their "sixteen million hands" would help in southern progress. If not, they would retard the growth of the whole South. "We shall constitute one-third and more of the ignorance and crime of the South," he said, "or one-third of its intelligence and progress; we shall contribute one-third to the business and industrial prosperity of the South, or we shall prove a veritable body of death, stagnating, depressing, retarding every effort to advance the body politic."

Booker T. Washington's advice to his own people was equally frank. They must work hard to win the friendship and respect of their southern neighbors, engaging "in agriculture, mechanics, in commerce, in domestic service, and in the professions." In particular, they should recognize that "when it comes to business, pure and simple, it is in the South that the Negro is given a man's chance in the commercial world."

Washington said blacks must not expect to achieve social equality with whites immediately. They should begin at the bottom and work their way up, as Washington had done in his youth and in the foundation of the Tuskegee Institute. "No race can prosper," he asserted, "till it learns that there is as much dignity in tilling a field as in writing a poem." They must learn to distinguish between "the superficial and the substantial, the ornamental gewgaws of life and the useful."

The ideal relationship between the races could be summarized in one image. The black people, he told his white listeners, will work hard, "interlacing our industrial, commercial, civil, and religious life with yours in a way that shall make the interests of both races one. In all things that are purely social we can be as separate as the fingers, yet one as the hand in all things essential to mutual progress."

Both races should recognize that each had much to offer the other. Whites should seek the new industrial labor force among native blacks. Blacks should build their enterprises on southern soil rather than seeking refuge in the North. Both races were like a ship at sea that called to another for water and was told, "Cast down your bucket where you are." The thirsty crew reluctantly dropped a bucket expecting to find only salt water, but the water was fresh, for without their knowledge they had drifted into the broad mouth of the Amazon River. "Cast down your bucket where you are," Washington told both races, "and you will find great opportunities lie before you."

Washington spun out these ideas in the best oratorical fashion of the times. He knew how to "sense" his audience, to recognize whether people were caught up in his ideas. Soon after he began the Atlanta address, his eyes shining in the sunlight, his feet planted firmly, his husky voice uttering the words in measured cadences, he knew that he had captured the crowd. People looked at him with admiration, some with tears in their eyes. When he came to the central metaphor in the speech, he held up his hand with fingers outstretched, then closed it into a fist as he said they would be "one as the hand in all things essential to mutual progress." Applause resounded through the auditorium. White gentry and black laborers alike jumped cheering to their feet.

When he had finished, applause again thundered through the hall. Governor Bullock rushed across the platform and clasped Washington's hand. Others followed. Clark Howell, editor of the *Atlanta Constitution*, wrote: "The address was a revelation. The whole speech is a platform upon which blacks and whites can stand with full justice to each other."

The Atlanta Exposition address catapulted Washington into local and national prominence, and after the address crowds gathered around him wherever he went in Atlanta. Washington was somewhat overwhelmed by the response and was glad to escape to Tuskegee on the following day. There congratulations also poured in. President Grover Cleveland commended his speech, and the press, both North and South, was laudatory. The ten-minute oration had made Washington the foremost spokesman for his race, a position he would retain for the remaining twenty years of his life.

There were some, however, who criticized Washington's formula for interracial harmony. Some African Americans felt he had conceded too much, put too much emphasis on the need for hard work and not enough on ending segregation and securing political rights. Even as Washington spoke, lawmakers in South Carolina were debating a measure that would disfranchise blacks in that state. In fact, within a few years every southern state passed such laws. . . .

Washington was, of course, aware of injustice. He had been segregated in hundreds of jim crow hotels, restaurants, and railroad cars during his lifetime. Even on the day of the Atlanta Exposition address he was staying in a segregated hotel. His students had a taste of the racial animosity underlying such policies in 1896 when Alabama Governor William C. Oates addressed Tuskegee's graduating class. Annoyed by the liberality of a previous speaker, the governor threw away his prepared address and, glaring at his audience, told them: "I want to give you niggers a few words of plain talk and advice. . . . You might as well understand that this is a white man's country, as far as the South is concerned, and we are going to make you keep your place. Understand that. I have nothing more to say to you." Such astonishingly arrogant words might have provoked Washington to rage, but he was well acquainted with such men and ideas. His eyes twinkled as he heard the governor; then he dismissed the assembly on the grounds that everyone was "fagged out" from so much speaking. One of the guests later wrote, "Mr. Washington's imperturbably good nature alone saved the day."

Booker T. Washington's "good nature" struck many observers as acquiescence to white racism. In 1905 one of his chief critics, W. E. B. Du Bois, helped organize the Niagara movement, a forerunner to the National Association for the Advancement of Colored People, to foster resistance to disfranchisement and segregation. Such men believed that Washington was more remarkable for the limitations he accepted than for the opportunities he announced. Although Washington condemned racial oppression in the Atlanta Exposition address, he conceded that it mattered little if blacks were barred from opera houses, and at Tuskegee he emphasized manual labor rather than the professions. He gave two reasons for such policies. Sometimes he claimed that these limitations were appropriate, even beneficial to an emerging people who needed to begin with the fundamentals. At other times he claimed they were forced upon him by necessity. If he had become an agitator for equal rights, he would have lost support for Tuskegee. "When your head is in the lion's mouth," he liked to say, "you have to stroke that lion."

In his Atlanta Exposition address Washington also courted white favor by embracing the mythology of the Old South as a paradise where masters were unfailingly noble and kindly and slaves were constantly loyal and grateful. This distortion was accepted as truth at the time in the North as well as the South. This legendary past was immortalized a few decades later in *Gone with the Wind*, one of the most popular movies of all time. When Washington spoke of "patient and faithful" slaves following their masters "with tear-dimmed eyes" to their graves, he was fueling the mythology of the genteel South. Undoubtedly, such scenes did occur sometimes under slavery, but in accepting such images as the essence of the slave South Washington was clearly stroking the head of that lion.

It was not Booker T. Washington's fashion, however, to rail against injustice, to demand that the outside world conform to his ideals. Not that he quietly accepted disfranchisement and segregation as some writers have mistakenly claimed: he fought the movement to take away the black vote, remarked on the absurdity of segregation in public facilities, and condemned racial prejudice as a force that injured both blacks and whites. But the main thrust of his policy was to draw out the capabilities of his own people. Political and cultural disadvantages could, he believed, strengthen blacks. "With few exceptions," he said, "the Negro youth must work harder and must perform his task better than a white youth in order to secure recognition. But out of the hard and unusual struggle through which he is compelled to pass, he gets a strength, a confidence, that one misses whose pathway is comparatively smooth by reason of birth and race."

In 1895, in the midst of an age of industrial progress and self-made men, his emphasis on individual initiative won admiration from both races. There were times of deeper insight when Booker T. Washington realized the terrible burden imposed on his people by racial prejudice. While he reigned at Tuskegee, hundreds of blacks throughout the South were burned to death or hanged by lynch mobs, and thousands were denied what he called "a man's chance" in business because of their color.

Despite these injustices, however, he continued to urge blacks to find strength in themselves and to make friends with their white neighbors. When those white neighbors did not merit his trust, Washington could still take consolation in the course of history. He had begun life, after all, as another man's property and had come a long way in material prosperity, public stature, and self-esteem. If he was not the white man's equal at least he was not his slave. In 1895 a man who vividly recalled sleeping in rags on a dirt floor in a slave cabin could be more impressed with what his people had achieved than by what they had been denied.

Washington's greatest strength—and his most serious limitation—lay in his ability to work within the historical situation. History freed him from slavery and allowed him to be a teacher: he worked hard and became a leading educator. History imposed barriers on him and his people: he encouraged them to live the fullest lives possible within those barriers. He would leave the removal of those barriers to other generations.

Bibliography

COBEN, WILLIAM. *At Freedom's Edge* (1991). On black mobility and the southern white quest for racial control, 1861–1915.

DU BOIS, W. E. B. *Souls of Black Folk* (1903 and later editions). Poetic history of the Reconstruction era by Washington's chief critic.

FREDERICKSON, GEORGE M. *The Black Image in the White Mind* (1971). Nineteenth-century attitudes about blacks and their future.

GILMORE, GLENDA ELIZABETH. *Gender and Jim Crow: Women and the Politics of White Supremacy in North Carolina, 1896–1920* (1996). Suggests that women were more open than men to allowing African Americans to vote.

HARLAN, LOUIS R. *Booker T. Washington: The Making of a Black Leader, 1856–1901* (1972). Fine biography revealing complexity of Washington and his times.

————. *Booker T. Washington: The Wizard of Tuskegee, 1901–1915* (1983). Extensive account of Washington's Tuskegee years.

————. *The Booker T. Washington Papers* (1972–1989). Includes many informative letters by Washington.

LITWACK, LEON F. *Been So Long in the Storm: The Aftermath of Slavery* (1979). Sensitive recreation of the experience of southern blacks and whites in the first years of freedom.

OSHINSKY, DAVID M. *"Worse Than Slavery": Parchman Farm and the Ordeal of Jim Crow Justice* (1996). Describes use of criminal justice system to reestablish unfree labor in Mississippi after Reconstruction.

RICHARDSON, HEATHER COX. *The Death of Reconstruction: Race, Labor, and Politics in the Post–Civil War North, 1865–1901* (2002). Argues that many northerners withdrew their support for Reconstruction because they felt that blacks would not make good workers in a free enterprise system—and that a key goal of Booker T. Washington in his Atlanta Exposition speech was to offset that impression.

ROSE, WILLIE LEE. *Rehearsal for Reconstruction* (1964). Describes northern efforts to provide a model at Port Royal for the economic and educational progress of ex-slaves.

STAMPP, KENNETH M. *Era of Reconstruction, 1865–1877* (1965). Survey of the period emphasizing loss of voting rights and lack of property as the chief black weaknesses.

TRELEAJE, ALLEN W. *White Terror* (1971). Account of southern vigilante groups, especially the Ku Klux Klan.

WASHINGTON, BOOKER T. *Up from Slavery* (1901 and later editions). Autobiographical account of Washington's life to the time of the Atlanta Exposition address.

WAYNE, MICHAEL. *The Reshaping of Plantation Society: From Slavery to Sharecropping in the Natchez District, 1860–1890* (1982). How emancipation changed plantation life.

WEST, MICHAEL RUDOLPH. *The Education of Booker T. Washington: American Democracy and the Idea of Race Relations* (2005). West explores Washington's effort to seek racial progress within the framework of segregation.

Study Guide

Summary

The essay begins by describing the opening of the 1895 Atlanta Exposition, where Booker T. Washington was about to address a predominantly white audience. It then takes us back to Washington's childhood, and we follow his rise from slavery in Virginia to prominence as a black educator. When he delivers his speech, advocating black progress through hard work, we can see the blending of Washington's experience and philosophy. Washington recommends to other blacks the course of self-help that has worked so well for him. The essay concludes by suggesting the problems this philosophy faced in an era of increasing segregation.

Identification Topics

Atlanta Exposition, jim crow laws, Emancipation Proclamation, Jane Ferguson, Hampton Institute, Reconstruction, the New South, "forty acres and a mule," Tuskegee, "Cast down your bucket where you are," W. E. B. Du Bois, Niagara movement, Samuel Chapman Armstrong

Study Questions

1. Booker T. Washington had a strong, almost naive, faith in the real and potential harmony of whites and blacks. What instances of interracial cooperation did he recall in his own life? How did his Atlanta Exposition address evoke the ideal of cooperation?

2. Why were some people on Booker T. Washington's plantation apprehensive about freedom?

3. How was Washington's life touched by racial injustice? What results did he predict if southerners did not treat blacks fairly?

4. Washington believed that African Americans' best route to progress was through self-help. How did his life reflect this principle? In what ways did he believe that some blacks were responsible for their own poverty?

5. The author argues that Washington is wrongly accused of uncritically accepting segregation and placing the full burden of self-help upon his own people. In what phrases does Washington's Atlanta speech call on blacks to help themselves? In what words does he demand that whites treat them fairly? On the other hand, in what respects did Washington accept limitations on black initiative and freedom?

6. Washington justified the emphasis on manual labor at Tuskegee on the grounds that blacks needed to build from the ground up. In distinguishing between the "gewgaws" and the "useful" was he making a valid point about black needs, or was he rationalizing his acceptance of segregationist limitations on his race?

7. Booker T. Washington said, "There is as much dignity in tilling a field as in writing a poem." Why did he feel it was important to make that point? Was this good advice for African Americans in 1890, or was it condescending?

8. Washington was an optimist in 1895 because he had progressed so far from his slave rags of thirty years before. What might he have thought of contemporary black history if he had been born in 1875? What disadvantages did blacks as a race suffer at the time of the Atlanta address?

9. What is your overall assessment of Booker T. Washington's career? Did he make the best of unalterable conditions? Or did he acquiesce in the growth of segregation?

10. In what ways did the federal government help the ex-slaves after emancipation? What potentially useful measures can you think of which might have been adopted, but were not?

Research Topics

1. Investigate how other slaves acted after emancipation. What did they do with their freedom? Were any other former slaves as successful as Booker T. Washington?

2. Study W. E. B. Du Bois and other critics of Booker T. Washington. Were their criticisms sound?

3. Explore Booker T. Washington's life after the Atlanta address. How did he use the prominence he gained from this speech?

4. Compare the journey of Booker T. Washington to Hampton Institute with the journey of Benjamin Franklin to Philadelphia. Describe the origins of each man and the challenges that lay ahead. Which man would face greater obstacles to rising in the world?

5. Study the successes and failures of the Freedman's Bureau.

CHAPTER 2

The New Industrial Era

The Rise of Andrew Carnegie

In three centuries, the character of American life has undergone several dramatic changes. In the colonial period, Euro-Americans replaced Indians as the dominant population on the eastern seaboard. During the Revolution, thirteen British colonies formed an independent nation. Early in the nineteenth century, a coastal people spread westward to the Mississippi. And after the Civil War, four million slaves were freed from bondage. Each of these epochal events affected the American environment, but no change was more influential than industrialization in the late nineteenth century. The growth of big business affected where Americans lived, what they consumed, how they worked, and what they thought. If Rip Van Winkle had slept from 1870 to 1910, he would have seen changes far greater than those wrought by the American Revolution. The men who had led the industrial movement, entrepreneurs like Andrew Carnegie, were the most influential people of their time. Their histories reveal the massiveness of the new enterprises and suggest that even the captains of industry had trouble adjusting to their own unprecedented power.

For two centuries America was a nation of wood. People came to the country in wood ships and moved about in carts, wagons, and coaches of wood. They used wood for their tables, chairs, plates, and bowls. They plowed their fields with wood plows pulled by oxen joined with wood yokes.

The economy built on wood was local, near to home. More than 90 percent of early Americans lived on farms. Most of what they ate, wore, and worked with they made themselves, lighting their dwellings with homemade candles and cutting their clothes from homespun cloth. Most of their products were just one step removed from nature. They wove the fleece from their sheep's backs into woolen cloth and ground the grain from their fields into bread. The fuel that warmed their houses came from nearby woods, as did materials for the houses themselves.

Wood may be said to symbolize something vital in early America: the comparative self-sufficiency of the family and the simple, close relationship to nature. By the same token, iron and steel were the basic ingredients of a new America that took form in the late nineteenth century. In the industrial age people traveled across the country behind an "iron horse" (locomotive) following iron rails. They crossed the oceans in steamships driven by iron machinery, fought their battles in ships protected by iron and steel armor, and constructed tall buildings with frameworks of steel. The dependence on these materials influenced new patterns in labor and business. Large companies began to replace individual enterprises; men and women worked in factories, not for themselves; and they worked upon and with materials made from minerals, not living plants.

Iron was only one of many growing enterprises that revolutionized American life, but its history illustrates industrialization as a whole; and one business, the Carnegie Steel Company, illuminates trends throughout the industry. The company was created by Andrew Carnegie, a remarkable man in an age of incomparable entrepreneurs. He became interested in iron after the Civil War and concentrated his energy on steel in the 1870s. Buying and leasing other businesses, he pushed his company to dominance over the industry, producing almost as much steel as the whole of the British Isles. In 1901 Carnegie sold his company, retired from business, and became the nation's leading philanthropist.

Entrepreneurs like Carnegie have been both lauded and vilified, some critics regarding them as the indispensable leaders of an age of industrial wonders, others seeing them as narrow and greedy "robber barons" who exploited people and resources for their private benefit. Certainly they changed America, but at what cost to themselves and their society? By studying Carnegie's career we can explore the kinds of personal qualities that went into creating giant industries and consider the effects of their businesses on those they employed and served.

Andrew Carnegie's life began in Dunfermline, Scotland, a town on high ground above the Firth of Forth, looking out on Edinburgh, fourteen miles to the southeast, and the North Sea beyond. A center for the damask cloth trade, the town housed hundreds of looms on which half the population wove linen cloth, decorated with intricate designs of thistles, roses, and portraits. For centuries a tradition of fine craftsmanship had been passed from father to son.

Andrew Carnegie's family was typical of the town. The father, William, was a weaver. Shortly after his wife, Margaret, gave birth to Andy in their small cottage on November 25, 1835, he moved to a larger house and purchased three additional looms, worked by apprentices. As the eldest son, Andrew might expect to follow his father's trade.

But this future was not to be. Ironically, Andrew Carnegie, one day the greatest industrialist in the world, first experienced the industrial revolution as one of its victims. Shortly after his birth a power loom was established in Dunfermline, heralding an end to the old way of life. A group of protestors disguised in costumes attacked and burned the new mill, but they could not hold out for long against the lower cost of machine-produced linens. During the winter of 1847–1848, six hundred of Dunfermline's weavers were out of work. William Carnegie had to sell his extra looms. His Scottish fortune ruined, he decided to take his family to America.

Years later Andrew would reflect on his Scottish legacy. He remembered relatives and friends who taught him a love for history and poetry and recalled simple childish pleasures such as raising rabbits. But along with these pleasant memories he had learned a painful lesson: how those unable to control their fortunes can be set adrift in the world.

The Carnegies left Dunfermline on May 17, 1848, setting sail from Glasgow for New York. Andrew was a bright and outgoing child. On shipboard he soon got to know the sailors and became so popular that he was invited to share their Sunday dessert. The family disembarked in New York City after fifty days at sea and continued on to Pittsburgh, whose history became thoroughly intertwined with Andrew Carnegie's.

Pittsburgh is located at the confluence of the Monongahela and Allegheny Rivers in western Pennsylvania. Early visitors frequently commented on the great beauty of the two rivers and the narrow valleys that had cut through steep bluffs and green rolling hills. An English visitor said of the pristine view that its only failing was that it lacked the noise and smoke of a great city. A century later an Englishman, Herbert Spencer, came to Pittsburgh in the company of Andrew Carnegie. By then the place was known as "The Smoky City." Clouds of coal dust darkened the skies, and torrents of factory waste discolored the rivers. Six months in Pittsburgh, Spencer believed, would justify anyone in committing suicide.

The transformation of this idyllic landscape into a commercial center is one of the great "success stories" in American urban history. Pittsburgh's favored location among huge supplies of iron and coal made it one of the fastest growing cities in the United States. Its population swelled from 1,565 to 49,221 between 1800 and 1860. As early as 1820 the city was known as the iron capital of America. In 1842 Charles Dickens included Pittsburgh in his tour of the United States. The city, he wrote, "certainly had a great quantity of smoke hanging over it, and is famous for its iron works."

Many resourceful businessmen had a hand in the early economic success of Pittsburgh. But none did more than the Scottish boy making his slow progress westward in summer 1848. The Carnegies' trip from New York took three weeks by river and canal. In Pittsburgh they were greeted by relatives and a friendly Scottish community. They settled in an area known as "Slabtown," an ugly assortment of factories, stores, saloons, and jerry-built hovels.

It is tempting to let Andrew Carnegie's first days in Pittsburgh be colored by his later success. But to do so is to ignore the true harshness of those years. In 1848 the Carnegies could not dream that one day they would be worth millions of dollars. Their reality was poverty. Worse still, William Carnegie was a broken man. He knew only one craft and attempted to pursue it, weaving linens and peddling them along the Ohio River; but in America, as in Scotland, one could not make a decent living from handwoven linens.

Andrew's mother was a strong, energetic woman. Shortly after their arrival in America she began to make money working for a shoe manufacturer and taking in laundry. But the skimpy parental earnings could barely support the family. Carnegie later wrote, "The prospect of want had become to me a frightful nightmare." The family fears burst to the surface one day in "the most tragic of all scenes I have ever witnessed." Andrew's uncle, visiting the family, tried to suggest ways for Andrew to help. He innocently suggested that the boy might get a basket of knick-knacks and peddle them on the wharves.

Margaret Carnegie, outraged at the idea of her son doing such a thing, sprang toward the uncle. "What! My son a peddler and go among rough men upon the wharves! I would rather throw him into the Allegheny River. Leave me!" The shaken man retreated and Margaret broke down. Holding Andrew and his younger brother, Tom, her voice choked with emotion, she told them they must become honorable and respectable and not remain in a lowly, impoverished condition.

Yet the means of escape were by no means clear. Andrew's first jobs hardly seemed better than a peddler's. To help support the family he went to work in a factory, laboring from sunrise to sunset at $1.20 a week. A second job took him to a bobbin factory, where he worked in a dark cellar stoking a boiler. He must watch the gauges carefully—too little fuel and the machinery would not run properly, too much and the boiler could explode. At home "begrimed with coal dirt," he was unable to sleep soundly, wakening often to watch imaginary gauges. A promotion of sorts brought him out of the cellar but exposed him to an equally nasty task, dipping the bobbins in a foul-smelling oil that often caused him to vomit.

It is easy to understand why Carnegie saw his next task, with the O'Reilly Telegraph Company, as a wonderful opportunity. In the days before the telephone the rapidest form of communication was the telegraph. Business and personal letters were sent from city to city over telegraph lines by Morse code, then copied down and carried by delivery boys to the addressee. Unlike Carnegie's previous jobs, this one demanded initiative and mental effort and gave him an introduction, although a humble one, to members of Pittsburgh's business community. He soon memorized not only the location of every business establishment but also the faces of all the proprietors so that when he was bearing a telegram he could identify them on the street.

Between trips, waiting in the telegraph office, he taught himself to take messages by ear from the wire. Most operators had to copy out the code letter by letter and translate it; Carnegie was one of the few operators in the country then who could receive by ear. It was natural that soon, in 1851, he was given a position as operator. "I felt that my foot was upon the ladder," he later wrote, "and that I was bound to climb."

Even as a bobbinboy he had begun to plan his economic ascent. He heard that a new form of bookkeeping called double-entry was useful in business. Although he was working long hours, he went to school in the evening to learn the system, and in addition began an extensive reading program including works by Macaulay, Bancroft, Burns, and Shakespeare. To develop his mind still more he joined the Webster Literary Club, which met to debate political questions and to study literature.

In these early years of his "career" (he was only sixteen in 1851) Carnegie might have been modeling his life on Benjamin Franklin's. He led a purposeful life, worked hard, advertised his abilities, and exploited every advantage that offered itself. But like most men on the make, Andrew Carnegie had little understanding of those who were unable to master their circumstances. Shortly after he became a telegraph operator, a sad event contrasted Carnegie's optimism with his father's tragic condition. Andrew had been sent out of town to help provide emergency telegraph service after a storm. By chance he met his father, who was going by ferryboat to Cincinnati to peddle his linens. Andrew was shocked to see that the old man was traveling not in a cabin, but on deck, exposed to the elements. William Carnegie admitted to his son that he could not afford a cabin. Andrew replied, "Never mind, Father, it won't be long before you and mother shall ride in your own carriage." His father paused for a long time, then, with difficulty, said, "Andra, I am proud of you." Andrew went back to work, and William went on to Cincinnati on the boat's open deck.

Without meaning to, without realizing that he had done so, the young man had humiliated his father as surely as if he had cursed him for a failure. William Carnegie died in 1855. He had known how to weave fine patterns in linen and to sing a good song. His son said of him, he was "one of the most lovable of men . . . not much of a man of the world, but a man all over for heaven." He had not known how to make his way in industrial America.

Andrew was very much a "man of the world," as he clearly proved in the decade before the Civil War. In the telegraph office he established a public reputation as a bright, industrious youth and met many of Pittsburgh's business leaders. One man he impressed was Thomas Scott, who in 1852 became superintendent of the Pennsylvania Railroad's western division. A year later Carnegie became his secretary and personal telegrapher.

The railroad was then an infant industry. By twentieth-century standards, the diminutive engines with their enormous polished lamps seem like carnival toys. The railroads at that time, however, were models of business efficiency—bigger and more carefully organized than any other enterprise. Formerly the largest economic units in the United States had been New England textile mills, some of them virtually occupying a whole town. The railroads were much larger, holding stations, warehouses, repair shops, offices, telegraph lines, and vast work forces. Even more impressive than their size was their organization. In order to operate efficiently—to move goods along the lines, collect payments, repair machinery, and regulate dozens of other activities—numerous functions had to be carefully planned and coordinated, requiring the collection of impersonal statistical data on costs and labor.

The railroad became almost universally the standard for efficiency and order. Even the great nineteenth-century admirer of nature, Henry David Thoreau, paid tribute to railroads, recognizing their contribution to human development. Trains passed near his cabin at Walden Pond, and he contemplated their place in the American scene. "They go and come with such regularity and precision," he wrote, "and their whistle can be heard so far, that the farmers set their clocks by them, and thus one well-conducted institution regulates a whole country. Have not men improved somewhat in punctuality since the railroad was invented? Do they not talk and think faster in the depot than they did in the stage office? There is something electrifying in the atmosphere of the former place . . . To do things 'railroad fashion' is now the byword."

Between 1853 and 1865 Carnegie learned to do things "railroad fashion." The well-organized line from which he learned, the Pennsylvania Railroad, was known as "the standard railroad of the world." Its president,

J. Edgar Thomson, and the superintendent of the western division, Thomas Scott, were two of the best managers of their day.

As Scott's right-hand man, Carnegie became familiar with all aspects of the railroad business. He observed the relationship between the railroad and its varied customers and learned about routing trains, maintaining equipment, and clearing wrecks. In 1859 Scott moved to Philadelphia as vice president of the line, and Carnegie became superintendent of the western division. He was now twenty-four years old and earning $2,400 per year, a substantial sum in those days. As superintendent, Carnegie had new ideas for increasing the railroad's efficiency: clearing lines quickly after wrecks by burning the ruined cars and regularizing traffic flow by moving company goods only when customer traffic was light. These innovations show that Carnegie had mastered the *mental* art of business. Just as he had assembled a mental map of the business establishments of Pittsburgh, Carnegie now had a picture of the Pennsylvania Railroad system. He knew its equipment, workers, and customers; and he knew how changes in one area would affect conditions in another. Many businessmen were inclined to play hunches, taking risks with partial knowledge of a situation, but Carnegie possessed the mental acumen to evaluate all the intricate variables in a business decision. This ability made him an effective manager and helped him in another kind of business activity, that of financier.

While working for Thomas Scott, Carnegie had learned that it was possible to buy stocks in American companies, paper that would produce revenue for the holder without his working. With Scott's help he had made a number of good investments, including a one-eighth interest in the first sleeping car company in the United States. Thanks to such stocks, Carnegie had an income of almost $50,000 a year in 1863.

In 1865 Carnegie resigned his position with the Pennsylvania Railroad to devote full time to his financial interests. During the next seven years he was involved in a number of business enterprises, including telegraph lines, an oil company, grain elevators, Pullman cars, and railroads. Realizing a transcontinental railroad was imminent, he organized the Keystone Bridge Company in 1865 and built a crossing of the Mississippi at Saint Louis and another of the Missouri at Omaha.

His widely ranging activities in these years enhanced his ability to evaluate business opportunities and showed him the many factors in capitalizing and running varied enterprises. He was now ready, as he later said, to "put all of his eggs into one basket and then watch that basket grow." There were many "baskets" from which to choose in post–Civil War America. Carnegie might easily have gone into Pullman cars, telegraph lines, or oil. But he was attracted to iron. It was a field that an entrepreneur might easily dominate. The oil business was too chaotic and speculative; in other fields, such as the telegraph, a single company, Western Union, already controlled the field. But the iron industry, though well established, was not monopolized by one large concern. In addition, iron seemed to be the essential material in a growing America.

When dealing with a person of Carnegie's stature, we run the danger of identifying the industry with the man, as if he had made a product where absolutely none had existed. But of course there was iron long before there was Carnegie. Man first began to work with iron some six thousand years before industrialists fashioned it into engines and ships and railroads. Early peoples made iron into tools and weapons that proved more effective— stronger and harder—than objects of copper, bronze, and stone. Over the centuries blacksmiths evolved better ways of working with their material and produced a widening group of products. By the mid-nineteenth century, new enterprises had placed heavy demands on iron producers.

Several variables affected the character of iron, especially the carbon content and the time allowed for cooling. Wrought iron and steel had a low carbon content and were malleable. Cast iron had a higher carbon content and was firmer, but was also more brittle. In 1856 an Englishman, Henry Bessemer, invented a blast furnace that produced a new metal with the best qualities of both kinds of iron. It was malleable but strong, hard but not brittle. It was precisely the kind of metal the new industries required. Bessemer's invention was soon put to use in the United States.

Carnegie became involved in iron in 1872 when he and several partners formed Carnegie, McCandless and Company, the predecessor of Carnegie Steel. Carnegie had been interested in the Bessemer steelmaking process for several years. At first it was not practical to build a Bessemer plant in Pittsburgh because it would require a kind of iron ore not generally available in the region. But the discovery of a suitable ore in Michigan solved the raw materials problem. Carnegie had a chance to observe the Bessemer process in England in 1872 and was impressed. An acquaintance later described Carnegie's reaction to the Bessemer converter: "Nothing that he had ever seen was so picturesque, so fascinating, so miraculous in its easily controlled force and fury. It was half a furnace and half a cyclone, yet it was obedient to the touch of a boy's hand. Give it thirty thousand pounds of common pig iron, and presto! the whole mass was blown into steel." It was a machine to match Carnegie's grand imagination.

Back in Pittsburgh, Carnegie began work on the plant that would become the J. Edgar Thomson Works. It was twelve miles from Pittsburgh on Braddock's Field, a pastoral area of farmland and virgin timber that had remained almost unchanged in the century and a quarter since Gen. Edward Braddock had met defeat there in the French and Indian War. The location took advantage of transportation facilities on two railroads and the Ohio River barges. At its completion in 1875 the plant was the largest and the best in America.

One would need only to observe the day-to-day activities of the Thomson Works to realize the remarkable difference between the old economy of home workshops and the new industry concentrated in giant plants. Every day tons of raw materials were shipped to Braddock. Ore was loaded into a furnace along with coke and limestone. The coke was ignited and blasts of air were forced through the mass; the iron became molten and was drained off into molds; later, with more refined technology, into giant ladles on freight cars. These were carried to a Jones mixer, a huge iron box capable of holding up to 250 tons of molten pig iron. In this vast cradle many loads of liquid iron were mixed to form a uniform composition. It was then transferred from the mixer to the Bessemer converter, which one of Carnegie's associates called "the most beautiful and perfect piece of mechanism ever devised by the human mind." In the converter, jets of air were blown through the liquid iron, forcing out impurities and thereby transforming iron into steel. Then the molten steel was poured into molds and formed into ingots, which were, in turn, moved under heavy rollers and pressed into the necessary shape for later use. Carnegie produced some finished goods such as rails and iron plate. Other products were made in independent factories.

Building the plant was only the first step in the creation of a steel company. For the next twenty-five years Carnegie devoted his energies to matters of management, marketing, and expansion. He was fortunate from the start in securing a Civil War veteran and experienced steelmaster, Capt. William R. Jones, as plant supervisor, the man who would be at the plant every day ensuring that work progressed smoothly.

Jones refused Carnegie's offer of shares in the company, preferring to receive "one hell of a salary." As a measure of his assessment of Jones's responsibilities, Carnegie gave him the same salary as that of President Ulysses S. Grant, $25,000 a year. Jones was bright and resourceful and could run and repair the machinery while identifying new equipment needs. The Jones mixer was his invention. Equally important, he was an incomparable leader. Known to the workers as "Captain Bill," he was an affable master who worked closely with his men. Pictures of him reveal a solid, handsome man with eyes of remarkable warmth. In his years as a steelmaster he occasionally knocked off work early to take his men to a baseball game. When he heard of the Johnstown flood in 1889, he closed the mill, and he and his men went to help with rescue operations. He died soon afterward while inspecting a "hang"—a block in the flow of molten iron in one of his furnaces; the furnace exploded, killing him almost instantly. Carnegie was reduced to tears by the news. The plant was closed for the day of Jones's funeral, and nearly ten thousand men marched in his funeral procession. Jones was replaced by a close friend, Charles M. Schwab, who eventually became president of the U.S. Steel Company and was, like his predecessor, a talented and affable steelmaster.

One of the reasons for Carnegie's success was his ability to identify and promote talented men like Jones and Schwab. He also devised

Steel plant and laborer. The raw human energy of industrialization was supplied by millions who worked long hours for low pay.

management techniques to evaluate the effectiveness of each stage of steel manufacture. Traditionally, iron- and steelworks kept records of their overall profits and losses but had no way of accurately measuring results at each stage to discover where improvements might be made. With detailed records Carnegie could replace ineffective parts, whether men or machines. He had learned the lessons of his early years well. Carnegie's was the first American manufacturing concern to do things "railroad fashion."

Careful management was an essential element in the growth of his steel interests. It enabled him to keep prices lower than those of his competitors and so to attract orders. Carnegie recognized, too, how valuable informal ties were in producing customers. Among his other talents, he was an accomplished salesman, telling amusing Scottish stories and cultivating his old friends from the railroad days. Businessmen would buy their steel from Carnegie for two good reasons: his prices were low and he was their friend. Carnegie was also able to anticipate new markets for steel. Late in the nineteenth century cities replaced railroads as the main buyers; Carnegie widened his contacts accordingly.

To careful management and imaginative marketing Carnegie added a third program, acquiring other companies. By this practice—known as horizontal integration—he increased his output and his domination of the industry. Among other businesses, he acquired the Homestead Works in 1889 and the Allegheny Bessemer Steel Company in 1890. In 1892 these interests were consolidated as the Carnegie Steel Company.

As he bought steel operations, Carnegie sought to control the businesses upon which steel depended. Producing steel required enormous supplies of coke, a hot-burning coal. In nearby Connollsville, a coal-rich region, Henry Clay Frick had gained control of 80 percent of the coke production. In 1889 Frick and Carnegie worked out an agreement whereby Frick became general manager of Carnegie's steel interests and Carnegie controlled Frick's coal. Carnegie gained a stronghold on another raw material, iron ore, by negotiating a long-term lease on ore lands in Minnesota's Mesabi Range, the richest in the world. To transport the ore he secured an interest in Great Lakes carriers and built a railroad from their Lake Erie terminus to his Monongahela furnaces.

By 1900 Carnegie accounted for one-fourth of the nation's steel output. In that year the company's profits were $40 million, of which $25 million went to Carnegie himself. Carnegie steel could be found throughout the United States in railroads, battleships, bridges, and skyscrapers. It went into the Brooklyn Bridge and the Washington Monument.

Carnegie might have built his business even further. In 1900 he was considering the idea of constructing railroad lines and acquiring plants to produce such finished products as steel tubes, rods, and wire. But Andrew Carnegie had another ambition. Early in life he had written an article entitled "The Gospel of Wealth," in which he had argued that the man who dies rich "dies disgraced." A rich man, he had said, should use his money for the benefit of others. Over the years Carnegie had made a number of philanthropic bequests; now he wanted to devote himself entirely to this end. To do so he must convert his industrial wealth into liquid capital.

It was, of course, one thing to sell a ton of steel and quite another to sell a half-billion-dollar steel company. Fortunately, at this moment the great financier J. P. Morgan was interested in expanding his steel interests.

In 1898 Morgan had organized the Federal Steel Company with capital of $200 million. In December 1900 Morgan told Charles Schwab he was interested in buying Carnegie Steel. Schwab's boss was ready to sell and came up with the figure $492 million. Schwab communicated the price to Morgan, who took one look at the figure and accepted it without further negotiation. In January 1901 the bargain was formalized in a fifteen-minute meeting between Morgan and Carnegie. As Morgan left Carnegie's house, he shook his hand, saying, "Mr. Carnegie, I want to congratulate you on being the richest man in the world!"

Morgan formed his holdings into U.S. Steel, capitalized at $1.4 billion—the world's first billion-dollar corporation. The company controlled 60 percent of the steel industry. Charles Schwab became its first president, and Carnegie turned his energy to giving away his fortune.

In liquid assets—holdings that could easily be converted into cash—Carnegie may well have been the world's richest man. But in the late nineteenth century he was by no means unique. In Pittsburgh alone were a dozen men whose talents rivaled Carnegie's, including George Westinghouse, a pioneer in air brakes and electricity; Andrew Mellon, a leading financier; and Charles Schwab. Many of Pittsburgh's business leaders were self-made men. The telegraph office where Carnegie had worked as a boy also spawned David McCargo, a superintendent of the Allegheny Valley Railroad, and Henry W. Oliver, an oil millionaire. In the United States as a whole were many other brilliant entrepreneurs—men like John D. Rockefeller, J. P. Morgan, Thomas Edison, and Cornelius Vanderbilt, each exercising as much power as the presidents of the United States. Today, Carnegie, Edison, and Rockefeller are at least as well known as Presidents Hayes, Garfield, Arthur, Cleveland, and Harrison.

They lived in years of unprecedented opportunity. Just as the great changes brought about by the American Revolution made provincial lawyers, planters, and legislators into the founding fathers of the republic, the industrial revolution of a century later created an environment in which entrepreneurs who might otherwise have been local businessmen became industrialists with national and international interests. The outline of Carnegie's entrepreneurial role is relatively easy to trace. By managing his businesses efficiently, seeking out resources at the lowest possible price, and using new and effective machinery, he produced good, inexpensive steel. But when we attempt to evaluate Carnegie's career, we should know not only what he did but also how his work affected people. We need to consider the importance of the product he produced, the influence of his industrial management on others, and his role as a philanthropist.

In Andrew Carnegie's mind there was no question that he and other industrialists served America by building their enterprises. He was perhaps the most articulate of the entrepreneurs, and in some characteristics he was atypical—he was more literate than most (he memorized long segments of

Shakespeare and Burns), and he devoted more of his resources and energy to philanthropy. But he typified the one characteristic most shared—the belief that the creation of wealth was a noble endeavor.

The nineteenth-century captain of industry was not merely a businessman; he was a miracle worker. No one believed more strongly than Carnegie in the "miracle" of modern civilization. His favorite motto was "all is well since all grows better." He wrote many essays reflecting his belief in human progress and frequently associated his confidence in mankind with his belief in America, as in his popular book, *Triumphant Democracy* (1886).

The philosophical basis of Carnegie's optimism was Social Darwinism. After Charles Darwin's *On the Origin of Species* was published in 1859, many businessmen applied a simplified version of Darwin's ideas to human society: the "survival of the fittest" would lead to higher and higher forms of civilization. Social Darwinism naturally appealed to successful businessmen who wanted to believe that their achievements were attributable to their own "fitness" and contributed to the elevation of all mankind. The man most associated with this idea was Herbert Spencer, an English philosopher, whose works Andrew Carnegie claimed to treasure above all others. Carnegie said that upon reading Spencer, "Light came in as a flood and all was clear." Spencer showed him that "Man was not created with an instinct for his own degradation, but from the lower he had risen to the higher forms. Nor is there any conceivable end to his march to perfection. His face is turned to the light, he stands in the sun and looks upward." In material achievement there can be no doubt that Carnegie contributed greatly to America's "march to perfection." America needed steel for buildings, ships, bridges, railroads—for the very sinews of the new industrial age—and Carnegie supplied it.

But at what cost? How did his career affect those it touched most closely, his business associates and laborers? Social Darwinism suggested that people succeed because they are virtuous, thus enabling businessmen to forget the brutal side of their success. Carnegie's unattractive side was his perpetual ruthlessness. He drove his managers and workers with all his energy, frequently playing off partners and plant managers against one another. Capt. Bill Jones parodied Carnegie's style: "Puppy dog number three, you have been beaten by puppy dog number two on fuel. Puppy dog number two, you are higher on labor than puppy dog number one." Those who could not stand the pace quit or were fired. Over the years Carnegie forced fifteen partners out of his steel business. Jones said of him, "Andy was born with two sets of teeth and holes bored for more."

If he was hard on his own colleagues, he was even harder on his competitors. When the Duquesne Steel Works began producing rails by a new, inexpensive process, Carnegie fostered a rumor throughout the railroad industry that the new rails lacked "homogeneity." It was a brilliant if unscrupulous propagandist's device. No one knew what "homogeneity" meant—in fact, it meant nothing at all—but the accusation inspired so much unwarranted suspicion that the market for the new product dried up. Soon afterward Carnegie bought the Duquesne Works at a bargain price.

Carnegie's opportunism was even more evident in his dealings with his work force. Many assume today that as soon as men were taken away from the loom and the blacksmith shop, where they made finished products, they lost the sense of pride in their work. Yet many of Carnegie's employees apparently shared their boss's excitement in the achievement of the mills. Bill Jones, who worked closely with his men, preferred the noise and activity of a large mill to rural work, which he found dull. He believed esprit de corps among the workers was vital. The workers appear to have been proud of their productivity. There was a spirited competition among the Carnegie furnaces to see which would produce the most iron. At the end of each week a broom was placed atop the chimney of the most productive, announcing the week's victors to the whole area.

Under the direction of men like Jones, with his love of baseball, the esprit de corps among Carnegie workers may have been high. But baseball games and intraplant competition could not cloak the hardships of industrial labor. Carnegie's huge profits were made possible in part by low wages and long hours. The workers usually put in twelve hours a day, seven days a week in the hot mills. Author Hamlin Garland wrote his impressions of the mill life. First, there were the poor neighborhoods where the workers lived: "The streets were horrible; the buildings were poor; the sidewalks were sunken and full of holes . . . Everywhere the yellow mud of the streets lay kneaded into sticky masses, through which groups of pale, lean men slouched in faded garments, grimy with soot and dirt of the mills." In the mills, Garland learned the difficulty of steelwork. One man told him he had lost forty pounds in the first three months he worked. Others spoke of their exhaustion when they returned home. Then, too, gruesome accidents maimed or killed workers in explosions of molten iron. "The worst part of the whole business," said one man, "is, it brutalizes a man. You can't help it. You start to be a man, but you become more and more a machine, and pleasures are few and far between. It's like any severe labor; it drags you down mentally and morally just as it does physically."

One of America's first industrial unions, the Amalgamated Association of Iron, Steel, and Tin Workers, sought to improve the workers' conditions. Carnegie had not allowed it to establish a foothold in his own plants, but the Homestead Works was highly unionized when he purchased it in 1889. Carnegie believed that the union contract that tied wages to production penalized the employers whenever they purchased improved equipment. In 1892 he authorized his tough manager, Henry Clay Frick, to break the union.

Frick began by lowering wages, which resulted in a strike. To secure the plant he hired three hundred men from Pinkerton's National Detective Agency as a private army. When the workers learned that these men were being moved to the plant in two barges, they lined the shore and opened fire on the Pinkerton men with rifles and a cannon; a battle continued through all of July 6, 1892. Finally the detectives, outnumbered by ten to one, agreed to withdraw. They were promised safe passage through the city by the union leaders, but the angry mob could not be restrained, and many of the Pinkerton men were badly beaten. The workers controlled Homestead for the next five days. Finally on July 12 state troops moved in and took over the plant. During the Homestead strike 14 men were killed and 163 wounded. But Carnegie had won. The plant reopened with a nonunion crew. Historians generally agree that the union defeat at Homestead was instrumental in delaying industrial unionism in the United States for almost half a century.

Despite his victory, this episode was perhaps the most tragic event in Carnegie's career. He liked to think of himself as a friend of labor. Although he lacked a close rapport with the workers and his wages were low in comparison with steel wages of sixty or seventy years later, his men were better housed and paid than many other nineteenth-century laborers.

Although Andrew Carnegie was in many ways a hard, even brutal man, he did not see himself this way. By his words and later by his deeds he drew a picture of another Andrew Carnegie—a loving, compassionate man who used his money to make the world a better place. His autobiography is full of tender memories: he makes a joyful, tearful return to Dunfermline; he tries to find a sailor who befriended him as a boy; he learns that a banker who knew him long ago remembers him with "deep affection." Carnegie even had a drawer in his desk reserved for appreciatory mail; it was marked, "Gratitude and sweet words."

There appear, then, to have been two Andrew Carnegies—one tender and caring, the other tough and greedy. The sensitive Carnegie was aware of his own ruthlessness and at age thirty-three, when his income was already more than $50,000 a year, he considered reforming his life. He chastened himself: "No idol [is] more debasing than the worship of money . . . To continue much longer overwhelmed by business cares and with most of my thoughts wholly upon the way to make more money in the shortest time, must degrade me beyond the hope of permanent recovery." When he wrote these lines, he was considering retirement in two years, but instead he devoted three more decades to business.

During those years of pursuing wealth he did seek to avoid "debasing" himself. He chose steel over finance because he wanted to make money by producing something tangible and useful. He took pride in the quality of his steel. And he used some of his money for other people, beginning with an occasional gift of a church organ or a municipal swimming pool. During the rise of Carnegie Steel, his gifts were limited by his policy of plowing most of his profits back into the business. But after selling his company to J. P. Morgan, Andrew Carnegie could devote the remaining nineteen years of his life to philanthropy. He began with a $5 million donation to the benefits and pension fund of his employees. He built 2,811 public libraries around the world, 1,946 of them in the United States. He did not usually attend church but liked religious music, and he gave away almost eight thousand church organs. A few of his grants seem frivolous, like the $400,000 he gave Princeton for an artificial lake to encourage rowing and to "take the young men's minds off football." But most of his gifts were well conceived to educate and edify mankind. He built the Palace of Peace at the Hague; he contributed to Tuskegee Institute; and he helped to finance the movement to grant independence to the Philippines. To organize and perpetuate his philanthropic activities he established the Carnegie Corporation of New York with an endowment of $125 million. When he died on August 11, 1919, he had indeed given away most of his money; he had set aside about 10 percent of this wealth for his wife and daughter.

Through his charitable donations and accomplishments in business Carnegie sought to make real his belief that "all is well since all grows better." He contributed to human progress by producing an important ingredient, steel, at a low price, as well as by building libraries and helping churches and universities. But his great resources came in part from the impoverishment of his laborers. A contemporary columnist, Finley Peter Dunne, questioned Carnegie's priorities by letting one of his characters, a workingman, say that it was all very well that Carnegie was giving away libraries, but that when his turn came to receive one, he would rather have food.

When we attempt to assess Andrew Carnegie, we are faced finally with contrasts. He was a ruthless businessman and a generous philanthropist; he built a great steel company but left his workers poorly clad and housed. He was so dynamic and complex that we seek underlying psychological explanations for his behavior. Historians have suggested that his father's failure and his mother's domination compelled him to seek continually to prove his manhood; or that his stature led him to compensate in business (he was four inches shorter than the average man of his time). It is possible that these factors helped form his personality, but other, more tangible qualities were there, too.

The poverty and helplessness of Carnegie's youth and the grim conditions of his early employment made him desire a good income and engendered the sympathy for the underprivileged that was reflected in his philanthropy if not in his wages. He engaged in business because he enjoyed it and was good at it. He liked creating a large steel company

Andrew Carnegie. Bill Jones said he was "born with two sets of teeth and holes bored for more."

that produced a good product. No doubt many other Americans wanted to do the same thing, but few had the skills of Carnegie: the memory that enabled him to survey every side of a business arrangement, the energy to manage dozens of enterprises, and the courage to take well-calculated risks. Such factors undoubtedly were much more important in Carnegie's triumph than his short stature or his father's failure.

The desire for wealth and native talent for business helped Carnegie and the other great industrialists of his age to prosper. The conditions of their age also facilitated their success: the exploding growth of new inventions, business techniques, and markets as well as the abundance of resources provided an enormous field of activity for the nineteenth-century capitalist. A half century later talented men would face a different world, dominated by large business, in which proportionately fewer poor youths would grow rich. The "organization man" became more common than the capitalist.

Men like Carnegie made possible this transition. One of his greatest achievements was applying careful management techniques to the production of material goods. The techniques of industry as well as its products, in turn, changed America.

Despite, or perhaps because of, the huge and impersonal character of his industry—the Bessemer converters with their gigantic cargoes of molten steel and the factories as populous as small cities—Carnegie tried to think of himself in human, even sentimental measures as the friend of humanity. The industrial world he made, however, was neither moral nor immoral in its own right. Great cities, industrial plants, transportation facilities, entertainment industries, and other features of twentieth-century prosperity grew out of the industrial revolution, radically altering the material conditions of American life. Later generations would address the problems that industrialism created, seeking to improve the rewards of labor and to reduce industry's harm to the environment. But in doing so they would modify rather than remove the new world that men like Andrew Carnegie had built.

Bibliography

BRODY, DAVID. *Steelworkers in America: The Nonunion Era* (1998). New edition of a classic work on steelworkers with seven essays on the significance of the book in labor history.

CARNEGIE, ANDREW. *Autobiography* (1920). Carnegie's interesting and somewhat romanticized history of his life.

———. *Triumphant Democracy* (1886) and *The Gospel of Wealth* (1890). Carnegie's thoughts about industry and the stewardship of wealth.

GUTMAN, HERBERT. *Work, Culture, and Society in Industrializing America* (1976). Focuses on the traditional values and work ethic laborers brought to the factory.

HAYS, SAMUEL P. *The Response to Industrialism* (1957). Influence of industrialism on American society.

HOFSTADTER, RICHARD. *Social Darwinism in American Thought* (1959). Analyzes the social philosophy espoused by Carnegie and other business leaders.

JOSEPHSON, MATTHEW. *The Robber Barons* (1939). Lively narrative history of the new industrialists.

KILMER, PAULETTE D. *The Fear of Sinking: The American Success Formula in the Gilded Age* (1996). Argues that popular culture reveals an emphasis on public service during the time of Andrew Carnegie.

KIRKLAND, EDWARD C. *Industry Comes of Age* (1967). General history of the growth of big business.

KRAUSE, PAUL. *The Battle for Homestead, 1880–1892* (1992). Explores the origins, course, and results of the Homestead strike.

LIVESAY, HAROLD C. *Andrew Carnegie and the Rise of Big Business* (2006). Fine brief biography of Carnegie.

STANDIFORD, LES. *Meet You in Hell: Andrew Carnegie, Henry Clay Frick, and the Bitter Partnership That Transformed America* (2005). A well-written account of the hard-driving entrepreneurial temperament that enriched Carnegie and Frick, sometimes at the expense of their workers.

VAN SLYCK, ABIGAIL A. *Free to All: Carnegie Libraries and American Culture, 1890–1920* (1995). A social and cultural history of the Carnegie libraries.

WALL, JOSEPH FRAZIER. *Andrew Carnegie* (1970). Excellent, thorough biography.
WYLLIE, IRWIN G. *Self-Made Man in America* (1954). Description and analysis of the American belief in the self-made man.

Study Guide

Summary

This essay describes the career of Andrew Carnegie: his youth in Scotland, his early business activities, his years as a steel magnate, and his life as a philanthropist. We encounter the personal qualities—intellect, ambition, and a strong dose of ruthlessness—that enabled Carnegie to succeed. We see how an economy of steel transformed the character of American life and labor, and we discover that even Carnegie himself had difficulty adjusting to the personal reality of the new business world: he became a philanthropist in part to appease his own conscience.

Identification Topics

Andrew Carnegie, Dunfermline, William Carnegie, Pittsburgh, Pennsylvania Railroad, Henry Bessemer, William R. Jones, Herbert Spencer, Homestead strike, Pinkerton's National Detective Agency, Carnegie Steel, U.S. Steel, Social Darwinism, Carnegie Corporation, "The Gospel of Wealth"

Study Questions

1. How did Andrew Carnegie's early life in Scotland influence his respect for industry and success?
2. What qualities enabled Carnegie to make the climb from laborer in a bobbin factory to Thomas Scott's personal secretary on the Pennsylvania Railroad?
3. What were the most important contributions Carnegie made to the growth of his steel company? Notice especially his part in management, salesmanship, and expansion.
4. Many factors besides Andrew Carnegie's entrepreneurship made possible the creation of U.S. Steel. Explain the role of the following: the influence of railroad management, Henry Bessemer, the location of Pittsburgh, the expansion of the iron and steel markets, related industries such as coke manufacture, William R. Jones, the Mesabi Range, J. P. Morgan.
5. What evidence is there that Carnegie was insensitive or cruel to other human beings, especially his father, executive staff, business rivals, workers?
6. What was the attitude of Carnegie's workers toward their jobs? In what ways did they display their enthusiasm? Their discontent?
7. How did Carnegie justify the sometimes harsh course of his business career? How did his belief in Social Darwinism and his philanthropy encourage his sense of self-worth?
8. What were Carnegie's main contributions to America as a businessman? As a philanthropist?
9. What was the value of Carnegie's philanthropy? Would he have achieved more for humanity if he had paid his workers more and had less to give away?

10. To what extent was Andrew Carnegie's success a result of his ability? To what extent was it made possible by his times?
11. Why did the federal government attempt to gain some measure of control over industries such as steel and men such as Andrew Carnegie? Were any of his actions harmful to society?
12. Are there any modern-day Andrew Carnegies?

Research Topics

1. Study other business leaders of Andrew Carnegie's time and compare their personalities, techniques, and achievements with those of Carnegie.
2. Explore the history of the labor movement in the era of Andrew Carnegie. Investigate more fully the history of the Homestead strike.
3. Learn more about Social Darwinism and the philosophy of the self-made man in this period.
4. Study the effect of the growth of the steel industry on Pittsburgh.
5. Read a few Horatio Alger stories. What similarities and differences do you note between the heroes of those tales and the life of Andrew Carnegie?
6. Consider whether Andrew Carnegie's career would be possible today. Evaluate how modern economic conditions and modern government regulations might have changed the course of his career.
7. Study the efforts in Andrew Carnegie's lifetime to regulate big business.
8. Examine the living conditions of industrial workers during this time.
9. Explore the career of Andrew Carnegie as philanthropist and evaluate the impact of his charitable activities.

CHAPTER 3

The Birth of Environmentalism

John Muir and the American Wilderness

The late nineteenth century was an era of business. Its heroes were men like Andrew Carnegie, who created giant industries, and its spirit was so strong that Booker T. Washington told his black students that in commerce they had "a man's chance" to prosper. In every age, however, some people oppose the prevailing values: Loyalists oppose a revolution; abolitionists reject an institution. In the age of enterprise, some Americans challenged the business ideal of unfettered individualism. Labor unions sought the right to bargain; farmers attempted to regulate railroads and grain elevators. Those years also brought American conservationism to fruition. John Muir was the foremost spokesman for that movement, a pastoral voice in an age of steel. He was as bright and energetic as any business leader, but he chose to celebrate nature rather than transform it. His life illustrates the course of the early conservation movement and provides an example of how some human beings influence history by choosing career paths contrary to the dominant ideas of their age.

One fine summer day in 1868 the young John Muir stood by a cliff edge hung over the Yosemite Valley. A half mile below, the land "seemed to be dressed like a garden—sunny meadows here and there, and groves of Pine and Oak." Nearby the Yosemite River cascaded through a channel in the rock, sped down a short incline, and sprang "out free in the air." Muir wanted a clear sight of the waterfall and began to work his way down the rock. Below he could see a narrow shelf that might support his heels over the sheer cliff. But he must slide down a steep incline to reach the ledge; if he missed, he would fall to his death. He wondered whether to go on.

The events of a lifetime, thirty years of growth in Scotland and America, had brought John Muir to this precarious position. As a child he had often taken chances for a better view of nature, and recently he had completed a solitary thousand-mile hike from Indiana to the Gulf of Mexico. He had risked his life before but had never faced danger as overwhelming as this Yosemite cliff. Still he would go on. He filled his mouth with artemisia leaves, hoping the bitter taste would prevent giddiness. He then worked his way down to the ledge; it held him, and he was able to shuffle twenty or thirty feet to the side of the falls. There he found what he wanted—"a perfectly free view down into the heart of the snowy, chanting throng of comet-like streamers, into which the body of the fall soon separates." Muir could not later recall how long he had stood over the falls or even how he had gotten back to the rim. But in camp after dark that night he recorded in his journal that "the tremendous grandeur of the fall" had smothered all fear. He had had a "glorious time."

Muir survived and wrote about this and hundreds of his experiences in the wilderness, making the Yosemite Falls episode part of his legend. Muir himself grew into the most popular and influential American conservation leader. Edwin Way Teale, another great figure in American wilderness history, said, "Of those who have written of nature surpassingly well . . . John Muir was the wildest. He was the most active, the most at home in the wilderness, the most daring, the most capable, the most self-reliant."

Despite such praise, Muir appears to have been out of step with his times. When he was born in 1838 the American population was barely sixteen million. Half the territory that would become the fifty United States was controlled by Native American tribal governments. In large sections of the country, buffalo, mountain lion, and grizzly bear roamed a wilderness hardly known to whites. The plow had barely crossed the Mississippi, and the Great Central Valley of California was "one bed of golden and purple flowers" clothing millions of acres. When Muir died three quarters of a century later, the population had reached nearly one hundred million. A quarter million miles of railroad tracks intersected the land, and the forty-eight contiguous states were part of a federal union that stretched from ocean to ocean. The buffalo was nearly exterminated, and the mountain lion and grizzly bear had retreated to remote mountain refuges. The great American prairies and valleys had been broken by the plow.

Muir's career and personality ran against the grain of all this progress. In an age when a frontiersman named Tom Nixon became a hero for killing 140 buffalo in forty minutes (and 7,000 in a month), John Muir argued that animals as well as human beings are God's creatures and have rights. Alive at the dawn of the automobile era, Muir complained that even the stagecoach moved too fast for passengers to see anything worthwhile. And in a nation that gloried in its ability to conquer nature—to convert redwoods into lumber and mountain meadows into grazing land—Muir held that wild nature must be preserved. Thus, while other men were inventing the light-bulb, building giant corporations, or laying railroad tracks, John Muir was exploring the American wilderness.

It is possible to see Muir as a cantankerous individualist, one of those men whom Henry David Thoreau described as marching to the beat of a "different drummer." Certainly he was exceptional. More perhaps than any other American, Muir sought continually to expose himself to the wilderness. He climbed a tree in a windstorm, rode down a mountainside on an avalanche, and stood in the open to watch the progress of a Yosemite earthquake. On his hiking expeditions he frequently carried only a metal cup, tea leaves, and some dry bread, preferring simple fare and a bed of pine needles to a cluttered campsite.

But John Muir was not a hermit or a misanthrope. In fact, he was to become one of the most influential men of his day. During these years when Americans were settling the last frontiers, respect for nature became part of the American credo. Muir helped make it happen. He wrote articles in national magazines, founded a wilderness preservation society, and fought for the protection of wilderness areas. Eventually his name would adorn campsites, lakes, mountains, and forests. It appears more often in California's nomenclature than that of any other man. The Muir Woods near San Francisco, the John Muir Trail along the Sierra Nevada crest, and the Muir Grove in Sequoia National Park are a few of the more famous sites bearing his name.

John Muir's life began in Dunbar, Scotland, in 1838. He was raised in a substantial house in the center of town, but most of his early memories were of expeditions into nearby fields and to the sea. In later years he wrote, "When I was a boy in Scotland I was fond of everything that was wild." He and other boys took long runs on country lanes and explored the rocks and pools along the shore of the North Sea. They grew hardy in scraps at school and in competitions to prove their bravery. As a boy John climbed down the sheer walls of a dungeon in the ruins of Dunbar Castle and scaled the steep roof outside his bedroom window. He later recalled sitting on the rooftop in the night and "looking at the scenery over the garden wall while the wind was howling and threatening to blow me off."

Muir remembered his youthful adventures as a wonderful beginning to a life lived close to nature. But unfortunately his complicated and over-bearing father thought otherwise. Daniel Muir was a merchant and a farmer by trade, but he was above all obsessed with religion. He constantly read the Bible and other religious works such as Foxe's *Book of Martyrs*. His view of the godly household was austere and forebidding. He allowed no pictures, considering them graven images forbidden by the Scriptures; he sprinkled his conversation with biblical allusions; and he frowned on gaiety. John's mother, Ann, a naturally cheerful person, was jovial only when her husband was absent. John said his father "devoutly believed that quenching every spark of pride and self-confidence was a sacred duty."

Daniel saw his son's wilderness forays as wasteful, devilish behavior. Every time John went exploring, he realized he might be severely beaten. But, as he later recalled, "no punishment, however sure and severe, was of any avail against the attraction of the fields and woods."

John spent his first eleven years in Dunbar. For education he received mainly lessons in French, English, and Latin, with some work also in spelling, arithmetic, history, and geography. He later compared his early learning with the "progressive" educational philosophies in vogue at the turn of the century. In Scotland, he said, "there was nothing said about making the seats easy or the lessons easy." If students failed to learn a lesson, they were beaten, "for the grand, simple, all-sufficing Scotch discovery had been made that there was a close connection between the skin and the memory." His father added to John's assignments the memorizing of several Bible verses each day, and before he was eleven John had learned most of the Scriptures "by heart and by sore flesh." Even in the schoolyard, however, the wilderness was not far away. From the playground the boys could look out over the sea and watch sailing ships moving past. "In stormy weather," Muir recalled, "they were all smothered in clouds and spray, and showers of salt scud torn from the tops of the waves came flying over the playground wall."

While John was learning lessons from man and nature, his father was formulating a plan to move the family to America. It is not entirely clear why he decided to leave Scotland, for he was able to provide well for himself and his family in Dunbar. His spiritual restlessness may have moved him. In recent years he had changed from one religious denomination to another before becoming a Disciple of Christ. He may have hoped to find more people with similar religious views in America, as well as more economic opportunities for his large family.

At any rate, one day he announced that they were going to America. He sold his business and booked passage on a ship from Glasgow. John was delighted. To him, America meant "no more grammar, but boundless woods full of mysterious good things." John enjoyed his first ocean voyage, climbing all over the ship and helping with the work when the crew would let him. But it was a hard voyage. For forty-five days they were on the ship, often in heavy seas making it too dangerous to light cook fires on deck or lanterns and candles below. They ate salt pork and potatoes and sometimes bits of candy their father had brought along. John's sister, Sarah, dreadfully seasick, stayed in her bunk for the whole trip.

They reached the United States in early spring 1849. Daniel carefully collected information on places to live and settled on Wisconsin after learning from a Buffalo, New York, grain dealer that most of his wheat was from that region. By packet boat, lake steamer, and horse-drawn wagon they traveled to Portage, a boom town on the path of a proposed canal that would unite the Fox and Wisconsin Rivers, providing a water route between the Great Lakes and the Mississippi River. With the help of a friend they located some land by Fountain Lake, ten miles from Portage. There they built a small shack and began to clear the land.

Fountain Lake, surrounded by forest and meadow, was a beautiful place. It was alive with wildlife, especially such birds as wood ducks, chickadees, nuthatches, prairie chickens, and bobwhites. The children played hide-and-seek in the fields and explored the countryside. Muir later recalled that there nature streamed "into us, wooingly teaching her wonderful glowing lessons . . . every wild lesson a love lesson, not whipped but charmed into us. Oh, that glorious Wisconsin wilderness."

But John's father was no more sympathetic to play in Wisconsin than in Scotland. He turned increasingly to religious studies and became a lay preacher in the local Disciples church. He left John and the other children to do most of the farmwork. They turned the virgin soil with a "breaking plow," then grubbed out the roots and bushes. When they burned these on a great bonfire, Daniel characteristically used the occasion to lecture the children on the terrors of hell. At twelve John was put to work guiding the heavy plow behind an ox team. Even the girls had to work in the fields. The boys slept upstairs in an unheated room, three in a bed, where the quilt froze by their faces on the cold mornings and they rushed downstairs in bare feet to dress before the kitchen stove. Their food was scanty. For a time Daniel Muir put the whole family on an unbalanced vegetable diet that slowly drained their strength. He allowed more food only after a neighbor accused him of ruining the family's health.

One of John Muir's worst experiences came in digging a well for his father. Day after day he had to chisel his way through sandstone down a hole three feet wide. Eighty feet down he was nearly killed by poisonous gas in the shaft. Neighbors told the Muirs how to clear out the gas, and John had to cut through another ten feet to strike water. It is no wonder that he later wrote, "Farming was a grim, material, debasing pursuit under Father's generalship."

Never close to his father, John did come to respect other adults in the neighborhood. One man lent him books, such as Scott's Waverly novels. Others loved to recite poetry and encouraged John's interest in literature. In these early years, his greatest achievements were in mechanics. He found that with a simple penknife and pieces of wood he could build clocks, barometers, and a waterwheel. His father allowed him no time during the day for such exercises but said he could work on them before breakfast. Delighted to have some time he could call his own, John began rising at 1:00 A.M. In the basement he built all kinds of gadgets. From an old iron wagon-box rod he fashioned a huge thermometer that could be seen from far out in the fields, so sensitive that it could record the heat change caused by someone approaching within five feet. He also built a contraption to raise a sleeper out of bed at a designated hour and another to feed the horses automatically.

Some of the neighbors thought John was a crank. Others recognized his inventive genius, and one of these encouraged him to exhibit at the Wisconsin State Fair and to enter a mechanical trade. John was now twenty-one and could legally determine his own course of life, but the choice was difficult. His father wanted him to stay at home and work on the farm. His friends encouraged his inventiveness. John was still drawn to the wilderness. But in those days before the National Park and Forest Services were created, there seemed to be no way to combine a love of wilderness with a career. John sometimes walked the roads around his house all night pondering his course. "I used to spend hours with my head up in the sky," he writes. "I soared among the planets and thought."

He finally decided to leave home, taking with him as many of his inventions as he could carry. His father refused to say good-bye, but his mother gave him a gold coin to help him on his way. At the station in Portage the conductor was impressed by Muir's collection of inventions and introduced him to the engineer. With the engineer's approval John rode across Wisconsin on the cowcatcher platform at the front of the train.

In Madison John exhibited his inventions at the state fair. They attracted large crowds and were reported enthusiastically in the local press. One paper called Muir a "genuine genius." When word of his success reached home, it provoked joyful congratulations from his mother, brother, and sisters—and a solemn letter from his father on the danger of vanity.

John was offered several jobs. He worked for a time with a man who had invented a steam-powered iceboat. But he soon came back to the University of Wisconsin at Madison. Muir gained incalculably from his college education. His good mind and buoyant personality made him popular on campus. He was slender and almost six feet tall. He let his light red hair and beard grow long—he never shaved and he bothered little about grooming. His sisters said that he looked "wild as a loon," which he took as a compliment. Those who knew him often commented on his eyes, and one of his admirers said that he had "the twinklingest blue eyes" she had ever seen. He soon became known for his inventions, which he set up in his room along with several new gadgets, including a desk with a mechanism that put books in front of him at intervals to keep his work on schedule, a contraption to light a fire in the morning, and a "loafer's chair" that fired off a pistol when anyone sat in it. Muir's room became a college showplace and was visited even by members of the state legislature.

Muir's years at the university might easily have led the inventive student into a career in mechanics, engineering, or business. Instead, higher education reinforced his taste for wilderness. Previously his relationship to nature had been recreational and intuitive. He enjoyed being outdoors and observing plant and animal life, but these pleasures had no apparent relationship to an adult world of thought and action. At the University of Wisconsin he learned that religion, science, and literature might all be involved in the study of the wilderness.

He studied geology under Ezra Slocum Carr, who had worked at Harvard under Louis Agassiz, one of the foremost scientists of the nineteenth century. Many geologists at that time relied on the biblical account of the Great Flood to explain characteristics of the earth. Agassiz and Carr argued that scientists should study the land itself with a "seeing eye." They believed such studies revealed that a "universal ice age" had helped shape the earth's contours. Taking to their studies a traditional faith in divine omnipotence, they relied more on God's handiwork than on Scripture. Agassiz wrote: "The glacier was God's great plow and when it vanished from the surface of the land, it left it prepared for the hand of the husbandman." To help his students read the land Professor Carr frequently took them into the country on field trips, and so he taught Muir that one could go into the wilderness for scientific and theological reasons as well as for recreation.

Muir took a similar lesson from his studies in botany. A fellow student, Milton Griswold, showed him how plants can be identified by their leaves and other organs. Muir remarked, "Why Griswold, that's perfectly wonderful!" He purchased a botany book and began to study the characteristics of, and relationships among, plants.

Another valuable lesson came from his literature professor, James Davie Butler, who introduced Muir to the works of Ralph Waldo Emerson and urged his students to keep "commonplace books" with accounts of the day-to-day events in their lives. Emerson's writings on nature revealed that the wilderness is a realm filled with literary and philosophic inspiration, and a journal gave Muir a way of recording the details of his wilderness experience for later literary use.

Muir also encountered men who were beginning the battle to conserve natural resources. In the early years of European settlement, America had so much land and so few people that no thought had been given to preserving the wilderness; it was considered something that could be taken for granted. But by the time Muir entered the university, American forests were falling with fearful rapidity. Railroads and steamboats alone used ten million cords of wood a year. Wood was the primary building material and fuel for thirty million Americans. A few farsighted individuals were warning against unchecked exploitation of the wilderness. Increase A. Lapham, Wisconsin's foremost conservationist, actively campaigned for restrictions on timber companies. Alexander von Humboldt, author and naturalist, claimed that destroying trees would eventually destroy the watershed. At the university Muir heard these ideas, and they helped develop his sensitivity to the wilderness as something to preserve as well as to cherish.

In retrospect, Muir's Wisconsin education was admirably suited to his later career. But in 1864 when he departed from the university, his course was by no means clear. Muir considered specializing in a branch of natural studies, such as astronomy; instead, for the next few years he combined short wilderness expeditions with work in factories.

In 1863 he explored sections of the Wisconsin and Mississippi Rivers, and in the following summer he walked through upper Michigan and Ontario, Canada, collecting plants and keeping a journal. But when it came to earning a living he turned to activities in which his mechanical ability and inventiveness were most useful. From 1864 to 1866 he worked in an Ontario sawmill and rake factory. He invented several machines that doubled production and was offered a partnership in the company. He refused, explaining frankly, "I love nature too well to spend my life in a work that involves the destruction of God's forests."

He moved on to Indianapolis, Indiana, in 1866 and went to work for Osgood, Smith, and Company, which manufactured hubs, spokes, and other carriage parts. Again he invented machinery and rose quickly in his employer's esteem. He was asked to write a report on the management of the factory, and he made a number of suggestions for more efficient operation. Once more he was offered a management position and a partnership.

John Muir clearly had the ability to become a successful businessman. His inventive and organizational abilities suggest that he might have become another Thomas Edison or Henry Ford. But the wilderness was always there. While working in Ontario and Indiana, Muir spent his weekends in the woods. His enthusiasm for the outdoors was so infectious that numerous friends in both places often accompanied him into the forests.

He later described these years as a time of great inner turmoil. The nation, recovering from the ravages of the Civil War, needed business leaders; his family might need financial help. His talents in manufacturing were apparent. Surely he could pursue a career in business and devote his spare moments to his wilderness avocation.

But then in March 1867 an event forced him to reevaluate once more what he wanted to do with his life. Late one day he was working with a sharp file on one of the machines. It slipped and pierced the cornea of his right eye. He recalled, "I would gladly have died where I stood." Both eyes were affected, and a doctor declared that Muir would not see again. For weeks he lay in a darkened room. "My days," he wrote, "were terrible beyond what I can tell, and my nights were if possible more terrible. Frightful dreams exhausted and terrified me."

One of his friends brought another doctor, a specialist who told Muir that the injured eye would recover and in time he would be able to see again with both eyes. Muir felt like a man "arisen from the grave." He now decided to delay no longer before going to the wilderness and wrote, "God has to nearly kill us sometimes to teach us lessons."

It was still not clear to Muir how he might spend his whole adult life in the wilderness, but he was determined at least to pass the next three years "botanizing." Afterward he would settle down, but the long stay in nature, he said, would be "sufficient to lighten and brighten my afterlife in the gloom and hunger of civilization's defrauding duties."

Before setting out he made a final visit to his Wisconsin home. There he affirmed his relationship to nature. Daniel Muir still identified wilderness with evil and told John his study of geology and botany was blasphemous. The son replied, "I'll tell you this, Father, I've been spending my time a lot nearer the Almighty than you have." In the years ahead he would continue to believe that he was close to God in the wilderness.

In fall 1867 Muir set out on his thousand-mile walk from Indiana to the Gulf of Mexico. "I wandered afoot and alone," he wrote, "with a plant-press on my back, holding a generally southward course, like the birds when they are going from summer to winter." He carried a few supplies and little cash. His route over the hills and mountains of Kentucky and Tennessee took him through country that had been devastated by the Civil War. He encountered bands of outlaws more than once. Along the way he collected botanical specimens that he sent to his brother in Wisconsin for safekeeping. His description of the journey in *A Thousand-Mile Walk to the Gulf*, an account published many years later, displays his youthful enthusiasm. His ability to justify this wandering life was exhibited in an encounter with a blacksmith in the mountains of eastern Tennessee.

He stopped at the man's house to seek lodging. The blacksmith appeared, "Hammer in hand, bare-breasted, sweaty, begrimed, and covered with shaggy black hair." He invited Muir to spend the night but during dinner questioned him closely about what he was doing. When he learned that Muir was wandering through the South collecting plants, he told him that he should be doing something more useful. "These are hard times," he said, "and real work is required of every man that is able. Picking up blossoms doesn't seem to be a man's work at all in any kind of times." John Muir was undaunted; he reminded the blacksmith that the great King Solomon had studied plants and that Christ had told his disciples to "consider the lilies." He asked his host, "Whose advice am I to take, yours or Christ's?" The blacksmith was impressed by Muir's reply, calling him "a very strong-minded man," and admitted that he had "never thought of blossoms in that way before." It was one of Muir's strengths that he could do things that were unusual and also persuade others that what he was doing was worthwhile. He used the "consider the lilies" text again in his later writings when he wanted to encourage his readers to visit the national parks.

John Muir's walk finally took him to the southern tip of Florida; from there he went by boat to Cuba where he spent several weeks in botanical explorations. He had intended to go to South America and visit the Amazon, but his funds were low. It hardly mattered. "All the world was before me," he wrote, "and every day was a holiday, so it did not seem important to which of the world's wildernesses I first should wander." He had seen pictures of the Yosemite Valley in California and decided he would continue his travels in the Far West. He took steerage passage on a crowded ship to the Isthmus of Panama and then traveled to San Francisco. He arrived on March 28, 1868, but did not linger. On the streets he asked a carpenter how to get out of the city. The man asked him where he wanted to go, and Muir replied, "Anywhere that is wild."

Once out of San Francisco, Muir crossed the coastal range by Pacheco Pass and looked down on the Great Central Valley, "level and flowery, like a lake of pure sunshine." He called it "the floweriest piece of the world." He camped there for a time and then walked on toward the Sierra Nevada. When he saw the mountain range, it was "so gloriously colored and so radiant, it seemed not clothed with light, but wholly composed of it, like the wall of some celestial city." He hiked up the Merced River to Yosemite Valley. "No temple made with hands can compare with Yosemite," he later wrote. "Every rock in its walls seems to glow with life." His health, damaged by the malarial swamps of the South, recovered quickly in the clean mountain air.

In the months and years ahead John Muir became as much a feature of Yosemite Valley as the forests and rocks. He spent his winters in a small cabin in the valley, sharing its snowy isolation with a few other white men and Indians. He worked intermittently as a shepherd and sawmill hand to earn his keep, but he spent most of his time exploring. He was an adventurer, a philosopher, a botanist, and a geologist. It was in this period that he stood on the brink of Yosemite Falls. That episode and others like it reflect his constant effort to see the whole region from every possible angle of vision and in every possible condition.

When an earthquake rocked the valley on March 26, 1872, and other men huddled in their beds in deathly fear, Muir was delighted. Here is how he describes the scene: "One morning about two o'clock, I was aroused by an earthquake; and though I had never before enjoyed a storm of this sort, the strange, wild thrilling motion and rumbling could not be mistaken, and I ran out of my cabin, near the Sentinel Rock, both glad and frightened, shouting, 'A noble earthquake!' feeling sure I was going to learn something." As Muir stood outside, he watched a great rock split away from a cliff and shower down on the valley, "making a terribly sublime and beautiful spectacle." Muir had theorized that the valley's sharp sides were fashioned by earthquakes. Now he had seen evidence.

In a less dramatic way he discovered how glaciers had shaped Yosemite Valley. In months of hiking and climbing in the region he saw on the rocks many signs of ancient glacial activity. At that time the leading theory on the valley's origins was that of Josiah D. Whitney, a Harvard professor who had been hired by the state of California to do a geological survey. Whitney spent many years on his work, publishing authoritative volumes on California's geology. He held that the Yosemite Valley had come into being when a section of the Sierra Nevada had sunk into a great hole beneath. Muir was unconvinced, remarking wryly, "the bottom never dropped out of anything that God made." While working at the sawmill in the valley, he had spent part of his time as a tourist guide. He used these encounters with visitors to state his views on the origins of the valley. In 1871, at the urging of friends, he published the first of several articles explaining his glacial theory. When Josiah Whitney heard of Muir's work, he vehemently dismissed his arguments as those of "a mere sheepherder" and "an ignoramus." It was several decades before scientists generally accepted Muir's views. But many important men were impressed with his work. The president of the Massachusetts Institute of Technology, one of the tourists he conducted around the valley, was so taken by Muir that he urged him to come east and teach at the institute. The great Louis Agassiz, among the first to propose the theory of universal glaciation, so admired Muir's work that he wrote, "Here is the first man who has any adequate conception of glacial action."

With all this recognition Muir once more had to reevaluate his choice of a career. He still had no vocation in the traditional sense, calling himself "an unknown nobody in the woods." He had planned to take up a conventional career after three years of wandering, but now those having passed, he saw no reason to leave the mountains, which so intrigued and inspired him. "I only went out for a walk," he wrote, "and finally concluded to stay out till sundown, for going out, I found, was really going in."

Fortunately, his new-found popularity as a writer was a way to earn a living from his wilderness travels. He did most of his writing while

John Muir's wilderness worlds. From Florida to California he visited the American wilderness, helping to create a conservation ethic.

living with friends in Oakland and San Francisco. He complained about these periods of forced absence from the mountains but nonetheless developed a fine flowing style that conveyed his enthusiasm for nature. A century later his word pictures still lure readers out of their urban homes into the mountains and forests he so beautifully described. His writing is characterized by strong adjectives and metaphors. On the ability of the juniper and the rock pine to resist the wind he says: "Their stiff, crooked roots grip the stormbeaten ledges." Sunrise in the Yosemite brings "another reviving morning. Down the long mountain-slopes the sunbeams pour, guiding the awakening pines, cheering every needle, filling every living thing with joy." The Bridal Veil waterfall is "clad in gauzy, sun-sifted spray."

Describing the flora and fauna of the wilderness led Muir to a philosophy of nature. He believed that civilization makes people competitive, narrow, and dull. The wilderness calls forth their more generous impulses and inspires them with its vitality. Humanity is out of tune with the whole cosmos, with the primary force that creates and sustains the world. Although Muir rejected the biblical idea of an anthropomorphic god, he did believe that the universe, and man with it, was guided by a great spiritual force. To see the force, all one has to do is go into the wilderness and observe how nature operates. He wrote: "Heaven knows that John the Baptist was not more eager to get his fellow sinners into the Jordan than I to baptize mine in the beauty of God's mountains."

In the 1870s Muir preached a gospel of the wilderness while continuing his wanderings. After his early explorations of the Yosemite region he began to travel farther afield. In 1873 he hiked the whole length of the Sierra Nevada. In the years following he explored sections of the Rocky Mountains, the Pacific Northwest, and Alaska.

As he approached his fortieth birthday his enthusiasm for wild nature was unabated, but he began to envy his brothers and sisters who had married and were rearing families. In 1879 he began courting Louie Strentzen, daughter of a wealthy fruit rancher in the Alhambra Valley, a few miles east of San Francisco. They were married on April 14, 1880, and the couple settled on her father's land, where John immediately became involved in running the orchards. Louie well understood John's need for nature and encouraged him to take the three months before the busy fall harvest to go on with his travels. He returned to Alaska in 1880 and 1881, exploring several regions where no white man had been before. Muir loved these forays into the wilderness but was ambivalent about leaving his family. When he was on a ship off the coast of Alaska in the midst of beautiful sea and mountains, he wrote Louie: "I was just thinking . . . of our warm, sunny home, and Annie [their infant] in her soft blankets . . . and of the red cherries down the hill. . . . Oh, if I could touch my baby and thee." During the next seven years John Muir spent most of his time managing the orchards, raising Bartlett pears and Tokay grapes. He worked hard and managed the business efficiently, so that he quickly became one of the most successful ranchers in his area. In 1886 a second daughter was born.

Muir sought to teach his children a religious creed quite different from that of his father's, encouraging them to revere God, "not as a person, but as a loving, intelligent spirit creating, permeating, and controlling the universe." In many ways John Muir was an ideal father and husband—devoted, resourceful, open. But the years as a rancher wore at him. He complained of "the eternal grind, grind, grind" and compared himself to a wild animal in a cage. His friends and his wife urged him to spend more time exploring and writing about the wilderness. Louie regretted what the ranch was doing to him and even urged him to sell it. His health began to deteriorate.

Finally in 1888 Muir took his first extensive trip to the mountains in many years. The high point of the journey was a climb to the top of Mount Rainier. ("Did not mean to climb it," he wrote to Louie, "but got excited and soon was on top.") In the next year he went to Yosemite with Robert Underwood Johnson, an editor for *Century* magazine, one of the foremost periodicals in the nation. Muir was shocked at the deterioration caused by sheep and tourists. At Johnson's urging he agreed to write a series of articles in *Century* arguing that Yosemite be made into a national park. At that time the valley belonged to California, and although it was a state park it was open to exploitation by timber and grazing interests.

By 1890 Muir's brother-in-law arrived in California to help manage the orchards. From then on he was able to devote more time to the wilderness. In that year, partly because of Muir's articles in *Century*, Yosemite became a national park. In the following years Muir enveloped himself more in conservation issues. In his youth he urged people to appreciate rather than to conserve the wilderness. In the 1870s, when many sections of the Sierra Nevada had not even been explored, men did not seem to pose a threat. But by the 1890s timber and livestock companies were tearing away at the mountains. By illegally claiming lands or by simply stealing trees from public lands, lumbermen destroyed some of the finest redwood groves in the mountains. Often they used dynamite to blast the big trees, wasting three quarters of the timber. Simultaneously, hundreds of thousands of sheep—which Muir called "hoofed locusts"—were destroying the native flowers and grasses of the mountain meadows.

When John Muir returned to the wilderness in 1890 after almost a decade away, he was not only a writer but a propagandist for conservation. In 1892 with a few friends he founded the Sierra Club, which planned outings in the wilderness and lobbied for conservation issues. Muir became associated with the National Forest Commission in 1897, appointed to survey the nation's wilderness areas. The most influential member was a young man named Gifford Pinchot. At first Muir and Pinchot got along well. Both loved the outdoors, and both opposed careless exploitation of the wilderness. But it soon was apparent that Pinchot's goal was planned use of the wilderness, not preservation. Muir told Pinchot he wanted nothing more to do with him after the younger man favored allowing sheep to graze in the forest reserves. The conflict between their ideals—planned use and preservation—would split the conservation movement for many years to come.

To promote his views Muir published a series of influential articles in the *Atlantic Monthly* in 1899. These were so popular that the editor, Walter Hines Page, declared that they improved the magazine's circulation enormously. The articles helped win support for the growing conservation movement and added to Muir's reputation as its foremost leader.

John Muir was at the height of his popularity and influence a few years later in 1901, when he made one of his most extraordinary visits to Yosemite. Over the years he had escorted many important men and women into the mountains. Now he learned that President Theodore Roosevelt wanted to visit the park in Muir's company. Muir may have anticipated no more than a few private minutes with the president, but Roosevelt had other plans. After traveling to Yosemite in a large party, Muir and the president rode away alone on horseback to a remote section of the park. They set out their sleeping bags and cooked over a large fire. "Now this is bully!" said Roosevelt. That night the president sat by the crackling flames and listened to Muir talk about the wilderness. They awakened with four inches of snow on their sleeping bags, but the president, undaunted, insisted on spending two more nights in the wilderness. At the end of the trip he told Muir, "I've had the time of my life!"

The trip with Roosevelt reflected Muir's national prominence as a conservationist and outdoorsman. He was now in his sixties and could not make the long backcountry trips that he had taken as a younger man. But he still traveled extensively. In 1901–1902 he made a trip around the world. He spent many hours in Europe's leading museums. ("A monstrous dose of civilization," he called it.) But he particularly enjoyed seeing new wildernesses—the Himalayas from Darjeeling, Australia from atop a stagecoach. Nine years later he made a long trip through South America and Africa. He also made many shorter trips to the Sierra Nevada and to the Petrified Forest in Arizona.

During these years he pulled together his notes from journals and articles written many years before and arranged them in a series of books. The *Atlantic* articles became *Our National Parks*. His other books in this period included *The Yosemite* and *The Story of My Boyhood and Youth*. These and other volumes helped spread Muir's philosophy of the wilderness.

He was also involved more and more in battles to preserve wilderness. The most important of these involved the effort to prevent a dam in the Sierra. To the south of Yosemite canyon lies another known as Hetch Hetchy. This valley consists of rock formations that rival Yosemite's, and in Muir's time its vegetation was even lovelier than that of its sister canyon. It was included in the boundaries of Yosemite Park, but influential

San Franciscans fancied it as a place to build a reservoir. Hetch Hetchy aroused a classic struggle between those who believe the wilderness should be preserved and admired and those who would "conquer" and use it. Arguments initiated by each side in this encounter have been repeated again and again in subsequent conflicts over the wilderness.

The dam's proponents claimed it was essential to create a reservoir in Hetch Hetchy to give San Francisco a stable water supply. They painted sensational images of people suffering in a city without water, argued that the canyon was a practical site for an inexpensive dam, and contended that the new lake would actually enhance the beauty of the region. They even said that the site could be easily acquired because it was public land.

Muir met their arguments at every point. Yes, he said, people have practical needs, but they also have spiritual needs. They should not attempt to make everything "immediately and selfishly commercial," for they need "beauty as well as bread." He argued that nature is essential to good health; it heals and cheers body and soul. Moreover, he pointed out that there were several alternative damsites—surely San Francisco could serve its utilitarian needs in some other region. Finally, he criticized the idea that the reservoir would increase the area's beauty; it would bury the lovely valley floor. His essay, which appears in *The Yosemite*, concludes: "Dam Hetch Hetchy! As well dam for water-tanks the people's cathedrals and churches, for no holier temple has ever been consecrated by the heart of man."

Muir fought the Hetch Hetchy battle in every possible arena. He wrote articles, organized a massive public campaign, and persuaded such friends as railroad magnate Edward H. Harriman to lobby against the bill. In his seventy-fifth year he was still fighting the dam. He wrote to one friend that be hoped the struggle would end soon; it was killing him. That year the conflict did end. Muir and his supporters met defeat when the dam proposal bill passed Congress in December 1913.

The old mountaineer took the loss well; many other wilderness areas would survive. He could also take comfort because his belief in the worth of wilderness was now shared by millions of Americans. The life that had begun with a personal love of nature had matured into a useful career and encouraged a historic movement.

Muir continued to write in the following year. At Christmastime he went south to visit his daughter, Helen. While with her, he caught pneumonia. He died on December 24, 1914. He had often reflected on death and had faced it many times in the mountains. He spoke of it as "going home." After death the soul would be free to wander through the wilderness uninhibited by a physical body and earthly cares. He once described how he would begin that pilgrimage: "My first journeys would be into the inner substance of flowers, and among the folds and mazes of Yosemite's falls. How grand to move about in the very tissue of falling columns, and in the very birthplace of their heavenly harmonies, looking outward as from windows of ever-varying transparency and staining!"

Bibliography

BADE, WILLIAM F. *The Life and Letters of John Muir* (2 vols., 1923). Especially useful for its selection of Muir letters.

HAYS, SAMUEL. *Conservation and the Gospel of Efficiency* (1959). Classic study of conservation in the early twentieth century.

HOLMES, STEVEN J. *The Young John Muir: An Environmental Biography* (1999). Argues that Muir's psychological development was important in shaping his relationship to the wilderness.

KRECH, SHEPARD, III. *The Ecological Indian: Myth and History* (1999). Explores ways that Indians shaped and sometimes abused the natural environment.

McCLELLAND, LINDA FLINT. *Building the National Parks: Historic Landscape Design and Construction* (1998). Explores the way landscape architects have influenced the way that tourists experience national parks.

McGEARY, M. NELSON. *Gifford Pinchot: Forester-Politician* (1960). Biography of leading advocate of planned use of the wilderness.

MILLARD, CANDICE. *The River of Doubt: Theodore Roosevelt's Darkest Journey* (2005). Theodore Roosevelt, the first environmentalist president, almost lost his life in the Amazonian expedition described in this book.

NASH, RODERICK. *Wilderness and the American Mind* (1967 and later editions). Excellent historical analysis of American attitudes toward the wilderness.

PETULLA, JOSEPH M. *American Environmental History* (1977). Survey of the exploitation and conservation of American natural resources.

RUNTE, ALFRED. *National Parks: The American Experience* (1979). How America's national parks came into being.

TEALE, EDWIN WAY, EDITOR. *The Wilderness World of John Muir* (1976). The best one-volume anthology of Muir's writings.

WOLFE, LINNIE MARSH. *Son of the Wilderness: John Muir* (1945). A well-researched and lively biography.

Study Guide

Summary

From the previous chapter on Andrew Carnegie we turn to an entirely different kind of man, John Muir. Like Carnegie, Muir was born near Edinburgh, Scotland, in the 1830s, and like him he had a knack for business and invention. But while Carnegie devoted most of his life to industry, Muir gave his to the wilderness. The essay discusses his boyhood in Scotland and Wisconsin, his decision to abandon a promising business career for nature, his wanderings in California and elsewhere, and his contributions to the environmental protection movement. This article and the Carnegie essay show that conservationism and industrialization, two movements that continue today to compete for national support, had their inception at roughly the same time in American history.

Identification Topics

John Muir, Tom Nixon, Dunbar, Daniel Muir, Portage, Wisconsin, Louis Agassiz, Yosemite Valley, Josiah D. Whitney, Gifford Pinchot, Hetch Hetchy, Sierra Club, "hoofed locusts"

Study Questions

1. What was John Muir's attitude toward formal religion? How did his father's religiosity affect him? In what sense did religion enter into his relationship with nature?
2. What is the evidence that John Muir could have been a successful inventor or industrialist? In what ways did he take his scientific interests and organizational skills into the wilderness?
3. How did Muir come to devote himself to the wilderness? Explain the role of the following: his boyhood, the university, business experience, a sharp file, the thousand-mile walk, writing, Louie, timber, and sheep interests.
4. In what ways did John Muir contribute to the preservation of American wilderness? Explain why he became a conservationist as well as a naturalist.
5. What is the difference between conservationism and planned use?
6. What arguments were voiced on each side in the Hetch Hetchy fight?
7. Compare and contrast John Muir and Andrew Carnegie, especially their relations with other people, their abilities, and their ideas of the good society. Which man contributed more to America?
8. Why did conservationism make a start as a national movement in the late nineteenth century? Would the movement have begun if John Muir had not lived?
9. Was John Muir an extremist? How would you compare him to William Lloyd Garrison and other reformers?

Research Topics

1. Compare John Muir with other contemporary environmentalists, especially Gifford Pinchot.
2. Study the origin and growth of the national park system in the United States.
3. Explore more fully the history of the Hetch Hetchy controversy. Try to understand both sides of the issue.
4. Investigate the Turner thesis. What was it? Is there a connection between the date of its publication and the height of John Muir's career?

CHAPTER 4

Imperial America

Dewey and Aguinaldo at Manila Bay

As former rebels against British imperial rule, Americans have opposed colonialism, believing that all people have the right to govern themselves. In attempting to support democracy abroad, however, America has frequently intervened in other countries. In 1898 the United States went to war with Spain ostensibly to end Spanish cruelty in Cuba, but within a year was using brutal Spanish tactics to maintain control over the Philippines. Many forces then at work in America—the racism that segregated and disfranchised blacks, the industrialism that expanded the nation's wealth, and the settling of the West that removed the last internal frontier, among others—affected American policy in the Philippines. Two men whose paths crossed in Manila Bay, George Dewey and Emilio Aguinaldo, symbolized the power of a rapidly growing America and the rising hopes of the long-colonized Philippines.

When the Spanish-American War began in April 1898, few Americans knew about the Philippines. The country had gone to war to drive Spain out of Cuba without giving thought to other Spanish possessions. Even President William McKinley professed ignorance about Spain's Pacific islands. But within a few weeks the Philippines would be front-page news in the United States, and in less than a year the islands would be an American territory. Why would the United States want to acquire a distant and obscure country seven thousand miles beyond her western shores? And how would her action affect the Filipinos themselves? The careers of the American admiral George Dewey and the Philippine leader Emilio Aguinaldo suggest answers to these questions.

In 1898 the American vitality that had forged democratic institutions, conquered a continent, and given birth to giant industries seemed to flow naturally into overseas expansion. Adm. George Dewey, whose Philippine exploits would make him a national hero, embodied the self-confident spirit that America took into the country's first overseas adventure.

Dewey was born in Montpelier, Vermont, in 1837. He entered the navy in 1854 as a student in the newly founded Naval Academy at Annapolis and received much of his early training from veterans of the War of 1812. At the beginning of the Civil War, Dewey became executive officer of the steam frigate *Mississippi*, a distinguished vessel that had served as Commodore Matthew Perry's flagship in Japan. In 1862 his ship was part of the fleet that wrested control of the Mississippi River from the Confederate forces. The commander of the fleet was David G. Farragut, a resourceful officer who won immortality at Mobile Bay for his order, "Damn the torpedos! Full steam ahead!" Almost a half century after serving under him Dewey wrote, "Farragut has always been my ideal of the naval officer, urbane, decisive, indomitable."

After the exhilarating years of the Civil War the navy entered a long, frustrating period of inertia. "It was easy then," wrote Dewey, "for an officer to drift along in his grade, losing interest and remaining in the navy only because he was too old to change his occupation." Dewey's description of one of his ships, the *Juanita*, reflects his feeling about the navy of the 1870s and 1880s. A round-bottomed sloop built in 1861, she rolled heavily even in light seas. Sailing her into the Mediterranean, Dewey was mortified to find that she and other dated American ships were "the laughingstock of the nations." While Europe was building armored battleships and fast cruisers, the typical American vessel was "a relic of a past epoch."

By 1890, however, Dewey had begun to feel a new "pulse" in the country as Americans grew more interested in their position in the world. The Reverend Josiah Strong reported that his countrymen had spread across their own land and now needed to expand overseas as an outlet for their energies. Capt. Alfred Thayer Mahan wrote a widely read book,

The Influence of Sea Power upon History, arguing that nations grew to greatness through control over the seas. Politicians Henry Cabot Lodge and Theodore Roosevelt claimed that strong nations were warrior nations. These ideas were translated into public policy in the building of a new "steel navy" in the 1890s.

George Dewey was stationed in Washington during the period of expansion, serving as president of the Board of Inspection and Survey, which examined new vessels for fitness. Although he was nearly sixty years old, he projected the optimistic, outgoing spirit of the era and thought of himself as "a man of action." While in Washington he won the respect of Theodore Roosevelt, then assistant secretary of the navy, who supported his promotion to commander of the Pacific squadron. At the time "not one man in ten" in Washington expected a war with Spain. But Dewey prepared for the possibility, knowing that the Philippines, a Spanish possession, would be an American target if war came. During his last month in Washington he studied charts and descriptions of the Philippines and, with Roosevelt's "vigorous support," arranged for more munitions for his fleet.

On January 3, 1898, Dewey, now a commodore, took command of the Pacific squadron in Nagasaki, Japan. The squadron was "hardly a formidable force," consisting of only two cruisers, a gunboat, and a Civil War paddlewheel steamer. Apart from the steamer, however, they were fine, up-to-date ships, well supplied with modern rapid-fire guns accurate at distances of five miles and more.

Pictures of Dewey standing on the deck of the flagship *Olympia*, a bright, trim vessel, show him to be a solid man, with short white hair, a thick walrus mustache, and warm, piercing eyes. We can hear him saying, as he later wrote, that he would go to Manila whether or not he had sufficient ammunition, "for such were our orders and such was the only thing to do."

Although war had not yet begun, on February 11, 1898, he set sail from Japan for Hong Kong, which he regarded as the "most advantageous position from which to move to attack." He arrived on February 17 and learned about the sinking of the *Maine* in Havana. War now seemed inevitable. Eight days later Theodore Roosevelt sent Dewey a cable advising him to "keep full of coal." Dewey sought information on Manila's defense, drilled his men, put his machinery in top condition, repainted his ships to make them less conspicuous, and loaded coal and other supplies. Since international law prevented neutrals from supplying armed belligerents in wartime, he established a base at Shanghai, reasoning that "so loosely organized a national entity as the Chinese Empire could not enforce the neutrality laws."

On April 25, 1898, he received a cable from Secretary of the Navy John D. Long telling him to "Proceed at once to the Philippine Islands.

Commence operations particularly against the Spanish fleet." Two days later, at two o'clock in the afternoon, the American fleet set out across the China Sea toward Manila Bay.

Commodore Dewey was confident that he could defeat the Spanish, but he was sailing toward a well-fortified position. The Hong Kong papers had frequently mentioned the presence of minefields at the entrance to the bay, and in the gambling clubs no one would bet on the Americans, even at heavy odds. The fleet proceeded toward Manila in two columns, fighting ships forward and auxiliaries twelve hundred yards behind, all lights extinguished in the night except a carefully screened lamp at the stern of each vessel, allowing others to follow. The only other illumination came from the phosphorescent wake at the bow and stern of each ship.

At daybreak on April 30, Luzon, the Philippines' main island, was in plain view. The fleet continued south along the coast, staying a safe three to four miles from shore. Dewey had received intelligence that the enemy was waiting in Subic Bay, a well-protected deep-water harbor thirty miles north of Manila Bay, but this information proved false. Pleased that the enemy had not elected to stand in this formidable position, he sailed toward the narrow channel leading into Manila. "Now we have them," said Dewey.

Waiting until dark, he approached the channel under a pale moon. Ahead several fortified islands were dimly visible. The passage reminded him of a night thirty-six years before when he had followed Farragut up the Mississippi toward New Orleans. As the ships passed El Fraile, the outermost island, the Americans braced themselves, expecting soon to encounter mines, torpedo launches, and cannon shot. The El Fraile battery opened fire but was quickly silenced by the American guns. The ships encountered no other resistance, and a little after midnight, marveling at their good fortune, they steamed unscathed into the wide expanse of Manila Bay.

Through the night they went on toward the city, planning to engage the Spanish fleet at dawn. Dewey allowed the men to sleep at their guns but awakened them for coffee at 4:00 A.M. The fleet approached Manila and discovered the Spaniards off Cavite Peninsula some five miles away.

Dewey was elated. "Before me now," he writes, "was the object for which we had made our arduous preparations, and which, indeed, must ever be the supreme test of a naval officer's career." He led his fleet of six vessels on an oblique course toward the Spanish position, keeping the guns on the enemy. The ships moved at eight knots, two hundred yards apart, "the dun, war-colored hulls of the squadron followed in column behind the flagship, keeping their distance excellently." The Americans were under fire from batteries in Manila, Cavite, and the Spanish fleet, but these shots were inaccurate. At 5:40 A.M. the distance to the Spanish fleet was five thousand yards. Dewey turned to the captain of his flagship, saying: "You may fire when you are ready, Gridley."

American shells rained down upon the Spanish ships; then Dewey circled and came past four more times, accurately raking the Spaniards. A single eight-inch shell struck the Spanish flagship, *Reina Cristina*, killing and wounding twenty men and destroying the steering gear. Another disabled the crews of four rapid-fire guns. Shells carried away the mizzenmast with the admiral's flag and exploded in the ammunition room and sick bay. The *Reina Cristina's* losses were 150 men killed and 90 wounded. Finding his ship almost completely disabled, Admiral Montojo ordered her abandoned and sunk. Five years later, when she was raised from the mud, she was found to have fifteen holes in her hull.

At 7:35 A.M. Dewey learned that he was low on ammunition and ordered his fleet to withdraw and evaluate the situation, but the information proved inaccurate. Taking advantage of the lull, Dewey ordered a meal prepared before returning to the battle.

Shortly after eleven o'clock the American ships approached the remnants of the Spanish fleet, quickly overwhelming the remaining ships. At about noon a Spanish flag on the government building in Cavite was lowered and a white flag raised. The Spanish had lost eight ships and 381 men, and Admiral Montojo was wounded. Dewey did not lose one man, and he now commanded Manila Bay. The Spanish offered to surrender their chief city, but the commodore refused to accept a capitulation until American land forces arrived.

After a day of intense action the Americans settled down to the comparatively dull job of blockading Manila. They occupied the military base at Cavite and disabled the guns at Corregidor in the mouth of Manila Bay. On May 4 Dewey sent a ship to the Chinese mainland with his report on the remarkable victory. The short, fierce Battle of Manila Bay was America's most successful encounter with a foreign foe since Andrew Jackson's lopsided victory over the British at New Orleans in 1815. Like Jackson's victory, Dewey's was overwhelming, and he received congratulatory cables from all around the world. One of his favorites, from Theodore Roosevelt, read: "Every American is your debtor."

By defeating the Spanish fleet, Dewey had won a bay, a city, and an empire. Like an efficient businessman he had surveyed the situation in advance, built up his resources, discovered his adversary's weaknesses, and seized the victory. The most significant thing about Dewey's action was its decisiveness. This success had been so simple that it seemed providential.

The victory at Manila Bay was deceptive, however. Dewey may have matched steel against steel, bested the enemy's ships, and cut off his capital, but the Philippines were not merely a navy and a city. The islands were crowded with people who looked on with curiosity as the Western powers blasted away at one another. Dewey would form only a dim idea of the Philippine people, and most Americans would never begin to comprehend them. But the Filipinos had a history and ambitions of their own that would soon disrupt the course of the American empire.

The Philippines consist of a long chain of several thousand islands. Most of the population is clustered on the eleven largest islands, particularly Luzon and Mindanao, both about the size of Indiana. Ancient volcanoes rise from the islands, and thick forests shelter cockatoos, parrots, iguanas, monkeys, and water buffalo. The natives are mainly Malays who came to the islands from the south thousands of years ago. Some of the islands are so remote that in the 1970s anthropologists would discover Stone Age tribes living in the thick forests.

The Filipinos first encountered Western man in 1521 when Ferdinand Magellan, claiming Spanish sovereignty over the islands, landed a small army in the face of fifteen hundred warriors led by the native chief Lapu-Lapu. The natives fought fiercely, killing Magellan and driving the Spaniards back to their ships. Lapu-Lapu is regarded today as a hero—the first Filipino to successfully resist foreign domination.

The Spaniards returned forty-four years later and, after six years of warfare, subjugated the natives and established Manila as their capital. They imposed their government, religion, and society upon the Filipinos for the next three centuries, Christianizing the natives and forcing them to build roads, churches, and convents. The Spaniards monopolized the most lucrative positions in the church, state, and economy.

In the nineteenth century Filipino life centered on small dusty villages with large churches and on farms whose chief crops were hemp, sugar, tobacco, coconuts, and rice. Village bands, religious processions, and cockfights added color to native life. The Filipino houses were sometimes large and well built, but more often the people lived in "nipa" huts made of bamboo. The Americans, who burned many of these huts after liberating the Philippines from Spain, reckoned they took five dollars' worth of material and three days' work to rebuild.

Emilio Aguinaldo, hero of the Philippine independence movement and in many respects a typical Filipino, was born on March 22, 1869, in Kawit, a few miles south of Manila, in a large house with a steep thatch roof. His father was a well-to-do landowner, lawyer, and town official. The imprint of Spanish rule was evident throughout the region. The towns bore Spanish names: Rosario, Las Piñas, Santa Rosa, Manila. The higher officers in church, army, and government were Spaniards. And life was highly flavored by Catholicism. Religious training had an important part in Aguinaldo's education. His mother taught him to "pray to the mysteries of the rosary every night."

While he was young Aguinaldo learned that as a Filipino he belonged to an inferior caste in his own land. Capable leaders like his father were not allowed to occupy high office. In contrast, the Spanish priest in Kawit was treated as if he were a monarch. After mass on Sundays a teacher took Aguinaldo and his classmates to Father Toribio Minguella to pay their respects. Aguinaldo recalls: "The priest was seated in a big armchair. One by one we would kneel down to kiss his hand which he would raise in a gesture of blessing us."

After attending school, Emilio went to work to help support his family. With his brother Críspulo he bought a *paraw*, a native sailing vessel. They transported cargoes between their home province and the adjoining islands of Mindoro, Panay, and Tamblas, carrying salt and *bolos*, large knives for which their region was famous, to exchange for forest products, tallow, cattle, and material for making fish traps. For several years they lived agreeably at sea, lying on the deck at night and watching "the twinkling stars," catching fish for their meals, looking at "beautiful maidens wading in the shallow seashore."

During his years as a trader Aguinaldo grew in stature in his home village of Kawit. When he was twenty he began holding local offices and at twenty-five he became municipal captain, thus occupying the highest office open to a Filipino. A year later he married Hilaria del Rosario, and in the fall of 1896 their first child was born, welcomed into the world with a celebration of fireworks, and baptized soon afterward in the local Catholic church.

Aguinaldo's life in the Spanish-ruled Philippines was pleasant but confining. He was a successful trader, a respected leader, a proud husband and parent. In a sense he was a free man; yet there were constant reminders that he and his people were regarded as inferiors by the Spanish. In May 1896 Aguinaldo and other town officials had just paid their respects to Father Fidél de Blas and were on their way to the council hall. A Spanish lieutenant saw Aguinaldo and called out to him, "Hey, you, Municipal Captain, come here. Prepare me a *calesa* right now, do you understand?" A calesa was a buggy, and the lieutenant was treating Aguinaldo like a lackey. Aguinaldo, humiliated and embarrassed, answered meekly, "Yes, sir." He asked his servant to fetch the vehicle and went on to the council chamber. After the meeting had begun, the lieutenant entered the room and shouted at Aguinaldo, again demanding a buggy. Aguinaldo lost his temper and shouted back, "We are holding a meeting. If you want anything, you may tell us about it after giving our meeting due respect."

The lieutenant replied, "To whom shall I pay my respects? Why should I salute any one of you?"

Aguinaldo lacked the confidence to tell the lieutenant he should show deference to the town meeting but pointed to a painting of the Spanish queen regent hanging behind the council, saying that the lieutenant should salute it. A few minutes later the Spaniard got his buggy. He then lodged a complaint with his superior against the Filipino for discourtesy to military authority.

Aguinaldo was not punished for his part in the affair, but neither was the lieutenant. The Spanish soldier had acted on the common assumption that a colonized people are inferior, that even their most constructive activities are foolish pretenses. Among his people Aguinaldo might be a municipal captain, but to the Spanish officer he was a servant.

After the buggy incident Aguinaldo went to Manila to join the Katipunan, a secret anti-Spanish fraternity. He recruited new members in his own province, meeting clandestinely with recruits in the fields and on his paraw. In summer 1896 Spanish authorities learned about the Katipunan, and on August 19 they began to round up its members.

Aguinaldo led an insurrection on August 31. He and his followers took over Kawit by disarming the town's three Filipino civil guards and confiscated the parish funds after the priest fled. Aguinaldo sent out a message declaring, "We have started to rebel against this tyrannical race" and urging others to join him in rising against Spain and breaking "the chains of slavery that have bound us with her all these hundred years."

He embarked upon the revolution in a spirit of determination mixed with trepidation. After resigning his civic post and changing into the rough clothes of a guerrilla, he found it difficult to eat. "As my heart pounded furiously," he recalled, "I could not swallow any morsel of food without gulping water." He fully expected to die within a few months.

Aguinaldo's fears were well founded. The Spanish forces used ruthless tactics to suppress the rebellion. At the beginning of the movement there were only some fifteen hundred Spanish troops in the Philippines, but within a few months this number had swelled to more than twenty thousand. At first the Filipinos were poorly armed, fighting chiefly with bolos and spears. But late in 1896 they won several impressive victories and captured many Spanish guns. For ammunition they collected un-exploded Spanish shells and removed the powder, picked up empty cartridges from the battlefields, and if necessary used nails and wire as projectiles. The revolution quickly gained momentum, the people supporting the soldiers with food and lodging and welcoming them to town with bamboo arches, bells, bands, and the singing of the *Te Deum*.

On December 30, 1896, the revolution gained its foremost martyr, José Rizal, the most respected Filipino of that time. Born in 1861, Rizal was a brilliant young man who had traveled in Spain, France, Italy, Germany, and England. A surgeon, philosopher, poet, and artist, his novel *Do Not Touch Me* became the *Uncle Tom's Cabin* of the movement for Philippine freedom. Rizal was not a revolutionary. A gentle, humane person, he favored gradual change. But when the revolution began, he was arrested and charged with sedition. Confronted in court with false confessions gained by torture, he was found guilty and condemned to die. On the morning of December 30 he was taken from his cell to face a firing squad. The walls around were crowded with picnicking Spaniards who regarded the execution as a great social event. Amid their laughter and applause, Rizal was killed.

The insurgents, meanwhile, had formed several independent governments. The people associated with Aguinaldo created an elective government, with Aguinaldo at the head of its military forces. This "little republic" controlled the province of Cavite. According to Aguinaldo, the government was patterned after that of the United States; the region was free from crime and disorder; and "everybody greeted each other as brothers and sisters."

Factionalism, however, damaged the Filipino position, and with the arrival of fresh Spanish troops in 1897 the regime was able to win back most of the insurgent territory in Cavite. Spain now clearly had the upper hand against the rebels. But problems at home, disease among the troops, and the possibility of a war over Cuba all inclined her to seek a quick negotiated settlement. On the promise that Spain would adopt reforms, Aguinaldo agreed to leave the country, departing for Hong Kong in 1897.

Emilio Aguinaldo and his fellow revolutionaries had hardly settled on the mainland when the Spanish-American War began. Aguinaldo reasoned that because the United States had gone to war to end Spanish oppression in Cuba, surely America would help the Filipinos. Already in November 1897, and again in January 1898, he had written to Washington appealing for help. The declaration of war against Spain and the Teller Amendment, promising that the United States would not annex Cuba, encouraged hopes that America would be equally generous to the Philippines.

At the outbreak of the war, the Spanish governor general of the Philippines sought to dissuade Filipinos from relying on America, claiming that the United States would destroy their churches and enslave them. But the people scoffed at Spanish warnings, even helping Dewey find his way into Manila Bay: the Spaniards had turned off all coastal lighting, but Filipinos built a huge bonfire on shore as a signal.

E. Spenser Platt, the U.S. consul to Singapore, encouraged Aguinaldo to expect American support for Filipino independence and cited the Teller Amendment as evidence of America's good intentions. On May 16, by Dewey's orders, Aguinaldo and seventeen of his followers were taken aboard the *McCulloch* at Hong Kong and brought to Manila. On May 19 Aguinaldo met with Dewey and slept aboard the flagship *Olympia*.

We have no record of their conversations. Aguinaldo claimed that Dewey assured him the United States would grant independence to the

Philippines and encouraged him to fight the Spanish. Dewey said he made no such promise, but he appears to have been sympathetic toward independence. He allowed Aguinaldo to occupy buildings the Spanish had abandoned and supplied him with arms. He avoided, however, any gesture that could be regarded as recognition of Philippine independence. On June 18, 1898, the insurgents proclaimed their independence; Dewey turned down an invitation to attend their ceremonies on the weak pretext that it was mail day. But when he sent news of the declaration home, he added, "In my opinion these people are superior in intelligence and more capable of self-government than the natives of Cuba, and I am familiar with both races."

The Filipinos gave credibility to their claim of independence by winning several victories over the Spaniards. By late June they had thirty thousand men under arms and were the de facto government of Luzon Island, except for Manila, which they had surrounded with trenches.

Dewey remained in the Philippines through the spring and summer of 1898, waiting for the arrival of the soldiers that would make possible the occupation of Manila. Most of his men stayed in the ships anchored off Cavite. The climate was hot and damp; periods of torrential rain were followed by steaming tropical heat and "lifeless air." The sailors subsisted on sea rations, supplemented occasionally with fresh fruit and eggs purchased from the natives, and meat, vegetables, and other "Chinese delicacies" brought from Hong Kong.

Despite the fact that they were thousands of miles from home, there was something natural about the presence of the Americans in the Philippines. As Dewey looked over the hills of Luzon from his flagship, they reminded him of the Green Mountains of Vermont. The harbor was now effectively a part of America, to be administered efficiently. "American supremacy and military discipline," wrote Dewey, "must take the place of chaos." Dewey did not address himself to the larger question of whether the Philippines should become permanently a part of America. This, he realized, "was a question to decide at home." Now he was required simply to provide for its stable government under a blockade.

Great as Dewey's victory was, it was comparatively simple in contrast to the problems that lay ahead. The Spanish fleet had been defeated, but what should be done with the Philippines? There were four apparent possibilities: they could be returned to Spain, declared independent, turned over to another foreign government, or retained by the United States. These options were represented by the presence of four forces in Manila Bay at the time: Americans, Spaniards, other Europeans, and Filipinos.

The United States appeared to be in charge. In his efficient leadership, which John Hay, the secretary of state, described as a mingling of "wisdom and daring," Dewey ably embodied America's claim to world power. He had been mortified by the knowledge in the 1870s and 1880s that the American navy could easily be demolished by a modern fleet. But the fight at Manila had won the admiration of foreigners and allowed Americans to respect themselves. The United States was now a power to be reckoned with.

What of the Spanish? They had occupied the Philippines for more than three centuries and had built Manila, and yet they had shown a curious lethargy in their defense. Heavy guns that should have been along the shore before Dewey's arrival were found unmounted. The gunners at the entrance to the bay had let Dewey's large fleet slip through with almost no resistance. No torpedo boats greeted him inside the bay, and the shore batteries at Manila and Cavite had been ineffective. Moreover, Admiral Montojo had chosen a curious position for his stand. Dewey believed he could have hurt the Americans had he confronted them in Subic Bay. Montojo had refused to fight in the deep water of Subic Bay because, as he put it, "Our vessels could not only be destroyed, but they could not save their crews." In other words, the timorous Spaniard was preparing for defeat.

If the story of the Battle of Manila Bay reflected the energy and ability of a new nation now a world power, it also displayed the indolence of an older country that had lost its confidence. The contrast was tragically dramatized by an incident the night after the battle. Crowds had gathered along the Manila waterfront to gaze at the conquering fleet lying offshore. Out of solicitude for the people, Dewey had the band play "La Paloma" and other Spanish tunes. Dewey writes, "While the sea-breeze wafted the strains to their ears the poor colonel of artillery who had commanded the battery, feeling himself dishonored by his disgraceful failure, shot himself through the head."

The Spanish were clearly demoralized and offered no more resistance. Dewey had to consider, however, another possible threat to his position from other nations whose navies were in the harbor. He was particularly worried about an increasingly large number of German vessels. He realized that it was common in wartime for neutrals to send naval vessels as observers, and some of the foreign ships in Manila seemed friendly enough. Along with the Germans there were small contingents from England, France, and Japan. But Germany's show of power was worrisome. Dewey recognized that the Philippines were "a rich prize for any ambitious power." Germany had more ships than needed for observation and, at one time, actually had a more formidable fleet in the bay than Dewey. Worse, the ships frequently disregarded common blockade rules. They steamed into the bay and dropped anchor without first reporting to Dewey, and they occupied small sections of territory around the bay, making surveys.

Dewey was frankly alarmed and sent urgent requests to the United States for more ammunition, later admitting that the German attitude was one reason for his worry about stores. When the time came to take the city of Manila, the English fleet, which had been much friendlier to Dewey, positioned itself between the Americans and the Germans, giving rise to rumors that if the Germans should attack the Americans the English and American fleets would "fire in the same language." It is more likely that the fleet wanted to observe the action from a favorable vantage point, but Dewey regarded their activity as an amicable gesture. Long after Dewey left Manila, German records were made public that proved Germany had not planned to attack the Americans but did intend to take the islands if the Americans decided not to. At the least, the presence of other foreign vessels in Manila Bay was a reminder of the international implications of the Philippine situation.

The fourth group at Manila Bay was the Filipinos, whose significance the United States was strangely reluctant to acknowledge. Aguinaldo's appeals to President McKinley asking him to guarantee the independence of his country went unanswered. Newspapers in the United States carried little news of Filipino activities, and Americans were either apathetic or hostile toward the natives. On May 15 Gen. Wesley Merritt, commander of an American army bound for the islands, wrote McKinley suggesting he might have to fight the Filipinos. Merritt's soldiers knew nothing about the natives, and aboard the transports they joked about the Filipino "cannibals" and referred to them as "niggers." When the American troops reached Manila, they were landed without regard to the Philippine army or government. The first American general in the Philippines, Thomas Anderson, sought to reassure Aguinaldo, telling him, "In 122 years we have established no colonies." Anderson wrote to Washington saying that the Filipinos "are not ignorant savage tribes, but have a civilization of their own." Yet nothing was done to establish formal relations with the insurgents.

One wonders how the history of America's involvement in the Philippines would have changed if Dewey had been able to work more closely with the people. At Subic Bay, Americans and insurgents had cooperated in taking a strategic Spanish gun emplacement. Surely Dewey and the rebels together could have taken Manila shortly after his arrival. He claimed he had no troops to occupy it, but why not let the Filipinos occupy their own capital? Apparently, America wanted to help the Filipinos on America's terms.

As more American troops arrived, they persuaded a reluctant Aguinaldo to turn over the Filipino trenches along the south side of Manila. By now his troops controlled most of Luzon. General Merritt, in charge of the army in the Philippines, was under orders to "avoid all sign of alliance with the insurgents." With sufficient support to hold

Manila, Dewey began negotiations with the commander of the Spanish forces, General Jaudenes. The Spaniards, surrounded by American and Philippine troops, bereft of their navy, cut off from contact with Madrid, and vulnerable to bombardment by the American fleet, were quite willing to surrender.

But the commander did not want to lose face by quitting without firing a shot. The two sides finally agreed that the American army would attack; Dewey would move his fleet into position but not bombard the city. In exchange, the Spanish shore batteries would not shell his fleet. The Spanish would resist for a time; then Dewey would signal a request for surrender, and the Spanish would comply. It would proceed like a military drill, but real ammunition would be used—and real lives would be lost.

On August 13 this drama was enacted. The Americans stormed Fort San Antonio outside Manila and took it. The fleet moved into position and demanded a Spanish surrender. A white flag appeared, and the Americans then occupied the city. As part of the capitulation agreement America promised not to allow any insurgents to enter Manila. The Spanish feared reprisals from the Filipinos, and the Americans were glad enough to occupy the capital themselves. One great power had thus supplanted another in the Philippines.

In America the conquest of the Philippines seemed a magnificent triumph. Dewey was the most popular man in the United States, the country's first military hero since the Civil War. Across the land stores were flooded with Dewey buttons and hats. A popular song celebrated his victory, and he was awarded a new rank, Admiral of the Navy.

What did Dewey's victory mean? On the one hand, it was a military achievement, plain and simple. The destruction of Spain's Pacific fleet and American control of the Philippines had given the United States an initial advantage in the war with Spain. Subsequent victories in the Caribbean would persuade Spain to accept peace terms favorable to the United States.

The war was fought for two explicit reasons: to end Spanish oppression in Cuba and to achieve political stability in the Western Hemisphere. One goal was humanitarian, the other political. Neither suggested the need to acquire territory, a fact underscored by the Teller Amendment. With victory in Manila, however, Americans began to think of new territory, justifying expansion on economic, humanitarian, and strategic grounds.

American business had not been enthusiastic about entry into the Spanish-American War, but with Dewey's victory a new attitude appeared, and the stock market rose sharply. Businessmen and politicians began to talk about the economic value of the Philippines. The islands were regarded as good sources of hemp, minerals, sugar, tobacco, and forest products; and they were a doorway to the great Chinese market. Henry

Cabot Lodge claimed that their "value to this country is almost beyond imagination."

While American businessmen were thinking of coaling stations and hemp, another group of Americans thought about Philippine souls. Humanitarians saw the Filipinos as backward people who should be elevated by Christian missionaries and educators. There were flaws in this argument. The natives were neither ignorant nor heathen. Three and a half centuries of Spanish rule had won most to Catholicism, and an extensive educational system existed on the islands. Nor was the United States in a good position to claim solicitude for nonwhite peoples. Ironically, the American mission to uplift Filipinos would occur at the same time as jim crow laws were removing the benefits of citizenship from American blacks. Apparently it was easier to aid nonwhites abroad than to bring about equality at home.

But the idea of America as defender of human rights had tremendous appeal. The islanders were frequently referred to as our "Little Brown Brothers." A poem by Rudyard Kipling, which first appeared in February 1899, called upon Americans to "Take up the White Man's Burden" and civilize the Filipinos. The Filipinos might not be grateful for American help, but President McKinley remarked, "Do we need their consent to perform a great act for humanity?"

Coupled with humanitarian and economic reasons for keeping the Philippines was a third strain of thought, a delight in expansion for its own sake. Taking new land was quite simply something that great powers did. Their activity was usually justified by the word "destiny"—Americans had been destined to spread across the continent and were now destined to take the Philippines. Albert J. Beveridge had summarized the expansionist idea in a speech several days before Dewey's victory. "We are a conquering race," he said. "We must obey our blood and occupy new markets, and, if necessary, new lands."

Events during summer 1898 encouraged the movement to annex the Philippines. Victories in Cuba and Puerto Rico as well as the army's entry into Manila confirmed American strength. President McKinley, a strong Methodist, decided to support annexation after spending many a late night walking the floor in the White House and kneeling in prayer. Finally one night, in a kind of revelation, as he reported to a meeting of fellow Methodists, he considered the alternative ways of disposing of the Philippines: we could not give them back to Spain or to another European power, he decided, nor could we allow them to govern themselves without preparation. And so, he decided, "There was nothing left for us to do but to take them all, and to educate the Filipinos, and uplift and civilize and Christianize them."

When the peace commission had convened in Paris, McKinley's original instructions on the Philippines had been vague, but on October 25 he cabled the American negotiators telling them to demand that Spain concede the islands to the United States. Spain reluctantly agreed in return for a payment of $20 million. According to the treaty that was signed on December 10, Spain relinquished sovereignty to Cuba and ceded Guam, Puerto Rico, and the Philippines to the United States.

The Paris negotiations had gone smoothly, but the treaty still had to come before the Senate. And despite the popularity of imperialism, a strong coalition of anti-imperialists had begun to form. McKinley himself had encouraged anti-imperialistic sentiments in a December 6, 1897, message to Congress on Cuba. "I speak not of forcible annexation," he had said, "for that cannot be thought of. That by our code of morality would be criminal aggression." McKinley was later embarrassed by these words.

By late 1898 "imperialist" and "anti-imperialist" had come to designate those who supported or opposed expansion. In fall 1898 anti-imperialist leagues were formed around the country, devoted to defeating the treaty in the Senate. Some members were veterans of reform campaigns—men and women who had fought for Native American rights, abolition, Prohibition, and civil service reform. This group included Carl Schurz, Charles Francis Adams, and Jane Addams. Others were educators and literary figures, among them President David Starr Jordon of Stanford, philosopher William James, and writers William Dean Howells and Mark Twain. Businessmen like Andrew Carnegie helped finance the anti-imperialists. Labor opposition was led by Samuel Gompers, president of the American Federation of Labor.

The anti-imperialists claimed that acquisition of colonies was contrary to the American ideal of government by the consent of the governed. Ever since the American Revolution, the United States had acquired territory with the usual expectation that the new land would become a part of the United States. The Philippines would be an exception, for even the supporters of annexation did not intend that the islands would join the Union.

The anti-imperialists reminded the American public of their cherished traditions. William Jennings Bryan, the Democratic presidential candidate of 1896, asked an audience in Omaha on June 14, 1898: "Our guns destroyed a Spanish fleet, but can they destroy that self-evident truth, that governments derive their just powers, not from superior force, but from the consent of the governed?" In another talk Bryan echoed Lincoln's "house divided" speech: "This nation cannot endure half republic and half colony—half free and half vassal."

Historians have questioned whether the apparently altruistic feeling for the Philippine people was the real reason for opposition to colonialism. Many Americans opposed annexation, not because of sympathy for, but out of prejudice against, the Filipinos. In the atmosphere of racial bigotry that prevailed in the late nineteenth century, it was assumed that Filipinos were unfit to become American citizens. Samuel Gompers called them a "semi-barbaric population, almost primitive in their habits and customs." A high proportion of the senators who opposed annexation were from southern states that had recently passed jim crow laws and disfranchised African Americans.

Practical considerations also led the anti-imperialist movement. Some businessmen feared competition from cheaper Philippine agricultural products, and labor leaders feared importation of cheap labor. Many anti-imperialists believed it would be too difficult to maintain and protect distant colonial possessions.

In the winter of 1898–1899 the opponents of annexation were strong enough to threaten the treaty, but they faced a difficult tactical problem. Should they refuse to support the treaty, thereby continuing the technical state of war with Spain? Or should they accept the treaty and then fight imperialism in a separate Philippine vote or in the elections of 1900? Many anti-imperialists wanted to block the treaty, but others supported it, planning to consider annexation separately. The result was a 57 to 27 Senate vote on February 6, 1899, only two votes more than the necessary two-thirds majority required for treaty confirmation.

The Senate then considered a separate Philippine measure, the Bacon Resolution, which would have granted independence to the islands. Hostility to annexation was so strong that the vote on February 24, 1899, resulted in a tie. Vice President Garret A. Hobart cast the deciding vote against the measure. In its place another bill, the McEnery Resolution, was adopted, promising that in "due time" the United States would "make such disposition of said islands as will best promote the interests of the citizens of the United States and the inhabitants of said islands." This vague statement was hardly comforting to the anti-imperialists.

The opponents of annexation had made a grave tactical error. There were enough of them to have insisted on a self-denying measure, such as the Bacon Resolution, before the treaty vote as a condition of their support for the treaty itself. By voting on the treaty first they failed to win any important concessions and badly divided their own movement.

In the presidential campaign of 1900 the Democrats nominated William Jennings Bryan and adopted a strong anti-imperialist platform. Bryan lost badly, but the election was not a mandate for imperialism, for the Democrat's domestic policies were at least as much of an issue as his foreign policy. Nonetheless, the election effectively ended the anti-imperialist movement. The American possession of the Philippines was now a matter of fact.

In the meantime, Philippine opposition to colonial rule had led to an insurrection against America. When it became apparent that the

United States was not planning to grant the islands their independence, the Filipino troops that had helped defeat the Spaniards began to rebel against their new rulers. In 1899 guerrilla war quickly spread throughout the islands, with Emilio Aguinaldo as the nominal leader of the Filipinos.

The rebellion was so formidable that the United States had to send seventy thousand troops, four times as many as had fought in Cuba, to suppress it. It dragged on for three years and took more American lives than the war with Spain. The United States soon adopted many Spanish antiguerrilla tactics, using torture and establishing concentration camps. The most successful officers were men like "Hell Roaring Jake" Smith, who told his men to make the island of Samar into "a howling wilderness" and to "kill everything over ten." A congressional investigation of the conduct of the war revealed the seamy side of America's endeavors to "uplift" the Filipinos.

The Philippine insurrection came to an end in 1901 with the capture of Aguinaldo. Frederick Funstan, a general in charge of a Kansas volunteer regiment, arranged to have himself and four other Americans taken to Aguinaldo's camp, deep in the Luzon mountains, in the guise of prisoners. Their "captors" were friendly Filipino scouts. Once the group reached Aguinaldo's camp they abandoned their pretense and took the rebel leader captive. In Manila the demoralized Aguinaldo signed a proclamation urging his people to end hostilities and enjoy their new lives under the "liberty promised by the generosity of the great American nation."

The United States had already begun to establish civil government in the islands. In 1900 William Howard Taft was inaugurated as governor. A few months later three Filipinos were added to the governing commission. The American record in the Philippines was considerably more liberal than the Spanish. American teachers were sent to the islands. Filipinos were allowed to fill important positions in the government. The United States attempted to "train" the Filipinos for independence. The islands became an American commonwealth in 1935 and were given full independence after World War II.

America's initial involvement in the Philippines had been a curious blend of humanitarianism and expansionism. Although United States rule was more liberal than Spain's and another power probably would have taken the islands if America had withdrawn, colonialism, even in its most benevolent form, brought economic opportunism and racial prejudice—and, of course, military conquest in the first place. Dewey's stunning victory made expansion seem simple but blinded America to Filipino aspirations.

Three days after United States forces captured Manila, Dewey visited the city and found the Americans well established. "The people had already resumed their peaceful avocations," he wrote, "and if it had not been for the colors over the citadel, the American sentries posted here and there, and the presence in the streets of the tall, stalwart, good-natured volunteers, who made the little Filipinos seem diminutive in contrast, one would never have imagined that a state of war had lately existed or that the sovereignty of the centuries had been changed."

Bibliography

AGUINALDO, EMILIO. *My Memoirs* (1967). Aguinaldo's autobiography.

BEISNER, ROBERT. *Twelve Against Empire* (1968). Studies twelve anti-imperialists, including Andrew Carnegie.

DELMENDO, SHARON. *The Star-Entangled Banner: One Hundred Years of America in the Philippines* (2004). Explores the role of the United States in the Philippines from the 1890s to the present.

DEWEY, GEORGE. *Autobiography* (1913). Interesting and well-written memoir of the admiral's career.

FREIDEL, FRANK. *The Splendid Little War* (1958). Focuses on the soldiers' experience in the Spanish-American War.

GOLAY, FRANK HINDMAN. *Face of Empire: United States–Philippine Relations, 1898–1946* (1998). Thorough account of the American intervention up to the time of Philippine independence.

LAFEBER, WALTER. *The New Empire* (1963). History of American expansion between 1860 and 1898.

LINN, BRIAN MCALLISTER. *The Philippine War, 1899–1902* (2000). Exhaustive account of the war.

PRATT, JULIUS W. *Expansionists of 1898* (1936). Explores American motives in annexing Hawaii and the Philippines.

SPECTOR, RONALD. *Admiral of the New Empire: The Life and Career of George Dewey* (1974). Standard Dewey biography.

TRASK, DAVID F. *The War with Spain in 1898* (1981). Lengthy, comprehensive account of the war.

Study Guide

Summary

The American conquest of the Philippines appears differently when viewed through the eyes of different cultures. When we trace the course of George Dewey's career, then the American victory over the Spanish fleet and the acquisition of the Philippines seem a glorious triumph for courage, industry, and humanity. Viewed from the perspective of Emilio Aguinaldo, however, the United States appeared to be stepping into Spain's imperialistic role. The essay describes the Battle of Manila Bay, the conquest of Manila, the debate over annexation, and the Philippine insurrection. It concludes by indicating the complexity of evaluating the moral and strategic validity of America's Philippine policy.

Identification Topics

George Dewey, Alfred Thayer Mahan, Theodore Roosevelt, the *Maine*, William McKinley, annexation, anti-imperialism, Manila Bay, Emilio Aguinaldo, José Rizal, Katipunan, Teller Amendment, "Hell Roaring Jake" Smith

Study Questions

1. How was the United States able to gain control of the Philippines? Evaluate the role of the following: American naval power, Spanish indolence, Dewey's preparation and skill.
2. Why did Emilio Aguinaldo and other Filipinos rebel against Spanish rule?
3. How did the United States treat the Filipinos at Manila Bay? In what ways did Americans encourage Filipino hopes for independence? In what ways were they insensitive in their treatment of the natives?
4. For what reasons did the United States decide to annex the Philippines? What evidence is there that some other power would have annexed the islands if America had not? What arguments were used to oppose annexation? Why did America annex the Philippines but not Cuba?
5. Why did the Filipinos rebel against the United States? How was the United States able to quell the uprising?
6. Should the United States have granted the Philippines their independence immediately after Dewey's victory? What would have happened to the Philippines if America had withdrawn? Were the Filipinos ready to govern themselves in 1898?
7. In what respect were the Filipinos in no better condition under American rule than under Spain? In what ways was the government more liberal?
8. Why did the United States want the Philippines in 1898? Would America have contemplated annexation in 1850? In 1980? Was the Spanish-American War an extension of western expansion and manifest destiny?
9. Do you agree with Secretary of State John Hay, who described the Spanish-American War as "a splendid little war"?
10. President McKinley justified annexation of the Philippines with the rhetorical question, "do we need their consent to perform a great act for humanity?" Evaluate that statement. Does the American political tradition involve other examples of "doing good" for people despite their resistance? How does this attitude fit with the principle of government by the governed?

Research Topics

1. Study the history of the Philippine insurrection. How did the United States suppress the insurrection? What was the reaction in the United States?
2. Explore more fully the controversy over the annexation of the Philippines.
3. Follow the course of American government in the Philippines. On the whole, was it beneficial or not?
4. Investigate the role of newspaper coverage in the history of the Spanish-American War.

CHAPTER 5

New Immigrants

Russian Jews in the United States

America has long been a place of refuge for the outcasts of other lands. Puritans fleeing religious persecution and Irish families escaping famine immigrated to the New World to begin their lives anew. Waves of immigrants from northern Europe peopled the United States in the early years, but the greatest influx came during the years 1880 to 1915 when millions of people from eastern and southern Europe came to America and created ethnic communities. The Russian Jews and other immigrants faced many hardships in the United States, but none more difficult than maintaining their cultural identity in an America that both stimulated and undermined their traditional ways.

Whenhen did America begin? The American national holiday celebrates the events of 1776 in Philadelphia, Pennsylvania. But the United States is not exclusively the product of the Revolution. America had many births— after 1776 as well as before; her origins lay in the streets of Dublin, the villages of Russia, the fields of China, and the fjords of Norway, as well as in the farms and towns of the thirteen colonies. In 1900, 15 percent of the people living in the United States had been born elsewhere. Between 1840 and 1914 more than thirty million people came from foreign countries to settle in the United States. The Great Migration of Puritans to Massachusetts Bay from 1630 to 1640 brought about forty thousand people; late in the nineteenth and early in the twentieth centuries, as many immigrants frequently passed through Ellis Island in a week. In the years 1905, 1906, and 1907 more people came to America than the whole population of the United States at the time of the Revolution. Ireland, Great Britain, Scandinavia, Russia, Italy, and Germany each gave birth to more than a million future Americans between 1840 and 1915.

These immigrants were changed by the United States, but America was changed by them at the same time. The story does not lend itself to neat chronological boundaries or to the listing of key episodes; it is much more subtle and amorphous than the history of an individual or event. But the story of one group will help clarify this gradual, fundamental change. The Russian Jewish experience is remarkable in itself, but is the more important because it is not unique; a dozen or more immigrant sagas have similar scope. The Chinese in San Francisco, the Irish in Boston, the Scandinavians in Wisconsin and Minnesota, and scores of other groups combined immigrant backgrounds with an American future.

The Russian Jews who began arriving in the United States in large numbers after 1880 were not the earliest members of the Jewish faith to arrive. The first Jews came to America in 1654 and settled in New Amsterdam. At the time of the American Revolution, some two thousand Jews were in the United States, with congregations in Newport, New York, Philadelphia, Richmond, and Savannah. In the next thirty years the population climbed slowly, but after 1820 Jewish immigration began to increase rapidly. By 1850 the Jewish population was 50,000; in 1860 it reached 150,000. Most of the new immigrants were refugees from political and social turmoil in Germany. They mainly engaged in trade and settled throughout the United States.

Just before 1900, immigration to the United States changed dramatically. Hitherto most immigrants, non-Jewish as well as Jewish, had been from central and northern Europe: France, Germany, Scandinavia, Great Britain, and Ireland. But now new immigrants began to arrive from southern and eastern Europe: Austria-Hungary, Poland, Russia,

Romania, Italy, and Greece. Most Jewish immigrants after 1880 were from eastern Europe.

At first the German Jews were ambivalent about the arrival of their religious fellows from eastern Europe. On the one hand, they sympathized with Jews escaping from oppression. On the other, they were embarrassed by the curious customs of the new immigrants: the men with long, curly beards; the women with wigs; the strange accents; the poverty; the reputation of some for radicalism. The old Jews commonly feared that the strange new immigrants would damage their own image of respectability. But despite these reservations, the German American Jews became active in immigrant aid societies and lobbied to keep immigration policies liberal. Between 1881 and 1914 more than two million Jews immigrated to America. More than three-fourths of these came from Russia; most of the remainder from other regions of eastern Europe, especially Austria-Hungary and Romania. Most new immigrants settled in, or at least passed through, New York's Lower East Side. Between 1880 and 1910 the Jewish population in New York City increased from 80,000 to 1,250,000.

The Jews who came to the United States had no nation of their own but lived scattered across Europe and throughout other quarters of the globe. Wherever they lived they depended on their host nation to allow them to worship in peace. In Germany, Italy, Austria-Hungary, Russia, and elsewhere, they provided services as artisans and businessmen and accordingly were tolerated. But their position was always precarious. They usually had no political power and often were oppressed by hostile citizens and rulers.

The Russian Jews were mainly the descendants of men and women who had settled in Poland in the thirteenth and fourteenth centuries. There they had become moneylenders, tax collectors, innkeepers, artisans, and grain merchants. For several centuries they lived in relative peace, but in the eighteenth century Poland was partitioned—divided among Russia, Prussia, and Austria—and many Polish Jews came under Russian domination.

Under the tsars the position of the Jews rapidly deteriorated. They were not allowed to live outside of a region known as the Pale of Settlement, which consisted of Poland, Lithuania, Byelorussia, and the Ukraine. Within the Pale itself, their political and economic activities were restricted. They were usually not allowed to own land, and they were barred from higher education by restrictive quotas and tests. Early in the nineteenth century, Jews were drafted into the Russian army for twenty-five-year periods of service and were expected to become Christians. Those who managed to preserve their faith through this long ordeal became heroes among their people.

For civilians as well as for soldiers, the challenge of maintaining Judaism in a hostile environment strengthened faith. Religion provided the Jewish people with a sense of community, integrity, and purpose. Being a Jew involved not only special forms of worship but also distinctive patterns of dress, behavior, and speech—most spoke Yiddish, a composite of Hebrew and other languages. They observed special holidays, prayers, and laws. Religious learning was the essential part of education: young men frequently spent many years studying Jewish law, and the scholar was highly esteemed.

Thus, the Russian Jews were effectively a nation within a nation, drawn together by a common faith and culture and driven together by Russian prejudice. But despite their disadvantages they established strong, healthy communities within the Pale. Most lived in towns that dotted the predominantly agricultural landscape. Barred from landownership, they provided goods for the agrarian population by working as artisans, small manufacturers, and merchants. In the Russian population as a whole, a much larger proportion of Jews than Gentiles was involved in manufacturing, commerce, and the professions. These economic activities provided a livelihood but not great riches. Some 5 to 10 percent of Russian Jews were moderately wealthy; 20 percent were impoverished; the majority lived in modest comfort with simple food, clothing, shelter, and furnishings.

Still, by several measures of achievement the Russian Jews may be said to have prospered. They maintained close family ties, had high standards of hygiene, and experienced no problem with alcoholism. These indications of personal and communal health are reflected in Russian vital statistics: the Jewish death rate was much lower than that of other Russians. The caliber of Jewish life is reflected also in a relatively high literacy rate: twice as many Russian Jews as non-Jews could read at the end of the nineteenth century.

The life of the Russian Jew with its mixture of hardship and triumph is told in the story of a girl who migrated from the Pale to the United States. After a few years of life in the New World she decided to write an account of her youth, not, as she indicated in her preface, because it was unique, but because it was "typical of many." Her American name was Mary Antin, and the title of her book was *The Promised Land.*

Mary was born in Polotzk, a village some three hundred miles west of Moscow. Her father was a prosperous merchant who provided well for his family: his daughter remembered embroidered linen, silver candlesticks, kitchen shelves "lined with copper and brass," and "featherbeds heaped halfway to the ceiling." It was a world in which matchmakers arranged marriages, and people wore a ribbon around the neck to ward off disease. Above all, it was a world tinctured by the Jewish faith. Religion touched almost every corner of Mary's life. Whenever her mother discovered a peculiar mark on a chicken she was preparing to cook, she would send it to the rabbi, who would "look in his big books" and decide whether the chicken could be eaten. The Antins observed the Sabbath with a rigor that even the early American Puritans could not have matched. On the Sabbath, Mary was not allowed to work or even to touch any instrument of labor or commerce, such as an ax or a coin. It was "forbidden to light a fire, or to touch anything that contained a fire, or had contained fire, were it only a cold candlestick or a burned match."

As a little girl Mary learned that "The world was divided between Jews and Gentiles." A girl named Vanka threw mud at her; her mother brushed off the dirt and explained that there was nothing to do because Vanka was a Gentile, and "The Gentiles do as they like with us Jews." Mary learned quickly, and later when Vanka spat at her she wiped her face and, she writes, "thought nothing at all. I accepted ill-usage from the Gentiles as one accepts the weather."

As she grew older, she saw other signs of prejudice. Jewish merchants had to pay special fees for the right to travel on business. A local capmaker went to a city to practice his trade, passed the proper tests, and paid his fees, but the authorities claimed he had not done so. He returned impoverished to Polotzk. The young men of Polotzk were drafted into an army that made no provision for their faith. Many sought to avoid the service by inflicting injuries on themselves. Mary Antin recalled that the resulting deformities were often permanent, so that "there were many men in Polotzk blind of one eye, or hard of hearing, or lame, as a result of these secret practices."

If such hardships were the daily bread of Jews in the Pale of Settlement, they lived always with the fear of much worse oppression. At any moment the Gentiles in a community might take it into their heads to massacre the Jews. These outbreaks of mass violence, known as pogroms, were frequently encouraged by priests, police, and even by the tsar. They were rare under the benevolent rule of Alexander II (1855–1881), but they occurred much more often after his assassination in 1881. In the following year the government instigated a massacre of Jews at Nizhny Novgorod. During the next few years Jews were slain or driven from their homes in scores of local pogroms throughout Russia.

Fear haunted the Jews in Polotzk, especially on Christian holidays; then they locked their doors and stayed inside, "knowing that the least disturbance might start a riot, and a riot lead to a pogrom." Mary Antin recalled seeing people who had been caught in pogroms. "Jews who escaped the pogroms," she writes, "came to Polotzk with wounds on them, and horrible, horrible stories, of little babies torn limb from limb before their mothers' eyes. Only to hear these things made one sob and sob and choke with pain. People who saw such things never smiled any more, no matter how long they lived; and sometimes their hair turned white in a day, and some people became insane on the spot."

To be a Jew in the Pale of Settlement was to be constantly humiliated and threatened by hostile neighbors and a hostile regime. Yet it was an economic crisis rather than fear of oppression that finally drove the Antins to migrate to America. During the nineteenth century large new industries had forced many eastern Europeans out of work. Simultaneously, the rapidly growing population strained the resources of food and shelter. The Jews were especially injured by these changes. Between 1800 and 1900 the number of Russian Jews increased from one million to four million. Many Jewish artisans lost their jobs when factories began to produce goods more cheaply than they could. At the same time, government regulations prevented most Jews from becoming industrialists.

Mary Antin's father was ruined by these changes. At first Antin was a successful merchant, but then he became ill and was no longer able to support his family. To survive, the Antins had to sell many of their belongings, and Mary's mother had to go to work as a peddler. When the father finally recovered, economic conditions were so bad that he could not reestablish himself in business. Like millions of other Europeans, he began to think of America.

Russian Jews could not go to Moscow, Kiev, or Saint Petersburg to improve their condition. But they could go to New York, Boston, or Chicago to find more economic opportunities and fewer prejudicial restrictions. Prior to 1880 very few eastern Europeans had come to America, but in the next thirty-five years one Russian Jew in three would make the trip. Steamship companies encouraged them by offering rapid passage at a low fare. The first settlers helped others by sending back information and money and by establishing households and neighborhoods in America where the immigrant could settle among friends.

After 1880 the migration developed at an astonishing momentum. Between 1881 and 1914, when World War I interrupted the flow of immigrants, more than 1.5 million Russian Jews came to the United States. migration became an obsession in the Pale of Settlement. Mary Antin recounts:

> America was in everybody's mouth. Businessmen talked of it over their accounts; the market women made up their quarrels that they might discuss it from stall to stall; people who had relatives in the famous land went around reading their letters for the enlightenment of less fortunate folk . . . children played at emigrating.

Mary's father listened carefully to such talk. If others could go, then so too might he. Finally he gathered his courage and set out alone for America. He could not afford to bring his family, but in America he borrowed the necessary money and wrote for the family to join him.

Mary was ecstatic. "So at last," she writes, "I was going to America! Really, really going at last! The boundaries burst. The arch of heaven soared. A million suns shone out for every star. The winds rushed in from outer space, roaring in my ears, 'America! America!'" Mary compared going to America with going to Jerusalem or crossing the Red Sea. It was not merely a journey—it was the fulfillment of life's promise.

With such thoughts, Mary Antin and hundreds of thousands of other East Europeans set out for America. The trip was filled with hardships. First one must pack together the few belongings that could be easily carried on a long journey by cart, rail, and ship. With these possessions—pots and pans, a samovar, and perhaps goose-down bedding—the emigrant departed from the native village into a world whose language and customs were unfamiliar. At every step were unscrupulous trainmen, innkeepers, and government officials who might prey on the ignorant. At the borders many had to cross illegally, because the tsar often denied passports to Jews. Many a refugee crossed into Germany or Austria in the black of night and on foot, following a guide through isolated fields or forests. Once outside Russia, the immigrants boarded trains, usually riding in fourth-class accommodations that were little better than boxcars, and journeyed on to port cities such as Hamburg or Bremen. Even then the ordeal was frequently prolonged, as they lived in prisonlike quarantine enclosures while waiting for their vessels. Finally, on the voyage to America the passengers were exposed to acute discomfort. They commonly traveled in crowded steerage quarters deep in the bowels of the ship, which were poorly ventilated and shook with the engines' vibrations. Many travelers recalled the poor food, filthy toilets, and the constant stench of vomit. One man echoed the feelings of many when he described the journey as "a kind of hell that cleanses a man of his sins before coming to the land of Columbus."

The Antins experienced many of these hardships on their travels. After journeying across Russia they learned that they could not enter Germany unless they purchased second-class rail tickets (instead of the fourth-class tickets they held). They could not afford the extra cost and had to remain in a border town until a friend helped them across. They then passed through Germany, packed like cattle into a fourth-class car. Once all the passengers were unceremoniously removed from the train and forced to take showers, apparently as a precaution against disease, though no explanation was given. At their destination they were herded into a building where they had to wait for many days before boarding a ship.

Finally they went to sea for a sixteen-day voyage. Crowded together with other passengers as seasick as themselves, they encountered storms that tossed passengers from their beds. "We frightened immigrants," writes Mary Antin, "turned our faces to the wall and awaited our watery graves." Despite such difficulties, the voyage was not entirely painful. When the weather cleared there were "happy hours on deck, with fugitive sunshine, birds atop the crested waves, band music and dancing and fun." And then there was the fine moment when the ship finally neared the American shore.

At Ellis Island, where most of the immigrants entered America, they came face to face with the first of the blunt realities that would shape their new lives. This immigrant depot, a huge brick edifice lying just off Manhattan in New York Harbor, was opened in 1892, a year after the U.S. government had taken over supervision of immigration from the states. As immigrants disembarked, they were given numbers and herded into a great central hall where they were formed into lines and led past several doctors who scrutinized them for disease. The laws of that time imposed no quotas on immigrants but did stipulate that entrants be in good health and be able to provide for themselves. Those who appeared to be sick with tuberculosis, venereal disease, ringworm, or other serious ailments were marked with chalk and held for further examination. The immigrants who passed the medical tests were then asked a barrage of questions about their character, politics, skills, money, and family status. Frequently their assimilation began here at the hands of clerks who simplified eastern European names into shorter Anglo-Saxon forms. Most were allowed to leave Ellis Island after a day. Others had to remain for one or two weeks for further examination. The least fortunate—between 1 and 2 percent of the immigrants between 1880 and 1914—had to return to Europe.

The ordeal at Ellis Island was softened for Jewish immigrants by the Hebrew Immigrant Aid Society, founded in 1892. Its representatives, identified by the letters HIAS on their blue caps, helped the immigrants answer questions and served as advocates for those the government sought to exclude. They also provided information on housing and jobs.

After completing their examinations on Ellis Island, the immigrants boarded one of the ferries that ran twenty-four hours a day between the island and Manhattan. A short voyage past the Statue of Liberty took the travelers to Battery Park. Behind them now were the loathsome railroad and steamship accommodations and intimidating customs and immigration officials. Disembarking amid the cries of seagulls and the throb of the ferry engine, the immigrants were finally set free in America.

But who were they now? Where would they go? How would they make a living? Because immigrants landed in New York with an average of only $8 in their pockets, the end of the long journey from Europe was only the beginning of a much longer struggle to make a living in America.

The Russian Jews who came to America were mostly young, and many came with their families. The majority were skilled laborers; 40 percent were clothing workers. After an abortive Russian revolution in 1905, a higher proportion of wealthy and educated Jews began to immigrate. Some artisans were able to use their European skills in

America, but many found that the industrial forces that rendered their crafts obsolete in Europe were also at work in America.

Whatever their backgrounds, the immigrants had first to search for shelter and work. Some went to other cities—Boston, Cleveland, Detroit, even Los Angeles—but most stayed in New York. Of the Jews who landed at Ellis Island, three-fourths remained in the city. New York was vital in shaping the eastern European Jewish experience in America.

New York had grown rapidly during the nineteenth century. In 1800 its population was 60,000; by 1850 it had climbed to 515,000; and in 1900, after it absorbed Brooklyn and other outlying areas, the population was more than three million. The city owed its growth in part to the forces that were redistributing the American population from farm to city across the country. With new railroads, telegraphs, and steamships, urban centers acquired greater importance. Cities became centers of manufacturing, distribution, and finance in an economy where interdependence was rapidly replacing self-sufficiency.

Even without the immigrants New York would have grown in the nineteenth century, but newly arriving Americans greatly accelerated the expansion. Once Russian Jews had arrived in Manhattan they had many reasons to stay. New York had jobs in manufacturing enterprises, department stores, and printshops. Opportunities for individual enterprise were there, too; one could easily become a street peddler or proprietor of a small store. Another attraction was one's fellow immigrants, a whole neighborhood with tens of thousands of men and women who had grown up in Russia, bringing with them Yiddish newspapers, plays, stores, doctors. They created a comfortable, familiar community in the midst of a strange land.

Most eastern Europeans lived on the Lower East Side of New York, an area that had become a Jewish ghetto during the past eighty years. Early in the nineteenth century a small colony of Jewish immigrants settled there. In the 1830s and 1840s, Dutch, German, and Polish Jews followed them. With the later arrival of eastern European Jews, the Lower East Side became a nation within a nation—or, more accurately, a cluster of nations within a nation. A map of the settlement patterns of Russian, Galician, Austro-Hungarian, Romanian, and Levantine Jews reveals boundaries among the groups as distinct as national frontiers. By 1900 the Lower East Side was one of the most crowded places in the world, with more than a half million Jews in concentrations of as many as seven hundred per acre. This was the most crowded section of the city, containing only about one-eightieth of the land, but one-sixth of the population. One observer wrote: "The architecture seemed to sweat humanity at every window and door."

Such crowding was made possible in part by new building techniques and in part by forbearance by the inhabitants. New York City lots were twenty-five feet wide and roughly a hundred feet deep. The first tenements consisted of private houses that were converted into apartments. But with increased crowding, a more efficient system was required. In 1879 a contest was held with the prize going to the best apartment design. The winning plan was the now infamous "dumbbell" tenement, so named because it was shaped like a weightlifter's bar and weights.

The typical dumbbell tenement had from six to seven stories, each floor with four apartments containing a kitchen, a sitting room, and one or two bedrooms. Only the rooms facing the street or the ten-foot-deep backyard had fresh air. Other rooms faced a foul air shaft or had no windows. One toilet served all the inhabitants on each floor. Under the best of conditions these rooms would seem confining, even for a small family. But many were occupied by families with five or six children. Also there were boarders, individuals or whole families, who shared an apartment with the renters, sleeping in the kitchen or sharing the other rooms and helping to pay the rent of $10 to $20 a month. Through the summer men and women slept in the yards or on roofs or fire escapes to avoid the stifling closeness of the tenement apartments. In one week during August 1896 the temperature averaged 90 degrees and 420 New Yorkers died of the heat.

With all its limitations, the tenement apartment still offered shelter, both physical and psychological, from the abrasive world in which the immigrant must find work. The search for steady employment was frequently the most trying and disorienting feature of immigrant life. Many artisan immigrants had to find work in new areas. Some went to work in sweatshops, small manufacturing establishments producing clothing, cigars, and other products. Others became small merchants—with a pushcart and a bushel of apples one could easily become a peddler on the busy ghetto streets. With a little more money, one could rent a small street-front store with a tenement apartment in the rear.

Mary Antin's father was one of many immigrants who drifted—or rather was beaten—from one job to another. Her family settled in Boston, but their experience coincided with that of Russian Jews in New York, Cleveland, and elsewhere. At first, Mary's father and a partner ran a refreshment stand on Crescent Beach, selling cold lemonade, hot peanuts, pink popcorn, and their own potato chips, which were "thin as tissue paper, crisp as dry snow, and salty as the sea." Mary writes: "I admired greatly our shining soda fountain, the rows of sparkling glasses, the pyramids of oranges, the sausage chains, the neat white counter and the bright array of spoons. . . . I thought my father looked very well in a long white apron and shirt sleeves. He dished out ice cream with enthusiasm. So I supposed he was getting rich."

Then a problem arose with the law—something about the business license and selling on Sunday, the Christian Sabbath. At any rate, the family had to abandon the beautiful refreshment stand. Mr. Antin rented a basement store, purchased a stock of sugar, flour, crackers, potatoes, kerosene, kindling wood, and penny candy, and again he was in business. But trade was slow. Mary's older sister and mother had to go to work. And even then they dreaded the landlady's weekly visits and the humiliating need to ask for more time to pay the rent.

Experiences such as these awaited many immigrants. Russian Jews frequently wrote boastful letters to their countrymen, saying that in America all people were equal, that the peddler was as respected as the capitalist. But the egalitarian dream could not hide the miserable working conditions of many immigrants. Ephraim Lisitzky, a poet, described a poignant scene in which he first encountered the reality of immigrant labor on the sordid fringes of the American economy. As a fifteen-year-old boy he traveled from Russia to the United States to join his father, who had immigrated eight years before. After a confusing search, he found the roominghouse in Boston where his father lived. There he waited at the doorstep for his father's return. "Suddenly," he writes, "a figure came towards me through a rosy mist. As it approached, the mist lifted and I saw it, radiant and compassionate. I leaped up—it was my father. In the dusk my father's face loomed up from the street. He walked heavily, bent under a sack filled with rags and bottles. His face was dark and hard with an expression of mingled humiliation and forgiveness." Like many other immigrants, Lisitzky spent his days picking through trash cans, selecting the few items that could be resold.

Soon the younger Lisitzky had to go to work himself. Unable to find other employment, he borrowed a peddler's basket and strove to make a living. He writes:

> I chose Tuesday, a lucky day in Jewish tradition, to embark on my peddling experience.
>
> It was a rainy autumn day. The wind shook my basket and whipped the shoelaces dangling from my hand into my face. I trudged down the street like a doomed man on his way to the gallows. Whenever anybody looked at me I lowered my eyes in shame. I approached a house whose number was the numerical equivalent of a verse of Scripture I had in mind, timidly mounted the stairs and couldn't bring my hand to knock at the door. At last I knocked diffidently. The door opened. I stood in the doorway with downcast face, and inquired clumsily in a low voice:
>
> "Maybe the lady wants matches?"
>
> "Matches?" The woman at the door responded sardonically. "Come in and I'll show you the piles of matches the peddler already supplied me with—enough to burn up all of the houses in Boston!"

Lisitzky moved on to other houses, but at the end of day he had not sold a thing. Not only was he forced to become a peddler, but he was not even good at it. At the synagogue he wept inwardly. Life was hard in the land of the free.

Most eastern European Jews on the Lower East Side made their livings in ways only slightly more rewarding than the Lisitzkys'. The majority eked out a humble existence as peddlers, small shopkeepers, or factory workers. In 1890 the garment trade alone employed thirteen thousand workers on the Lower East Side. In 1900, 50 percent of the city's industrial labor force worked in the area, toiling many hours for small wages.

With poor housing and employment, one would expect the Lower East Side to have been a depressing place. And yet, despite its crowds and poverty, the area displayed an impressive vitality. Jacob Epstein, one of America's finest artists in this century, traced his creativity to his youth among the ghetto's "unique and crowded humanity." Bertha, a character in Henry Roth's classic novel, *Call It Sleep*, preferred the ghetto to her small European home because, she said, "There's always a stir here." Even William Dean Howells, a distinguished visitor well acquainted with the wealthiest and most cultivated homes in America, was impressed with the vigor of New York's Jews. "I found them," he wrote, "usually cheerful in the Hebrew quarter. . . . I was struck by men's heroic superiority to their fate, if their fate is hard."

Observations such as these suggest that our account of poor housing and hard work only touches the surface of the immigrant experience. Despite these hardships an infectious vigor enlivened the Lower East Side. Its people were among the healthiest in the city; drunkenness, suicide, and crime rates were relatively low. Their families were strong. An energy affected the newcomer and startled the visitor who walked among the merchants on Hester Street who hawked trinkets, food, and clothes; through crowded streets with their signs in Yiddish and Hebrew, where Christian missionaries sometimes sought to win converts; past the tenement apartments, so closely packed that one could smell the neighbors' cooking and hear their arguments; and among the shops and theaters of the Lower East Side.

What was the source of this energy? In part it was a sense of expectation: a better world was at hand. America meant freedom and opportunity. We may read that same anticipation in a letter written by John Winthrop in frontier Boston almost three centuries before. Settled among people who were ill fed, poorly housed, and wracked by disease, he had written home to his wife, "We are here in a Paradise." Like the Puritans before them, the eastern European Jews believed that they were on the brink of a better life.

Sometimes this confidence was broken by too many days spent picking rags from gutters and trash cans or by too many nights of hunger and crowding. But it could feed on many things: the sight of exotic new objects such as a rocking chair; the availability of inexpensive goods—peaches for a penny a quart, eyeglasses for thirty-five cents, fancy underwear for less than a dollar. And then, too, the chance to prosper was there. The man with the cart might own a store. The storekeeper could build a chain of stores. The tenement dweller might one day have a real tub, hot running water, an inside toilet, and—to vanquish winter's chill—"stimm hitt."

Around them were indications that such visions were not entirely fanciful. Already a few German Jewish merchants had become fabulously wealthy in merchandising. Isidor and Nathan Straus had built Macy's into the largest department store in the world. Julius Rosenwald increased sales at Sears, Roebuck to $50 million per annum. Other Jews entered the professions. By 1900 New York City had five hundred Jewish doctors. Jewish intellectuals included philosophers Felix Adler and Morris Cohen, social scientists E. R. A. Seligman and Franz Boas, and journalists Walter Lippmann and Joseph Pulitzer.

Signs of success appeared on the Lower East Side. Physicians and dentists occupied fancy brownstone houses along East Broadway, the grand boulevard of the new community. The avenue was also the Jewish newspaper row, commanded by the ten-story *Jewish Daily Forward* building on Seward Park. Nearby were the Educational Alliance and the Jewish Maternity Hospital. On Grand Street were several large department stores, and the Bowery had the world's largest savings bank. Few immigrants, of course, ever became department store owners, or newspaper editors, or doctors. But for them there were other rewards. After becoming a citizen, one could vote just like any other American. On the Lower East Side, as in the rest of New York City, celebration bonfires were lit on election day. One could move freely from one part of the country to another and send one's children to free public schools. If one's own dreams seemed unattainable, one could at least provide the children a chance for advancement. One of the most eloquent passages in Mary Antin's *Promised Land* tells of her father's taking his three daughters to their first day in school. Business success, even the ability to learn English, had eluded Mr. Antin. But his daughters could aspire to a better life. She writes:

> So it was with a heart full of longing and hope that my father led us to school on that first day. He took long strides in his eagerness, the rest of us running and hopping to keep up.
>
> At last the four of us stood around the teacher's desk; and my father, in his impossible English, gave us over in her charge, with some broken word of his hopes for us that his swelling heart could no longer contain. . . .
>
> I think Miss Nixon [the teacher] guessed what my father's best English could not convey. I think she divined that by the simple act of delivering our school certificates to her he took possession of America.

By entering the public schools, Jewish children gained the opportunity to learn American language and customs. At home, in the street, and in the Jewish *cheder*, which supplemented public education with Jewish training, they met the rich culture of their own ancestors. Like the Puritans and other early American immigrants, the Russian Jews hoped to keep alive their heritage while living a fuller life in a new country. This aspiration nourished the remarkable cultural activity of the Lower East Side, with its journals, clubs, and plays. One of the foremost agencies of Jewish culture at the turn of the century was the Yiddish theater, with the finest drama in New York for its time. The shows were inexpensive, exciting, and responsive to audience interests. In 1900 New York had three Yiddish theaters—the Jewish Peoples, the Thalia, and the Windsor. The plays usually revolved around leading stars, such as Jacob P. Adler and Bertha Kalish, Sigmund Feinman, David Kessler, and Boris Tomashefsky, all idols of the Lower East Side, onstage and off. The plots dealt with stock situations, and one of the foremost writers, "Professor" Horowitz, could write a play a day. The plays often dealt with a topic of paramount interest to immigrants in a new land, the tension between Jewish traditions and a more secular America. Many plays pitted unfaithful children against parents who had sacrificed for them.

For many years Yiddish theater performances were more compelling than anything on Broadway, which mainly featured light musicals and vaudeville. Musicals fared best with the Yiddish audience when songs inspired by Russian cantors' chants were added to programs. The Yiddish theater began its decline only when the American mass media began to draw the best Jewish theatrical talents: men such as the Warner brothers, Sam Goldwyn, Douglas Fairbanks, and Louis B. Mayer, who became pillars of the motion-picture industry.

Other agencies of Jewish culture came along: social clubs where people went for company, debate, and intellectual discussion; the Young Men's Hebrew Association; and various charitable associations. When Jews were denied access to Christian hospitals, they formed their own, including Mt. Sinai in New York and Beth Israel in Boston. Other cultural activities took place in cafes, centers for talk, of which there were three hundred in New York in 1905.

The most important Jewish cultural agency was, of course, the synagogue. As new immigrants came and new religious beliefs spread, the number of synagogues spread rapidly. In New York there were 14 in 1854, 150 in 1890, and 300 in 1900. Many were simply storefronts and were administered from day to day by a *shamas*, a religious functionary with little status, because rabbis were in short supply. The work of shamas and rabbi was supplemented by that of other religious figures, notably the *shohet*, or ritual slaughterer; a *mohel*, who performed the traditional circumcision; and the *maschgiach*, who oversaw dietary regulations.

Despite the proliferation of synagogues and religious functionaries, religious devotion declined. Proportionately fewer rabbis than laymen migrated, and a tendency to reduce the number of the essential elements of the faith spread. And so, too, followed a trend toward religious apathy. Many men and women became actively antireligious—secular in their outlook on life. Mainly socialists, anarchists, and freethinkers, they claimed that organized religion was reactionary and took the fervor of faith into advocacy for secular reform. At their most extreme, they scoffed at Jewish religious laws and customs, and even held Yom Kippur balls on the night of the recitation of the *Kol Nidre*, when most Jews were in the synagogue praying and fasting.

Such events were exceptional and transitory. For the most part, immigrants sought to perpetuate their traditional lifestyle. After all, for centuries they had preserved a distinctive Jewish culture in a hostile European environment. In New York they formed the largest concentration of Jews anywhere in the world and throughout America were comparatively free to worship, think, and behave as they pleased. In newspapers, cafes, clubs, and the theater they now had the freedom to fulfill their traditions as Jews.

But despite these influences for continuity, the American experience began subtly to undermine Jewish traditions. Even if the adults tried to maintain the old traditions, the children were frequently drawn away. The free public schools, which gave them opportunities undreamed of in Russia, taught them a new language and exposed them to a new religion—the Lord's Prayer and other Christian customs were observed in many schools. Children who used Yiddish rather than English were laughed at, and they quickly learned English, sometimes even refusing afterward to speak Yiddish at home. Immigrants established schools to provide supplementary Jewish training, but they were often poorly taught and ill attended. Many boys would attend special classes only for a few weeks before the bar mitzvah, the ceremonial observance of their passage to manhood. But in 1908 only 28 percent of New York's Jewish children were receiving any Jewish training. As the children grew up, most did not support the Yiddish journals and theater.

For some immigrants this casting off of the old ways was a matter for self-congratulation. Mary Antin considered that she had been reborn in America. She was pleased to have abandoned the "medieval" practices and beliefs of her native Russian village and to have adopted the seemingly wider vision of her new land. She did not even object to saying the Lord's Prayer in school, and she called herself by the Christian name, Mary, given her by the immigration officials.

As the twentieth century progressed, the Jewish standard of living improved until it matched that of other Americans. Many Jews moved out of the Lower East Side to other communities and to the suburbs. In 1892, 75 percent of New York's Jews lived on the Lower East Side; by 1916 the proportion was only 23 percent. These were signs of material success, but some of the best Jewish spokesmen feared that success might debase the immigrant, that American materialism might be more damaging than Russian tyranny, that a priceless heritage might be lost.

Ironically, these laments found their counterpart among white Anglo-Saxon Protestant Americans, who worried that their own heritage would be undermined by Jews and other nonwhite or non-Protestant Americans. The new immigration with its heavy concentration of eastern and southern Europeans brought to America millions of people who seemed disturbingly different from the descendants of earlier, northern European immigrants. In 1916 Madison Grant published the classic statement of these fears, *The Passing of the Great Race*. Grant claimed that ethnic minorities were undermining primitive American virtues.

Prejudice against the new immigrants found its way into public policies. Restaurants, hotels, clubs, jobs, even whole neighborhoods were closed to Jews. Organizations such as the Immigration Restriction League lobbied to curtail immigration to the United States.

During the 1920s hostility to Jews, as well as to other ethnic minorities, was formalized in prejudicial quotas in educational institutions and hospitals. It found the highest sanction in the adoption of the National Origins Act of 1924, a law restricting immigration to the United States to 150,000 annually and establishing quotas that favored the northern European peoples over the new immigrants of the previous fifty years. It remained substantially unchanged until 1965 when a new system, based on America's need for skills, was adopted.

The enactment of the National Origins Act should remind us that American nativistic hostility targeted many immigrant groups. Italian, Irish, Greek, Chinese, and Japanese immigrants hoped to improve themselves by becoming Americans. Like the Jews, these other groups have retained ethnic characteristics in their religion, culture, food, and holidays. And all have had to overcome the prejudice spawned by that side of the American character which fears change or diversity. For years many employment ads included the warning, "No Irish Need Apply." Chinese and Japanese immigrants faced even worse persecution: in Tacoma, Washington, all the Chinese were driven out of town in 1885, and throughout the West in the 1940s hundreds of thousands of Japanese Americans were interned in detention camps.

Despite the enormity of such events, the constructive relationships between old and new Americans have been many. Historians and sociologists have argued about the correct way of describing this accommodation. One description, using the image of a melting pot, suggests that all Americans have merged into a common national character, composed of its many antecedents. Another thesis suggests that America is a pluralistic society or a mosaic consisting of many kinds of people. Surely there is truth in each of these propositions. Jewish Americans, Irish Americans, Chinese Americans, Anglo Americans, African Americans, and Native Americans all have distinctive heritages. But at the same time, radio, television, and films, as well as mobility, democracy, and business have formed an amalgamated society in which all Americans take some part.

We miss some of the richness of American history, however, if we move too quickly from the early to the late twentieth century. For history is not only what people become. It is also what they are and were. And not so long ago, when Admiral Dewey conquered the Spanish fleet in Manila, and Theodore Roosevelt was elected president, and John Muir advocated a Yosemite National Park, America was the home of ten million men, women, and children from other quarters of the globe. We might close with a picture of the sons and daughters of the Russian Jewish immigrants teaching public school or producing Hollywood films. Let us leave them, rather, in history—attending classes in the cheder, shopping in the open-air markets on Hester Street, hurrying to a Yiddish play at the Thalia—part Jewish, part Russian, part American.

Bibliography

ANTIN, MARY. *The Promised Land* (1912). Autobiography by a young woman who adapted readily to American life.

CUTLER, IRVING. *The Jews of Chicago: From Shtetl to Suburb* (1996). A story that parallels the history of New York's Lower East Side.

DANIELS, ROGER. *Guarding the Golden Door: American Immigration Policy and Immigrants Since 1882* (2005). American immigration policy from the Chinese Exclusion Act (1882) to the present.

DINNERSTEIN, LEONARD, AND DAVID REIMERS. *Ethnic Americans: A History of Immigration and Assimilation* (1982). Good overview of immigrant history.

GODLEY, ANDREW. *Jewish Immigrant Entrepreneurship in New York and London 1880–1914* (2001). Comparative study of Jewish experience, arguing that more Russian Jewish immigrants in New York than in London became entrepreneurs.

HANDLIN, OSCAR. *The Uprooted* (1951). Evocative re-creation of immigrant experience.

HIGHAM, JOHN. *Strangers in the Land* (1955). Classic history of American nativism.

HOWE, IRVING. *World of Our Fathers* (1976). Thorough and beautifully written account of eastern European Jewish immigration.

RISCHIN, MOSES. *The Promised City* (1970). Focuses on Jews in New York City, 1870–1914.

ROTH, HENRY. *Call It Sleep* (1934). Haunting novel about Jewish immigrant life in New York.

SALZ, EVELYN, EDITOR. *Selected Letters of Mary Antin* (2000). Provides a window of the complexities of Mary Antin's life, including her later mysticism.

SCHULBERG, BUDD. *What Makes Sammy Run* (1941 and later editions). Lively account of an unscrupulous second-generation American who claws his way from New York poverty to Hollywood splendor.

TAKAKI, RONALD. *Strangers from a Different Shore* (1989). Describes the Asian American immigrant experience.

Study Guide

Summary

The essay explores the history of the Russian Jews, one segment of the massive influx of immigrants into the United States in the period 1880–1915. We begin with a discussion of Jewish life in Russia using the experience of Mary Antin as a focal point. We then observe Jewish efforts to establish new communities in America, especially on New York's Lower East Side, where a Jewish nation within a nation grew up in the late nineteenth century. The essay indicates the stunning diversity of the American people in this era and suggests the problems immigrants faced in preserving traditional cultures in an American environment.

Identification Topics

Mary Antin, Pale of Settlement, pogroms, Ellis Island, dumbbell tenement, Lower East Side, Hester Street, the Thalia, Madison Grant, National Origins Act of 1924, "No Irish Need Apply"

Study Questions

1. In what respects did Jews prosper in Russia? In what ways did they have a distinct culture? How were they discriminated against?
2. Why was Mary Antin so enthusiastic about going to the United States? What did America mean to her?
3. In general, why did Jews in eastern Europe have such an exalted image of the United States? In what ways did they regard it as a promised land?
4. The author claims that despite their hardships the Russian Jews built strong, healthy communities in the United States. What hardships did they encounter? How were they discriminated against? What evidence do we have of their vitality?
5. In what respects were Jewish immigrants able to preserve their traditional cultures in the New World? In what ways did the new environment undermine their traditions?
6. In what ways, if any, was life for Jews better in the United States than in Russia? In what ways, if any, was it worse?
7. Why was the National Origins Act passed in 1924? Since America is an immigrant nation, why was there so much hostility to free immigration early in the twentieth century?

8. The United States has been described as a melting pot and as a mosaic. Which analogy best summarizes the early experience of the eastern European Jews? Explain your answer.
9. In what ways were the experiences of immigrants similar to and different from those of blacks in America?
10. From your own observations, do you consider America to be a "melting pot"?

Research Topics

1. Study the history of other immigrant groups in America in 1900. Did they encounter the same problems and discover the same opportunities as the Russian Jews?
2. Explore the history of the evolution of immigration restriction sentiment in the United States and the reasons for the passage of the National Origins Act of 1924.
3. Why did some immigrants prosper in the United States and others not? Study the lives of immigrants who became famous and others who barely survived.

CHAPTER 6

Expanding American Democracy

The Woman Suffrage Victory

Critics of woman suffrage predicted dire consequences if men abandoned their monopoly on politics. Women's weak minds and delicate temperaments could not survive the hurly-burly of public life. The complexity of politics and the rough election-day crowds would either frighten women into simpering fools or transform them into unnatural amazons. Gone would be the charm and serenity of the tender sex, the woman's capacity to create havens of domestic tranquility in a tumultuous world. With such arguments, many Americans sought to deny women the ballot. But woman suffragists said "Nonsense!" to the romantic fiction of the female incapacity for electoral politics. In a democracy, they argued, it was outrageous to leave half the citizens unrepresented because of their sex. These reformers, men as well as women, fought seventy years for woman suffrage. Their campaigns won success at the height of the Progressive Era, and yet many Progressives, while embracing other reforms, were reluctant to support woman suffrage. A woman's right to vote would soon seem as natural as her right to live, but the change came only after a long struggle.

On the bright cold afternoon of March 4, 1913, hundreds of thousands of spectators crowded the streets of Washington, D.C., hoping to catch a glimpse of a colorful parade. This was inauguration week for Woodrow Wilson, the country's first Democratic president in sixteen years, but the pageant was designed to impress rather than honor Wilson. Planned by women's rights activists, it advertised women's accomplishments and dramatized the need for woman suffrage.

The affair began with an allegory presented by dancers and an orchestra on the steps of the Treasury Building. The air was chill, but the sky overhead was a perfect blue. Thousands stood watching as the performers, dressed in rainbow-colored robes representing Justice, Charity, Liberty, and Hope, moved across the steps. The dancers paused, and a woman in pure white depicting Peace appeared from behind one of the massive columns of the Treasury. While the orchestra played the *Lohengrin* Prelude, she held out her hands and released a dove into the bright sky. The cold wind blew ripples through the light, airy costumes of the dancers, and detractors predicted that the whole cast would be confined to their beds the following day. But, according to a *New York Times* reporter, "The real suffragists said it was heroic."

When the pageant ended, the suffrage advocates, five thousand strong, took their places in the women's parade. This was one of the most elaborate processions ever assembled in the national capital. Floats depicted the worldwide struggle for woman suffrage; the history of the American quest for equality; and the activities of women in households, farms, the professions, and government. Some of the women rode on the floats; others marched between them carrying their state flags or yellow banners with the slogan "VOTES FOR WOMEN."

The marchers had come from all over the United States. Illinois women reserved a whole train and employed women porters; their "manless special" attracted much attention, and at every stop along the route the women gave speeches and poured tea for visitors. Among the women in the parade were all the notable leaders of the suffrage movement, including Dr. Anna Howard Shaw, president of the National American Woman Suffrage Association. The most popular figure with the crowd was "General" Rosalie Jones, who had left New York several weeks before, leading her women on a long march to the capital. Now she walked along briskly with her followers, carrying a yellow pilgrim staff and a large bouquet of roses. Among the marchers were contingents of writers, artists, physicians, lawyers, businesswomen, and "just wives."

A group of women rode on horseback at the front of the parade, led by Inez Milholland, a striking figure in a white broadcloth cossack suit. As she turned on to Pennsylvania Avenue, she beheld an astonishing sight. Along the route hundreds of thousands of spectators filled the

Mall. The crowd surged on to the avenue, pressing upon the marchers. The police, not having anticipated so many people, were virtually helpless.

The proximity of marching women and audience elicited a range of responses to the suffrage cause. Everywhere there were signs of support. Houses were decorated with yellow bunting, representing the women's movement, intertwined with the patriotic red, white, and blue. Thousands of spectators wore yellow "VOTES FOR WOMEN" buttons. Men expressed their support by wearing badges or marching with the National Men's League for Woman Suffrage. Boy Scout troops and National Guard units helped control the crowd. Maj. J. M. Shindel of the Pennsylvania National Guard threw flowers in the path of Rosalie Jones and her pilgrims, shouting, "Nothing's too good for you!"

There were, however, other men and women who were less friendly to the suffragists. Some wore satirical badges proclaiming "VOTES FOR MEN" or depicting men's trousers with "VOTES FOR WOMEN" patches sewed over the bottoms. Others jeered or threw cigarette butts at the marchers. Drunken men tried to climb aboard the floats. A policeman shouted at Genevieve Stone, the wife of an Illinois congressman, "If my wife were where you are, I'd break her head."

The sun set before the last of the parade moved down Pennsylvania Avenue, marking the end of a day both exhilarating and exhausting. One of the featured speakers, Helen Keller, was so tired that she was unable to take part in the concluding ceremonies. The parade and its audience had symbolized better than its planners might have wished both the excitement and the frustration of the woman suffrage movement.

Although the pageant and march had been successful productions, the opposition along the route had best represented the predominant mood of the American people. One hundred and forty years had passed since the beginning of the American Revolution, but in 1913 women still did not enjoy equal rights. The American democracy was primarily a male democracy.

There were many reasons for the long postponement of woman suffrage. Political machines that ran many state and local governments were reluctant to introduce a new set of voters into the electoral system. Organizations like Tammany Hall in New York were accustomed to working with traditional male clientele and considered women voters an unknown force that might threaten their power. Businessmen feared the influence of women's votes on working conditions in their factories: nonvoting women and children could be employed in poor conditions at low wages, and their bosses feared that woman suffrage might damage this profitable arrangement. The liquor interests felt threatened by sexual equality at the polls because the Prohibition crusade drew much of its strength from women.

All these groups considered woman suffrage a direct challenge to their power. Other Americans opposed the movement on ideological grounds. Voting would overtax women's inferior intellects. Popular journals ran articles on such subjects as "Why the Vote Would Be Injurious to Women" and "Famed Biologist's Warning on the Peril in VOTES FOR WOMEN." A woman's proper place was in the home. Here she should create a comfortable atmosphere, a haven of decency sheltered from the abrasive struggles of the outside world. All these advantages could be lost if women began to vote. When women went to the polls, they would be exposed to the corrupt influence of dissolute men. Worse, by choosing their own political candidates they might become independent of their husbands and lose their traditional attitude of subservience. The pillars of civilization would come crashing down, and all would be chaos.

It was ironic that such attitudes toward woman suffrage should come out in a time generally known as the Progressive Era. During the presidential administrations of Theodore Roosevelt, William Howard Taft, and Woodrow Wilson, the government passed many laws designed to reform American society. Roosevelt's "trustbusting," along with his creation of the Department of Commerce and Labor, curtailed some abusive actions of big business. The Pure Food and Drug Act and the Meat Inspection Act guaranteed a better diet for Americans. Other acts strengthened the Interstate Commerce Commission, regulated the railroads, and provided for equitable use of the national forests. Taft extended these reforms to include regulation of telephone companies and to break up monopolies in tobacco and oil. Wilson continued the earlier Republican reform momentum with new trust regulations, the Federal Reserve Act, and laws protecting labor.

The apparent interest of progressivism in the underdog makes the delay in woman suffrage seem inexplicable. But the continuing opposition to expanding the electorate was not entirely inconsistent with the Progressive impulse. Reforms early in the twentieth century were understood mostly from a conservative point of view. Political reform would return the government to middle- and upper-middle-class leaders. Business regulation would restore the traditional competitive marketplace. The ideal Progressive world was mostly white, male, and native. It mattered little to the reformers that in the early twentieth century most African Americans lost the chance to vote and that restriction of immigration gained popularity. Blacks and immigrants were not part of the traditional ruling elite.

Some women's leaders even tried to capitalize on the prevailing mood of ethnic conservatism to strengthen their demands for woman suffrage, arguing that their votes would strengthen the white middleclass electorate, because proportionately fewer immigrants than natives had wives. Others took part in reform programs, advocating Prohibition and conducting social welfare programs, thereby gaining administrative experience and wider support for suffrage.

Despite such efforts, however, the suffrage movement had failed to register many gains in the early Progressive period. In fact, the history of woman suffrage in the sixty-five years since the demand for votes was first made at the Seneca Falls Convention in 1848 had been painfully slow. At that gathering Elizabeth Cady Stanton had introduced a resolution stating: "It is the duty of women of this country to secure to themselves their sacred right to the elective franchise." The meeting and its suffrage resolution had been ridiculed by the press, but once the issue was raised Stanton devoted much of her life to the suffrage cause. In 1850 she met Susan B. Anthony, the Quaker daughter of a local mill operator, and tried to win her over to the cause. Anthony was a temperance reformer who initially showed little interest in women's rights issues. But when she was barred from speaking at a major temperance convention because she was a woman, she recognized the significance of Stanton's interest. In 1852 the two women formed a partnership that would be the most important factor in the first half century of the suffrage movement.

They campaigned for a broad program of reform, organizing meetings, speaking, distributing pamphlets, and circulating petitions. In 1860 they won a major victory in persuading the New York Legislature to adopt a law giving married women the right to their wages—which had formerly belonged to their husbands—and allowing them for the first time to sue in court. With the beginning of the Civil War they turned to the cause of emancipation, identifying their own aspirations for liberation with that of the slaves.

When constitutional amendments were proposed guaranteeing rights to former slaves, they hoped they would be so worded as to encompass women's rights. But many male abolitionists refused to support their demands, holding that "This is the Negro's hour," and the amendments did nothing for women. Despite this setback, women pursued a variety of strategies to publicize their cause. In 1866 Elizabeth Cady Stanton ran for Congress as an independent, and Susan B. Anthony presented a suffrage petition to Congress with several thousand signatures. Stanton lost by 12,000 votes to 24, and Anthony's petition failed to persuade Congress to act. In 1867 the two women campaigned unsuccessfully for a state woman suffrage law in Kansas. In the following year they persuaded a supporter to introduce a woman suffrage amendment in Congress, but the bill received no support. Defeat followed upon defeat, but the women continued their work.

In 1869, twenty-one years after the Seneca Falls Convention, the two women founded the National Woman Suffrage Association, with Stanton as president. Stanton's keynote address to that organization was one of her most forceful statements on behalf of women's rights. She compared

Susan B. Anthony. For almost sixty years, she was one of the most dedicated and skillful leaders of the women's rights movement.

women with peasants, serfs, and slaves. "Of all kinds of aristocracy," she declared, "that of sex is the most odious and unnatural; invading, as it does, our homes, desecrating our family altars, dividing those whom God has joined together, exalting the son above the mother who bore him, and subjugating, everywhere, moral power to brute force."

Stanton, Anthony, and other members of the new association traveled throughout the country speaking on women's rights and forming suffrage organizations. Stanton was the more eloquent speaker; Anthony was particularly adept at arranging meetings, hiring halls, and handling the other details of administration. But progress was slow. During the first two decades of their organization they won only a few, widely scattered victories. In 1869 the Territory of Wyoming, where men greatly outnumbered women, became the first region in the United States to adopt woman suffrage. (In 1890 Wyoming was admitted to statehood and so became the first state to permit women to vote.) In 1876 Stanton won publicity for the cause by drafting the Woman's Declaration of Rights at the Philadelphia Centennial Exposition. Two years later she and Anthony persuaded California Senator Aaron A. Sargeant to introduce the federal woman suffrage amendment into Congress. The amendment would be reintroduced periodically until 1919.

In 1890 the National Woman Suffrage Association joined forces with a rival organization, the American Woman Suffrage Association, to form the National American Woman Suffrage Association (NAWSA) with Stanton as president. She retired two years later, and Anthony followed in the office until 1900. During the last decade of the century many suffragists attempted to capitalize on the nativistic mood of the times and emphasized their deep roots in the nation's past. Many had felt cheated by the Civil War experience, where they had supported the African Americans, only to have the ex-slaves receive freedom before they did. They were less willing now to take up the cause of the immigrant.

By 1900 both Stanton and Anthony were in their eighties and had to curtail their suffrage activities. Stanton died in 1902, and Anthony died in 1906, a few weeks after delivering an address to a Baltimore suffrage convention in which she declared, "Failure is impossible." During the final years of the founders, new suffragists began to emerge on the national scene. The most important was Carrie Chapman Catt, who had grown up in Iowa, where she was a teacher, school principal, and journalist. In 1890 she attended the first convention of the National American Woman Suffrage Association and immediately became one of its foremost members. Her husband, a wealthy California civil engineer, supported her reform interests and even signed a personal contract with Carrie allowing her to spend two months in the spring and two more in the fall devoted entirely to the suffrage movement. In the 1890s Catt assumed many of Susan B. Anthony's administrative responsibilities, raising funds and organizing branch offices for the NAWSA. In 1900 when Anthony retired, Carrie Chapman Catt took over as president. She immediately worked to strengthen the nationwide organization and to build up the suffrage treasury. She remained president until 1904, when her husband's illness required her to retire temporarily.

Catt's successor, Anna Howard Shaw, was a licensed preacher and physician who had received a theological degree from Boston University in 1886. She is generally credited with being one of the ablest and sincerest suffrage orators of her day, and under her guidance the NAWSA grew from seventeen thousand to two hundred thousand members. But she was less adept at administration than Anthony and Catt. During the eleven years of her presidency, the NAWSA lost much of its administrative control over local activities.

The fortunes of woman suffrage were not dependent, however, solely on the activities of the national president. The movement gained strength early in the twentieth century through the activities of hundreds of local suffragist organizers and thousands of workers. Pauline Agassiz Shaw, for example, became one of the movement's great financial supporters. Her husband, a New England mining magnate, encouraged her to use the family fortune for many benevolent activities, including experimental kindergartens and day-care centers. Through the child-care centers Shaw became acquainted with the problems of working mothers and began to think about the larger issues of women's rights. She regarded woman suffrage not only as a desirable goal but, more importantly, as a means to greater ends. If women could vote, she believed, they would reform politics, improve working conditions, and increase chances for world peace. In 1901 she founded the Boston Equal Suffrage Association for Good Government.

Jane Addams, the best-known social worker of the Progressive Era, also came to see woman suffrage as a way of achieving wider social reform. She believed that the greatest problem in city life was the dismal condition of urban households; because women were closest to the problems of home life, they would be most likely to rectify them if they had the power to vote.

Another suffragist, Harriot Stanton Blatch, was brought up with sensitivity to women's issues by her mother, Elizabeth Cady Stanton. Harriot Blatch lived in England for many years with her husband before returning to the United States in 1902. She brought with her appreciation for the more dramatic tactics of the British woman suffrage movement, and she organized such activities as parades, political campaigns against suffrage opponents, and the organization of working women.

The suffragists represented a wide gamut of political sensibilities. Some, like Bell Kearney of Mississippi, believed that woman suffrage would help maintain the superiority of America's traditional rulers. She argued that woman suffrage with a literacy requirement would greatly increase the ratio of white to black voters in the South. The South, she said, should "look to its Anglo-Saxon women as the medium through which to retain the supremacy of the white race over the African." Others, however, like Jane Addams and Pauline Shaw, believed that suffrage would help elevate the poorer classes.

In the early 1900s the movement gained increasing support from poorer women laborers. Caroline A. Lowe, a suffragist from Kansas City, Missouri, and a wage earner herself, presented an eloquent appeal on behalf of seven million working women to the 1912 NAWSA Convention. "From the standpoint of wages received," she said, "we wage earners know it to be almost universal that the men in the industries receive twice the amount granted to us although we may be doing the same work. We work side by side with our brothers; we are children of the same parents, reared in the same homes, educated in the same schools, ride to and fro on the same early morning and late evening cars, work together the same number of hours in the same shop and we have equal need of food, clothing and shelter. But at 21 years of age our brothers are given a powerful weapon for self-defense, a larger means for growth and self-expression."

Lowe argued that this weapon, the vote, being denied to women, left them victims of the economic marketplace.

Relying on the activities of thousands of local organizers like Caroline Lowe, the suffragist movement pinned its hopes on local victories. Throughout the United States suffragists delivered speeches from automobiles and on street corners, lobbied in state legislatures, published tracts, and circulated petitions. In 1915 they nearly won one of the most important local contests, the fight for the vote in New York. In that campaign they held block parties and street dances; established special days for visiting firemen, policemen, railroad workers, and other groups of men; and campaigned from door to door in every section of the state. To dramatize the prejudice that gave new immigrants the vote before women, they sent delegates of university women to sit in the audience clad in cap and gown, unenfranchised, as new males were sworn in as citizens. On the morning of election day when the suffrage issue went before the voters, they sent poll watchers to every voting place, armed with coffee and sandwiches for themselves and for male poll workers, and watched to see that the election was honest. But on election eve they learned that they had been defeated. In New York City when the news arrived, there was a moment's silence, then one of the women declared, "Who'll go with me now and start a new campaign with a street meeting?" Manhattan soon had its first suffragist rally of the new campaign.

Elsewhere the local campaigns had already produced suffrage victories. At the time of the great 1913 Washington suffrage parade, nine states had adopted laws allowing women to vote. The suffrage states— Wyoming, Colorado, Utah, Idaho, Washington, California, Arizona, Kansas, and Oregon—were all western states with relatively small populations in which men generally outnumbered women. Altogether, the suffrage states commanded only fifty-four electoral votes.

It was a start, but some of the suffragists felt that the movement was going too slowly and that more should be done on the national level. The foremost leader of the militant suffragists was a young woman named Alice Paul. Like many other women's rights leaders, she was reared in a Quaker household. In 1908 she had gone to England to do research for a doctorate in social work from the University of Pennsylvania. She joined the British suffragist movement and became acquainted with its leader, Emmeline Pankhurst.

English suffragists employed tactics far more radical than those of their American counterparts. They planted bombs, destroyed mail, burned men's clubs and social pavilions, damaged golf courses, and even attempted to take the royal jewels from the Tower of London. Alice Paul did not engage in these more violent forms of protest, but she did become a suffragist speaker and attempted to interrupt public meetings with suffrage demands. She was arrested seven times, including once in Norwich when she attempted to deliver a suffrage speech outside a hall where a young politician, Winston Churchill, was delivering a speech. "You didn't have to be a very good speaker," she once reflected, "because the minute you began you were arrested."

Upon returning to America in 1910 she joined the National American Woman Suffrage Association. She was disappointed by the organization because of its lack of militancy and its failure to push for the federal suffrage amendment, but through the influence of Jane Addams in 1912 she was appointed head of the NAWSA congressional committee. At the time she was only twenty-seven years old.

Her appointment at such an early age indicated the relative unimportance of the committee. Although it was responsible for encouraging congressional suffrage action, it had received a budget of only $10 during the previous year, and the former chair had managed to return change from that! Alice Paul inherited a list of suffrage supporters with her new job and found that most were either dead or had left the capital. The suffrage amendment, introduced so many years before through the influence of Susan B. Anthony and Elizabeth Cady Stanton, had not been reported out of committee since 1896.

Alice Paul was challenged rather than discouraged by the situation. With the help of Lucy Burns, whom she had met in prison in England, she instigated a vigorous suffrage campaign in the capital. With the approval of the NAWSA she organized the great Washington parade of 1913, sending invitations across the country, lining up families in Washington to house the visiting suffragists, and handling the details of parade organization. When a group of southern suffragists refused to march in the parade with black representatives of the National Association for the Advancement of Colored People (NAACP), she appeased their delicate racial sensibilities by placing a men's contingent between them and the NAACP marchers. Alice Paul marched in a university section among scores of voteless women dressed in caps and gowns. Sixty years later in an interview for *American Heritage* she remembered the parade with fondness. The crowd was boisterous but friendly, she said. "Of course, we did hear a lot of shouted insults, which we always expected. You know, the usual things about why aren't you home in the kitchen where you belong."

In the following year Alice Paul established the Congressional Union for Woman Suffrage to raise funds for her congressional committee. Because the NAWSA provided almost no money for the federal campaign, she believed that she needed a separate budget. She soon established a strong organization, and with the help of fellow lobbyists she was able to persuade Congress to bring the suffrage bill to the House floor. The Congressional Union popularized the measure by calling it "the Susan B. Anthony Amendment." The bill was defeated that year in both the House and the Senate.

The leaders of the NAWSA observed the Congressional Union's activity with some apprehension. The parent organization was committed to a state-by-state movement and emphasized the grass-roots education of the voters. Alice Paul preferred the national approach, reasoning that Congress provided a smaller and more manageable group of people with which to work. In 1914 the NAWSA required Paul to resign her leadership of either the congressional committee or the Congressional Union. She chose to remain in charge of her own organization. Soon afterward the Congressional Union was deprived of its affiliation with the NAWSA and went its separate way.

The Congressional Union thrived as an independent organization. After the suffrage bill's congressional defeat in 1914, the Union campaigned against Democrats seeking reelection, contending that the party in power should be blamed for the failure of the suffrage amendment. Many of the women's targets were defeated, and suddenly the suffrage movement acquired political clout. In 1916 historian Charles Beard wrote an admiring description of the organization—now called the National Woman's party—in *The New Republic*. "It has ideas," he said, "but it does not wear them on its sleeve . . . . It does not beg, it does not wheedle, it does not whine. It wages a trench warfare with exactly the kind of weapons that men use. It knows that no other kind is effective. It speaks a language which the most seasoned and cynical politician can understand. It has money and organization and will and votes."

In 1916 woman suffrage states elected one-fifth of the Senate, one-seventh of the House of Representatives, and one-sixth of the presidential electors. In that year, under heavy pressure from women's groups, both major parties adopted woman suffrage planks in their national platforms. But they both hedged their support by advocating state-by-state decisions rather than supporting the national suffrage amendment.

Acting on the principle that the party in power should be blamed for suffrage failure, the National Woman's party campaigned against Woodrow Wilson. In so doing they gained the first martyr to their cause. Inez Milholland, who had led the Washington parade, was considered by the suffragists to be the most striking of their supporters, and they customarily placed her at the head of their parades. Her suffrage activism had begun in her undergraduate days at Vassar, where she held an illegal women's rights meeting in a local cemetery after the college president refused to allow the meeting on campus.

Inez Milholland was not struck down by bullets or bayonets, but she died dramatically, nonetheless. She and her sister Vita were touring the western states in 1916, campaigning against Wilson, when she collapsed from exhaustion while delivering an address in Los Angeles. Her legendary last words were: "Mr. President, how long must women wait for liberty?"

Woodrow Wilson would see those words hundreds of times in the next two years, for the National Woman's party had them embroidered on suffrage banners and displayed them before the White House along with their party's purple, white, and gold standards. On January 7, 1917, Wilson, who had ridden to victory on the slogan "He Kept Us Out of War," received a delegation from the National Woman's party but told them that he continued to favor a state-by-state approach to the suffrage question. On the following day the women created a "perpetual delegation" to the White House. Wilson refused to meet with any more delegates, claiming that the impending war required all his time. And so the women sent pickets to the White House from 10:00 A.M. to 5:30 P.M. six days a week. President Wilson was gracious enough, removing his hat and bowing to the women when he left the White House grounds for his daily drive, but he still refused to support the Anthony Amendment.

On April 6, 1917, the United States entered the war with Germany, and many suffragists believed that women should postpone their activities until the end of the war. But the National Woman's party, recalling that the same logic had damaged the women's movement during the Civil War, insisted on maintaining their daily vigil at the White House. They now came to be regarded as disloyal and suffered abuse from opponents, some of whom tore up their banners. The police made periodic sweeps of the picket lines, arresting several hundred women before the year's end for allegedly obstructing traffic.

On October 20, 1917, Alice Paul was arrested. She spent five horrifying weeks in prison, first in stuffy overcrowded cells with other suffragists, and then alone in a psychiatric ward. She was already so weakened by poor prison food that she could hardly walk, but she decided to dramatize her cause by going on a hunger strike. The prison hospital responded by force-feeding her through hard tubes pushed into her nose, a tactic that had been used in British prisons to break suffragist hunger strikes. Alice Paul knew that women had received permanent damage to their nasal passages and eyes from this technique. But she persisted.

Her situation was all the more intimidating because the prison doctors implied to her that she would be committed to an insane asylum, a move they could make without intervention by judge, jury, or lawyers. In the mental wing of the hospital she was further intimidated by an "observation" procedure that involved awakening her with a bright light once every hour all night long. Her cell window was boarded up.

Alice Paul was cut off from all friends and attorneys for several weeks, but finally Dudley Field Malone, one of the country's foremost lawyers, had the opportunity to see her. As often happens when a government abuses a well-known person, the tide of public sentiment shifted strongly in favor of Paul and her fellow suffragists. Through President Wilson's influence they were released from prison on November 27 and

28, 1917. Less than two months later, on January 19, 1918, Wilson came out in favor of woman suffrage. The next day the House of Representatives passed the Anthony Amendment. But there remained the problems of winning Senate support for the measure and of persuading the necessary three-fourths of the states to ratify.

Alice Paul's contribution to the woman suffrage movement was more dramatic than that of the moderate suffragists. But while she was capturing national headlines with confrontation tactics, thousands of suffragists were at work winning support state by state, city by city, and precinct by precinct. In New York City, Lillian D. Wald, who ran the Henry Street Settlement House on the Lower East Side, was especially influential. She took her commitment to suffrage into meetings with immigrants, housewives, and politicians. Her settlement house ran a visiting nurse program that sent one hundred nurses on 250,000 house calls throughout New York City in 1917. By their activity the nurses showed immigrant wives that a woman could be as resourceful as a man, and they frequently encouraged them to support the suffrage movement. The wives, in turn, influenced their husbands. When New York adopted woman suffrage in 1917, the Lower East Side approved by better than two to one.

The National American Woman Suffrage Association also took a crucial part in the final suffrage battles. In 1915 Carrie Chapman Catt again became president of the organization. Under her direction the NAWSA adopted the "Winning Plan" in its national convention in 1916. This was a combination of local and national activity. In Washington, Catt was an effective lobbyist, winning even President Wilson's personal admiration. In the states her workers helped win an impressive series of victories between 1916 and 1918.

The war also helped the women's cause. It required hundreds of thousands of women to fill "men's jobs" when male workers joined the armed forces. The idealistic Wilsonian war rhetoric, stressing human rights, further aided the suffragists. Alice Paul, in particular, turned the Wilsonian demand for justice abroad into another reason for justice to women at home. Moreover, woman suffrage now appeared to be on the threshold of worldwide approval. Russia and England had already given women the vote by 1918, and most Canadian provinces had enfranchised women. (England, however, required a woman to be thirty before she could vote.)

In May 1919 President Wilson called a special session of Congress to consider the suffrage amendment. Six more states had passed suffrage bills. The Eighteenth Amendment, prohibiting the sale of alcoholic beverages, had already passed, removing the incentive for the liquor lobby's opposition to woman suffrage. The momentum was now clearly on the side of ratification. On May 20, 1919, the House again voted its approval. On June 4, after a sometimes bitter debate, the Senate finally added its consent.

Carrie Chapman Catt. In the 1890s she and her husband agreed that she could devote four months a year to women's rights activities.

The states soon began to ratify the Anthony Amendment. Many had already approved state laws for woman suffrage and ratified almost immediately. But the Deep South was strongly opposed, and it would be necessary to sweep the rest of the country to win the necessary three-fourths majority required for ratification. The issue was in doubt until the bill came before the Tennessee house on August 26, 1920. With that body almost evenly divided, the youngest representative, twenty-four-year-old Harry Burns, cast a decisive vote in favor of the amendment. His mother, an ardent suffragist, had written him, "I've been watching to see how you stood but have noticed nothing yet. Don't forget to be a good boy and help Mrs. Catt."

With the passage of the Nineteenth Amendment, women through-out the United States were able to vote in the presidential election of 1920. For many who had longed for enfranchisement all their lives, the first opportunity to vote seemed the verge of a new age. One of the suffragists, Charlotte Woodward, had been in the movement since a June day in 1848 when she had ventured forth from her farm to attend the Seneca Falls Convention. She alone of the members of that first women's rights convention lived to see the nationwide enfranchisement of her sex.

Victory was particularly sweet to those who had worked for it as active suffragists. But it was pleasing also to millions of other women who enjoyed the fruits of the suffrage victory. One was a woman named Sally

Gold, who had been born in Austria when John Adams and Thomas Jefferson were still alive. She remembered that in Austria there had never been any talk of woman suffrage; in fact, she could remember seeing women "harnessed to carts like donkeys." When she was about sixty she immigrated to the United States and came to live in New York City. When woman suffrage was adopted in New York, she lived in an apartment behind a small store where she sold eggs, butter, and other groceries. On the first election day under the new law, her granddaughters urged her to go right out and vote. But Sally Gold was more than a hundred years old and knew how she wanted to observe this day. She carefully washed the dishes and swept the floor. Then she went out to cast her ballot.

The suffrage victory was a product of many factors. Although it took place in an era of broad social reform, it existed, ironically, in an uncomfortable relationship with the Progressive movement. Its members gained experience by working in Progressive causes such as temperance unions and settlement houses. But the male leadership of the Progressive movement was generally slow in embracing woman suffrage. The movement benefited, however, from the atmosphere of reform in the United States in the early twentieth century. Suffragists saw reform occur in other areas and were encouraged that they, too, might accomplish their goal.

The suffrage victory drew on women with many backgrounds and temperaments. The more liberal members of the movement had to work side by side with suffragists who welcomed the disfranchisement of blacks and restrictions of immigrants. The movement also divided between militant and moderate suffragists. The mix of characteristics was apparent in the personalities of the movement's two best-known leaders. Although they favored different tactics and headed different organizations, Alice Paul and Carrie Catt needed one another. The National Woman's party dramatized the cause and revealed the political power of women. The NAWSA was more active in organizing the local campaigns that were essential to ratification. Both recognized, moreover, that women could not achieve full social and political equality simply by the fact of having the vote. After ratification Catt lent her energies to the newly created League of Women Voters, an organization designed to help women make the most intelligent possible use of their ballots. And Paul began to work for an equal rights amendment, guaranteeing women full equality with men. In 1919 women tended to feel that other feminist reforms would follow naturally on the suffrage victory. But discrimination in property laws, employment practices, and other areas continued unaltered and did not come under effective attack until the 1960s.

Looking back on the disparate forces that contributed to the suffrage movement, its long history, and its unfinished business, we find that Alice Paul's assessment a half century after the passage of the Anthony

Amendment is particularly apt: "I always feel . . . the movement is a sort of mosaic. Each of us puts in one little stone, and then you get a great mosaic at the end."

Bibliography

BUHLE, MARI JO, AND PAUL BUHLE, EDITORS. *The Concise History of the Woman Suffrage Movement* (1978). Documentary overview of suffrage movement.

CATT, CARRIE CHAPMAN, AND NETTIE ROGERS SHULER. *Woman Suffrage and Politics* (1923). Suffrage history by foremost NAWSA administrator.

DANIELS, DORIS. "Building a Winning Coalition: The Suffrage Fight in New York State." *New York History* (January 1979): 59–80. Emphasizes role of settlement house workers, especially that of Lillian Wald.

FLEXNER, ELEANOR. *Century of Struggle: The Women's Rights Movement in the United States* (1970). Standard survey on the feminist movement.

GALLAGHER, ROBERT S. "I was arrested, of course. . . . " *American Heritage* 25 (February 1974): 16–24 and 92–94. Illuminating interview with Alice Paul focusing on the suffrage battle.

GRAHAM, SARA HUNTER. *Woman Suffrage and the New Democracy* (1996). Argues that the National American Woman Suffrage Association was one of America's most effective single-issue pressure groups.

GREEN, ELNA C. *Southern Strategies: Southern Women and the Woman Suffrage Question* (1997). Explores the history of southern women who favored and those who opposed woman suffrage.

IRWIN, INEZ HAYES. *The Story of Alice Paul and the National Woman's Party* (1964). Popular account of Paul's suffrage activities, 1913–1920.

KRADITOR, AILEEN S. *The Ideas of the Woman Suffrage Movement, 1890–1920* (1965). Analysis of arguments for and against woman suffrage.

LUNARDINI, CHRISTINE A. *From Equal Suffrage to Equal Rights* (1986). Alice Paul and women's rights.

MEAD, REBECCA J. *How the Vote Was Won: Woman Suffrage in the Western United States, 1868–1914* (2004). Explores why the Western states enfranchised women well in advance of the East and the South.

SHAW, ANNA HOWARD. *The Story of a Pioneer* (1915). Autobiography of a NAWSA leader.

STANTON, ELIZABETH CADY, ET AL. *The History of Woman Suffrage* (6 vols., 1899–1922). Extensive account by participants.

STEVENS, DORIS. *Jailed for Freedom: American Women Win the Vote* (1995). Carol O'Hare edited this new edition of an account written in 1920 by one of the many women who went to jail for the suffrage cause.

Study Guide

Summary

This essay surveys the history of the woman suffrage movement from its inception at the Seneca Falls Convention to the passage of the Nineteenth Amendment.

The article focuses on the activities of Alice Paul and Carrie Chapman Catt, both of whose distinctive tactics contributed to victory in 1919. The essay argues that Progressives were often opposed to the amendment but that many women nevertheless gained political experience in the Progressive movement. It concludes by showing that both Paul and Catt felt that much work lay ahead in the women's rights movement.

Identification Topics

"General" Rosalie Jones, Inez Milholland, Elizabeth Cady Stanton, Susan B. Anthony, National American Woman Suffrage Association, Jane Addams, Alice Paul, National Woman's party, Carrie Chapman Catt, Nineteenth Amendment, progressivism

Study Questions

1. For what reasons did people oppose woman suffrage? Why did many Progressives, who supported other reforms, oppose it?
2. In what ways did women not enjoy equality in law and custom in 1910?
3. In what ways did Elizabeth Cady Stanton and Susan B. Anthony foster the suffrage movement?
4. Why was Alice Paul dissatisfied with the NAWSA program, and what was her contribution to the suffrage movement?
5. Describe the contribution of each of the following to the suffrage movement and mention the factors you consider to have been most important: Alice Paul, Carrie Chapman Catt, local suffragist workers, World War I, the Progressive Era, Woodrow Wilson. Explain your answer.
6. Why did Alice Paul and Carrie Catt believe that the battle for women's rights could not end with the passage of the Anthony Amendment? What further measures did they advocate?
7. Who contributed more to the woman suffrage victory, Alice Paul or Carrie Chapman Catt?
8. Of the conditions faced by women at the time of the passage of the Nineteenth Amendment, which have changed the most and which have changed the least?

Research Topics

1. Trace the history of the women's rights movement after 1919. Why was so little achieved in the next half century?
2. Explore more fully the biographies of prominent women in the Progressive and woman suffrage movements.
3. Investigate fully the arguments for and against woman suffrage.
4. Examine the history of the Equal Rights Amendment. Why has it failed to pass?
5. Read about and compare the suffrage movements in England and America.
6. In what ways do modern supporters of women's rights employ the ideas and tactics of the early suffrage movement? In what ways are the opponents similar?

CHAPTER 7

American Volunteers in World War I

The Lafayette Escadrille

In 1914 Europe was engulfed in general war. Before the last shots were fired in 1918, some twenty million combatants and civilians would lose their lives. The United States at first pursued a course of neutrality, but was drawn into the conflict in 1917 after Germany began a campaign of unlimited submarine warfare and sank several American vessels. While late on the scene, the United States arrived with so many troops as to tip the balance of the war toward the Allies, including England and France. Long before American soldiers arrived on European soil, however, American volunteers by the hundreds had gone to war for France and other Allied countries as soldiers and airmen. They exhibited the same thirst for adventure and the same belief in democratic values that characterized many of the millions of inductees who would enter the American service after war was declared. Most famous of these volunteers were the members of the Lafayette Escadrille.

Mildred Aldrich, an elderly American expatriate, arose each morning at dawn during the summer of 1914, wrapped herself in a cloak, and went to her lawn to gaze over the French countryside. Each morning the sun illuminated the same lovely valley: "miles and miles of laughing country, little white towns just smiling in the early light, a thin strip of river here and there, dimpling and dancing, stretches of fields of all colors."

For years Aldrich had lived in Paris as a theater critic for the *New York Times*. But age and declining health had changed her. She moved to the country to find "a quiet refuge" and "the simple life." In retirement Mildred Aldrich liked to look over the countryside as she worked in her garden. Winding through the fields and villages, the Marne River made a "wonderful loop" to within a mile of her hilltop house. Aldrich's American friends chided her for abandoning her native land, but even while gazing at the French countryside, she had not forgotten the United States. She reported: "I turn my eyes to the west often with a queer sort of amazed pride." The United States was, however, a country for "the young, the energetic, and the ambitious." Aldrich had once been all of those, but now she cherished the calm life of rural France.

From her dreamlike locale, the world itself seemed a kind of dream. One morning a paper arrived with the news that the crown prince of Austria had been assassinated at Sarajevo, Serbia. Considering the event from her hilltop, Aldrich reasoned that "Austria will not grieve much" because Archduke Franz Ferdinand was "none too popular" with his people.

If Mildred Aldrich had been an active political reporter rather than a retired drama critic, she might have sensed that the assassination in Sarajevo would not be so easily forgotten. Within a few weeks there were a series of threats, first by Austria against Serbia, then by Russia against Austria, then by the other major powers of Europe, including England and France, against each other. These threats, once acted upon, would drive Europe into World War I, the most bloody conflict in history. And the first great battle of that war would soon take place along the Marne River, in the very countryside that Mildred Aldrich viewed from her front yard.

A few weeks after her first mention of Sarajevo, Aldrich was writing home, "It is a nasty outlook. We are simply holding our breaths here." On July 30, 1914, she envisioned the looming warfare: "It will be the bloodiest affair the world has ever seen—a war in the air, a war under the sea as well as on it, and carried out with the most effective manslaughtering machines ever used in battle." A few days later a man walked up and down the rural lanes near her farmhouse beating a drum and calling on the men to mobilize. All day long Aldrich could watch airplanes flying from Paris to the frontier to observe the German movements. Airplanes! She had attended an exhibition just fourteen years before where a model of an airplane was on display: it had never flown nor had any other heavier-than-air machine gone aloft at that time. Two years later, in 1903, Wilbur and Orville Wright flew a plane a few hundred yards at Kitty Hawk, North Carolina. The progress in flight during the next decade had been astonishing. Sitting in her garden, where she watched airplanes flying overhead, "so steady and so sure," Aldrich reflected, "It is awe-compelling to remember how these cars in the air change all military tactics." No longer would an army be able to move unobserved.

With war imminent, friends urged Mildred Aldrich to retire from her country home to a safer distance from the German border, to Paris or better still the United States. But she chose to stay in her new home. The German armies moved quickly during the first weeks of the war, through Belgium and across the French border. Still Aldrich stayed. One morning Aldrich heard a tremendous explosion and learned that the bridges over the Marne River were being dynamited to delay the Germans. French and British troops began moving past the farmhouse headed for the front, and Aldrich served up tea and biscuits to some of the soldiers. Officers surveyed the countryside from her front yard.

The contending armies—Germany invading and England and France resisting—came over the horizon, and Aldrich could hear the cannon and see smoke in the distance. She wrote: "To my imagination every shot meant awful slaughter, and between me and the terrible thing stretched a beautiful country, as calm in the sunshine as if horrors were not." That night the Germans came closer. With their artillery they set fire to grain stacks and buildings visible from the farmhouse. These fires "stood like a procession of huge torches across my beloved panorama."

From her hilltop Mildred Aldrich was witnessing a portion of the Battle of the Marne, one of the most important fights of the war. If the French and English failed to hold, the Germans would likely occupy Paris. But the Allies did hold. On September 7, 1914, Aldrich noticed that the cannon fire seemed more distant. An English soldier on a bicycle wheeled up to her house and told her, "Everything is all right. Germans been as near you as they will ever get. Close shave." She learned that the Germans had come within four miles of her hilltop, where they were stopped and retreated back a few miles to defensive positions. Aldrich had endured the sound of cannon for three days—pounding "on every nerve in my body"—but she realized that others had sacrificed much more: "Out there on the plain, almost within my sight, lay the men who had paid with their lives—each dear to someone—to hold back the battle from Paris."

Three months after the Battle of the Marne, Mildred Aldrich toured the war zone by car. She passed through village after village where houses had been shelled to rubble and through forests where huge trees had been snapped like twigs by cannon fire. She came to a broad field where some of the dead were buried, all the graves marked by French flags, floating "like fine flowers in the landscape. They made tiny spots against the far-off horizon line, and groups like beds of flowers in the foreground, and we knew that, behind the skyline, there were more."

Tens of thousands of soldiers fell at the Battle of the Marne. Millions more would die before the end of the war. Mildred Aldrich would continue to observe the conflict from her hilltop and send reports in letters to friends—the basis eventually for three books. Other Americans, young men driven by idealism or the thirst for adventure, would become more actively engaged in the fighting.

With the opening of World War I the United States began a policy of neutrality that was to last into 1917. At the onset of the war President Woodrow Wilson urged Americans to remain "neutral in fact as well as in name, impartial in thought as well as action." Wilson believed that Americans could set a standard for world peace by remaining above the conflict. But other citizens identified from the start with the Allied cause: they thought of England and France as fellow democracies and read with horror stories of the German army sweeping across Belgium toward Paris. Hundreds of individual Americans served as volunteers, driving ambulances and fighting in combat units. The most famous of the volunteers, Ernest Hemingway, was wounded while engaged as an ambulance driver for the Italian army. His *Farewell to Arms*, while fiction, draws on his actual experiences on the Italian front. Most American volunteers served with the Allies—France, Britain, and Italy. But a few served as ambulance drivers for the Germans. Many of these Americans went to war to take part in what they considered a righteous cause. An American volunteer named Alan Seeger, who would die in 1916 at the Battle of the Somme, wrote a poem in which he thanked France for giving him and his fellows "that rare privilege of dying well." Another American volunteer was described as devoted to "the cause of Liberty and Righteousness throughout the world."

Most of the Americans who served in France joined the Foreign Legion and helped defend a line of trenches that ran from the North Sea four hundred miles to Switzerland. Other trenches, occupied by Germans, ran parallel to the Allied line, sometimes several hundred yards distant, sometimes much closer. In these trenches millions of men served during World War I. After the early engagements in the war, including the Battle of the Marne, armies on the western front seldom moved more that a few hundred yards in an attack. Sometimes one side would attempt a breakthrough, gaining a few miles of the other's territory. But on the whole, both sides were literally bogged down for most of the war.

The men in the trenches lived in mud, exposed to rain, cold, and enemy bombardments. During the night they made excursions into "no man's land," the dangerous ground between the lines. In larger attacks, the soldiers were called upon to make near-suicidal frontal assaults, walking across open ground toward the enemy trenches. Such maneuvers had been dangerous enough for troops during the eighteenth century, when an enemy soldier could barely fire one bullet per minute. Against modern rapid-firing machine guns frontal assaults were murderous. In a single attack at the Somme River the British suffered sixty thousand casualties in one day. In and around the line of trenches between 1914 and 1918 millions of men died.

For a few thousand soldiers World War I opened a new field of combat, a war waged above the trenches in airplanes. In a sense, the third dimension of warfare had been introduced more than a century before with the use of observation balloons in the Napoleonic Wars and later in the U.S. Civil War. By 1914 armies regularly employed such balloons to provide information about the enemy's position for the artillery—on the western front gunners were firing shells so far that often they could not even see their targets. The Zeppelin also made its appearance in the war. Named after a German count who produced the first effective models, these lighter-than-air craft could carry bombs far behind the enemies' lines. But the most important innovation of the war was the use of the airplane for collecting intelligence, conducting bombing runs, strafing enemy troops, and engaging other aircraft.

The Italians had pioneered air warfare in 1911 by using nine planes in a war against the Turks in Libya. Their firsts included intelligence gathering, a bombing run, and the wounding of one of their pilots by a bullet fired from the ground. The United States used planes for reconnaissance during a short-lived occupation of Vera Cruz, Mexico, in 1914. With these exceptions and a few others, the airplane was largely untested as a military weapon at the beginning of World War I.

The planes that Mildred Aldrich saw flying above her farmhouse near the Marne had been gathering intelligence on German movements—the one activity that would obviously benefit from air power. At first observation planes from opposite sides simply flew past each other, their pilots sometimes even waving cheerfully, invoking a kind of fraternity of the air. But it was soon apparent that enemy planes were helping to kill one's own countrymen, and tactics were developed to enable pilots to destroy enemy observers. Initially these consisted of arming pilots with pistols, but small arms had little effect in aerial combat. Other early suggestions for the military pilot's arsenal included hand grenades, harpoons, and hooks. Machine guns were at first too heavy to be useful in early aircraft, but in 1911 an American army officer, Isaac N. Lewis, developed a machine gun weighing only twenty-five pounds. Lewis guns were subsequently mounted on the planes, making aerial combat deadly.

Pilots were provided various tactical assignments and appropriate planes. Fast, maneuverable chasse (hunting) planes guarded slower observation planes. Bombers were designed to carry increasingly large payloads, and chasse planes were assigned to protect them. Methods of aerial combat included elaborate formations in which one plane protected another, and maneuvers in which planes turned, climbed, and swooped in death-defying maneuvers in order to shoot down an enemy plane or avoid being shot down themselves. In 1903 Wilbur and Orville Wright had flown only a few dozen yards above the ground. By 1918 combat pilots could reach heights of twenty thousand feet. The planes themselves added to the risk of combat. Made mainly of wood, canvas, and wire, they could easily break apart or be set afire in combat. Moreover, the pilots in World War I went aloft without parachutes.

Despite the dangers of combat flight, many young men were intrigued by the idea of becoming pilots. In addition to the Americans who served in the French infantry, a few enlisted in the French Flying Corps. One young American, Norman Prince, hoped not simply to fly for France, but to fly for France in a distinct American squadron. Prince hailed from Massachusetts but had spent many vacations at Pau in southern France, where he hunted, made friends, and learned to speak French. A polo-playing Harvard graduate, he was born to wealth, like many other future American volunteers in the French Flying Corps. During autumn 1914, at the beginning of the war, Prince was enrolled in a flight school in Marblehead, Massachusetts. There he developed the idea of creating a separate unit within the French Flying Corps composed of Americans. A few months later he set sail for France aboard the *Rochambeau*, an ocean liner named appropriately for a Frenchman who had served in America during the Revolution. On shore at La Havre, Norman Prince wrote his mother, "I believe I can find a place to do some efficient and useful work for the cause to which I am so deeply devoted."

At first it was difficult for American volunteers to find places in the French Flying Corps at all, to say nothing of creating a separate unit. The chance to pilot one of a relatively small number of planes went first to Frenchmen. Eventually, however, many of these pilots were killed and more planes were built, making room for American volunteers. Norman Prince was one of those airmen. In May 1915 he went to the front to replace a disabled pilot. He wrote home, "I saw the battle lines and heard for the first time the never-ending boom of guns. This is war in dead earnest and right at hand." Prince flew for several months and was then given leave with two other American airmen to return to the United States and tour the country on a kind of goodwill mission for France. The German embassy demanded that these Americans in French uniforms be interred for the duration of the war, but Prince and his comrades slipped aboard a ship and returned to France in winter 1916.

By then the idea of a separate American unit within the French Flying Corps was bearing fruit. An American expatriate doctor, Edmund L. Gros, who was already working for the American Ambulance Corps in France, helped persuade acquaintances within the French Ministry of Foreign Affairs that they could gain propaganda benefits by creating a unique American unit within the French Flying Corps. Gros was part of the Franco-American Committee, a collection of French and American citizens devoted to bringing Americans and ultimately America itself into the war. While Gros and his colleagues politicked, American pilots such as Norman Prince had fought well in French units. Before leaving for America Prince had been cited as an "excellent military pilot who has consistently displayed great audacity and presence of mind." Another American, William Thaw, stayed aloft over the front during one especially perilous mission, guiding French artillery fire despite taking so many hits that when his plane landed it was beyond repair. Such American exploits proved that the volunteers could actually contribute to the war effort as well as create favorable publicity in the United States. Finally on March 14, 1916, a separate American escadrille (squadron) was created within the French Flying Corps. It began with nine members, one of whom was Norman Prince.

Many of the American volunteers in the Flying Corps were the sons of wealthy families and graduates of prestigious colleges, but at the training camps not all the men fit that description. As one volunteer noted: "There is a fine crew in this school, men from all colleges and men who don't know the name of a college, . . . men sticky with money in the same barracks with others who worked their way over on ships." He went on to describe an African American in the barracks—most likely Edward Bullard of Columbus, Georgia. At the time the American army was segregated, but that was not the case with the French forces. Although the American pilot described his African American compatriot in terms that today would be considered racial stereotypes, he still demonstrated a healthy respect for his fellow pilot:

> This democracy is a fine thing in the army and makes better men of all hands. For instance, the corporal of our room is an American, as black as the ace of spades, but a mighty white fellow at that. The next two bunks to his are occupied by Princeton men of old Southern families. They talk more like a darky than he does and are the best of friends with him. . . . This black brother has been in the Foreign Legion, wounded four times, covered with medals for his bravery in the trenches, and now uses his experiences and knowledge of French for the benefit of our room.

The American volunteers, along with other airmen in World War I, were pioneers in a new kind of warfare. As one trainee wrote, "I am now

in a French aviation school and learning how to imitate the birds."
Among the pilots who would join the Flying Corps was a young
American who would become one of the most famous writers of his
time, James Norman Hall. Along with another American pilot, Charles
Nordhoff, Hall would author *Mutiny on the Bounty*. In 1917 and 1918
Hall wrote a series of articles for the *Atlantic Monthly* based on his experience as an airman. The articles formed the basis for his book about the
air war, *High Adventure*. A good writer as well as a skilled pilot, Hall
was able to capture the experience of flight in the early years.

On his first day of flight training, James Hall listened carefully to
the advice of fellow Americans: wear all your flight gear including goggles and fur-lined boots—it's cold up there. Eager to get it right, Hall
dressed for high altitude and made his way to the airfield, where he saw
his first "airplane." Called a Penguin, this class of planes had clipped
wings, a twenty-five-horsepower engine, and was incapable of even leaving the ground. Seasoned aviators, French and American, laughed at the
joke on Hall and left the overdressed novice to his education.

The Penguin, James Hall learned, could build up just enough speed
for the tail to lift, giving the pilot practice in steering with a rudder.
"Never have I seen a stranger sight than that of a swarm of Penguins at
work," wrote Hall. "They ran along the ground at an amazing speed,
zigzagged this way and that, and whirled about as if trying to catch their
own tails." As Hall watched, two of the Penguins rushed at each other "as
though driven by the hand of fate" and crashed head-on. Hall's turn came
and he charged down the field at full speed, lifted the Penguin's tail,
seemed about to flip over, cut his engine, and spun around in a circle.
Later in the day, he was able to steer a straight course with the rudder, and
he sped down the field to a flag marking the end of the course. There a
man turned his machine 180 degrees, and Hall headed back, having mas-
tered the Penguin—"compelled it to do my bidding."

James Hall taxied proudly to the starting point, anticipating congratulations. But instead the other airmen were looking up at a plane high overhead. As they watched, it turned straight up into the sky, hung for a
moment, then dropped into a nosedive, turning as it fell "like a scrap of
paper." The French called this maneuver a *vrille*, "the prettiest piece of aerial acrobatics that one could wish to see." After seven or eight turns, the
pilot came out of his dive, gathered speed, and made two quick loops, followed by a *retournement*—turning over in the air and reversing his direction. He then spiraled down over the onlookers and landed so perfectly that
it was "impossible to know when the machine touched the ground." The
"birdman" removed his helmet and goggles and was recognized at once as a
former instructor, taking the afternoon off from the front to visit old
friends. For him those death-defying maneuvers were more than aerial
sport—under other circumstances they might save his life or enable him to

shoot down an enemy. Mounted on the hood of his plane was a machine gun with a long belt of cartridges—a reminder of the war.

After the pilot went off with his friends, James Hall examined his plane carefully, looking into the cockpit. He noted that the gun was mounted so that it would fire directly through the propeller, which rotated at speeds of up to 1,900 revolutions per minute. Hall looked back at his little Penguin and realized how much he had to learn.

The French course in military aviation undertaken by most Americans usually consisted of a sequence of increasingly complex solo flights, unlike modern flight training where the instructor goes aloft with the pupil. At first trainees flew up and down the runway barely leaving the ground; then they mounted to about one hundred feet, shut off their engines, and glided back to earth. Next they added a turn to their flights, climbing above the airdrome, and circling around to land. Still close to the training field, a student then flew to 3,000, shut off his engine, and glided down to a predetermined spot. Another test required the trainee to climb above 6,500 feet and remain there for a full hour. Finally, he would make several cross-country flights.

The program made good sense, but every stage brought surprises—some troublesome and some deadly. The commandant at Avord, where most Americans were trained, was killed when a student flew into his plane, knocking off a wing. The commandant's plane crashed to the ground, but the student managed to land safely, although the wing of the other plane stuck to his machine. Another pilot crashed into the roof of the camp bakery, ending up hanging from the ceiling, uninjured. Others were less fortunate; about 1 percent of all student pilots died in flight training.

The first real flight by the novice, beyond simply cruising down the runway, was called the *tour de piste*. The solo trainee had to climb high over the airdrome, make his first-ever turn, and land. If he failed to coordinate hands and feet on the controls, he could easily crash into a hanger or the runway. One American took off from Avord, flew over a row of haystacks indicating where he should turn, and dipped his left wing according to instructions. But he was unprepared for the sensation: he felt as if he were falling out of the open-cockpit plane. Distracted, he misjudged the turn and went sailing across the space of another class and toward a nearby village. By the time he managed to turn again, his landing field was in the "dim distance." The novice barely skimmed a row of trees, "trespassed" through the air space of another class, and landed.

"What did you do?" said the instructor.

"God only knows," the student replied.

Told to try again, he managed two good tours. But on the second he learned another lesson about flight: "I struck a bump and received an awful jolt, which to say the least startled me considerably." Seasoned pilots knew, and beginners soon learned, that unseen air currents could unexpectedly lift or drop a plane a hundred feet and more. "My machine was seized and turned sideways," one pilot recounted:

> Then, as though tossed by a giant who had instantly changed his mind, it was dropped into a hole, perhaps 100 feet deep. Gusts strike you in front, sideways, behind; up you go over a mountainous wave; then down, falling over the other side. So it goes, gently easing each bump with the controls, sideways, forwards or backwards, with a delicate touch that comes by instinct.

James Hall's instructor explained that the air could be turbulent at one level and yet calm at another—a fact known to any modern air traveler—but the young trainee was "incredulous" until he actually experienced the change in winds. Hall had not until then lost his "boyhood belief that the wind went all the way up."

After developing a feeling for air currents, trainees practiced more complex maneuvers including flying spirals and landing without an engine—"a very difficult thing to do," one pilot recounted, "as the field from 3,400 feet appears as small as your back yard." After this test the trainee would be required to pass the high altitude test. One pilot, who held his plane at 8,000 feet for the required hour, regretted that he had taken only a sweater for warmth. He "nearly froze" during the flight and even after landing he was "chilled through for a long time afterwards."

In the classroom the trainees received instruction in navigation by map and by compass. Then came their *brevet* flights, journeys of about two hundred miles. The trainee flew to an assigned destination, landed, and flew home. James Hall's flight papers included a list of prices to be paid to farmers in case of forced landings on their crops. Hall particularly treasured the official orders telling him to proceed "by the route of the air" from Avord to Châteauroux and Romorantin. He read this "with feelings which must have been nearly akin to those of Columbus on a memorable day in 1492 when he received his clearance papers from Cadiz. 'By the route of air!' How the imagination lingered over that phrase!"

Hall donned a fur-lined flight suit, climbed into his craft, and took off. His plane was at first buffeted by the winds. Then he reached 2,500 feet and smooth air. As he flew on he saw with wonder the land from the open cockpit of his airplane. Beneath was a cathedral he had often visited in a town near the airdrome:

> Looking down on it now, it seemed no larger than a toy cathedral in a toy town, such as one sees in the shops of Paris. The streets were empty, for it was not yet seven o'clock. Strips of shadow crossed them where taller roofs cut off the sunshine. A toy train, which I could have

put nicely into my fountain-pen case, was pulling into a station no larger than a wren's house.

James Hall climbed to 6,000 feet: "It seemed a tremendous altitude." He could see scores of villages and châteaus, forests and farmland: "It looked like a world planned and laid out by the best of Santa Clauses. . . . For untold generations only the birds have had the privilege of seeing and enjoying it from the wing. Small wonder that they sing." Hall followed a straight road, heading southwest toward Châteauroux. His motor ran smoothly and for a while he reflected that flying was "the simplest thing in the world." But the young pilot would soon learn to be more respectful of the dangers of flight.

Hall's trip into Châteauroux went well. In the distance he could see the spires and red roofs of the town; nearby were barracks, hangers, and a landing field. Hall reduced speed. His motor purring gently, the landscape coming closer: "shining threads of silver became rivers and canals, tiny green shrubs became trees." He saw people in the streets and then spotted a mother spanking a small boy in her yard. She stopped spanking to look up at the approaching plane, and the boy escaped. Hall was pleased to have done the child an unintentional favor.

After refueling, he continued on toward Romorantin, the second point in his triangular route. He was following the correct compass course, when suddenly he realized that something was wrong. Glancing at his map Hall discovered that he had been blown far off course. His instructors had cautioned against being "certain about anything while in the air." But Hall had failed to take into account the unseen, unfelt force of a sidewind. He flew on, looking for landmarks, but he was soon flying over an unbroken bank of clouds. He later wrote, there is "no isolation so complete as that of the airman who has above him only the blue sky, and below, a level floor of pure white cloud." Hall was still confident, however, that he could use his compass to correct his course to Romorantin. But now the clouds came upon him in "heaped" masses, soon surrounding him on all sides. "I made a hasty revision of my opinion as to the calm and tranquil joys of aviation, thinking what fools men are who willingly leave the good green earth and trust themselves to all the winds of heaven in a frail box of cloth-covered sticks." James Hall could no longer avoid flying into the clouds, and in a moment he was "hopelessly lost in a blanket of cold drenching mist." He could not even see his own wings and lost all sense of direction.

Then Hall fell into a dive while thinking he was flying level, an illusion common in low visibility flight—one that killed John Kennedy Jr. on a flight near Cape Cod in 1999. The air screaming through the wires of James Hall's plane may have saved his life. Startled by the sound, he looked at his "speed-dial," saw that he was flying too fast, and knew that he must be falling earthward "at a terrific pace." Suddenly dropping out of the clouds he saw the world tilted at such a crazy angle that he half expected to see "dogs and dishpans, baby carriages and ash-barrels roll out of every house in France, and go clattering off into space."

Hall pulled desperately at the "broom-stick" and brought his plane level with the horizon. Relieved to be alive, and not wanting to fly over "half of France" looking for Romorantin, he chose one of a dozen villages within view—one surrounded by wide level fields—shut off his engine, and glided toward the ground. Barely clearing a row of fruit trees, he touched down. Hall's plane rolled down a hill and stopped a few feet short of a small stream. He decided to wait by his plane, hoping someone had seen his descent. Soon a small boy appeared shouting triumphantly to friends that he had found the downed biplane. "*Bonjour, mon petit*," said Hall, but the shy youngster said nothing. Soon several score children appeared along with women and old men. As in other villages throughout France, the young men were dead or fighting at the front.

The crowd made a circle around the machine, waiting politely for Hall to speak. He in turn pretended to be attending to his plane while in reality he was trying to "screw up my courage" to say something in French. The mayor of the town arrived and Hall tried without success to communicate. Unable to express himself in words, Hall invited each of the boys to sit in the cockpit. Eventually, despite the language problem, Hall learned the correct direction to Romorantin. Then with the help of the boys, he pushed his biplane to level ground and took off.

After a short flight, Hall landed safely in Romorantin, completing the second phase of his triangle. Soon he climbed again into the sky for his final flight. The weather had improved and Hall enjoyed skimming through broken clouds, sometimes skirting them so closely that the current of air from his propeller "raveled out fragments of shining vapor, which streamed into the clear spaces like wisps of filmy silk." Suddenly Hall saw a "fantastically painted" twin-engine plane going in the opposite direction:

> The thing startled me, not so much because of its weird appearance as by the mere fact of its being there. Strangely enough, for a moment it seemed impossible that I should meet another avion. Despite a long apprenticeship in aviation, in these days when one's mind has only begun to grasp the fact that the mastery of the air has been accomplished, the sudden presentation of a bit of evidence sometimes shocks it into a moment of amazement bordering on incredulity.

The brief appearance of the other plane set Hall thinking about the reality of flight and of his own vulnerability. Listening to the "swish of the wind through wires and struts" he reflected that if only "a few frail wires should part" his ingenious biplane would tumble to the ground.

Then in the distance he saw the barracks, hangers, and machine shops of Avord. Feeling as if he had been away for many years instead of just a few hours, he brought the plane to a halt and greeted a "monitor," the man who would confirm that James Hall had completed his triangle. That night he sat at a rickety table and wrote by candlelight his account of the day's adventure. In the distance he could hear the sound of heavy guns: "the very ghost of sound, as faint as the beating of the pulses in one's ears." Many of the men whose absence had been so conspicuous in the village of Hall's forced landing would have been fighting among those cannon—or dead already in combat along the western front.

James Hall's preliminary flight had been an adventure, made memorable by his own skill in capturing in words the wonder and terror of flight. Other pilots tackled these brevet flights with varying degrees of success. One American, a man named Millard, made three attempts at his brevet flight, crashing each time. James Hall noted that the man "could never find the towns where he was supposed to land, so he would keep on going until his gas gave out. Then the machine would come down of itself, and Millard would crawl out from under the wreckage and come back by train." Eager as they were to train American pilots, the French finally gave up on Millard.

Forced landings were more common than crashes, and many a pilot, like Hall, came to ground in a farmer's field. One American lost power during a brevet flight and landed several kilometers from the nearest town. A suspicious farmer "collared" him as a possible German spy and took him to a nearby chateau. There the owner, speaking English, learned that the pilot was an American. He treated the airman to a meal and lodged him in an elegant chamber. Pilots sometimes returned to their planes after a forced landing to find them covered with flowers. At least one American, returning to his craft after a forced landing, discovered that young girls of the village had written amorous messages on the wings.

Some pilots were less fortunate than James Hall when it came to taking off after a forced landing. An American persuaded a group of boys to hold his plane while turning the propeller by hand to start the engine. The motor roared to life, frightening the boys into letting go before the pilot could scramble into the cockpit. The plane sped across a field with the pilot running behind. He caught up after the plane came to rest ignobly nose down in a ditch, looking "like a duck hunting bugs in the mud."

Other pilots were, like Hall, struck by the sheer beauty of the earth and clouds, seen for the first time from high in the sky. Their sense of wonder was not unlike that of the astronauts about a half century later, looking down on the earth from outer space. In letters and articles pilots tried to find words to describe the new element. The subject could be as simple as the clouds: "The view ahead and on the east side was like snow-fields of soft wet snow, with here and there hillocks rising in it with blue shadows." And the subject could be as grand as a flight into the mountains. One American pilot wrote this account of a flight into the Pyrenees in southern France:

> Turning eastward, I passed over some of the outer peaks which, snow-capped and bare of all foliage, were scarcely three hundred meters below me. I saw no one moving above the snow-line. It looked bleak, but very splendid in the sunlight. . . . I drank in the chilling, pure air with delight and fixed the picture so firmly in my mind that I shall never forget it.

Eventually these training flights came to an end. Soon after his difficult first triangle, James Hall made a second brevet flight, this one in three hours and without problems. That exercise completed the first stage of his training, and Hall was advanced to the rank of corporal. At a local tailor shop he had wings and a star sewn to his collar, designating him a *pilot aviateur*. He was now a brevetted military pilot. But before he could fly in combat he needed to complete another level of training to prepare him to fly among enemy pilots, whose purpose would be to destroy him and his craft. Most Americans learned marksmanship at Cazaux, which they called "Kazoo," where they began by firing shotguns at clay pigeons and balloons. Next they fired machine guns at a target pulled by speedboat across a nearby lake and fired rockets from the air at silhouette targets on the ground. The course in "acrobacy"—learning the maneuvers for aerial combat—involved moves that would have been thought impossible at the beginning of the war. These included the barrel turn, "a series of rapid, horizontal, corkscrew turns," and the *vrille*, a spinning nose dive that killed more than one novice pilot "for the reason that one could not know, beforehand, whether he would be able to keep his head, with the earth gone mad, spinning like a top, standing on one rim, turning upside down."

After learning these maneuvers and others James Hall flew practice fighter missions with fellow pilots. Sometimes three planes would fly in a mock attack on a village or a train. They were forbidden to fly over Paris during these outings, and so, Hall remarks, "we took all the more delight in doing it." Hall saw Paris "in all its moods: in the haze of early morning, at midday when the air had been washed clean by spring rains, in the soft light of afternoon." Such flights may have seemed all the more satisfying at that time because they came before the real work of being a World War I pilot. Soon enough James Hall would join other pilots in a new exercise where the scenery would include not only landscapes and clouds, but also enemy pilots bent on their destruction.

American volunteers would serve in many French units during the war, but they were best known for their participation in the one distinctively American squadron, Escadrille N-124, called originally the

Escadrille Américaine. When Germany protested that the squadron's name was a violation of American neutrality, the name was changed to the Lafayette Escadrille in honor of the Marquis de Lafayette, a young Frenchman who had won distinction leading French troops in the American Revolution. These pilots and a larger group of Americans fighting in French units were known collectively as the Lafayette Flying Corps. The members of the Lafayette Escadrille would eventually adopt as their insignia the head of a Sioux Indian, resplendent in feathers, copied from the picture on a box of Remington rifles.

The initial members of the unit gathered at Luxeuil-les-Baines in northeastern France in April 1916. This was a quiet sector of the front where they formed themselves into a combat squadron, complete with administrative personnel and mechanics. They also began to accumulate a collection of pets that would eventually include cats, dogs, foxes, and two lion cubs whom they named Whiskey and Soda. Their planes arrived from Paris—Nieuport 11 scouts with a wingspan of twenty-seven feet, a maximum speed of just over 100 miles per hour, and armament consisting of Lewis machine guns. The leader of the squadron was a Frenchman named Capt. Georges Thenault, an early supporter of the idea of a distinct American unit. Among the original members of the escadrille was Norman Prince, who had at first proposed such a squadron, and Victor Chapman, a descendent of John Jay, first chief justice of the U.S. Supreme Court.

On May 13, 1916, five planes of the Lafayette Escadrille climbed into the sky, formed into a V, and flew the squadron's first mission. They headed over a section of Switzerland and into Germany, where they encountered antiaircraft fire and buzzed a German airdrome but found no enemy planes. Five days later Kiffin Rockwell, a North Carolinian, was flying alone when he encountered an enemy aircraft. Taking it by surprise, he brought the plane down with four well-placed bullets. His comrades, having heard of the kill before he landed, hoisted Rockwell in triumph from his cockpit. At the height of the celebration that night, Rockwell pulled out an eighty-year-old bottle of bourbon, given him by his brother, and took a drink. Rather than finish the bottle then and there, the pilots decided to keep it in readiness for other Americans to drink after they downed enemy planes—one drink per kill. Many of the pilots who took that draught later died themselves in aerial combat, and so the flask came to be known as "The Bottle of Death."

A few days later the Lafayette Escadrille was transferred to Behomme in the Verdun region of the front, where Germany was attempting to break through the Allied lines. The French would hold on at Verdun throughout 1916, but before the German offensive ended, roughly one million soldiers would die. Soon the American pilots found themselves in daily combat with German planes above the battlefield, and several

Raoul Lufbery, the foremost ace of the Lafayette Escadrille. His plane is emblazoned with the symbol of the escadrille, a Sioux Indian head, and with a swastika. The swastika, an image made notorious a generation later by Nazi Germany, was a design borrowed from Native Americans by the escadrille.

Americans were almost killed. Kiffin Rockwell took a direct hit on his windshield and was half blinded, but managed to bring down an enemy aircraft and land safely. One of the bravest of the pilots, Victor Chapman, attacked two observation planes and their three escorts. He shot down one of the planes, but the others then turned on Chapman. One bullet grazed his skull and another shattered the control for the right aileron. Chapman's plane dropped like a stone while he struggled to fix the broken mechanism. Finally he regained control and glided to a safe landing.

At Behomme the squadron gained several more pilots including Clyde Balsley, a shy Texan, and Raoul Lufbery, who would become the squadron's ace with seventeen kills. In the air Lufbery was a fierce and innovative fighter; on the ground he liked to roam the local forests in search of mushrooms. In time it was inevitable that one of the American pilots would be killed in combat. Clyde Balsley was almost the first: his machine gun jammed when he attacked a German plane. The German then turned his guns on Balsley and sent bullets into his pelvis and legs. Balsley managed to crash land behind the French lines. He was hospitalized and retired from the air corps as an invalid.

While Balsley was in the hospital, Victor Chapman flew to visit him, bringing along a basket of fruit. At the last moment Chapman, though recently wounded himself, decided to join three comrades on a morning patrol. He fell behind the others and four Germans attacked him, damaging his plane so badly that it fell apart as it plummeted toward the ground. This first death in the ranks of the Lafayette Escadrille shocked the other pilots. "We could read the pain in one another's eyes," wrote one. At a ceremony on July 4, 1916, the French prime minister took note of Chapman's death, calling him and his squadron "the living symbol of American idealism." The prime minister was aware of the value of Victor Chapman's sacrifice as an example to other Americans, perhaps to the United States as a whole. "France will never forget this new comradeship," he said, "this evidence of a devotion to a common ideal." After the funeral ceremony, most of the American airmen went to Lafayette's grave for a July Fourth commemoration of the Frenchman's contribution to the American Revolution.

More deaths soon followed. September 1916, Kiffin Rockwell, who had recorded the squadron's first kill, took a bullet in the throat and died before his plane hit the ground. Friends called him the "soul" of the escadrille, and Captain Thenault shed tears as he proclaimed that the "best and bravest of us all" is no more. Soon afterward the squadron took part in a raid on the German arms works at Oberndorf-am-Neckar. On the way back Norman Prince, who had first suggested the creation of an American squadron, tried to land at dusk at an unfamiliar air field. His plane struck a high tension wire, catapulting Prince to the ground. Raoul Lufbery, who had landed just before Prince, rushed to his side. Although both of his legs were broken and he had suffered from massive internal injuries, Prince was still conscious. "Hurry up and light the flares," he said, "so that another fellow won't come down and break himself up as I have." Lufbery reported:

> I placed him in an ambulance, urging the driver to hurry him to the hospital at Gerardmer. Throughout the trip, Norman did not cease to talk and chat with the good humor that was one of his charming characteristics. . . . He spoke of his desire to be back with the squadron soon. But in the meantime, he began to suffer horribly and at times his face would be distorted with pain. His hand, which I was holding between my own, was wet with sweat. His endurance was remarkable and when the pain became so intense that he grew faint, he sang to keep from losing consciousness. My own heart was torn to see the struggle within him.

Norman Prince died the next day.

Death was a constant companion in the French Flying Corps; cots were cleared regularly of one man's gear for another to replace him. When the specter of death was not too overwhelming, the pilots sometimes sang a grim song, "The Dying Aviator," as they attempted to laugh in the face of death:

> The young aviator lay dying
> And as 'neath the wreckage he lay,
> To the mechanics assembled around him,
> These last parting words he did say:
> "Two valve springs you'll find in my stomach,
> Three spark plugs are safe in my lung,
> The prop is in splinters inside me,
> To my fingers the joy stick has clung.
> Take the cylinders out of my kidneys,
> The connecting rods out of my brain;
> From the small of my back get the crankshaft,
> And assemble the engine again."

Soon after Norman Prince's death the Lafayette Escadrille was transferred to Cachy, near a great battle by the Somme River. This engagement, like the Battle of Verdun, would take roughly one million lives. But during their three months at the Somme, bad weather kept the planes on the ground most of the time: one American described the visibility as so poor that "even the ducks were walking." The squadron lost no more members, and their Nieuports were replaced by the SPADs, tougher, faster aircraft, the equal of any planes the Germans could bring against them. In view of the new aircraft, the unit's official name gained a SPAD designation: SPA-124.

James Hall completed his training and joined the Lafayette Escadrille after it had become a seasoned squadron. Veteran pilots warned him that he would soon be exhausted by the work: he should plan on getting ten or twelve hours of sleep per night when he could. He discovered that many of the pilots' waking hours were spent scanning maps of the sector over which they would be flying and swapping tales with fellow aviators. Almost always there was the drone of motors overhead as planes took off or landed in a series of patrols lasting from dawn till dark.

Then came the morning of James Hall's first patrol. An elderly man known as the "messroom steward" came to his cot with a lighted candle. "*Beau temps, monsieur*," he said, and left the candle on the bed table. Through the oiled cloth that served as a window, Hall saw no light at all outside. In the messroom, where he would eat breakfast, there was a fire. The mingled aesthetics of French and American pilots appeared in the music from the phonograph: "*Chansons sans Paroles*" followed by "Oh, movin' man, don't take ma baby grand."

Outside there were clouds at about ten thousand feet, with stars shining through the gaps. Hall learned that his squadron would be flying over the sector on high patrol, as much as three miles above the front. He finished his hot chocolate and waited anxiously for departure time. In *High Adventure* he describes the scene: "The canvas hangars billowed and flapped, and the wooden supports creaked with the quiet sound made by ships at sea. And there was almost the peace of the sea there, intensified, if anything, by the distant rumble of heavy cannonading." Mechanics clustered around the machines, arming the machine guns, polishing the windshields, and starting the engines. "In a moment every machine was turning over." The pilots wore a variety of gear including woolen helmets, leather helmets, fur helmets; one pilot even wore for a helmet a silk bonnet that made him look like a "dear old lady."

Finally the machines rolled out onto the field, a mechanic running beside each one, every plane in the formation sporting an Indian head. One by one the pilots turned into the wind, gathered speed, and climbed over the airdrome. They rose together with the lead planes diving and climbing to keep James Hall, whose craft lagged behind, in the formation. "Sometimes we seemed, all of us, to be hanging motionless, then rising and falling like small boats riding a heavy swell." Then the sun crested the horizon, bathing the clouds in "shades of rose and amethyst and gold." Beneath the beauty of the clouds, Hall saw the killing grounds of the front:

> It was still dusk on the ground and my first view was that of thousands of winking lights, the flashes of guns and of bursting shells. . . . The lights soon faded and the long, winding battle-front emerged from the shadow, a broad strip of desert land through a fair, green country. . . . I knew that shells of enormous caliber were wrecking trenches, blasting out huge craters; and yet not a sound, not the faintest reverberation of a gun. . . . To look down from a height of more than two miles, on an endless panorama of suffering and horror, is to have the sense of one's littleness. . . . The best the airman can do is to repeat, "We're here and we look at it like blind men."

Until now Hall had been in sight of the other members of the escadrille, but suddenly they were gone. Eventually he learned that such was the nature of aerial combat, with planes appearing and disappearing suddenly and fights often over in a few seconds. Hall spotted one of the squadron diving sharply and pointed his own plane down. A seasoned pilot in a hurry to lose altitude would fall into a vertical dive; Hall had not yet developed the confidence for that maneuver and dropped more slowly, falling farther behind his comrades. Suddenly an artillery shell passed close by his plane, reached the top of its arc, and dropped downward. Then bombs began exploding around him, jolting his craft with their concussions. The explosions came closer, bursting "in clouds of coal-black smoke." One seemed to have ruined his tail: "My feeling was not that of fear, exactly. It was more like despair." He knew he should head for home, but could not get a compass reading without flying straight for at least thirty seconds, which would have made him a perfect target for the Germans gunning for him from the ground.

Then a plane piloted by a friend came into sight and guided the novice Hall back to the airdrome.

Back on the ground the other pilot chided Hall: "If I had been a Hun! Oh, man! You were fruit salad! Fruit salad, I tell you! I could have speared you with my eyes shut."

Hall protested that he would have been able to fight his way out of the jam. The man shot back,

"Tell me this: did you see me?"

"Yes."

"When?"

"When you passed over my head."

"And twenty seconds before that you would have been a sieve, if either of us had been a *Boche* [a German]."

During the next few months, James Hall made forced landings—twice. Late one afternoon he was flying over Germany, delayed to watch a pretty sunset, and lost track of the rest of his squadron. As night fell he flew in the direction he thought would bring him back into France. In the distance he saw a large building, well lit, and decided to land near it. He glided down, barely missing a huge factory chimney and a line of tele-graph wires before landing in a field of sugar beets. He was safely on the ground, but was he in France? The first words he heard were German, and soon his plane was surrounded by Germans. As casually as possible he reached for matches, hoping to set his plane afire so that the enemy could not use it. Then a voice rang out in French, "*Qu'est-ce-que vous faites là? Allez! Vite!*" ("What are you doing there? Go! Quickly!") The Germans moved away from the plane, and a Frenchman approached. Soon Hall learned that the Germans were war prisoners, harvesting French sugar beets. He had landed in friendly territory.

The next time he was forced down Hall was not so fortunate. On patrol over Germany, the cloth fabric began ripping away from his right wing, and soon afterward he was hit by an antiaircraft shell. His engine dropped for-ward in its mounts and the plane fell quickly toward the earth. On impact the motor and landing gear dropped away and the fuselage skidded along the ground. The crash broke one of Hall's ankles, sprained the other, and injured his nose. This time the voices he heard were not French.

During his imprisonment, the Germans treated Hall well. Shortly after the crash he was invited to join German aviators at lunch. One had been in Hall's gunsights when his wing started to give way. Hall found himself "heartily glad" he had not killed the man. In prison he and other Allied pilots could indulge themselves on a "splendid little library" of history, biography, essays, and novels. Hall's time in the hospital, before being sent to prison, may have encouraged him to reflect on the war as a whole. At any rate, in a historical novel he later co-authored with Charles Nordhoff, there is a revealing scene. In *Falcons of France* an American pilot crashes behind enemy lines and suffers injuries very like Hall's. In the hospital the airman is given a private room, but not so remote as to shield him from the screams of badly wounded German soldiers. The narrator reflects on these men and on the injured men he had encountered at Neuilly, France, where he had received treatment for injuries from a previous crash:

> Their moans and cries, echoing and reechoing along the hallway, froze my blood. There is a quality scarcely human in the screams of a man crying out in sheer animal terror and pain. Once again, as at the American hospital at Neuilly, war was stripped for me of all its romance and glory. Many a time I wished that politicians, munitions makers, breeders and abettors of war of whatever sort, might be forced to make the rounds of such hospitals so that they might see with their own eyes the horrible suffering they had brought to pass.

James Hall concludes his autobiographical account of the war by noting that in Germany, although individual Americans were treated well, "bitterness towards America there certainly is everywhere, and an intense hatred of President Wilson." By then America had entered the war on the side of the Allies, following Woodrow Wilson's war proclamation in which he promised to make the world "safe for democracy." The United States proclaimed war on Germany in 1917, but did not engage in any large-scale operations until 1918. In the meantime the Lafayette Escadrille continued to function as a unit of the French Flying Corps, and other Americans fought in other French air squadrons.

Edmund Genet was one of the escadrille pilots who watched with enthusiasm the entry of the United States into the war. Genet was the great-great grandson and namesake of Edmond "Citizen" Genêt, who had served as minister from France to the United States when George Washington was president. This Genêt had gone far beyond the traditional role of diplomat in the United States, giving speeches to large crowds in which he encouraged Americans to support the French Revolution. He married an American woman and settled in the United States. His great-great grandson, was equally idealistic in his support for France—so much so that he deserted the U.S. Navy at the outbreak of the war in order to fight for France. At first Edmund Genet fought in the trenches along with Kiffin Rockwell, another future pilot.

Genet joined the Lafayette Escadrille in January 1917. A fellow pilot described him as a youth who "didn't look a day over fourteen. His peach-bloom complexion showed no traces of ever having met a razor socially."

Edmund Genet. This Lafayette Escadrille pilot deserted the U.S. Navy in order to fight for France. He was the first American to die after the United States entered the war.

Genet quickly distinguished himself as one of the escadrille's most aggressive pilots, going out in weather that kept other airmen on the ground and finding Germans. When he heard on April 4, 1917, that the United States had entered the war and that "Paris is decorated with Old Glory everywhere," he was at first elated and pinned a small American flag on his coat. "I wish we could fling out in sight of all the Germans the glorious stars and stripes to defy them," he wrote in his diary. Later that night his humor changed to depression—he had recently lost one of his best friends, who died flying for the escadrille, and in addition he had just learned that his girlfriend back in the United States had fallen in love with another man. In this dark mood, Edmund Genet wrote these lines in his diary:

> Somehow I've given away completely this evening. I feel sure there is something very serious going to happen to me very soon. It doesn't seem any less than Death itself. I've never had such a feeling or been so

saddened since coming over to battle for this glorious France. I tore into shreds a little silken American flag which I've carried since the beginning of my enlistment. Somehow it seems a mockery to rejoice over the entrance of our country into the conflict with the Entente when we have been over here so long giving our all for the right while our country has been holding back.

A few days later on April 16, 1917, Genet went out on patrol with Raoul Lufbery, the ace of the Lafayette Escadrille. Lufbery saw antiaircraft fire exploding near Genet's plane and saw him bank as if to return home. Thinking his friend was all right, Lufbery headed back to the airdrome. But Genet did not return. Reports from French soldiers and an investigation of his remains told the story. At 4,000 feet Edmund Genet was severely wounded by shell fire. His plane dropped into a violent spin, losing one of the wings. The plane hit a road at full speed. One of Genet's fellow pilots visited the scene of the wreck and reported, "I have never seen so complete a crash."

Edmund Genet became thus the first American to die in France after the United States entered the war. At his funeral service, Captain Thenault, the leader of the escadrille spoke of Genet and America: "Respectfully I salute your memory which we shall cherish, and before the grave of the first soldier fallen for the two flags—the Stars and Stripes and the Tricolor—in the great war, we say, Thanks to America for having given sons such as thou. Farewell."

Soon afterward Genet's mother received letters of condolence from President Wilson and Secretary of the Navy Josephus Daniels. Daniels told her that since her son had died fighting for an ally, his service with the U.S. Navy would be "considered in every respect an honorable one."

The Lafayette Escadrille continued as a distinct squadron until February 18, 1918, when it was transferred to the American Expeditionary Force as part of the 103rd Aero Pursuit Squadron. During its existence it had grown from a showcase squadron, viewed by the French as most valuable for its propaganda value, into tough-fighting escadrille playing an important part in the war. Including the Americans who fought for other French squadrons, 180 Americans flew for France during World War I. They undertook thousands of sorties and shot down 199 German planes. Fifteen of the volunteers were captured and fifty-one died in action.

The Lafayette Escadrille's top pilot was Raoul Lufbery, who brought down seventeen German planes. In 1918 after the squadron had been absorbed by the United States, the government decided that Lufbery was too important as a living war hero to be risked in combat. He was assigned to a desk job, but he persuaded his superiors to allow him to return to combat. On May 18, 1918, he attacked a German plane at about 2,000 feet in sight of his own aerodrome. Lufbery was close to bringing down the enemy when a bullet struck his own fuel tank, and his plane burst into flames. Lufbery was only slightly wounded and might have parachuted to safety—if he had had a parachute.

Parachutes had been in existence for more than a century, ever since a French inventor had tested one from a balloon—first on his dog and then on himself. And parachutes were routinely issued to men in observation balloons on the front. But during World War I, pilots went aloft without parachutes. Some authorities said that they were too bulky to be worn in fighter cockpits; some said that would encourage pilots to desert craft that might be brought down safely; some said that only a coward would want one. To a pilot in a burning plane thousands of feet above the ground, none of these reasons made much sense. For that reason an Italian instructor told his students that if their plane caught fire, "Shut off the gas and commend your soul to God." In quarters Raoul Lufbery had debated with fellow pilots about what to do in a flaming aircraft: he advocated staying with the plane. But now as other pilots watched Lufbery from the ground, they could see him pull himself from the cockpit of his burning craft and jump. Later some speculated that he had hoped to hit a stream far below, with some slight chance for survival. But instead he landed in a garden behind a French house and died instantly.

With the United States fully engaged in the war, other American heroes—notably Billy Mitchell and Eddie Rickenbacker—came to the fore as the great aces of the conflict. But although they appear in the record books with more kills than Raoul Lufbery, the escadrille pilot likely shot down more Germans. Differences between French and American methods of confirming victories diminished Lufbery's total. Pilots who knew all three said that Lufbery was the best of the American airmen.

Raoul Lufbery and other American volunteers who flew for France were forerunners of the larger American participation in World War I. In fact, soon after the American declaration of war, pilots in the Lafayette Escadrille were allowed to fly the American flag, making them the first airmen to fight in World War I under Old Glory. Like the millions of U.S. soldiers who eventually enlisted, the early volunteers thought of themselves as taking part in a great adventure and offering their lives for a glorious cause.

During one of his early flights, when he made a forced landing outside a French village, James Hall had sensed the larger meaning of his fighting for France. "*Vous êtes Anglais, monsieur?*" ("You are English, Sir?"), a Frenchman had asked. "*Non, Monsieur,*" Hall replied, "*Américain.*" The reaction was impressive:

> That magic word! What potency it had in France. . . . I might have had the village for the asking. I willingly accepted the role of ambassador of the American people. Had it not been for the language barrier, I think I would have made a speech, for I felt the generous spirit of Uncle Sam

prompting me to give those fathers and mothers, whose husbands and sons were at the front, the promise of our unqualified support.

With America's entry into the war, that "unqualified support" had arrived.

Bibliography

ALDRICH, MILDRED. *A Hilltop on the Marne* (1915). Personal account of France at the beginning of World War I by an American woman. Aldrich followed *Hilltop* with *On the Edge of the War Zone* (1917) and *The Peak of the Load* (1918).

BROWN, WALT, JR., EDITOR. *An American for Lafayette* (1981). The war diaries of Lafayette Escadrille pilot Edmund Genet.

BRUCE, ROBERT B., *A Fraternity of Arms: America and France in the Great War* (2003). Focuses on the key role of the French in preparing American soldiers to fight in World War I.

DEVLIN, PATRICK. *Too Proud to Fight: Woodrow Wilson's Neutrality* (1974). The philosophy behind American neutrality.

ELLIS, MARK. *Race, War and Surveillance* (2002). African American soldiers in Europe were treated poorly during World War I, and at home black dissenters were stigmatized as subversives.

FLAMMER, PHILIP. *The Vivid Air: The Lafayette Escadrille* (1981). Well-researched history of the escadrille.

HALL, JAMES NORMAN. *High Adventure: A Narrative of Air Fighting in France* (1918). James Hall's beautifully written account of his experience in the Lafayette Escadrille.

HALL, JAMES NORMAN, AND CHARLES NORDHOFF. *Falcons of France* (1929). Vivid fictional account of the Lafayette Escadrille written by two of its pilots.

HALL, JAMES NORMAN, AND CHARLES NORDHOFF, EDITORS. *The Lafayette Flying Corps* (2 vols., 1920). History of the corps including photos, biographical sketches, and documents.

HYNES, SAMUEL. *The Soldiers' Tale: Bearing Witness to Modern War* (1997). Comparative examination of combat narratives written by soldiers in World War I, World War II, and Vietnam.

MCKAY, ERNEST A. *Against Wilson and War, 1914–1917* (1996). Exploration of Americans who opposed entry into the war by an author who believes these supporters of neutrality were right.

ZEIGER, SUSAN. *In Uncle Sam's Service: Women Workers with the American Expeditionary Force* (1999). Roughly sixteen thousand served overseas in World War I, but mainly in traditional "domestic" roles.

Study Guide

Summary

This essay tells the story of a particular group of Americans, volunteers who fought for France in the air before the United States entered World War I. The article describes also the dawn of a new technology, aviation, describing how one became a pilot and what it was like to be among the first human beings to leave the ground and "imitate the birds." The essay describes the brutality of the war, both high above the ground in aerial combat and on the ground in trench warfare. Finally, the story of the Lafayette Escadrille reveals the idealism of young Americans fighting for France—an idealism that the nation as a whole would eventually embrace.

Identification Topics

Lafayette Escadrille, Lafayette Flying Corps, Mildred Aldrich, Battle of the Marne, western front, Norman Prince, Edmund L. Gros, James Norman Hall, Penguins, Nieuports, SPADs, Victor Chapman, Edmund Genet, Raoul Lufbery.

Study Questions

1. For what reasons was World War I more deadly than previous wars? How was this apparent to Mildred Aldrich? What other information do you learn from this essay about the brutality of the war?
2. Why did President Woodrow Wilson embrace neutrality at the outbreak of World War I?
3. Why did some Americans decide to fight for the Allies before America entered the war?
4. What was the difference between the Lafayette Flying Corps and the Lafayette Escadrille? Why was the Lafayette Escadrille founded?
5. How were young Americans taught the new skill of flying planes in combat?
6. For novice pilots at the birth of the aviation age, flight was little short of miraculous. Give some examples of their sense of wonder.
7. Describe the wartime experiences of these American airmen: Norman Prince, James Norman Hall, Raoul Lufbery, and Edmund Genet.
8. James Hall said that *Américain* was a "magic word" in France. Why would that be true?

Research Topics

1. Study the careers of other American pilots in World War I.
2. Explore the other experiences of the American volunteers: in the ambulance corps and in the trenches, for example.
3. Investigate whether the idealism exhibited by volunteers for the Lafayette Escadrille was also apparent among the soldiers who fought for the United States after American entry into the war.
4. In what ways were the escadrille volunteers typical of Americans at this time? In what ways were they unusual?

CHAPTER 8

Modernity Versus Tradition

The Scopes Trial and the American Character

Americans have always admired both progress and tradition. Frequently, while remodeling their lives and their society, they have looked with nostalgia to earlier times. Puritans created a new commonwealth in America, but claimed that their civil and religious innovations restored ancient Christian practices. American Revolutionaries built a new republic, but believed that they were regaining traditional liberties they had enjoyed as colonists. Similarly, many Americans in the 1920s walked forward while looking backward, enjoying the marvels of industrial technology, but longing for the simplicity of a preindustrial, prescientific age. Their anxieties came to the surface when a young man was brought to trial in Dayton, Tennessee, for teaching about evolution. Even as they disapproved of his conduct, the townspeople were curiously divided about the relative merits of tradition and the modern world.

In our imaginations the 1920s is a decade of fun and fads. It is the Jazz Age, the Roaring Twenties, or as columnist Westbrook Pegler styled it, "The Era of Wonderful Nonsense." Unlike the previous decade and the two that followed, no one event shaped life in the 1920s, no Great War or Great Depression. The people focused instead on a string of mini-events. It was an age in which thousands sought to outdo each other in sitting atop flagpoles or setting records in marathon dances. When we think of the 1920s, our minds turn immediately to such glamorous icons of popular culture as bootleg whiskey, Babe Ruth, and the Charleston.

Certainly beneath the surface glitter large forces were at work. But even these came to notice and were dramatized by colorful episodes, tawdry as the Leopold–Loeb murder case or triumphant as Charles Lindbergh's transatlantic flight. One of the decade's most talked-of events was the trial in Dayton, Tennessee, of the young John Thomas Scopes, who had committed the crime of teaching evolution to his high school biology class. In the hot summer of 1925 more than a hundred reporters would converge on Dayton and send out a million words of news to a fascinated nation. Two of the most renowned public figures in America, Clarence Darrow and William Jennings Bryan, argued the case.

In part America was fascinated by the "Great Monkey Trial" because of its carnival atmosphere and its famed protagonists. But the nation also paid attention because the trial was one of those episodes in which America attempts to define itself. It dramatized several important conflicts: urban versus rural values, progress versus tradition, modernism versus fundamentalism.

To see what the Scopes trial meant, we must begin by examining these underlying tensions. Between 1900 and 1925 dozens of new products became standard fixtures in American life. Thousands of families had replaced their horse and buggy with an automobile. Electric power was available throughout the nation. People could hear music and news on radios in their own homes. New buildings called skyscrapers had changed the profiles of big cities. And airplanes carried people into the hitherto impregnable skies.

These abundant signs of material progress encouraged confidence in American technology. Individual productivity increased rapidly, and new selling devices such as time payments helped expand the American market. The American businessman was the hero of the day. An author, Bruce Barton, even ventured to compare successful entrepreneurs with Christ: After all, wasn't the Lord the greatest salesman of all time? Barton's *The Man Nobody Knows* was enormously popular. The people's glib confidence in the inevitability and rightness of American business prosperity found an apt representative in laconic Calvin Coolidge, the last American president to enjoy a two-hour nap every afternoon.

Among the young, the materialism of the 1920s found expression in relaxed moral standards. In the past girls had been the guardians of social virtue. Now young ladies frequently went out on dates unchaperoned, wearing rouge, sleeveless dresses, and stockings rolled down to the knee. They danced cheek to cheek with boyfriends to passionate jazz rhythms and scoffed when their parents called the saxophone an instrument of the devil. They smoked, drank bootleg whiskey, and rode—or parked—in autos till sunrise, kissing and petting freely. Their sexual exploits may seem tame to a more jaded age, but compared with their parents they were scandalously unrestrained. In 1900 a kiss had implied a promise of marriage. In 1925 a girl in an F. Scott Fitzgerald novel could brag, "I've kissed a dozen men. I suppose I'll kiss dozens more." A college newspaper featured the rhyme: "She doesn't smoke / she doesn't pet / she hasn't been / to college yet." Everywhere the old standards seemed to be breaking down.

Some Americans happily embraced the freedom and materialism of the 1920s. Others were more cautious. Few objected to such conveniences as the radio and the telephone, but many rejected the new permissiveness; they emphasized traditional values and sought to combat change. Some supported legislation aimed at improving public behavior, including the proper length of skirts. Others demanded enforcement of Prohibition laws, restricted immigration, and subordination of minorities. They frequently identified virtue with small towns and vice with cities.

Some opponents of change joined the Ku Klux Klan (KKK), which claimed to protect white Anglo-Saxon Protestant America from threats to traditional morality. Klan members met in white robes and hoods, burned crosses, beat up gamblers and prostitutes, and lynched blacks—all in the name of morality. In 1925 the organization had about three million members throughout the United States and helped elect at least sixteen U.S. senators and eleven governors.

The fundamentalist movement was less inclined to racism and violence than the KKK but did share many of the Klan's aims. Both emphasized Scripture, the American heritage, rural life, and the common man, while fearing intellectuals and change. Fundamentalism was distinguished, however, by one elemental issue, the truth of Scripture, especially the biblical view of Creation, the Virgin Birth, and the Resurrection. These beliefs were the underpinning of personal morality. If people doubted the sacredness of their history, they would behave like beasts. Accordingly, fundamentalists sought to influence school curriculum by preventing the teaching of anything contradictory to the Bible. They identified the Darwinian theory of evolution as their foremost enemy.

Since the publication a half century before of Charles Darwin's *On the Origin of Species*, scientists had come to accept his view that human life had evolved over millions of years from more primitive forms of life. Their theories did not necessarily undermine the belief in God, because evolution could be seen as God's way of peopling the earth. Christians who accepted evolutionary theory were called modernists and believed the Bible should be reconciled with modern science. These religious progressives saw God as the first cause or absolute energy. Their weakness lay in making God so abstract as to be unapproachable. One New England modernist clergyman confessed that when he thought of God he imagined a "sort of oblong blur."

The modernist creed proved less compelling than the fundamentalist views, and in the 1920s the latter group captured many Christian denominations and passed resolutions upholding a literal understanding of the Bible. To further protect their children from competing ideas, fundamentalists campaigned against evolution in the schools. In Oklahoma and Florida they passed laws banning Darwinism from public education, and they sponsored thirty-five other anti-evolution bills between 1921 and 1929. Tennessee was not the first state to pass such legislation, and the great test case heard there might easily have taken place in hundreds of other towns. Fundamentalism was as much a part of the American scene in the 1920s as the Charleston or the automobile.

Tennessee joined the anti-evolution crusade in 1925 when an obscure legislator, John Washington Butler, a Macon County farmer, introduced a bill in the state house of representatives making it illegal in a state-supported school to "teach any theory that denies the story of divine creation of man as taught in the Bible, and to teach instead that man has descended from a lower order of animals." No significant opposition confronted the measure, even from the University of Tennessee, and the bill passed in the House and Senate by a wide margin.

With the passage of the Butler Act, the American Civil Liberties Union (ACLU) decided that the time had come to fight the anti-evolution movement in the courts. Holding that such laws threatened freedom of speech, the ACLU announced that it would provide legal and financial assistance to any teacher who wanted to test the act.

This was a tempting offer, for it promised not only support for the defendant but also publicity for his community. The test case might have come from anywhere in Tennessee, but the small rural community of Dayton provided the first case. One afternoon in April 1925 two local attorneys who supported the law and a mining engineer who opposed it discussed evolution while relaxing at the soda fountain in Robinson's drugstore. One evolutionist, George Rappelyea, suggested that Dayton stage a test case; he was seconded enthusiastically by F. E. Robinson, the drugstore proprietor, who exclaimed that the case would put Dayton on the map.

Anyone who taught biology in Tennessee might have served as defendant, for the state-required biology textbook, written in a more liberal era, included material on evolution. The men decided to ask John Thomas Scopes to challenge the law. Scopes was a twenty-four-year-old biology teacher at Dayton High School and, because he was an intelligent, modest, and popular young man, known to the townspeople as "Professor," he would represent the community well.

One of the men went out and fetched Scopes from a tennis court. Back at the drugstore, Scopes readily admitted that he could not teach biology without teaching evolution, whereupon Rappelyea urged him to help overturn an unjust law. Scopes was at first reluctant to expose himself to legal action but was soon persuaded to help. A few days later he was charged with breaking the law.

The trial rapidly took shape. Rappelyea contacted the ACLU, which promised its support, agreeing to take the case to the U.S. Supreme Court, if necessary, "to establish that a teacher may tell the truth without being thrown in jail." The prosecution sought to identify attorneys who could best argue—and publicize—the case. William Jennings Bryan was a logical choice.

Bryan was a leading spokesman for the fundamentalist movement. After passage of the Butler Act he had written to the governor of Tennessee, Austin Peay, telling him: "The Christian parents of the state owe you a debt of gratitude for saving their children from the poisonous influence of an unproved hypothesis." Sue K. Hicks, a Dayton attorney (whose unlikely first name came from his mother, who died giving him birth), invited Bryan to take part, anticipating that he would attract international attention to the case. In reply to Hicks's telegram, Bryan wired back his enthusiastic acceptance.

Although no longer an active politician, Bryan was still one of America's best-known public figures. Born in Salem, Illinois, in 1860, he practiced law in Illinois and Nebraska for eight years before being elected to Congress in 1890. He served for two terms, then tried unsuccessfully to win election to the U.S. Senate. Between 1894 and 1896 he was editor of the *Omaha World Herald*.

In 1896 Bryan was already known as a capable public speaker and a popular politician, but nothing in his career suggested the fame he would win overnight at the Democratic Convention in Chicago that year. The convention was controlled by "Silver Democrats," who identified themselves with that elusive figure, the common man, and claimed that a currency based on silver would save the people from oppression by an economic elite. Bryan, a pro-silver delegate to the convention, gave a speech that electrified the delegates. He identified his party with the farmers, the "plain people," and "the producing masses" of the nation. Blaming the gold standard for the country's ills, he thundered, "You shall not press down upon the brow of labor this crown of thorns, you shall not crucify mankind upon a cross of gold."

The speech joined the handful of American rhetorical masterpieces. High school students across the country soon recited the talk in speech contests. Bryan himself repeated it thousands of times to rapt audiences long after the campaign of 1896 was over. The convention was so moved by the "Cross of Gold" speech that the young and hitherto unknown Bryan was chosen on the third ballot as the Democratic presidential candidate.

Bryan appeared in Dayton almost three decades after his first presidential campaign; yet a continuity between the two episodes is evident. In each case a basic moral issue seemed to be at stake. In each Bryan proposed a simple, even a simplistic, solution to a complex problem. And both times he inspired a devoted following.

In the campaign of 1896 and in subsequent campaigns and activities Bryan won a reputation as defender of the plain people. After losing the 1896 election he returned to Lincoln, Nebraska, and established *The Commoner*, a journal that spread his political views for almost three decades. His personality so dominated Democratic politics that he was chosen as the party's presidential candidate in three elections: 1896, 1900, and 1908. He lost all to more popular Republican candidates, but he held a large following within the party. He might even have secured a fourth nomination in the badly deadlocked convention of 1912 had he not bent his energies to supporting the New Jersey Progressive, Woodrow Wilson.

Wilson became the first Democratic president in sixteen years and rewarded Bryan for his service by offering him any post in the administration. Bryan chose the most prestigious, secretary of state, and undertook to educate himself on foreign affairs. His uncompromising standards were soon apparent. A teetotaler, he substituted mineral water and grapefruit juice for wine at diplomatic functions. A man of peace, he negotiated thirty treaties providing for peaceful resolution of disputes. With the outbreak of World War I, Bryan threw all his influence behind neutrality and objected to any act that might draw the United States into war. When Woodrow Wilson insisted on sending two harsh notes to Germany after its submarine sank the British ocean liner *Lusitania*, Bryan resigned rather than sign the second one. In retirement Bryan was free to campaign for peace, an enterprise he undertook with evangelical fervor.

But when he learned that Congress had declared war, he immediately wired Wilson offering to serve as a private in the armed forces. Although he did not find his way to the trenches—the army would have little need for a fifty-seven-year-old private—he did throw his support behind the war. Now that the majority had decided for war, he declared, dissent was no longer proper. In *The Commoner* he quoted Thomas Jefferson's maxim: "Acquiescence in the will of the majority is the first principle of republics." Such would be his position later in the Scopes case. During the war Bryan was most conspicuous as a campaigner for Prohibition, which he called "the greatest moral reform" of the generation.

In his work for neutrality and Prohibition, Bryan implicitly associated religion and politics. In later years he turned increasingly to religious activities. He was encouraged to abandon his lifelong preoccupation with politics by his failure to lead the 1920 Democratic Convention as he had guided others. In politics his influence was waning, but in religion he might still play a role in leading America to righteousness. The new emphasis was hardly a radical shift from his earlier views. His religious roots were deep. As a child in Illinois he and his father had memorized sections of the Bible together. There was even something of the religious prophet in his appearance. His fervor, his commanding presence, and his powerful voice invited comparison with spiritual leaders. He had been called a "Moses come to lead the people from the wilderness" and a second Saint Paul. Theodore Roosevelt said of him, "By George, he would make the greatest Baptist preacher on earth."

In his last years Bryan stridently advocated the Bible's literal truth and moral precepts. In Miami, Florida, where he spent the winter, he taught an adult Sunday school class in a city park. Thousands of men and women sat in the open air beneath the palm trees and listened as the earnest, gray-haired evangelist held forth each Sunday from a wood bandstand. After the meetings he distributed copies of his books to likely converts, even pursuing some to their own doorsteps. On one mission to deliver a book to a young man who had said he wanted to begin a Christian life, Bryan came upon a muddy street torn up for sewer construction. His wife urged him to return when the road was fixed, but he continued on foot. "The boy may need the book," he said. "We cannot tell." It was typical of Bryan to see a chance to improve the world in even a small gesture.

Bryan was ever alert to occasions to save a soul or cure a nation. By 1923, six years after he had begun delivering Sunday lectures, they were being reprinted in 110 newspapers with more than twenty million readers. Bryan had also become an important figure in the Presbyterian church and a leader of its conservative element against such modernists as Harry Emerson Fosdick. In 1924 he was elected vice moderator of the national Presbyterian Convention.

At this time he came closer to the fundamentalist movement. He began to publish tracts with titles like *The Menace of Darwinism* and *The Bible and Its Enemies*, and he attacked both the scientific basis and the moral implications of Darwinism. The theory of evolution, he said, is simply a theory. Its scientific basis is questionable, and it is contrary to common sense as well as opposed to the Bible. In comparing humans with monkeys, Darwin confused the superficial with the essential. Certainly there are superficial similarities between people and beasts, but in men and women the body was less important than the mind, and the mind inferior to the soul. The human intellect and the human spirit argue for a unique divine creation. "We are not the progeny of the brute," he wrote, "We are the handiwork of the Almighty."

Darwinism was thus inaccurate. It made bad science; worse still, it made bad morality. Bryan claimed that Darwinism replaced Christian love with elemental hate as "the law of development." When translated into Social Darwinism, it justified economic oppression and class pride and so undermined democracy itself. Bryan insisted that people's beliefs about the origins of life affect their actual behavior. Only "a sense of responsibility to God" could make individuals aspire to "that which is highest and best."

Darwinism, Bryan contended, was sapping traditional American values. "The greatest menace to the public school system today," he told the 1920 Nebraska Constitutional Convention, is "its Godlessness. We have allowed the moral influences to be crowded out." Because Darwinism had infected the public school curriculum, its influence must be fought in the legislature and on the school board as well as in the private conscience. He constructed an ingenious rationale for this restriction on intellectual freedom. The individual, he said, will remain free to study evolution, but only as a private citizen. In the schoolroom one must accept the limitations set by school board and legislature. Quite simply the people, who pay the taxes that support the schools, have a right to determine what is taught. It is a simple matter of majority rule. For once, after years of political defeat, Bryan was confident that the majority was on his side.

After each Sunday school lecture or public address, people crowded around Bryan, eager to tell him how his faith had encouraged them or their children.

"I have been slipping away from the church," a young man told him, "but you have brought me back."

"My daughter is a student at the University," a father told him, "and your lecture has steadied her."

Their comments assured the white-haired patriarch of fundamentalism that his cause was just. Each of Bryan's many causes had held the promise of a better world, with peace, democracy, and temperance, but this final crusade absorbed and transcended all the others. If people would follow God with simple faith in His Word and strong determination to do His will, all war, oppression, and injustice would end—so Bryan believed.

He began to see progress when the Florida legislature, at his urging, passed a law in 1924 forbidding instructors to "teach *as true* Darwinism or any other hypothesis that links men in blood relationship to any other form of life." When the Tennessee legislature met a year later to consider a similar law, Bryan was in touch with several legislators, one of whom distributed five hundred copies of his pamphlet, *Is the Bible True?* to his colleagues.

When the test case was prepared at Dayton, it was natural that Bryan should be identified as the man who could best publicize the fundamentalist cause as well as prosecute the case. Immediately after he agreed to participate, he was showered with letters from wellwishers. His senior in the Presbyterian hierarchy, the Reverend Mr. J. Frank Norris, wrote him: "You are now in the great work of your life and are rendering ten thousand times more service to the cause of righteousness than a dozen presidents."

While Bryan reaped encouragement from his fundamentalist supporters, the opponents of the Butler Act had identified an equally fitting representative of their cause. A brilliant trial lawyer, Clarence Darrow, had offered his services to the defense as soon as he learned that Bryan had agreed to assist the prosecution. The Scopes case appealed to Darrow because throughout his legal career he had defended the underdog. He thought of himself as a representative of the people against all forms of oppression.

Perhaps he inherited this trait from his father, Amirus Darrow, an Ohio furniture maker and undertaker who had rejected Christianity after testing it as a student at Meadville Theological Seminary. Clarence was born in 1857 and reared on his father's rationalistic principles. While Bryan was learning about the Bible, Darrow was learning about science. After attending Allegheny College and the University of Michigan, Darrow was admitted to the Ohio bar in 1878. Following nine years of practice in Ohio, he moved to Chicago, where he quickly established a reputation as an adept civil lawyer and involved himself in local politics.

In 1894 his career was given direction by two cases. First he handled an appeal for young Robert Prendergast, who had shot and killed the mayor of Chicago. Darrow lost and Prendergast was executed. The experience appears to have solidified Darrow's opposition to capital punishment. People should not be held entirely responsible for their acts, he believed, because they were shaped by their birth and upbringing. The state might imprison a bad person to prevent injury to others, but there is no justice in executions. After the Prendergast assassination case Darrow tried fifty more capital cases and never again lost a client to the death penalty. In a second important case, he defended Eugene Debs, who had refused to honor a court order in the Pullman boycott. Darrow lost the case but defended Debs so ably that he was much sought after in other labor cases.

Darrow's reaction to World War I suggests several similarities to Bryan. He had considered himself a pacifist, but "when Germany invaded Belgium," he wrote, "I recovered from my pacifism in the twinkling of an eye." He favored support for England and France but believed that people could in good conscience oppose the war. Whereas Bryan believed that there were issues on which all reasonable people should agree, Darrow was suspicious of the tyranny of the majority.

Clarence Darrow (left) and William Jennings Bryan. They represented not only opposite sides in the Scopes trial, but also different views of American character and purpose.

If Bryan's contribution to the war had been saving soldiers from vice, Darrow's involved saving dissenters from jail.

After the war Darrow faced his most difficult case, which he called the "Leopold–Loeb Tragedy." Nathan Leopold was a brilliant eighteen-year-old in his second year at the University of Chicago Law School. In summer 1924 he persuaded a friend, Richard Loeb, to help him commit the "perfect crime." They abducted fourteen-year-old Robert Franks, killed him, dumped the body in a culvert, and sent a ransom note to his father. A few days later they were apprehended, traced by a pair of eye-glasses Leopold had dropped near the body. When the boys confessed the crime, there seemed little chance of saving them from the death penalty. The crime was reprehensible, and Leopold and Loeb were the sort of people many Americans disliked anyway—they were wealthy, intellectual, Jewish, and homosexual. But Darrow attempted to show that their minds "were not normal." After a long trial, which he said, "exhausted all the strength I could summon," he finally heard Chicago Judge John Caverly sentence the murderers to life in prison.

After the moral ambiguities of the Leopold–Loeb trial, the Scopes case must have strongly appealed to Darrow. Here the "crime" was teaching an important and widely accepted scientific theory, and the "culprit" was a personable young man. Moreover, Darrow was as partial to the principle of scientific inquiry as Bryan was to the Bible. Darrow had helped form an intellectual club in Chicago that regularly heard local professors lecture about life and the universe. He had already challenged Bryan on the Bible's reliability as a source of scientific truth in an article in a Chicago newspaper.

Darrow and Bryan held opposing views about dissent and science, but both thought themselves champions of the oppressed. Their difference lay in their perception of reality. Bryan believed that the plain, honest people of America were threatened by big-city intellectuals who scoffed at their traditional virtues and their traditional God. Darrow believed that intelligent, honest Americans were thwarted by bigots and ignoramuses who preferred make-believe truths to reality.

As the attorneys for both sides prepared to come to Dayton, the town prepared for its moment in the national spotlight. The people, fundamentalists and modernists alike, were jubilant at the publicity they would receive. Dayton was a small town that had flirted once with the chance to grow. Twenty years earlier it seemed destined to become a major industrial center. But the blast furnace on which expansionists had pinned their hopes had been forced to close. Dayton's dream had faded, and nearby Chattanooga had grown into the regional metropolis.

Dayton had remained a small town, hub of an agricultural county whose chief products were peaches, tomatoes, and strawberries. It was a stable, conservative community where, as in most small towns, blacks "knew their place" and women were excluded from public affairs. The town had no saloons, gambling, or whiskey. The Scopes trial would bring people, publicity, and business to the town—put it on the map. But even while growing, Dayton could preserve its values. In fact, it would call attention to itself precisely because it was defending its values.

Late in spring 1925 the trial obsessed Dayton. When news arrived that Chattanooga might upstage Dayton with an earlier trial, the outraged people held a meeting where feelings ran high. Modernist George Rappelyea sought to strike a blow for Darwinism and Dayton by declaring, "there are as many evolutionists in Dayton as there are monkeys in Chattanooga." In response the owner of a local barbershop, outraged at Rappelyea's support of a doctrine that appeared to associate his family with the beasts, attacked—and bit—the evolutionist.

Rappelyea and Dayton survived the evening's excitement, and Dayton's leadership in the evolution test was soon fixed when Judge John T. Raulston convened a special grand jury to hasten the trial. Raulston was a native of the region, born in Gizzard's Cove in the nearby mountains. He dreamed of higher office and reckoned the trial would aid his promotion. In various ways scores of other Dayton residents calculated their personal stake in the trial. Businessmen repainted their stores; innkeepers prepared extra rooms. With typical opportunism, a businessman by the name of Darwin posted a large sign outside his shop reading "DARWIN IS RIGHT" and added, in small letters underneath, "inside."

Despite such preparations, the reporters who began to arrive early in July were more impressed with Dayton's pastoral qualities than its entrepreneurial ambition. Many had traveled by train and bus from the crowded streets of New York and other large cities; they were impressed by Dayton's trim houses, cool lawns, and stately trees. They commented on the beautiful hills and rich fields surrounding the town. They were intrigued by the soft-spoken farmers who strode about in felt Stetsons. The reporters stayed in places like the Aqua Hotel, named for the clear spring water bubbling from the surrounding hills, where all guests were awakened by a rap at the door at quarter to seven, calling them to a communal breakfast. The citizens, eager to create a good impression, shook hands and smiled affably; chairs lined the streets outside the stores, beckoning the visitors to settle into Dayton's leisurely pace.

Sooner or later the strangers found their way to Robinson's drugstore, now the most famous landmark in town. Inside, discussion of the trial, the attorneys, evolution, and the Bible never stopped. John Scopes usually came to the store in the late afternoon after swimming in a local pond. His good nature and serious demeanor seemed to characterize the local citizenry's attitude toward the trial.

Two sides of the American temperament—religiosity and curiosity—existed comfortably in Dayton. A walk through the town revealed its dedication to Christianity. A dozen churches, including Southern Methodists, Southern Baptists, and Presbyterians, competed among themselves and with smaller denominations. Outside town the fields bore religious signs as naturally as they produced potatoes and strawberries. "Take care lest thy sins find you out," read one. Farther on in the hills strange sects practiced curious rites learned from a literal reading of the Bible. In Dayton the people told of a farmer who had *seen* God and a minister who had wrestled with Him.

Although most of the people did not claim to have seen, much less to have wrestled with, the Lord, nearly all were church members. Religion gave them recreation, communal spirit, topics of discourse. One reporter, seeming to be overwhelmed by the atmosphere, wrote in astonishment, "The whole region is saturated with religion."

Still, sentiment in Dayton was curiously tolerant of Scopes and evolution. Even H. L. Mencken, America's greatest contemporary critic of the "small town mentality," was impressed that no "poisonous spirit" surrounded the trial. The majority may have been fundamentalists and disapproved of teaching evolution in the schools, but most were also interested in learning more about the world. Several jurors admitted after the trial that they had looked forward to free lessons in science from Darrow's expert witnesses.

The first of the major protagonists to arrive in Dayton was William Jennings Bryan, who came into town by rail on July 7 aboard the *Royal Palm* from Florida. The people caught an initial glimpse of their famous guest when he appeared on the rear platform of the train dressed in black coat and tie and white tropical helmet. Bryan was cheered by a crowd of three hundred spectators. After disembarking, he removed his coat and strolled among them under the hot sun to Robinson's drugstore, where he ordered an ice cream soda and chatted with his admirers.

Two days later Clarence Darrow arrived. No crowd like Bryan's greeted him, but he was not disappointed. He realized that his opponent, and not he, was the "ruler of the Bible Belt." A few supporters were there, however. One, a local banker, turned over his house to Darrow for his headquarters. Darrow settled in and went to work on his case. He noticed a collection of framed mottoes on the wall assuring him "Jesus loves you" and "The Lord will provide."

In the next few days Bryan and Darrow quickly impressed themselves upon the region. Bryan told the Dayton Progressive Club, "the contest between Christianity and evolution in Dayton is a duel to the death." The next evening he delivered a lecture from the wood porch of a hotel in the hills; he stood in lantern light, speaking in his melodious voice to a crowd of country people who gazed at him with adoration. A storm of thunder and lightning in the hills blended well with his solemn and majestic presence.

The people in Rhea County had expected to like Bryan. They were surprised to find they also liked Darrow. Perhaps they had expected him to be overbearing and harsh. Instead, he impressed them with his homespun manners and modest demeanor. They liked his way of saying complicated things in a few simple words. If Bryan impressed Dayton as a spokesman of their own comfortable beliefs, Darrow excited them by his familiarity with science and the modern world.

The two attorneys were well chosen to represent the opposite sides in the trial. They were joined by other lawyers who would help present the case. In defending Scopes, Darrow had the assistance of Dudley Field Malone, a fashionable divorce lawyer; Arthur Garfield Hayes, perhaps the brightest attorney at the trial; and John Randolph Neal, a law school dean and proponent of academic freedom. Bryan would work with a battery of local attorneys including Sue Hicks, who had initially invited him to Dayton; and his son William Jennings Bryan Jr., a thirty-six-year-old Los Angeles attorney.

The basic strategy for each side was relatively simple. The prosecution would attempt to limit the trial to the simple question: Had John Thomas Scopes violated the law against teaching evolution in Tennessee schools? The defense would try to broaden the inquiry, claiming that the law violated the First and Fourteenth Amendments by writing a religious doctrine into law and that it was unreasonable because it forbade the teaching of a widely accepted scientific theory.

Such were the apparent legal boundaries of the trial, but it was inevitable that other issues would arise: evolution versus fundamentalism, modernity versus tradition, freedom of thought versus established values. These were expected. The reporters in Dayton, the townspeople and visitors, and the attorneys themselves recognized and welcomed the broad implications of the trial. Because the case touched such fundamental issues, the town was full of people of every sort: evangelistic preachers who held forth in the streets, showmen with pet monkeys, popcorn vendors. All had a stake in Dayton.

As Clarence Darrow walked through the crowded town to the courthouse on the hot first morning of the trial, he was aware that he was taking the case into the enemy's territory. Along his way he passed religious placards and banners attached to fences and buildings; they counseled him: "Read Your Bible Daily" and "Prepare to Meet Thy Maker." Then he came to a two-acre park with more banners hanging in its oaks and maples. In the middle of the park stood a large brick building, the Rhea County Courthouse.

Darrow was surprised at the size of the courtroom. On the morning of Friday, July 10, it was packed with spectators. Reporters from a hundred domestic and foreign newspapers sat at makeshift desks at the front of the room. A telegraph wire connected the courtroom with the outside world. The benches, aisles, and walls were jammed with townspeople and farmers. Darrow noticed that "Read Your Bible Daily" banners hung by the bench, the jury box, and throughout the courtroom. "It looked as though there might have been a discount for ordering a wholesale lot," he quipped.

Through most of the day the two sides questioned prospective jurors. Several were excluded as too conservative in their faith, but even so eleven of the final twelve professed to read their Bibles. (The twelfth was illiterate.) Reporters were as intrigued by Darrow's attire as by the day's proceedings. In the close heat of the courtroom Darrow had stripped off his coat, revealing his bright suspenders. Bryan cooled himself with a large heart-shaped palm fan. When he wasn't questioning jurors, Darrow reflected on the temperature: "Tennessee must be very close to the equator," he thought, "or maybe the crust is thin under this little sin-fearing section."

After the long day the court adjourned for the weekend. While Darrow prepared his case, Bryan used the time to proselytize. On Sunday morning he delivered a lecture at the Methodist church, and in the afternoon he addressed a large audience on the courthouse lawn. In these talks he stressed the priority of religion over intellect and education. Christ's doctrines provide "so complete a moral code that no scholar has dared add a word to it." He denied that evolution laws restricted freedom of speech; they simply enabled parents "to guard the religious welfare of their children."

On Monday morning the trial began. Microphones had been installed to carry the arguments to loudspeakers outside the courtroom and to a nationwide radio audience. Thus technology would aid in publicizing the battle between tradition and evolution. The day was given over mainly to technicalities, but Darrow introduced a note of drama when he moved that the indictment be quashed. The evolution law was a "foolish, mischievous, and wicked act," he said; it was "as brazen and bold an attempt to destroy liberty as was ever seen in the Middle Ages." The motion was denied.

Darrow startled the court again next morning when he objected to the customary prayer that opened the day. In forty years of practice he had never seen such a ceremony. Because the case had strong religious overtones the practice seemed to favor the prosecution. He argued vehemently, but his motion was denied, and each morning a minister delivered a prayer before the court.

By now Darrow had impressed the spectators with his particular style. His bright suspenders and sense of humor gave him a casual air, but at the proper moment he could make sharp inquiries and rebuttals. In the early days of the trial Bryan's style contrasted sharply with Darrow's alert probing. He sat back, constantly fanning himself, and seemed to Darrow the portrait of indolence.

Darrow later amplified that portrait in his autobiography. "There sat Bryan," he wrote, "fanning himself, looking limp and martyr-like between assaults upon the flies that found a choice roosting-place on his bald, expansive dome and bare, hairy, arms. He slapped away at them with the big fan, constantly and industriously. Somehow he did not look like a hero. Or even a Commoner. He looked like a common flycatcher." The hostility and contempt that burns through this description would increase as the trial progressed. Although Bryan and Darrow had initially attempted to be civil to each other, the tension between them was bound to grow, for each believed that the other was not only wrong but morally wrong.

The prosecution had an easy time presenting its case. On Tuesday and Wednesday they showed that Scopes had taught evolution in his biology courses, a fact he never denied. In response, Darrow and Dudley Field Malone declared that they would prove there was no conflict between evolution and the Bible. On Thursday, July 16, the court considered whether the defense should be allowed to present the testimony of expert witnesses. Scopes's attorneys had gathered fifteen clergymen and scientists who could discuss evolution research and its relationship to the Bible. If the judge would allow the defense to explore the validity of the evolution law, this testimony would be crucial.

In opposition Bryan rose to present his first real address to the courtroom. He took a long drink of ice water and then began his argument. The experts were irrelevant, he argued. Their testimony might have been appropriate in the legislature when the law was being drafted, but now the law was a fact and the only issue was whether Scopes had broken it.

Bryan was perfectly correct in seeking to limit debate to Scopes's actual behavior and to skirt the issue of the evolution law's validity. But he incautiously abandoned this stable ground as he continued his oration. Palm fan in hand, gazing at the hundreds of Bible-reading Christians who regarded him as the protector of their faith, he felt compelled to engage the evolution question.

He held up a copy of George Hunter's *Civil Biology*, the text Scopes had used, and turned to a diagram of animal life. "We are told just how many animal species there are, 518,900," he began. Then he explained that the book divided the animals into groups, each represented by a circle. From the large circles representing protozoa, fish, and sponges, he came at last to a tiny circle containing man.

"Then we have mammals," he said, "3,500, and there is a little circle, and man is in the circle. Find him, find man."

Now Bryan's voice rose in indignation at the thought of this belittling of God's chosen creature.

"There is that book! There is the book they were teaching your children, teaching that man was a mammal and so indistinguishable among the mammals that they leave him there with 3,499 other mammals—including elephants!"

The audience was delighted. After five days the contest they had anticipated was finally taking shape. They laughed and applauded. Bryan continued.

"Talk about putting Daniel in the lions' den! How dare those scientists put man in a little ring like that with lions and tigers and everything that is bad?

"Tell me that the parents of this day have not any right to declare that children are not to be taught this doctrine. . . . Shall we be detached from the throne of God and be compelled to link our ancestors with the jungle?"

Here was an essential point in Bryan's critique of Darwin. By associating man with the beasts, evolutionary theory appeared to deny the divine origin of life and the existence of God. Bryan now held up a copy of Darwin's *Descent of Man*. To ease the tension in the room he complained facetiously that Darwin claimed man had descended, "Not even from American monkeys but from Old World monkeys."

Then he grew more serious. He complained that the evolutionists failed to consider the first cause of life.

"Did he tell you where life began? Did he tell you that back of all there was a God? Not a word about it. . . . They want to come in with their little padded-up evolution that commences with nothing and ends nowhere."

Bryan's gestures and intonations were so effective in the hot, stuffy courtroom that John Thomas Scopes was reminded of a symphony.

Bryan now came to his final point. Without the divine creation, the essential link between God and man, there could be no moral standards. If man were merely a beast, he might as well act like a beast.

"The facts are simple," he said. "The case is plain, and if those gentlemen want to enter upon a larger field of educational work on the subject of evolution, let us get through with this case and then convene a mock court, for it will deserve the title of mock court if its purpose is to banish from the hearts of the people the word of God as revealed."

Bryan's speech was greeted with applause. Although he had begun and ended by claiming that the court should not go into larger questions of evolution, religion, and morality, he captivated the crowd by transgressing the boundaries he himself had established. The people wanted to hear about the broader issues.

The defense now followed with its own view of these larger issues, especially intellectual freedom. In a brief statement Darrow argued that risks are always involved in new ideas and inventions and that young people should be encouraged to "learn and choose." After this statement he turned the defense over to his co-counsel, Dudley Field Malone, who proved master of the occasion.

Malone, the New York attorney, had till now resisted the informality of the courtroom, but when he rose to speak he paused and removed his jacket, folding it carefully and placing it on the defense table. He then addressed the court with an air of deference.

"If the court please," he said in a low voice, "it does seem to me that we have gone far afield in this discussion. However, probably this is the time to discuss everything that bears on the issues that have been raised in this case; because, after all, whether Mr. Bryan knows it or not, he is a mammal, he is an animal, and he is a man. . . .

"I have been puzzled and interested at one and the same time at the psychology of the prosecution, and I find it difficult to distinguish between Mr. Bryan the lawyer in this case; Mr. Bryan, the propagandist outside this case; and the Mr. Bryan who made a speech against science and for religion just now. . . .

"Mr. Bryan, Your Honor, is not the only one who believes in God; he is not the only who believes in the Bible."

Malone's voice rose, and each idea fell neatly into place as he continued with what most observers believed the oratorical masterpiece of the trial. The audience hung on his words as his voice filled the courtroom and boomed through the loudspeakers outside in the park.

Malone told of times in the past when authorities, believing they possessed absolute truth, had hindered science. The Muslims had burned the great library at Alexandria because it contained books contrary to the Koran. The Catholic Church had tried Galileo because his astronomy appeared to contradict the Bible. In each case, history had repudiated the intolerant act. This should not happen again, Malone argued. Science and religion must be allowed to prosper side by side. He continued:

"These gentlemen say: 'The Bible contains the truth. If the world of science can produce any truth or facts not in the Bible as we understand it, then destroy science but keep the Bible.' And we say: 'Keep your Bible. Keep it as your consolation, keep it as your guide. But keep it where it belongs, in the world of your own conscience, in the world of your individual judgment.'"

Here Judge Raulston interrupted to ask Malone if he believed that the theory of evolution was compatible with the theory of "divine creation as taught in the Bible." Malone replied that he did so believe. God could have created the first single life cell and allowed man to evolve "serially." But whatever the actual process, men should be free to learn what they could through science.

Malone then turned to the question of morality. "What is this psychology of fear?" he asked. "I don't understand it." Science would not hurt the younger generation. "The children of this generation are pretty wise," he said. They did not produce the Great War that killed twenty million people. If they are allowed to think, he argued, "They will make a better world of this than we have been able to make of it."

By now Malone had the courtroom on his side. Fundamentalists as well as modernists hung on his words and interrupted him with applause. After twenty minutes Malone turned to the question at hand, admission of the expert testimony. Malone urged the court to admit it, to promote the free exchange of ideas.

"The truth always wins," he said, "and we are not afraid of it. The truth is no coward. The truth does not need the law. The truth does not need the forces of government. The truth does not need Mr. Bryan. The truth is imperishable, eternal, and immortal and needs no human agency to support it. We are ready to tell the truth as we understand it, and we do not fear all the truth that they can present as facts."

Malone now turned to Bryan. "We are ready," he said. "We feel we stand with progress. We feel we stand with science. We feel we stand with intelligence. We feel we stand with fundamental freedom in America. We are not afraid. Where is the fear? We meet it! Where is the fear? We defy it! We ask Your Honor to admit the evidence as a matter of correct law, as a matter of sound procedure, and as a matter of justice to the defense in this case."

Malone was finished, and now as he returned to the defense table, a remarkable thing happened. The courtroom exploded with cheering and applause. Even the policemen by the bench joined in the uproar, and people climbed over the rail to shake Malone's hand. Darrow exclaimed, "Tennessee needs only fifteen minutes of free speech to become civilized!" The cheering was reported to have been twice as long and twice as loud as that which greeted Bryan's earlier speech. Bryan, knowing he had been outdone, was gracious. "Dudley," he said, "that was the greatest speech I ever heard."

Malone's address was undoubtedly a masterful oratorical performance, and this was an age that admired good speeches. But even then the response was puzzling. Why should fundamentalists, who were surely in the majority that day, show such enthusiasm for a spokesman of the opposition? Their behavior gives us a clue to one thread of the conservative temperament in the 1920s. Curiously, Malone rather than Bryan had articulated their deepest anxieties.

Were they worried about their children? So was he. But he had confidence that they would grow up into wise and caring human beings. Did they want to believe in God? So did he. But he assured them that God could have chosen evolution as His method of creating human life. Did they wish to face the future with confidence? So did he. But in place of fearful rejection of the modern world, he offered them a vision of triumphant progress. The unfettered search for truth, he assured them, would bring mankind to a better future.

Here was a synthesis combining traditional values with confidence in the future, a simple credo of optimism, morality, and progress. Its appeal in the 1920s was enormous. The world was changing—that was plain. And much of the progress—the telephone, the Ford car, the radio—was exciting, even to the people of Dayton, Tennessee, and thousands of towns like it. But where would it lead? What would it do to the children's morals, to their faith in God? Didn't parents need to take control, to put boundaries on freedom, even freedom of thought? Such worries had led some Americans to favor Prohibition, the KKK, and fundamentalism.

To all these anxieties, Malone had an answer. "Where is the fear?" he had said. "We meet it! Where is the fear? We defy it!" His breastplate in the struggle against fear was a simple belief in progress. Like Charles Lindbergh, who to his contemporaries a few years later seemed to combine frontier simplicity and mechanical wizardry, Malone believed that America could have the best of its past in concert with the best of the future.

If history were simply a fantasy written by a playwright, we might let down the curtain over Dayton, Tennessee, with this account of triumph—Scopes vindicated, Bryan and the fundamentalists converted, freedom of thought restored. But historical events seldom resolve themselves into such tidy endings. Even Malone's great oratory could not sweep away the Dayton of 1925, the America of 1925, or the niceties of courtroom procedure.

After the wave of enthusiasm for Malone's address finally subsided, Judge Raulston concluded the day's proceedings, and the people filed out into the real world that ebbed and flowed around the courthouse. Malone's speech had surely impressed many people with the idea that one could have evolution and the Bible, progress and tradition.

But there were also one's daily functions to perform. Farmers and laborers returned to their snug houses and to chores they had postponed to watch the trial. On the streets boys sold ice cream and popcorn. The men with monkeys moved aimlessly about. Evangelical preachers sought to attract audiences. The moist hot air muted the sounds and thoughts of men and women.

When the court convened again the next day, Friday, July 17, Judge Raulston ruled that the testimony of expert witnesses could "shed no light" on the questions before the jury and should therefore be excluded. But after further argument he modified the ruling to permit the witnesses to speak to the court with the jury absent. The defense therefore could put the expert testimony in the record for the purpose of appeal. The court then adjourned for the weekend.

By now both sides were becoming impatient. Bryan issued a statement on Saturday claiming he was fighting a "conspiracy against the Bible Christianity." Darrow replied that the scientist did not need "to call the aid of the law to enforce belief in his theories." Both men gave lectures that weekend to local groups, while Scopes, surprisingly relaxed, told reporters he hoped to return to college when the trial was over.

On Sunday evening the defense attorneys gathered at Darrow's lodgings—known as the "Monkey House"—and discussed strategy. They were particularly intrigued by a new idea: Why not call Bryan himself as an "expert witness"? They felt sure that Bryan would be unable to resist the temptation to express his views and that he would discredit himself and the fundamentalists. To perfect the plan they practiced questions and answers, with one of the expert witnesses playing Bryan.

On Monday, July 20, the court convened for what many assumed would be the last day of the trial. The room was even more crowded than usual, and some worried that the floor might give way. After the midday break the judge reconvened on the lawn outside. He sat at a table on a platform built against the courthouse wall; hundreds of spectators assembled on benches in the park; boys climbed on tree branches above the crowd or circulated among the people selling soda pop.

The afternoon began with the reading of affidavits taken from the expert witnesses. Then the defense dropped its bombshell and called Bryan as a witness. Everyone was startled, including Bryan, who sat motionless as his fellow attorneys objected. He could easily have refused to testify; he was, after all, an attorney for the prosecution. But he was reluctant to appear timorous, and he was confident he could defend his position.

Bryan took a seat on a wood office chair on the narrow platform. Darrow, standing opposite him, began, "You have given considerable study to the Bible, haven't you, Mr. Bryan?"

"Yes, sir," Bryan replied, "I have tried to."

"Do you claim that everything in the Bible should be literally interpreted?"

"I believe everything in the Bible should be accepted as it is given there. Some of the Bible is given illustratively; for instance: 'Ye are the salt of the earth.' I would not insist that man was actually salt, but it is used in the sense of salt as saving God's people."

Darrow proceeded, pacing, leaning against a table, running a hand through his hair; occasionally he looked into a Bible for a reference. He mused, listened, and probed. What about Jonah and the whale? Did Bryan believe in that?

"It is hard to believe for you," said Bryan, "but easy for me. A miracle is a thing performed beyond what man can perform. When you get beyond what man can do, you get within the realms of miracles; and it is just as easy to believe the miracle of Jonah as any other miracle in the Bible."

Thus far, Bryan was doing well. The crowd applauded his answers. The other prosecuting attorneys appeared pleased. Darrow continued:

"Do you believe Joshua made the sun stand still?"

"I believe what the Bible says," Bryan replied. "I suppose you mean that the earth stood still."

Darrow: "The Bible says Joshua commanded the sun to stand still for the purpose of lengthening the day, doesn't it? And you believe it?"

Bryan: "I do."

Darrow: "Do you believe at that time the entire sun went around the earth?"

Bryan: "No, I believe the earth goes around the sun."

Darrow was making progress. Bryan now had to admit that the authors of the Old Testament did not understand the world as well as modern man. Even Bryan would not claim that the sun moved around the earth.

Now Darrow asked about the Flood. Could Bryan give its date?

Bryan seemed muddled. He gave an answer but could not recall whether the information was in the Bible. The prosecution again objected, but Bryan wanted to continue, and Judge Raulston agreed. Agitated, Bryan turned to the audience. "These are the people whom you insult!" he said.

Darrow glared and shook his finger at Bryan: "You insult every man of science and learning in the world because he does not believe in your fool religion!"

The atmosphere grew more tense. Darrow continued his questions about the Flood. Bryan claimed that some four thousand years ago the only life on earth had been among the fish and on Noah's Ark. Then

Darrow pointed out that some civilizations had existed for more than five thousand years.

Bryan was now forced to claim that all the world's civilizations must have sprung up after the Flood.

"Do you know a scientific man on the face of the earth that believes any such thing?"

"I cannot say," said Bryan, "but I know some scientific men who dispute entirely the antiquity of man as testified to by other scientific men."

"Oh," continued Darrow, "that does not answer the question. Do you know of a single scientific man on the face of the earth that believes any such thing as you stated, about the antiquity of man?"

Bryan faltered and replied, "I don't think I have ever asked one the direct question."

Bryan was obviously on the defensive now and tried to belittle the question. He said he had had more important things to do than "speculate on what our remote ancestors were." He seemed to forget that this was precisely the question that had brought them all to the crowded park in Dayton.

Darrow pressed on, exposing Bryan's ignorance of history, anthropology, and comparative religion.

"Did you ever read a book on primitive man? Like Tylor's *Primitive Culture*, or Boas, or any of the great authorities?" he asked.

"I don't think I have ever read the ones you have mentioned," answered Bryan.

"Have you read any?"

"Well I have read a little from time to time," he said weakly, "but I didn't know I was to be called as a witness."

"You never in your life made any attempt to find out about the other peoples of the earth—how old their civilizations are, how long they had existed on the earth, have you?"

"No, sir; I have been so well satisfied with the Christian religion that I have spent no time trying to find arguments against it."

"You were afraid you might find some?"

"No, sir; I am not afraid now that you will show me any—I have all the information I want to live by and to die by."

No phrase in Bryan's testimony more aptly summarized his view of science and religion. In affairs that mattered, the Bible provided enough information "to live by and to die by."

Darrow probed still further into Bryan's creed. Bryan believed that all the world's languages could be dated from the Tower of Babel, but had he read any scientific works on languages? Bryan admitted that he had not.

Once more a fellow attorney sought to rescue Bryan. "I want to interpose another objection," he said. "What is the purpose of this examination?"

Bryan was now feeling the strain of his ordeal. He shouted, "The purpose is to cast ridicule on everybody who believes in the Bible!"

Darrow snapped back, "We have the purpose of preventing bigots and ignoramuses from controlling the education of the United States!"

Now Bryan shook his fist at Darrow: "I am simply trying to protect the word of God against the greatest atheist or agnostic in the United States."

The audience burst into applause. Still the questioning continued. Darrow asked about Eve: Had she really come from Adam's rib? Bryan said yes. And what of Cain's wife: Where did she come from? Bryan had no answer.

Now Darrow returned to the creation of the world. He asked Bryan whether the six days of the biblical creation were twenty-four-hour periods. Bryan said probably not. They were "periods" of undetermined length. Here, as in the sun's standing still for Joshua, Bryan was admitting that the Bible could not always be understood literally.

Now Darrow came to his final line of questioning. He introduced Eve's temptation in the Garden of Eden. Did Bryan believe that women were compelled ever afterward to suffer childbirth pains because of Eve's sin?

"I will believe just what the Bible says," replied Bryan.

And did he believe that snakes were compelled to crawl on their bellies because the serpent tempted Eve?

"I believe that," said Bryan.

Darrow smiled. "Have you any idea how the snake went before that time?"

"No, sir."

"Do you know whether he walked on his tail or not?"

"No, sir, I have no way to know . . ."

Before Bryan finished, the audience broke into a roar of laughter at the image of a snake walking on its tail. Bryan had finally had enough— he leaped to his feet and, in an angry, quivering voice, said, "Your Honor, I think I can shorten this testimony. The only purpose Mr. Darrow has is to slur the Bible . . ."

Darrow broke in, shaking his fist and shouting back, "I object to your statement. I am examining you on your fool ideas that no intelligent Christian on earth believes!"

As the two men glared at each other, the whole audience rose and joined in the noisy tumult. Realizing that things had gone too far, Judge Raulston immediately adjourned the court for the day. And so the interrogation of Bryan ended as abruptly as it had begun.

As the crowd dispersed, many spectators came forward to congratulate Darrow. He had proved that even Bryan could not defend a consistently literal interpretation of Genesis. Bryan had seemed a fumbling and ignorant defender of an embattled creed. He knew nothing about the scientific theories that he so glibly rejected, and even his support for the Bible was full of inconsistencies. At one moment he claimed it should be understood as literal truth; at another (the "days" taken to form the world), he showed it was susceptible to other interpretations.

When Darrow left the park, he looked back at the tired, deflated Bryan. "I was truly sorry for Mr. Bryan," he later wrote. "But I consoled myself by thinking of the years through which he had busied himself tormenting intelligent professors with impudent questions about their faith, and seeking to arouse the ignoramuses and bigots to drive them out of their positions."

That night both sides made plans for the final day of trial. Judge Raulston, fearing that violence might occur if it went on much longer, was eager to see the trial concluded. Bryan hoped to put Darrow on the stand in a reversal of the afternoon's roles in order to expose his agnosticism. But his associates saw no advantage in prolonging the trial. The defense attorneys also wanted to conclude. They had made a case for freedom of thought but realized that Scopes would be found guilty by the letter of the law. They hoped to overturn the conviction on appeal.

On Tuesday, July 21, Bryan and Darrow went to the courthouse under a rainy, leaden sky. The great drama of the trial was over. In the courtroom Darrow declared that to "save time" he would ask the jury to bring in a guilty verdict. Bryan was crushed: he would be unable to present a carefully prepared summation that he had been working on for days. But the prosecution gladly accepted the suggestion. A moment later the jury filed out, and in eight minutes they returned. Scopes was guilty.

No one was surprised; the jury could not change the law. The greater issues raised in the trial would have to be resolved in a higher court and by the American public. In the meantime, the hundreds of people who had been drawn to Dayton by the trial began to resume their ordinary lives.

John Thomas Scopes lost his job and had to pay a $100 fine for disobeying the law, but a committee was formed to raise money to send him to the University of Chicago. There he would study geology and embark on a new profession.

Bryan remained in Dayton to work on the address he had planned to deliver to the jury. This was typical of Bryan's career. He might suffer setbacks, but if he believed in a thing, he stuck to it with bulldog tenacity. He had arranged to have the speech printed in the *Chattanooga News*, where it appeared a few days later. And so it survives as testimony to his fundamentalist faith.

The undelivered address to the jury begins with a description of the simple virtues of Dayton. Bryan contrasted "the disturbing noises of a great city with the calm serenity of the country." In words that recalled his "Cross of Gold" speech, he drew together the land, the Lord, and the Bible in a web of righteousness: "I appreciate the sturdy honesty and independence of those who come into daily contact with the earth, who, living near to nature, worship nature's God, and who, dealing with the myriad mysteries of earth and air, seek to learn from revelation about the Bible's wonder-working God."

He did not oppose scientific progress. "Give science a fact and it is not only invincible, but it is of incalculable service to man." He praised science's contribution to humanity. Had it not produced the phonograph, the telephone, the sewing machine, the harvester, and "artificial ice"? Nor did he oppose freedom of thought. Atheists, agnostics, and evolutionists should be regarded as members of "sects," and like those in other religious groups they should be allowed to have their own schools.

But evolution must not be given the dignity of public support in the nation's classrooms. As in the trial, he complained that evolution associated humans with the beasts and that it undermined morality. It replaced the wonderful, miraculous world of the Bible with a cold, sterile, godless universe. It depicted "a cold and heartless process." It left people to face a meaningless death. "Christ," he said, "had made of death a narrow, star-lit strip between the companionship of yesterday and the reunion of tomorrow; evolution strikes out the stars and deepens the gloom that enshrouds the tomb."

Bryan had not been able to deliver this address, but he spent the days after the trial working for the cause it celebrated. He visited the site of a proposed fundamentalist university on a hillside outside Dayton. He made a whirlwind tour through the region, speaking from the rear platform of a train to some fifty thousand people; the Scopes trial, he told them, had been a great victory for Christianity.

One day he drove through the Tennessee countryside with his wife, Mary. On a gravel road beside a cornfield he posed for a picture; standing in a dark suit beside the square black limousine with his face screwed up in a look that was half grin and half grimace, with his large farmer's hands at his side and his necktie slightly askew, he easily assumed the pose of the righteous, if aging warrior. His wife, whose confidence in Bryan was exceeded only by Bryan's confidence in himself, later wrote a description aptly describing the Great Commoner in these, his last days. "He met wave after wave of prejudice and animosity," she wrote, "as an old weathered rock will stand against angry seas."

On the Sunday morning after the trial Bryan delivered a sermon at Dayton's Southern Methodist church. After Sunday dinner he went upstairs to take a nap. In the late afternoon when Bryan had not reappeared, Mary began to worry. The room was checked, and Bryan was found dead. The heat and tension of these weeks had weakened him. But he was already an old man, aged beyond his years by diabetes.

Bryan's body lay in a house in Dayton overnight, while hundreds of tearful mourners gathered outside. On Monday morning the body was placed on a special train bound for Washington, D.C. As the train carried Bryan's body through the farmlands and hills of Tennessee and Virginia, crowds gathered in all the little towns along the way; people waved flags and sang hymns. In the capital, Bryan's body lay in state, visited by thousands of mourners. On the afternoon of July 31, a day of fog and heavy rain, he was buried in Arlington Cemetery, hailed as a "great hero of the common people."

There was a dramatic fitness in Bryan's death. He had regarded Dayton as the scene of one of his greatest battles; its people were the plain, rural Americans he most loved. Some writers felt that the Dayton experience had crushed him, that he had died of a broken heart. But that was not Bryan's way. He had spent his life fighting for beleaguered causes. His undelivered speech to the Dayton jury concluded with the words of a hymn that conveyed this sense of pride in adversity: "Faith of our fathers, living still/in spite of dungeon, fire and sword." Others might have thought of the fundamentalist Bryan as bearer rather than victim of "dungeon, fire and sword." But Bryan was impervious to such doubts. His eyes had seen the glory of the Lord, and he held fast to the truth he found in the Bible.

Although Darrow was older than his opponent, he outlived Bryan by almost thirteen years. After the trial he gave a number of speeches on evolution, and in 1931 he narrated a full-length film on the subject entitled *The Mystery of Life*. He also handled several more important cases. Darrow, no less than Bryan, regarded himself as a protector of human dignity. A few months after leaving Dayton he was in Detroit, successfully defending a black family who had resisted with force when attacked by a white mob.

In 1928 Darrow returned to Dayton, where he was warmly received by friends he had made during the trial. His hosts drove him to the site of the new Bryan University. The fundamentalist backers had failed to provide the necessary money, and all that could be seen was a large hole in a Tennessee hillside. A few years later Darrow wrote: "My latest information is that the hole is still there on the lovely hillside, wide enough, long enough, and deep enough for a fitting grave for the monster project. Bigotry and opposition to learning are not a good foundation for any university in these modern times." Where Bryan had seen spiritual grandeur, Darrow could see only narrowmindedness.

The fundamentalist movement appeared to lose heart after the death of its best-known spokesman. But other evolution bills were debated in the next few years, and several were passed. The movement, however, never achieved the universal acceptance Bryan had anticipated. The spirited Scopes defense emboldened politicians and journalists elsewhere to denounce evolution laws. In Tennessee the law fell into neglect and was finally repealed in 1967.

In retrospect, it is remarkable how much Bryan and Darrow had in common. Each saw himself as a defender of the oppressed. Each represented a major cultural force in the 1920s. At Dayton each presented a program for American development. But where Bryan identified truth with tradition, the Bible, and rural America, Darrow embraced a creed of intellectual and social emancipation.

America observed the proceedings at Dayton with such avid interest because the trial brought out so many issues: parental authority, conventional morality, freedom of speech, science and the Bible. At times it seemed that the two forces would come to blows in the hot, muggy, hectic days of the trial. But somehow Dayton absorbed both sides. The crowd that applauded Bryan on the Bible also cheered Malone and Darrow on freedom of speech. The people seemed to want both sides to be right. They wanted the moral anchor and the spiritual certainty of the Bible, but they also wanted the personal freedom and scientific progress that were so alluring in the 1920s.

Bibliography

ALLEN, FREDERICK LEWIS. *Only Yesterday* (1931). Lively social history of the 1920s.

BOYLE, KEVIN. *Arc of Justice: A Saga of Race, Civil Rights, and Murder in the Jazz Age* (2005). Shortly after the Scopes trial, Clarence Darrow defended an African American who was mobbed after moving into a white neighborhood in Detroit.

BRYAN, WILLIAM JENNINGS. *The Memoirs of William Jennings Bryan* (1925). Bryan's autobiography.

CAUDILL, EDWARD, AND EDWARD J. LARSON. *The Scopes Trial: A Photographic History* (2000). Vivid pictures of the courtroom, the major players in the trial, and the town of Dayton, Tennessee.

DARROW, CLARENCE. *The Story of My Life* (1932). Darrow's autobiography.

FASS, PAULA S. *The Damned and the Beautiful* (1977). American youth in the 1920s.

FURNISS, NORMAN F. *The Fundamentalist Controversy* (1954). History of the fundamentalist movement.

GINGER, RAY. *Six Days or Forever?* (1958). Fine history of the Scopes trial.

LARSON, EDWARD J. *Summer for the Gods: The Scopes Trial and America's Continuing Debate over Science and Religion* (1997). Especially strong on the cultural forces at work in Dayton.

LEVINE, LAWRENCE W. *Defender of the Faith* (1965). Biography of William Jennings Bryan covering 1915–1925.

SINGAL, DANIEL J. *The War Within: From Victorian to Modernist Thought in the South, 1919–1945* (1982). The intellectual context for the Scopes trial.

SMOUT, KARY DOYLE. *The Creation/Evolution Controversy: A Battle for Cultural Power* (1998). Explores the rhetoric of three controversies over evolution: Wilberforce v. Huxley (1860), the Scopes trial (1925), and the Arkansas creation science trial (1981).

TIERNEY, KEVIN. *Darrow: A Biography* (1979). Probing explanation of Darrow's career and personality.

Study Guide

Summary

This article tells the story of the Scopes trial. We learn about the various elements in the trial: the antagonists, William Jennings Bryan and Clarence Darrow; the town of Dayton, Tennessee; the issue of evolution; and the American impulses toward fundamentalism and modernity. Then we follow the course of the trial itself, watching the interplay of all these elements as the lawyers argue about science, God, and human destiny. In the crucible of the Scopes trial they and the townspeople of Dayton articulated the hopes and fears of Americans torn between the allure of science and the longing for tradition.

Identification Topics

Scopes trial, Ku Klux Klan, fundamentalism, Charles Darwin, American Civil Liberties Union, Butler Act, John Thomas Scopes, William Jennings Bryan, Clarence Darrow, Leopold–Loeb case, Dudley Field Malone.

Study Questions

1. What features of modern American life did most Americans, fundamentalists as well as modernists, accept and enjoy? What did fundamentalists dislike about modern America?
2. Why did the teaching of evolutionary theory create such a stir? Why did fundamentalists object to it? Was the theory really likely to undermine morality and civilization? How did modernists reconcile Darwinism and religion?
3. In what ways did Bryan's earlier career make him a natural choice for joining the prosecution in the Scopes case? In what ways did Darrow's career prepare him to defend Scopes?
4. Describe Dayton, Tennessee. In what ways did the town display fundamentalist conservatism? In what ways was it sympathetic to intellectual freedom? Why did the people in Dayton applaud Dudley Field Malone's speech on intellectual freedom?
5. Why did William Jennings Bryan feel that he could do more for his country as a religious leader than he ever had as a politician?
6. What were the main issues in the Scopes trial? Why did Bryan condemn the theory of evolution? What was achieved in Darrow's examination of Bryan? Why was Scopes convicted?
7. Do you think that people in Dayton were really threatened by the theory of evolution? Or were their real fears based on other social and cultural currents, such as the relaxing of sexual mores and unprecedented material change?

8. The author claims that despite the cultural schism revealed at Dayton, the opposing sides in the Scopes trial shared many values. What were their differences? On what issues were they in accord?

Research Topics

1. Study more fully the history of the fundamentalist movement.
2. Explore H. L. Mencken's criticisms of the fundamentalists and other forms of conservatism in the 1920s.
3. Learn more about the social history of the twenties. To what extent was the old moral code really breaking down?
4. Conservative religious movements gain followers in periods of rapid material change. Explore this theory. Can you apply it to other nations or to other periods in American history?
5. Investigate recent conflicts between "creationists" and "evolutionists." What are the similarities and differences between this modern conflict and that of the 1920s?

CHAPTER 9

The New Deal

*Eleanor Roosevelt and the
Politics of Compassion*

The Great Depression of the 1930s damaged the United States both physically and psychologically. In a land whose resources had seemed boundless and where technology had promised unlimited progress, the depression destroyed dreams as well as jobs. Breadlines and shantytowns appeared around the nation, making visible the plight of the unemployed. During this time of social and economic dislocation, a remarkable first lady came to the White House. Eleanor Roosevelt embodied in a deeply personal way the compassion for disadvantaged Americans that would be a hallmark of American politics during the next half century. Her story also reveals the turmoil experienced by someone seeking her own place in a world that was reluctant to allow women a significant role outside the home.

"I, Franklin Delano Roosevelt, do solemnly swear that I will faithfully execute the office of President of the United States." On the cloudy morning of March 4, 1933, these words boomed over loudspeakers to a vast audience standing on the grass, clinging to trees, and sitting on bleachers high on the roof of the Capitol building. Millions more listened to radios across the country. In that moment Franklin Roosevelt became president of the United States; in the same moment, Eleanor Roosevelt, without an oath of her own, became first lady of the land. That day she wore a blue silk dress, a dark blue coat, and an orchid corsage. On the inaugural platform she was one woman among eighty dark-suited men. She stared into her lap during most of the ceremony, as if trying not to call attention to herself. Reporters remarked that she was curiously passive.

Franklin Roosevelt completed the oath of office, removed his hand from the family Bible, then began to speak, his voice firm and reassuring. Eleanor already knew what Franklin would say. He and his advisors had worked on the speech the night before in the Mayflower Hotel. Franklin sent a copy to an adjoining room where Eleanor was staying with a journalist friend, Lorena Hickok. "It's a good speech," she told Hickok, "a courageous speech. It has hope in it. But will people accept it? Will they believe in him?"

The problems facing the new president were enormous. During the past four years, American industrial production declined by 50 percent; national income fell from $81 billion to $41 billion per year. The number of unemployed rose from four million in 1930 to fifteen million in 1933. People who had made fortunes in business now sold apples on street corners. Makeshift villages of wood and cardboard sprang up in parks and vacant lots across the country. Men and women foraged for food in garbage cans; some actually starved to death. Confidence in the nation's institutions was so low that thousands of depositors took their money from banks, assuming that it would be safer under floorboards or in mattresses. Unable to keep pace with the withdrawals, many banks closed their doors. In the crowd that assembled for the inauguration that day under a cold, gray sky there were men and women who had lost their savings or were unemployed; most had relatives and friends who were out of work. Looking at the faces before her, Eleanor wondered, "How much can people take without blowing up?"

Franklin continued his address. "This great nation will endure," he said, "as it has endured, will revive and will prosper." America's problem was mainly spiritual: "The only thing we have to fear is fear itself— nameless, unreasoning, unjustified terror which paralyzes needed efforts to convert retreat into advance." The presidency that began that day was to be one of the most notable in American history. Franklin Roosevelt would win four presidential elections, twice as many as any other president. He would serve during two great crises: America's worst depression and deadliest foreign war. During the 1930s Roosevelt would preside over a revolution in domestic policy, the New Deal, a series of reforms that radically altered the government's role in creating jobs, regulating businesses, protecting workers, and providing pensions.

As significant as Franklin Roosevelt's achievement was, Eleanor Roosevelt's career was just as distinctive. She redefined the role of first lady, and arguably, she set a standard that has not been matched in the half century since she left the White House. During her dozen years in Washington, Eleanor Roosevelt shook more hands, gave more teas, and attended more public functions than any other first lady before or since. These social activities were the sort of thing that president's wives were expected to do. More importantly, Eleanor Roosevelt devoted her time to dozens of activities that went well beyond the traditional sphere. She wrote newspaper columns, delivered hundreds of speeches, and served as an advocate for various causes. One of Eleanor Roosevelt's many nicknames was "America's public energy no. 1." A popular *New Yorker* cartoon in the 1930s showed two miners deep in the bowels of the earth, looking at an approaching figure. One miner was saying to the other, "Oh, my God, it's Mrs. Roosevelt!" Just as her uncle, Theodore Roosevelt, recognized that the presidency is a "bully pulpit," Eleanor Roosevelt demonstrated that the position of presidential spouse provided opportunities for promoting the public good.

Her energy allowed Eleanor Roosevelt to make contact with thousands of people: out-of-work coal miners, impoverished sharecroppers, and wounded soldiers. She seemed to be perpetually in motion, but at the same time she could immerse herself in each new moment as if nothing else mattered. Greeting the one hundredth guest at a reception, she could make the person standing in front of her sense that they were the most interesting person in the room. Leaning over the bed of the fiftieth soldier in a hospital ward, she could manage to make that patient feel that he was uniquely important.

This capacity for sympathy with her fellow men and women seemed natural in Eleanor Roosevelt, as if some inward peace must have made possible her outward serenity. Her grace, however, was nurtured by turmoil; it grew out of her own sorrows and was reinforced by her keen awareness of human suffering. On the day of her husband's inauguration, Eleanor Roosevelt was troubled by the challenge before her. The problems facing the nation were daunting, and she also faced a personal crisis.

During the past two decades she had created a role for herself in politics, education, and manufacturing—unusual activities for a woman at that time, especially for a married woman with children. These accomplishments were fundamental to Eleanor Roosevelt's sense of self-esteem, and she knew that they were threatened by her new role. Traditionally, first ladies were ornamental figures—fit symbols of womanhood in a nation that still held that a woman belonged on a pedestal, isolated from the real world. Women had gained the right to vote, but during the 1930s few held office or entered the professions. In a nation endangered by economic chaos, would Eleanor Roosevelt be able to play an active role in national affairs? The answer to that question would be important not only to the well-being of the first lady, but also to the health of the nation as a whole.

On the surface, Eleanor Roosevelt's early life was sheltered from hardship. She was born on October 11, 1884, in New York City, to Elliott and Anna Hall Roosevelt. Elliott's grandfather, Cornelius Roosevelt, made a fortune in banking and left his son, Theodore, $2 million—a huge sum at a time when an American laborer typically earned about $1,000 per year. Elliott's father was a big-chested, square-jawed bear of a man with firm convictions and a generous spirit. One of New York's leading philanthropists, he helped found the Metropolitan Museum of Art and the Museum of Natural History. He took a special interest in the plight of New York's newsboys, many of whom were orphans.

Elliott Roosevelt shared his father's generous heart, and he was so popular himself with the newsboys that when he came to visit their shelter, they stamped their feet in applause. He was also a favorite of New York's "smart" society. After returning from a world tour in 1881, he joined the fashionable Meadowbrook Country Club on Long Island, played polo, went on fox hunts, and quickly established himself as one of New York's finest horsemen. Soon afterward he was smitten by Anna Hall, a young woman who was widely regarded as the most attractive debutante in New York. In the fall of 1883 Elliott and Anna were married. The ceremony was described by a reporter as "one of the most brilliant social events of the season." The Roosevelt's first child, Eleanor, was born ten months later.

During her early childhood, Eleanor's parents were leaders in a young social set known as the "swells." They attended the most fashionable balls, polo matches, and yachting cruises. The Roosevelts had friends, social prestige, a modest fortune, and a romantic attachment that grew stronger with each year.

Their warmth extended naturally to their daughter. In the fashion of the times, Elliott and Anna often left Eleanor with servants. Eleanor's first language was French, which she learned from her nurse. The couple also shared many tender moments with their daughter, including sleigh rides in Central Park. Elliott called Eleanor, "father's little golden hair." As Elliott tucked her into bed on her fourth birthday, Eleanor told him, "I love everybody, and everybody loves me."

The Roosevelt marriage was strained, however, by Elliott Roosevelt's personal problems. His temperament was ill suited to the business world, and he felt inadequate in the face of more successful friends. He may also have suffered from comparison with his astonishingly successful brother,

Theodore, who in his mid-twenties was already serving in the New York legislature and writing the definitive history of the naval war of 1812.

Elliott's life began a downward spiral when he badly injured his ankle and was treated with laudanum—an opium-based medicine. He became addicted to drugs and alcohol, and in this unstable condition he became involved with one of the household servants, and she became pregnant. His brother, Theodore, demanded that Elliott be sent into exile in Virginia. There Elliott worked for a family friend and sent poignant letters back to his daughter with advice and love.

Elliott hoped to win his way back to his family, but while he was away Anna Roosevelt grew sick and died. In his sorrow Elliott seemed all the more solicitous of Eleanor. In one letter he urged her to think of her mind as an "Education House." "You surely always wish to live in a beautiful house," he wrote, "and not an ugly one." He urged her to attend to the "big" virtues: "unselfishness, generosity, living tenderness, and cheerfulness."

Soon afterward Elliott too died, broken by alcohol and despair. Throughout her life Eleanor Roosevelt felt a powerful bond to her charming but troubled father. She kept his letters close to her and reread them many times.

Left an orphan at eleven, Eleanor was raised with her brother, Hall, at the home of her maternal grandmother, Mary Hall. She was a well-meaning guardian but was struggling to preside over a household that included several of her own somewhat troublesome adult children. In her teens, as in her childhood, life was a paradox to the orphaned Eleanor: she was born to wealth and social position, but also to bereavement and loneliness.

For the adolescent Eleanor Roosevelt, a wonderful change came when she was sent to England in 1899 to attend Allenswood School, near London. With fifty-four other girls, Eleanor lived in a rambling brick schoolhouse ruled by a large, silver-haired Frenchwoman, Marie Souvestre. At first Eleanor felt "lost and alone," as the aunt who had accompanied her to England drove away from the school. But she soon found that Allenswood suited her better than any home she had known since early childhood. The whole school seemed designed to encourage and nurture the young American.

Eleanor was particularly fortunate in forming a close friendship with the headmistress. In the evenings Mademoiselle Souvestre sometimes invited her favorite pupils into her study, where she read them French poems and talked about public affairs. She stimulated Eleanor by arguing in favor of unconventional political positions, such as the cause of the Boers in their war with the English in South Africa.

In Marie Souvestre's company, Eleanor came to a firsthand knowledge of that wider world. Years later she wrote, "Mlle. Souvestre shocked me into thinking, and that on the whole was very beneficial." Under other

Eleanor Roosevelt as a teenager. Her life was a contradiction: She was born into wealth and prestige, but she was left an orphan at eleven.

circumstances she might herself have become a teacher at Allenswood. This was Mademoiselle Souvestre's hope. But when Eleanor reached seventeen, her grandmother called her back to New York and introduced her to society.

For many young socialites coming out was the fulfillment of a dream. But for Eleanor Roosevelt the life of a debutante seemed foreign and frightening—she described one ball as "utter agony." Years later she wrote, "I knew I was the first girl in my mother's family who was not a belle, and . . . I was deeply ashamed." But Eleanor underestimated her own charm. She was blessed with a glowing complexion, a graceful figure, and a quick wit. One of the most handsome and popular young men of the day, her fifth cousin Franklin Roosevelt, had the good sense to recognize Eleanor's loveliness.

During the debutante season they fell in love, and in 1903 after taking Eleanor to a Harvard–Yale game, Franklin proposed. His mother, Sara Roosevelt, was cool to the marriage and persuaded her son to postpone the wedding, but in 1905 the couple was married in New York City. Eleanor's uncle Theodore, then president of the United States, gave her away.

After an extensive honeymoon in Europe, the couple settled in New York City, where Franklin began his professional life as a lawyer. Sara Roosevelt, at first reticent about the marriage of her only child, soon became a constant fixture in the Roosevelt household. She took Eleanor on daily drives, organized the young couple's household, and built side-by-side townhouses for herself and her children. This closeness—which would eventually become suffocating to Eleanor—was at first welcome. Motherless since childhood, she was as eager for Sara Roosevelt's presence as Sara was eager to be present.

In quick succession Eleanor Roosevelt bore six children: Anna, James, Franklin, Elliott, and John. (There were two Franklins, the first of whom died in infancy.) Servants and Sara tended to isolate Eleanor from responsibility for the children, but with so many to care for, she was still active as a mother.

In 1910 a new phase of her life began when Franklin ran for the state legislature in Dutchess County, the location of the Roosevelts' estate at Hyde Park. Although he was running as a Democrat in a heavily Republican district, Franklin won the election. Two years later he attracted the attention of Woodrow Wilson at the Democratic Convention. After Wilson's election to the presidency, Franklin Roosevelt became assistant secretary of the navy.

In his new position, Franklin helped direct one of the most powerful navies in the world. As the assistant secretary's wife, Eleanor filled the less demanding role of visiting the wives of navy officers and trading pleasantries about life in the capital. Years later in her autobiography Eleanor declared that the life of politician's wife had left her unfulfilled: "I looked at everything from the point of view of what I ought to do, rarely from the standpoint of what I wanted to do. . . . So I took an interest in politics. It was a wife's duty to be interested in whatever interested her husband, whether it was politics, books, or a particular dish for dinner."

Certainly giving teas and exchanging calling cards were trivial pursuits in comparison to her later activities. But at the time, Eleanor Roosevelt was well liked as a society matron, and she enjoyed conversations with the important politicians and diplomats who often dined with the family. She might have gone through life contentedly enough as a bright, somewhat conventional, politician's wife, but in her early thirties, two events destroyed the worlds, both public and private, that she had known.

The first was the Great War. When America entered the war in 1917, Eleanor Roosevelt became active on several fronts. She organized the navy wives to knit sweaters and scarves for seamen, and she worked in a little corrugated tin shack at a "canteen" in the local railway station, passing out sandwiches and coffee to soldiers. While many other volunteers contributed only an hour or so a week to such activities, Eleanor gave hundreds of hours to the effort. Later she became engaged in more important—and more troubling—activity. She helped in the hospital wards, working among servicemen wounded in Europe.

Standing beside a man driven crazy by shell shock or critically injured by bullet or shrapnel, she became aware of suffering as a public phenomenon—inflicted by human beings on other human beings in a world gone wrong. The mother of one soldier, whom Eleanor often saw at St. Elizabeth's Hospital in Washington, wrote her after her son's death: "He always loved to see you come in. You always brought a ray of sunshine with you. . . . I know when you go to the hospital, it is in a spirit of love."

While Eleanor Roosevelt was growing more aware of the vulnerability of humanity, she also suffered a painful turn in her personal life: she discovered that her husband was having an affair with Lucy Mercer, Eleanor's personal secretary. In another age Eleanor and Franklin might have divorced, but in 1919 there were compelling reasons to stay together: their children, Franklin's career, and the awkward position Eleanor would have faced as a divorced woman. There was also, despite differences in their temperaments, a strong bond between Eleanor and Franklin. They never again shared the same bedroom, but they stayed together, and during the years ahead in their demanding public lives they were fiercely loyal to one another.

The new bond was tested in 1921 when Franklin contracted polio. He would never walk again without heavy metal braces and crutches or a cane and even then only for short distances. In the next five years he devoted much of his time to convalescence.

During the 1920s Eleanor became Franklin's surrogate. He could not travel easily, but he and his political advisor, Louis Howe, wanted to keep Franklin's political career alive by keeping the Roosevelt name in the public arena. So out of necessity, Eleanor Roosevelt was thrust upon the public stage as a leader in the women's division of the New York Democratic party and as a public speaker. She thrived in her new roles, gained self-confidence, and was soon known as one of the most influential women in New York. Interviewed in 1927 by *Success* magazine, she declared, "I suppose if I were asked what is the best thing one can expect in life, I would say—the privilege of being useful."

Eleanor found kinship with other women who had entered into unusual spheres of life. With two of her friends, Nan Cook and Marion Dickerman, she created Todhunter School in New York City and established a small furniture factory on the family's Hyde Park estate. With Franklin's encouragement, Eleanor built her own house at Hyde Park, called Val-Kill, where she often entertained her closest friends while he entertained his at the main house.

They continued to live much of their lives separately, and yet as parents, friends, and political colleagues they remained close. In 1928 Franklin was elected governor of New York, building in part on the goodwill Eleanor helped create. In Albany a reporter asked her about her marriage; he was writing an article on the subject "What is a Wife's Job Today?" Eleanor declared that mutual respect was the essential ingredient of a good marriage; noting that there were some marriages where a "vampire husband" or "vampire wife" ruled over their partner, she praised marriages in which each spouse was free to mature. "It is entirely through the interests that a man and woman share," she said, "that the light of a true marriage shines."

When Franklin was elected governor Eleanor had feared that she would have to abandon the public roles she had filled during the past few years. She did resign from the Democratic State Committee, but in many other respects her public role actually increased. Eleanor remained a consultant to the Women's Division in state politics; and she was active in the Women's Trade Union League. She also traveled throughout the state, even visiting remote farming regions in upstate New York. When Franklin won reelection by a landslide in 1930, his political advisor, James Farley, credited Eleanor Roosevelt with making possible his victory in the hitherto Republican north.

In 1932 her individuality seemed threatened again when Franklin Roosevelt was elected president. Most women would have been delighted at the chance to be first lady of the United States, but reporters noted that on election eve Eleanor seemed unhappy and withdrawn. At the time, first ladies were expected to do little more than attend state dinners and look radiant. During Franklin's years as governor, Eleanor had been able to continue teaching, but that was no longer possible.

During the painful months of transition to the White House, Eleanor Roosevelt was attracted to an Associated Press reporter, Lorena Hickok. They met during the presidential campaign, and Lorena sensed Eleanor's fears about her new life. Soon they became confidants. On the night of the inauguration Eleanor had one friend, Lorena, to whom she could confide her true feelings. Three days after the inauguration, on Lorena Hickok's fortieth birthday, Eleanor Roosevelt wrote her friend, "All day I've thought of you. Oh, I want to put my arms around you; I ache to hold you close." In reply, Lorena Hickok could write, "There have been times when I've missed you so that it has been like a physical pain."

Reading such letters, some historians have argued that Eleanor Roosevelt had a sexual relationship with Lorena Hickok; others reject the idea. Rather than "read between the lines" of Eleanor Roosevelt's sometimes passionate letters to friends, it would be wiser to read the lines themselves. In the case of Lorena Hickok—and later in Eleanor's friendship with her biographer Joseph Lash and her doctor, David Gurewitsch—what the letters do show is that Eleanor Roosevelt was sometimes drawn powerfully to another human being. The letters do not speak of sexual contact, but they do bespeak longing, love, tenderness, and kinship. Perhaps such relationships made possible Eleanor

Roosevelt's sympathy for out-of-work laborers and wounded soldiers—all that love for humanity was balanced by a more intimate love for a few individuals.

Lorena Hickok had not gone to the inauguration. She was waiting for Eleanor Roosevelt at the White House in the room that had been Lincoln's bedroom during the Civil War. It would soon be Eleanor's study; it was filled with ugly mahogany wardrobes and a clutter of old White House furniture. While the inauguration ceremony was drawing to a close a mile away, Hickok looked out the tall windows at the Washington Monument and listened to the thumping and hissing of a faulty radiator. Then she heard motorcycles and cheers; a few minutes later the first lady strode into the room.

Eleanor had promised Lorena an exclusive interview after the inauguration—the first she would give in the White House. Eleanor presented to her friend in a few brief sentences a kind of inaugural address of her own. "One has a feeling of going it blindly," she said. "We are in a tremendous stream, and none of us knows where we are going to land. The important thing, it seems to me, is our attitude toward whatever may happen. It must be willingness to accept and share with others whatever may come and to meet the future courageously, with a cheerful spirit."

A few minutes later, Eleanor Roosevelt was involved in her new responsibilities: she greeted some of the three thousand guests who came to the White House for an inaugural tea. Next there was a family dinner—with seventy-five in attendance. Then she went to the inaugural ball. In such ways, Eleanor was immediately drawn into the traditional role of the first lady: hostess.

Franklin Roosevelt was not burdened with the self-doubt that troubled Eleanor. As the new president his challenge was formidable, but at least it was concrete: he must lead the United States out of the depression. During his first three months in office—the Hundred Days—he took before Congress an ambitious legislative program including the National Industrial Recovery Act and the Emergency Banking Act. These bills were passed by Congress along with legislation creating the Civilian Conservation Corps, the Public Works Administration, and the Civil Works Administration. At no previous time in American history had so many important acts been passed in so little time.

During the Hundred Days Eleanor's achievements could hardly match her husband's, but by no means did she slip into the mold of a conventional first lady. Her servants, many of whom had overseen White House protocol for three decades, soon found Eleanor overturning traditions that she considered too formal. When her furniture arrived, she startled moving men by shoving desks and beds across the room in her eagerness to get settled. Laborers were told to work around her rather than wait for her to leave her study. She wanted a phone in her office and wondered why one had not been installed. The phone man was in the hall, she was told, waiting for a convenient moment to do his work. "Oh, spinach!" said Eleanor—for her, a salty expression—"Tell him to come in and get started!"

Many of Eleanor Roosevelt's innovations were designed to make the White House and its occupants more accessible to the people. By tradition servants greeted guests to the presidential mansion and then announced them to the first lady. Eleanor liked to answer the door herself, just as she would in any other house. The most innovative of Eleanor's actions during her months as first lady was in her handling of the press. Other presidential wives had stayed aloof, refusing even to grant interviews. Eleanor instituted press conferences that were open only to women. A few days after the inauguration she held one of these meetings—before Franklin's first conference. She greeted the newswomen by sharing with them a box of candies.

In such ways Eleanor made herself more accessible to the public than any previous first lady. But at the same time, she fought to preserve a private realm where she could simply be herself. She refused to be accompanied on her travels by Secret Service agents and insisted on driving her own car without a police escort. The Secret Service fretted; only a few months before an assassin in Miami had fatally wounded Chicago's Mayor Cermak as he stood beside Franklin. Nonetheless, Eleanor continued to value privacy above safety, and she refused protection. Finally a frustrated Secret Service agent placed a gun on the desk of one of the president's advisors and told him to make sure that the first lady carried it. Eleanor took the gun, and she learned to shoot it. But there her compliance ended: she carried the gun unloaded in her glove compartment.

During the summer of 1933, Eleanor Roosevelt tested the bounds of her liberty. She purchased a light blue Buick roadster, a sporty convertible with a rumble seat. Then she and Lorena Hickok set off on a trip through New England and around Quebec's Gaspé Peninsula. They drove along the south bank of the St. Lawrence River on one of the loveliest roads in North America.

Back in the United States, they spent a night in a Maine farmhouse. They sat out on a porch swing, and soon the farmer appeared and sat on the steps nearby. Eleanor Roosevelt began talking knowledgeably about potato prices and local agricultural conditions. The farmer's wife came out and sat in a rocking chair; as darkness settled over the farmland the four of them went on talking. Lorena sensed the farmer's growing admiration for Eleanor. At about eleven o'clock they went into the kitchen for a snack of doughnuts and milk. In their room Hickok asked Roosevelt how she happened to know so much about farming in Maine. Eleanor explained that she had looked at a local newspaper; she also gained information from the farmer as she went along: "something I learned to do when I was very young," she said, "to cover my ignorance."

When the two women returned to the White House, Franklin Roosevelt began a tradition he would observe throughout his presidency: he dined informally with Eleanor so that she could tell him what she had learned. How did the people live in Quebec? he asked. What were their houses like, what did they eat, and did the Catholic Church control education? And what about Maine: How were the farmers getting along, what had she learned about the local Indians? Eleanor Roosevelt answered these and other questions. It was soon apparent to Lorena Hickok that although Eleanor had relaxed on the vacation, she had constantly registered information for herself and Franklin, even making mental notes about the state of laundry hanging on the lines—any detail that would help them both understand more fully the condition of the nation they served.

During the presidential years many of Eleanor's best times with Franklin came during their discussions of the condition of the nation. Because Eleanor could travel more freely than Franklin—she covered 33,000 miles in 1933 alone—she became his "eyes and ears," bringing him personal reports from around the world. Franklin developed the habit of throwing arguments at Eleanor to test her reactions, sometimes adopting her point of view, sometimes not. As she left the room after one conversation, he told an adviser, "There goes the opinion of the average man in the streets."

Along with her reports, Eleanor Roosevelt also brought advice to her husband. She was Franklin's political advisor, even some would say, his conscience. She urged him to adopt measures to support minorities and the poor. In some instances, as in the case of her efforts to persuade him to sponsor antilynching laws, Franklin ignored her advice on the grounds of political expediency. The southern Democrats, he told her, would never allow such an intrusion in their affairs. But in many instances Franklin encouraged Eleanor to take an active role in his administration.

In the summer of 1933 Lorena Hickok went to work for the Federal Emergency Relief Administration, the agency created during the Hundred Days to provide a half billion dollars in assistance to the nation's poor. She was to travel across the country investigating the accomplishments of the relief program and writing reports to her boss, Harry Hopkins. Hickok's reports were vivid accounts of the war waged by the New Deal against the depression, and Hopkins often passed them on to congressmen and the president. Hickok also wrote daily letters to Eleanor, some extending to ten and twelve pages, giving her a personal glimpse of American locales blighted by the depression. One of her letters introduced Eleanor Roosevelt to Scott's Run, West Virginia, the place that became for her the quintessential example of what poverty and relief were all about.

After World War I the coal-mining districts of West Virginia had prospered with the industrial growth of the 1920s. Men sold out their small homesteads and came to work in the mines for $10 to $25 a day—enormous wages for that time. But with the depression the demand for coal fell, and many of the mines shut down. Thousands of workers were left jobless in dreary mining camps.

Lorena Hickok toured West Virginia in August 1933. She saw miners living in tents because they had been driven from company housing after a strike; babies with distended bellies and eyes vacant from hunger; children who took turns wearing the only pair of shoes in the family. She heard about a mother of eight who was dying of appendicitis and was denied admission to a hospital because of her poverty. Hickok came to Scott's Run, a scattering of mining camps along a tributary of the Monongahela River. A primitive dirt road followed a dirty little stream; steep hills rose on either side. Clusters of shacks, black with coal dust, stood beside slag heaps from the mines. Outhouses hung over a filthy stream that flowed down the mountain, and yet the people washed in the creek and used its water for cooking. The houses were small, ramshackle, leaky. "And in those houses," Hickok wrote, "every night children went to sleep hungry, on piles of bug-infested rags, spread out on the floor."

Eleanor Roosevelt heard about conditions in West Virginia from Hickok, and she arranged to visit Scott's Run. There she found the houses "scarcely fit for human habitation." In some the parents and younger children slept together on the only bed—often bare springs covered with a blanket—and the older children slept on rags on the floor. In one town, the entire populace drew water from a single spigot. "You felt as though the coal dust had seeped into every crack in the houses," Roosevelt later wrote, "and it would be impossible to get them or the people clean." The families were large, but most had no more than two or three chipped cups and plates on the shelves. Children missed school because there was only one dress or pair of pants between them, and so they had to take turns dressing and going to class.

When Eleanor visited Scott's Run, the place became for her the embodiment of economic hardship in America. She went to the coal fields often, as if to immerse herself in their dirt, their poverty, their despair. A Quaker worker remembered Eleanor sitting in a dirty hovel, talking to a bedraggled mother, listening intently to her story. The woman's baby sat on Eleanor's lap. She noticed a little boy holding a pet rabbit fondly in his arms. The boy's sister remarked mischievously, "He thinks we are not going to eat it, but we are." At that the boy fled down the road clutching the doomed bunny. When Roosevelt returned to Washington she told the story of the pet rabbit to friends at a dinner party. One of the guests sent her a check the next day for $100, hoping she would use the money to keep the animal alive.

Through this generosity the rabbit may have lived to a ripe old age, but Eleanor realized that the hardships of Scott's Run could not be cured one by one. She continued to visit poor people there and elsewhere, and she made personal contributions to charity. But she believed that the government must intervene on behalf of the needy, and that the nation as a whole should develop a higher sense of responsibility for human welfare. Fortunately, Congress had already passed a bill that would provide assistance to places like Scott's Run. One section of the National Industrial Recovery Act set aside $25 million in loans for "Subsistence Homesteads" for people who could not afford to buy their own houses. The homestead program was designed to demonstrate the value of government planning and provide a way for "stranded populations"—people thrown out of work by industrial decline—to make a living. The program's backers anticipated that families settled by the government on small plots of land could combine subsistence farming with work in small manufacturing plants.

More than fifty subsistence homestead communities would be established throughout the United States during the New Deal. The most famous of these, Arthurdale, became Eleanor Roosevelt's pet project. She realized that a resettlement community would be ideally suited to help the people of Scott's Run, and she met with presidential advisor Louis Howe and Secretary of the Interior Harold Ickes to discuss the matter. Roosevelt had an advantage because of her firsthand knowledge of the conditions in West Virginia and persuaded them that a community should be established near Scott's Run. "I'll buy the houses," said Howe. "Ickes, you buy the land. And Eleanor, you'll put the families in the houses."

Arthurdale became an attractive town. Neat white houses, each with its own barn, stood side by side on five-acre plots. A community center housed a school, auditorium, post office, and shops for local crafts. Esther Clapp, a distinguished educator, established a progressive school for the village. Near the school was an old log cabin where the children learned crafts and built a loom, a spinning wheel, and wooden dishes. The first lady often visited Arthurdale during the 1930s, taking part in village square dances and attending high school commencement.

Because of Eleanor Roosevelt's interest Arthurdale attracted the attention of the press. Soon stories began to circulate about the flaws in the utopian community: the houses cost more than they should have, and no major businesses located near the town. Eleanor Roosevelt would eventually admit that Arthurdale was not the panacea she had hoped for. But she knew another side to the experiment. Some reporters saw only a picturesque village that was costing the government a lot of money. Eleanor Roosevelt had seen what came before. One woman's experience told the whole story: she was a homesteader whom Eleanor visited shortly before Christmas, 1934. The woman had three small girls and carried a baby in her arms. She was living in an attractive house with a cellar full of canned goods. Last Christmas, she told Eleanor, she had occupied a hovel with two rooms and no windows. Christmas dinner had consisted of carrots. Because she and her husband had no money for presents, she had not even told the children it was Christmas. "This year," she said, the children "will each have a toy, and we have a chicken, one of our own, that we are going to eat."

"Oh, yes," Roosevelt noted, summarizing her feelings about Arthurdale, "the human values were most rewarding, even if the financial returns to the government were not satisfactory." Throughout her time as first lady, Roosevelt revisited Arthurdale so often that she knew practically everyone by name.

In such episodes as her work with Arthurdale, Eleanor Roosevelt displayed a character that was one part practical politician and one part spiritual healer. She also worked for social justice closer to home, in Washington, D.C. In addition to holding women-only press conferences, she struck a blow at the prestigious Gridiron Club, which allowed only male journalists as members. When the club held its annual banquets she presided over dinner for female journalists, called the "Gridiron Widows." At her press conferences she sometimes gave the women stories of important news before her husband released the same news in his conferences. Roosevelt also advocated the appointment of women to government positions. A woman who had spent many years in the capital remarked that when women administrators had wanted to dine together in the past, a small club could seat them all. "Now there are so many of them," she remarked, "that we need a hall."

One of Eleanor Roosevelt's most appealing gestures as first lady was to help arrange a concert by the great soprano Marian Anderson. Anderson was to have appeared at the Daughters of the American Revolution (DAR) concert hall in the capital, but being black, she was barred from performing there. The DAR was not at all unique in its policy of segregation; most of Washington's theaters were segregated at the time. But the affront to Marian Anderson so offended Eleanor that she resigned from the DAR and arranged for Anderson to sing instead at the Lincoln Memorial. The concert was attended by 75,000, many times more than could have crowded into the DAR hall. Harold Ickes, who attended the concert, called it "the most moving occasion of my life." Years later Marian Anderson remarked, "It seemed that everyone present was a living witness to the ideals of freedom for which President Lincoln died. When I sang that day, I was singing to the entire nation."

Through such acts Eleanor Roosevelt became identified with disadvantaged Americans of all kinds. Because of her stands on controversial issues, she became the most hated as well as the most loved of first ladies, but her ratings in polls often stood higher than those of her popular husband. During the Second World War, Eleanor visited American troops in England and the South Pacific as well as throughout the United States. One indication of her international stature was an article that appeared in the *Auckland Star* during her visit to New Zealand. Eleanor Roosevelt's name, the paper declared, "carries its own title. . . . There is no better known woman in all the world." The *Star* described her as a woman dedicated to "the quest for a better way of life, not only for her own people of the United States, but for all the peoples of the world."

It is still difficult to assess—and hard to overestimate—Eleanor Roosevelt's importance as first lady of the United States. One measure is her many activities, but even more important was the example she set as a compassionate woman motivated by a deep sense of justice. Because of who she was, she empowered other people—women, blacks, the poor—with a sense that their needs were recognized at the highest levels of the land. All that would end, however—or so she thought—with the death of her husband in 1945.

For two years after Franklin Roosevelt's death Eleanor wore black; she even discarded bright suitcases that seemed inconsistent with her mourning. Such gestures were common during that period, but they were more than formal observances in Eleanor's case. She and Franklin had loomed large in one another's lives—never more so than during their years in the White House when they became the most important political couple in American history. Despite their estrangement, Eleanor Roosevelt would often remember her husband fondly. After Franklin's death, she took care of his devoted Scottie, Fala. She remarked that the dog "never really forgot" Franklin—neither did she.

After Franklin's death, Eleanor declared, "The story is over." She even claimed that she expected to settle in front of a fire, an old lady in a shawl. But instead she entered upon nearly two decades of public service. Eleanor divided her time between her cottage at Val-Kill and a New York apartment in Washington Square. During the average week she received a hundred invitations to make public appearances. Her activities on one spring day illustrate her busy schedule: she began with a breakfast at Bryn Mawr College, took a train from Philadelphia to New York for a fundraising luncheon for a boy's school, drove to Poughkeepsie to deliver a late-afternoon talk at Vassar College on the United Nations, went home to Hyde Park for a quick supper, and returned in the evening to Poughkeepsie to attend a Girl Scout pow-wow. A good day's work.

In her sixties and seventies Eleanor Roosevelt was one of the most popular speakers in America. *Variety*, the entertainment magazine, said her talks ranked with the "finest pieces of speaking ever done by a woman on the air." She also wrote a daily newspaper column, "My

Day," and a monthly magazine column consisting of answers to readers' questions. In order to find the time for all her engagements she stayed up late every night and made up for lost sleep with catnaps taken inconspicuously at public gatherings.

Because of Eleanor's popularity, people often suggested that she should run for office, even for the vice presidency in 1948 under Harry Truman. She always discouraged such suggestions, but continued to exercise considerable influence within the Democratic party. Her reform interests were best expressed in her support for Americans for Democratic Action, which drew together liberals within the Democratic party.

In such ways, Eleanor Roosevelt continued to play an important role in American life after her husband's death; but her most significant achievement came at the United Nations, where she served as a delegate appointed by President Truman. During the winter of 1946 she attended the first meeting of the UN General Assembly, then convening in London. Soon afterward she became chair of the United Nations Human Rights Commission. In that role she presided over the drafting of one of the most important documents in history, the Universal Declaration of Human Rights—the Bill of Rights of the United Nations.

Eleanor Roosevelt recognized that different nations had different views on human rights. The United States would want a list of political freedoms: free speech, freedom from arbitrary arrest, the right to a fair trial. The Soviet Union, on the other hand, would emphasize the economic freedoms embraced by communism: the right to a decent standard of living, universal medical care, and adequate housing. As chair of the Commission on Human Rights, Eleanor would have to mediate between conflicting views.

Sitting at the head of a conference table with seventeen other delegates, Eleanor Roosevelt was said to remind some observers of a "favorite aunt." She could make her points by delivering them with humility: "I am probably the least learned person around this table," she would say. "So I have thought of this article in terms of what the ordinary person would understand." She could flatter the egos of her male fellow delegates: "Now, of course, I'm a woman, and I don't understand all of these things, and I'm sure there's a great deal to be said for your arguments, but don't you think it would be a good idea if . . . " In such ways, Eleanor Roosevelt played the role of a deferential and well-meaning woman, somewhat at a loss in a man's world. But beneath her self-effacing demeanor was the strength she had gained from thirty years of public service. When the need arose, she could cast off all pretense to meekness and whip her committee into line.

After two years of deliberation, the Universal Declaration of Human Rights was finally ready to be sent to the General Assembly during the fall of 1948. On the night of December 10 the measure was adopted without any opposing votes. In her diary Eleanor Roosevelt noted, "long job finished."

The sources of the Universal Declaration of Human Rights were many: the Magna Carta, the American Bill of Rights, the *Communist Manifesto*. The document also bears the stamp of Eleanor's own personality. The opening lines—"Recognition of the inherent dignity and of the equal and inalienable rights of all members of the human family is the foundation of freedom, justice and peace in the world"—echo words she wrote in her book *The Moral Basis of Democracy*: "There is a spring that flows for all humanity."

The Universal Declaration of Human Rights, like the American Declaration of Independence, is a moral rather than a legal document. It has no standing in law, but during the 1950s and 1960s it became the cornerstone of the constitutions of many emerging nations. Nobel laureate Alexander Solzhenitzyn said it was the "best document" ever produced by the UN, and UN Secretary-General U Thant called it "The Magna Carta of Mankind."

During her time at the United Nations, Eleanor Roosevelt added to her worldwide reputation as a friend of humanity. When the UN met in Geneva police had to hold back the crowds that flocked to see her. She came to be known as the "First Lady of the World." And yet throughout her life, she retained a sense of surprise that she should be so popular. On a trip to Pakistan in 1952, she landed in Karachi and beheld a crowd of ten thousand people at the airport. She wondered why so many were there and was astonished to learn that they had come to see her.

In her seventies Eleanor Roosevelt's hair was gray; her arms were plump; and she was beginning to look somewhat like the old lady in a shawl she had once expected to become. But she continued to follow a rigorous schedule of exercise and public appearances. At seven o'clock in the morning she arose, did sit-ups, and moved, according to one observer, "at the speed of light." She continued to deliver one hundred speeches a year and kept fifteen to twenty appointments a day.

In her mid-seventies she remarked, "At present I look like Methuselah, but I feel no older than my youngest friends." In 1961 with the inauguration of John Kennedy, Eleanor Roosevelt was again appointed a delegate to the United Nations, and she chaired the President's Commission on the Status of Women. Long a crusader for human rights, she was alive on the eve of the great Washington march and Martin Luther King's "I Have a Dream" speech. Many of the humanitarian reforms Eleanor had called for would be enacted during the next decade. But she would not live to see those changes.

During 1960 she fell ill from a deadly disease known as aplastic anemia. In 1962 it was discovered that she was also suffering from a rare form of bone-marrow tuberculosis. On the evening of November 7, 1962, Eleanor Roosevelt died at her home in New York City. The tributes she received are one measure of her achievement. She was said to possess an ability to "walk with kings and keep the common touch." Adlai Stevenson declared, "She would rather light a candle than curse the darkness, and her glow has warmed the world."

Only a few intimates realized that Eleanor Roosevelt's sense of kinship with the peoples of the world grew in part from her inner loneliness. "Behind tranquility," she once wrote, "lies conquered unhappiness." The woman who became a friend of humanity had been an orphan as a child and slept alone during most of her adult life. And yet Eleanor Roosevelt's life was certainly a triumph. Few people in public life have ever combined so well the practicality of a politician and the charity of a saint. A wonderful Bill Mauldin cartoon, published shortly after Eleanor's death, best suggests the devotion which she inspired: a cluster of cherubs in heaven are looking shyly from behind the clouds at an approaching figure. Awestruck, one of them remarks, "It's her!"

Bibliography

BEASLEY, MAURINE H., ET AL., EDITORS. *The Eleanor Roosevelt Encyclopedia* (2001). Excellent collection of entries on many facets of Roosevelt's life.

BLACK, ALLIDA. *Casting Her Own Shadow: Eleanor Roosevelt and the Shaping of Postwar Liberalism* (1996). Roosevelt's impact on politics after Franklin's death.

COHEN, ROBERT, EDITOR. *Dear Mrs. Roosevelt: Letters from Children of the Great Depression* (2002). First-hand perspective on the depression as experienced by children.

COOK, BLANCHE WIESEN. *Eleanor Roosevelt* (1992–). As of 2006, two volumes of this definitive multivolume biography had been completed, taking the story of Roosevelt's life to 1938.

EDENS, JOHN A. *Eleanor Roosevelt: A Comprehensive Bibliography* (1994). Includes information on writings by and about Roosevelt.

GLENDON, MARY ANN. *A World Made New* (2001). The definitive account of Eleanor Roosevelt's contribution to the drafting of the Universal Declaration of Human Rights.

GOODWIN, DORIS KEARNS. *No Ordinary Time: Franklin and Eleanor Roosevelt, The Home Front in World War II* (1995). Pulitzer Prize-winning account of the Roosevelt partnership in American public life.

HAREVEN, TAMERA K. *Eleanor Roosevelt: An American Conscience* (1968). Focuses on Roosevelt's role in politics.

LASH, JOSEPH P. *Eleanor and Franklin* (1971). A fine account of their relationship and their accomplishments by one of Eleanor Roosevelt's best friends.

ROOSEVELT, ELEANOR. *The Autobiography of Eleanor Roosevelt* (1961). Roosevelt's superb account of her own life.

SCHLUP, LEONARD C., AND DONALD W. WHISENHUNT. *It Seems to Me: Selected Letters of Eleanor Roosevelt* (2001) Excellent collection of letters focusing on Roosevelt's public life.

YOUNGS, J. WILLIAM T. *Eleanor Roosevelt: A Personal and Public Life* (2005). A narrative history of Eleanor Roosevelt's life and career.

Study Guide

Summary

This essay begins by showing Eleanor Roosevelt at the inauguration in 1933 of Franklin Delano Roosevelt as president. The moment serves as a point of departure for exploring Eleanor's tragic childhood, her marriage to Franklin, and her emergence during the 1920s as a leading public figure. The essay then moves ahead to her role as first lady, where she becomes an advocate for the victims of prejudice and poverty—her "politics of compassion." The last section traces her activities as a widow, especially her contribution to the Universal Declaration of Human Rights.

Identification Topics

Elliott and Anna Roosevelt, Sara Roosevelt, Lucy Mercer, Todhunter School, Scott's Run, Federal Emergency Relief Administration, Marian Anderson, Marie Souvestre, Hyde Park, Val-Kill, Lorena Hickok, Arthurdale, subsistence homesteads, Gridiron Widows, Universal Declaration of Human Rights

Study Questions

1. What was the extent of the Great Depression in 1933, when Eleanor Roosevelt became first lady?
2. Eleanor Roosevelt's grace "was nurtured by turmoil; it grew out of her own sorrows and was reinforced by her keen awareness of human suffering." Explain.
3. From an early age, Eleanor Roosevelt was dissatisfied with the traditional role of a woman. What are some specific examples of this dissatisfaction, and how did she confront them?
4. How did Eleanor Roosevelt's personal and war-related experience during World War I draw her into public life?
5. In what ways did Eleanor Roosevelt expand her role in public life during the 1920s? How did she justify such activities for a woman?
6. How did Eleanor Roosevelt change White House protocol during her own tenure as first lady?
7. In what ways did Roosevelt work for economic and racial justice from her "bully pulpit" as first lady?
8. How did Eleanor Roosevelt's relationships, notably with Franklin Roosevelt and with Lorena Hickok, contribute to her effectiveness as a public servant?
9. Evaluate the marriage of Eleanor and Franklin Roosevelt. What were its strengths and weaknesses? In what ways did they work together in fostering reform?
10. What is the significance of Arthurdale as an example of New Deal policy? Of Eleanor Roosevelt's contribution to reform?
11. In what ways did Roosevelt promote human rights?
12. What were Roosevelt's most important achievements after her years as first lady?

Research Topics

1. Compare Eleanor Roosevelt's career as first lady to that of other presidents' wives before and since.

2. Explore the world into which Eleanor Roosevelt was born. How did New York's upper class live at the turn of the century, and what was their influence in public life?

3. Eleanor Roosevelt's many writings include newspaper articles and an autobiography. Write an essay about her ideas and accomplishments based on one or more of her writings.

4. Eleanor Roosevelt played an active role in the conceptualization and implementation of Arthurdale and other resettlement communities. Explore whether she played a similar role in other facets of New Deal policy.

CHAPTER 10

Total War

The Bombing of Hiroshima

etween 1941 and 1945, the United States took part in the most destructive war in history. During those years, men who might otherwise have been factory workers, carpenters, lawyers, and businessmen became trained killers with one goal: to defeat Japan, Germany, and the other Axis powers. The United States went to war against these nations because they were ruled by totalitarian regimes; because they fought against our allies; and because, finally, one of them bombed Pearl Harbor. The war came to a close after America exploded two atomic bombs, the most destructive weapons ever used in warfare. The story of Hiroshima, the first target, shows the horror of total war, and the experience of the bomber crews reveals how warfare can convert ordinary men into agents of ghastly terror.

In the predawn hours of August 6, 1945, three American B-29s droned through the darkness bound north from the Pacific island of Tinian toward the Japanese coastal town of Hiroshima. They flew at four thousand feet, where the air was close and humid, to avoid colliding with one of the hundreds of B-29s returning from bombing runs over Japan. Such massive raids were common. In the past year the balance of terror in the Pacific had swung irreversibly to the American side, and in summer 1945, B-29 Superfortresses could blast and burn Japanese cities almost at will. In comparison to such huge congregations of destruction, the three low-flying planes seemed unobtrusive, all but harmless. Not only were they few, but they did not bristle with guns like the other B-29s. Among them they carried only one bomb. Aboard the three planes there was little to suggest the historic character of the mission. *The Great Artiste*, so named for its commander's reputed prowess in love, carried a cargo of scientific instruments. A second ship, called simply *Number 91*, was full of photographic equipment. The third craft, named *Enola Gay* after its pilot's mother, carried the bomb. Until recently only the lead pilot, Lt. Col. Paul W. Tibbets Jr., had known the character of this strange object they were soon to drop on Japan.

Tibbets was the commander of the 509th Composite Bomb Group, the first military unit ever trained in atomic warfare. He was a slender man with dark hair and heavy eyebrows. Despite his youthful, almost boyish appearance, he was a seasoned airman, the veteran of many B-17 bombing runs over Germany and Africa. He had trained his group with all the rigorous efficiency demanded of his unique mission. And he had guarded well the secret of the bomb. Through months of training with dummy prototypes, the crews had known their cargo simply as the "gimmick." The realization that they were to drop a weapon of enormous power had come slowly: it was implied first in the secrecy of their training and more fully revealed at a preflight briefing on Tinian. They now knew that the bomb had the potency of twenty thousand tons of TNT.

But even at takeoff several crewmembers had not been shown the last piece of the puzzle, the actual source of the bomb's power. In the first hour of the flight, Tibbets briefed the remaining men, scattered in various parts of the long, heavy aircraft. He sent William S. Parsons, his naval ordinance officer and a bomb expert, forward to explain the cargo to two men there, while he worked his way back through a narrow passage to the tail where the gunner, George Caron, sat in an isolated perch staring out at the darkness from under the visor of a Brooklyn Dodgers baseball cap. The gunner, who Tibbets described as a "pretty sharp type," was not surprised when he learned that the "gimmick" was an atomic bomb. He had heard people speculate about atomic-powered ships before the war, and he had guessed that the new bomb must have something to do with "splitting the atom." In the forward compartment the men who listened to Parsons were less communicative; they just raised their eyebrows in mute surprise.

After talking to Caron, Tibbets attempted to take a short nap. Expecting immediate orders to begin their mission, he and his men had been on edge for three or four days. He had not slept for twenty-four hours. Now he would try.

Parsons must have been tired, too, but he had a job to complete that banished all thought of sleep. The *Enola Gay* had taken off with an "unarmed" atomic bomb; the parts were all there, but some final adjustments had to be made before the bomb could be exploded. Ideally, the bomb would have been fully armed before the flight, but in the early days of August several B-29s had crashed during takeoff from Tinian. An accident with an atomic bomb would have destroyed half the island. Despite their fear that tools or parts might be left behind, the project commander, Gen. Thomas Farrell, had decided to let Parsons, an older man and much respected as a bomb expert, arm the bomb while in flight. Parsons had practiced for hours on the ground the day before and was ready to prepare the bomb for its final plunge over Japan.

He lowered himself slowly into the bomb bay and was followed by Lt. Morris Jeppson, another weapons expert. They stood in the narrow, pleasantly cool enclosure and began their work. The bomb had an unusual, almost makeshift form, as if it had been built as a high school shop project. Squat and diminutive, it gave no outward sign of the huge destructive power within. It measured ten feet from its blunt nose to its square tail and was twenty-eight inches in diameter. On its polished sides the ground crew had written messages cursing the Japanese and commemorating comrades lost at sea: "To Hell with the Emperor" and "This is for the boys on the *Indianapolis*."

Millions of hours of work had gone into devising the intricate mechanism of the bomb. The underlying physical principles had been anticipated almost a half century before, when Pierre and Marie Curie had argued that the atom, which had formerly been considered indivisible, could be broken. In 1905 Albert Einstein announced his famous formula, $E = mc^2$, which indicated that enormous energy lay in every particle of matter. Thereafter scientists throughout the world attempted to devise means to release and harness the energy of the atom. Some of the most famous of these—including Niels Bohr, Enrico Fermi, and Einstein—were Europeans who fled to the United States to escape Hitler or Mussolini.

At the beginning of World War II many of the best nuclear physicists in the world lived in the United States. On August 2, 1939, Einstein, the most famous of these exiles, wrote President Franklin D. Roosevelt that atomic research could lead to the creation of "extremely powerful bombs of a new type" and warned him that scientists in Germany were already seeking to develop an atomic bomb. The United States, then, was drawn into the nuclear race by the fear of atomic power in other hands as well as by the lure of possessing the "ultimate weapon" itself.

When America entered World War II in 1941, President Roosevelt established a scientific advisory committee, including Secretary of War Henry L. Stimson and Harvard president James B. Conant, to begin considering development of an atomic bomb. This group in turn established a committee of scientists, including Enrico Fermi and J. Robert Oppenheimer. In 1942 the "Manhattan Project" was organized, and work began on an atomic bomb. At its peak, the project employed 125,000 workers scattered among three top-secret plants: in Oak Ridge, Tennessee; Hanford, Washington; and Los Alamos, New Mexico. Most of the employees did not know what they were working on. The project's $2 billion budget was raised secretly without congressional authorization.

On December 2, 1942, a controlled chain reaction was produced at the University of Chicago, establishing an early milestone for the project, but it was not until two and a half years later that the first atomic bomb was ready for testing. The site chosen was an airbase at Alamogordo, New Mexico, a remote place of desert and mountains 120 miles from Albuquerque. In mid-July 1945 scientists and military men from around the United States gathered at Alamogordo. Among them were James B. Conant; Gen. Leslie R. Groves, director of the Manhattan Project; J. Robert Oppenheimer, the scientist most responsible for the bomb's creation; and U.S. Army Air Corps Col. Paul Tibbets.

At Alamogordo they assembled at an old ranch house near a 120-foot-high steel tower at a remote corner of the base. The bomb was to be exploded atop the tower. In the early hours of July 16 they waited anxiously as torrents of rain and streaks of lightning delayed the firing. As the time for the blast drew near many lay face down with their feet toward the tower. Tibbets flew above in a B-29. No one knew what to expect. Even among the scientists who had developed the bomb, some harbored a fugitive hope that it would not work.

Then at 5:30 A.M., while darkness still hung over the stormy Southwest, the bomb was detonated. The steel tower disappeared, vaporized by the massive explosion. A tremendous flash appeared to Tibbets above the clouds. A brilliant light illuminated the desert and the mountains: "It was golden, purple, violet, gray, and blue. It lighted every peak, crevasse, and ridge of the nearby mountains with a clarity and beauty that cannot be described." Thus Gen. Thomas Farrell described the "searching light." Oppenheimer, stunned, recalled words from the Hindu epic Bhagavad Gita: "If the radiance of a thousand suns were to burst into the sky, that would be the splendor of the Mighty One."

The light was followed by a shock wave, a tremendous sustained roar that knocked down men five miles from the bomb site and reverberated over the desert across thousands of square miles. In El Paso,

Albuquerque, Socorro, and Gallup buildings shook and windows rattled. Above the bomb site a great, multicolored cloud rose eight miles into the air. Beneath, where the tower had stood, was a huge saucer-shaped hole in the hard earth.

Finally, after the light and the shock, after a few seconds that had seemed an eternity, the men jumped to their feet, shook hands, embraced, and shouted. It had worked. Their achievement was staggering: never before had men harnessed energy with such dramatic results. And yet, even in this time of scientific triumph, there were feelings also of shock and dismay. Farrell felt that "we puny things were blasphemous to dare tamper with the forces heretofore reserved to the Almighty." And Oppenheimer recalled a second line from the Bhagavad Gita: "I am become death, the shatterer of worlds."

All this had happened only three weeks before. Now the "shatterer of worlds" would soon explode over people and houses instead of desert and cactus. The weapon sat snugly in the bomb bay while Parsons and Jeppson continued their work. They had plenty of time and moved carefully. First Jeppson removed the safety plugs and replaced them with arming plugs. (Even while doing this task, he thought of the importance of the mission and pocketed the safety plugs as souvenirs.) Then he and Parsons ran wires from the bomb to the electric monitoring equipment at the front of the plane. They finished the job within half an hour. Parsons later recalled that his hands were dirty, "as if I had changed the carburetor and distributor of my car." The two men then climbed to the forward compartment and settled down to watch the instruments. They were quiet, each thinking his own thoughts. Tibbets had been unable to sleep. He came forward to relieve his copilot, Maj. Robert A. Lewis, who was watching the plane's automatic pilot. The plane rumbled on toward the north through intermittent clouds and starlight. She rocked gently over patches of turbulent air and passed through light showers. Occasionally the sky was clear and the men could watch the moonlight on the sea.

It was fifteen hundred miles from Tinian to Hiroshima. The flight would take six and a half hours, and now there was nothing to do but wait. It should be a safe mission; the planes would be too high for enemy fighter planes or antiaircraft fire to reach them. But always on bombing runs there was fear. The three planes had only six fifty-caliber guns among them, and they would go over Japan without a fighter escort. Then, too, there was the bomb itself, a curious device. Some of the men wondered uneasily whether the bumping of the aircraft would cause it to explode prematurely. Along with such thoughts for their own well-being, some of the men thought about the enemy. Aboard the *Great Artiste*, radio operator Abe Spitzer wondered vaguely what it would be like to be a Japanese pilot carrying an atomic bomb toward San Francisco.

In these ways the uniqueness of the mission impressed itself on the men. But for the most part they occupied themselves as hundreds of other crews had done on the long bombing runs over Japan. Maj. Theodore J. Van Kirk, the navigator, had flown with Tibbets in Europe and attended to his job with routine efficiency. He did not appear to Tibbets to be particularly worried about the cargo: "He was a navigator: 'Where do you want to go, and when do you want to get there?'" The nineteen-year-old radio operator, Pfc. Richard Nelson, read a book about boxing. Lt. Jacob Beser, the radar countermeasures operator, was apprehensive about the mission but was reassured by Parsons, who seemed to "exude confidence." He lay on the floor and soon fell asleep, providing entertainment for some of the other men who rolled oranges and tried to hit him on the head. In the forward compartment the men watched in the dark as St. Elmo's fire, an eerie blue light common in the South Pacific, seemed to envelop the plane's four engines and clear plastic nose shield.

Despite the prosaic quality of these hours—Tibbets called it "the dullest trip anyone ever took"—the mission itself was the culmination of thousands of hours of preparation. In fact, the 509th Composite Bomb Group had been put together with the same care that had gone into fashioning its deadly cargo. In mid-1943 the Manhattan Project had reached the stage where it was necessary to contemplate the means of bomb delivery. The Allies had no sophisticated missiles comparable to the German V-1 and V-2 rockets, and at one time it was thought that the bomb would be so large that it would have to be taken into enemy harbors on shipboard. By 1943, however, it was apparent that the bomb could be carried by a plane.

After a period of preliminary planning, Col. Paul Tibbets was appointed in early fall 1944 to organize a new bomb group, the 509th, drawing men from other groups. He was assigned to an isolated base in a parched, treeless desert near the small town of Wendover, Utah. He assembled fifteen hundred men—mechanics and engineers as well as pilots and crews.

There were really two jobs to attend to at Wendover: creating a bomb capable of containing a nuclear armament and developing flight techniques to deliver the bomb. The metal shell, the nuclear cargo, the B-29, and the flight crews had to be adjusted to one another. The B-29s were modified to carry one large bomb, and test bombs were dropped so that they could be modified for accuracy. At first the stabilizing fins on the bombs were so weak they collapsed under the stress as the four- and five-ton bombs hurtled downward. The fins were rebuilt. Then there was the problem of adjusting the fuses. One of the lightly armed bombs exploded just after being dropped; had it been an atomic bomb, it would have demolished the plane. Finally, there was flight training. The crews practiced dropping bombs until they could come within nine hundred feet of a target from a height of six miles. After each drop they made a sharp, jarring turn, followed by an accelerated dive that took their craft far away from the falling missile.

During the months of training, emissaries traveled between Wendover, Oak Ridge, Los Alamos, and Hanford. Every activity was cloaked in unprecedented secrecy. The workers at Los Alamos did not know about Wendover, and those at Wendover did not know about Los Alamos. They called back and forth over a coded phone system to mysterious colleagues working at Y and K. Most of the men in the 509th Bomb Group did not know they were being trained to drop atomic bombs. Moreover, they were warned to say nothing about their work, and they were watched by security agents. The phones out of the base were tapped. Sometimes government spies were sent aboard buses and trains to lure airmen on leave into talking. Those who failed these security tests were removed from the group.

This thick blanket of secrecy continued to shroud the 509th as the time came to transfer the operation to Tinian. The ground crew traveled in isolated cars on troop trains and ate only after all other soldiers were cleared out of the dining cars. They traveled across the Pacific in a special naval transport and were isolated in a dock warehouse during a stop in Hawaii. The movement of the planes was equally secret. Once the planes and crews reached Tinian, the bomb parts were transported covertly. After the Alamogordo explosion several transport planes flew nearly empty to Tinian carrying nothing but one or two couriers with parcels containing bomb mechanisms in their laps. The cruiser *Indianapolis* was called up to transport the bomb casings in closely guarded wood cartons on a fast voyage from San Francisco.

On Tinian all the pieces were put together. It was an unlikely place for such an enterprise. Recently captured from the Japanese, the island measured a bare five by twelve miles. But it was now home base for more than five hundred B-29s that daily rumbled three abreast down its long runways to climb over its coral shores toward Japan. Thirty-five thousand men and a thousand nurses were stationed on Tinian.

The 509th Bomb Group settled uneasily into an isolated special compound along with a group of scientists. Their separation annoyed the other airmen, who sarcastically called them the "Glory Boys" and pelted their barracks with rocks when they left on missions in the middle of the night. One of their rivals wrote them a poem:

In the air the Secret rose,
Where they're going nobody knows.

The men of the 509th had little time to worry about such teasing. They flew several practice missions over the Pacific and continued their training with dummy bombs. Meanwhile, the scientists and engineers worked on completing the real bombs. The commanding air corps officer, Gen. Curtis LeMay, had received orders to send out the first bomb as soon as the weather cleared over Japan. On August 5 LeMay learned that the weather over the target areas would be clear on the following day. The first bomb was moved from a shed into a concrete pit; the *Enola Gay* backed carefully over it; and hydraulic lifts raised the bomb into her metallic belly. Guards stood by the plane as Parsons worked inside, learning to arm the bomb in the crowded bay.

That night the crews had gathered under the curved roof of a metal Quonset hut. They sat on wood benches while Tibbets, dressed in khaki shorts and an open-necked shirt, spoke quietly about the mission. For the men it was a familiar scene; they had met here several times on previous days while Tibbets, pipe in hand, had discussed the mission—told them how important it was, how it would shorten the war by six months, how proud he was to be associated with them. In this room they had seen slides of the Alamogordo explosion and had been told that President Truman would release the news about their mission. Now there was little more to say. Tibbets simply told them that the mission would begin shortly and discussed the weather reports and provisions for rescue of downed aircraft. Chaplain William Downer closed the meeting with a prayer, a formality usually, now a solemn occasion. "We pray Thee that the end of the war may come soon," he said, "and that once more we may know peace on earth. May the men who fly this night be kept safe in Thy care, and may they be returned safely to us."

Following the days of anxious expectation, an atmosphere of calm deliberation had come over the group. In the last hours before the flight men ate sandwiches, drank coffee, and talked about how long the war would last and what they would do afterward. Radio operator Abe Spitzer noticed the serious tone of the conversations; there was no joking about women, the staple topic of the airmen's discourse, only these contemplative exchanges.

After midnight the men assembled by the planes. The *Enola Gay* was surrounded with floodlights and guards; the scene reminded some of the crewmen of a Hollywood set. They posed for photographs and waited for the order to depart. At 1:37 A.M. three weather planes lifted off to scout the targets. At 2:45 A.M. the *Enola Gay* was on the runway; her engines labored as the huge sixty-five-ton plane gained speed. Then came an anxious moment. She accelerated to 180 miles per hour, but was still on the ground with the sea rushing nearer. She was "gobbling up too much runway," copilot Lewis shouted. At the end of the runway the plane finally left the ground. In the control tower the observers sighed heavily.

After the brief drama of the takeoff the flight assumed the routine character that allowed men to work, sleep, play, and think almost as they would on an ordinary mission. Caron might remind himself that this was "the one we had come over for," but the very fact of the months of training gave the early morning routine its almost commonplace quality.

They were approaching the halfway point in their flight. Tiny streaks of light crept up beneath the clouds, then swiftly a curtain of light spread blue and purple across the sky, and it was day.

Ahead lay Iwo Jima, halfway to Japan, where the three planes would rendezvous and fly in close formation the rest of the way to the target. The *Enola Gay* began to circle above the tiny Pacific island. Iwo Jima looked peaceful in the early morning light, but just recently it had been a place of unspeakable horror. It was already a legend in American military history and an essential link, strategically and psychologically, in the chain of events that brought the atomic bomb to Japan. In a sense, the dusty island lying below the planes symbolized the history of mutual aggression that had led to the day's mission.

At the beginning of the war Iwo Jima had been of little strategic importance to Japan. In 1941 the perimeters of Japan's vast empire stretched well beyond this island through Korea, China, Indochina, Indonesia, Borneo, and the Solomon and Gilbert Islands. Japan was on the offensive throughout the Pacific and could launch the surprise attack on Pearl Harbor that all but obliterated the American Pacific Fleet and killed 2,300 seamen. At first it had been an easy matter to overwhelm the Americans and to occupy the Philippines and the outer Aleutians.

Within two years, however, the Americans had beaten the Japanese navy and recaptured lost territory. In 1944 they took the Mariana Islands, including Guam and Tinian. The fall of the Marianas placed American bombers within range of Japan and changed the status of Iwo Jima. Suddenly the island, at the middle of the bombing route, assumed enormous strategic importance. In Japanese hands it served as an observation point for warning the homeland of impending raids and as a base for fighters to harass the B-29s. In American hands it could serve as a fighter base and emergency landing field.

Twenty thousand of Japan's best troops were assigned to Iwo Jima. They honeycombed the island with bunkers protected by thick concrete walls and connected by miles of tunnels. From these positions machine guns and artillery could fire upon every part of the island. In an attempt to counteract these preparations the Americans dropped 6,800 tons of bombs and 22,000 shells on the dusty island. On February 19, 1945, following seventy-four consecutive days of bombardment, the U.S. Marines landed. Stumbling ankle deep through volcanic ash, they were hit by withering fire from hidden Japanese positions. In the first two days the marines, clinging to the beaches, lost 3,650 men killed and wounded. Battle-hardened war reporters were appalled at the carnage: they saw arms and legs blown far from their bodies, men cut in half by flying steel, faces and bodies mangled by machine-gun fire.

On Iwo Jima the marines suffered their worst casualties in the history of the corps. They fought their way across the island yard by yard, attacking the pillboxes with rifles, bazookas, flamethrowers, and bayonets. Although the Japanese were overwhelmed, they fought bravely for every inch of ground. In the end, more than 20,000 of them gave their lives, and only 218 were captured. The marines suffered 20,000 casualties, including 6,821 killed. In less than a month 40,000 men had been incinerated by flamethrowers; blown apart by explosives; or cut by bullet, knife, and bayonet. Five men died for every acre of land on this desolate island.

In such places as Iwo Jima the Japanese showed themselves as tenacious in defeat as they had been forceful in victory. Each battle cost thousands of lives. On Okinawa, for example, where the two nations fought from April through June 1945, the Japanese lost 110,000 killed and 9,000 captured; the Americans lost more than 10,000 killed.

Such statistics testified to the Japanese resolve to die rather than surrender. The kamikazes gave further proof of Japanese persistence. In the final months of the war thousands of Japanese pilots agreed to become living bombs, flying heavily armed planes directly into American targets. During the fight for Iwo Jima the kamikazes fell upon the *Bismarck Sea* and the *Saratoga*, two light carriers, blasting huge holes in the first and sinking the second. In other battles the "Divine Wind" sank 29 ships, damaged 307, and killed almost 5,000 American seamen.

When Americans thought about ending the war with Japan, they thought about kamikazes and places like Iwo Jima. There were two million imperial troops in Japan, all of whom might fight as doggedly as their compatriots. Certainly the Japanese would lose, but at what cost to themselves and to their conquerors? Estimates of American losses in an invasion ranged up to half a million. Inevitably, any alternative to an invasion was attractive, and the long and bloody years of war had schooled the world in a brutal logic of violence, which encouraged the choice of harsh alternatives. In Hammurabi's Code it had been written that there must be "an eye for an eye." This code was rewritten many times during the war. The Russians had sworn that they would take "two eyes for an eye" in revenge for German depredations. In a less vengeful but equally stern spirit, Allied strategists, contemplating the bombing of German cities, had concluded that one eye now, even a civilian eye, could save two later. In 1939 such callous reasoning had been rare. But a new philosophy of warfare had grown with experience. Across the globe hundreds of thousands of planes, ships, buildings, and houses had been destroyed. For six years men, women, and children had been killed by gun, bomb, knife, and gas. In all, some twenty million people had died. Gross violence had become the accepted path to victory—and ultimately, to peace and the cessation of violence.

In this atmosphere it had been easy to justify saturation bombing of German towns at the end of the war. The culmination was a massive raid on the refugee-swollen town of Dresden on the night of February 13–14, 1945. Eight hundred planes had leveled the town and inflicted between

250,000 and 400,000 casualties. Brutal? Yes, but the bombing had hastened the end of mutual brutality. So it was reasoned.

This cruel logic did as much as any scientist, engineer, pilot, or politician to hasten the *Enola Gay* toward Hiroshima on the morning of August 6. It had nourished the technology that built Japanese warships, German missiles, English planes, and American bombs. And it justified the use of each new instrument of destruction. Once the atomic bomb was available, it was a foregone conclusion that it would be dropped. Germany escaped because it surrendered before the bomb was ready, but Japan was less fortunate.

The final decision to use the nuclear weapon had been made in late July by President Harry S. Truman. It was ironic that the responsibility was his, because he had learned about the new weapon only after his first cabinet meeting in April 1945, when Secretary of War Stimson called him aside to tell him about the Manhattan Project. Truman was at the Potsdam Conference when he learned about the Alamogordo explosion. Jubilant with the confidence that the new bomb would force Japan to surrender without an invasion, he issued a statement calling for immediate unconditional surrender, threatening Japan with "prompt and utter destruction" if resistance continued. The Japanese government sent no reply but announced to their people on July 28 that the Potsdam Declaration was "unworthy of public notice."

Hearing of Japan's reaction, Truman called for use of the bomb as soon as possible. Most of his staff were enthusiastic about the decision, but a few advisers had objected. A group of scientists, including Albert Einstein, warned Truman that use of the weapon against Japan would increase the possibility of future atomic warfare. A naval adviser suggested a blockade. A few men proposed demonstrating the bomb to the Japanese as an alternative to destroying a city. But after six years of total war, none of the alternatives was persuasive. The weapon that would kill and wound several hundred thousand Japanese could be seen as a blessing, a means to end the war and save lives. In this belief Truman had given the order to drop the bomb.

Now as the three B-29s made their rendezvous above Iwo Jima, all the threads of atomic policy—the research, the flight training, the history of mutual violence, the strategic planning—came together in a fabric of cold resolve. The *Enola Gay* carried the instrument of that resolve, rumbling toward its culmination in a moment of unimaginable horror.

After circling three times abovse Iwo Jima the *Enola Gay* joined the other planes and climbed to ten thousand feet. Navigator Van Kirk gave instructions to Tibbets for speed and altitude as the men ate a simple breakfast. Later they put on flak suits and checked the arc welder's goggles that would protect them from the atomic glare.

The men now showed signs of anxiety. In the tail section George Caron smoked cigarette after cigarette. He found that he was sweating from the waist up and freezing from the waist down. He fumbled nervously with a chain of rosary beads given him by his mother.

On the *Great Artiste* radio operator Abe Spitzer waited anxiously for the weather report from the targets. At 7:00 A.M. the three reconnaissance planes were supposed to send information on visibility over Hiroshima, Kokura, and Nagasaki. The planes were in range of all three targets, fast approaching the Japanese coast, but no message had arrived. Spitzer hunched over as chills ran through his body. At 7:10 A.M. there was still no word. Had he missed the signals? Was his radio broken?

Then at 7:20 A.M., when the planes were fifty miles from Japan, the first message arrived. Spitzer grabbed for a pencil but could not hold it in his shaking hand. It fell to the floor. He clutched another and wrote down the Hiroshima report: the target was clear. Soon similar reports followed from Kokura and Nagasaki. Weather conditions were good over all three cities. But Hiroshima was the primary target, and toward Hiroshima the *Enola Gay* now headed.

The planes climbed slowly to thirty thousand feet. Through the haze they could make out the coastline. They were flying over clouds at first, but fifty miles from the city they could see a large, clear space over Hiroshima. Tibbets conferred with Parsons. "Do you agree that's the target?" he asked. Parsons nodded yes. As they drew closer to Hiroshima, *Number 91* fell back to take pictures. The *Great Artiste*, preparing to drop its cargo of instruments, stayed alongside the *Enola Gay*. Twenty miles from the target bombardier Thomas W. Ferebee fixed the doomed city in his bombsight.

Hiroshima stood out ahead in the sunlight: a triangle of buildings and houses, occupying six islets in the delta of the Ota River, nestled between green hills and the blue, island-studded waters of Inland Sea. At that moment in the city 245,000 men, women, and children were beginning their day.

Until recently Hiroshima had been an important point of embarkation for hundreds of thousands of imperial troops headed overseas. They had filled the town with a festive atmosphere and a sense of inevitable victory. Now, however, that atmosphere was changed. The town's war industries and the presence of the Second Army headquarters were reminders of war. But there were no more troop ships. The Americans had brought local shipping to a halt by mining the approaches to Hiroshima. All around were signs that Japan was losing the war. Bread was rationed. Coffee and good whiskey were unobtainable. Every day B-29s flew overhead.

With the remarkable buoyancy of youth the children of Hiroshima were proud of their ability to identify the hostile aircraft by sight and sound. They who had once thrilled at the parades of soldiers were now excited by the daily passage overhead of B-29s, calling them "B-san" or "Mr. B."

Thus far Hiroshima, alone of Japan's major cities, had been spared a major bombing. Five months before, on the night of March 9–10, hundreds of B-29s had swooped over Tokyo with incendiary bombs, burning sixteen square miles of the city, killing 97,000 people, and leaving more than one million homeless. Other raids had crippled most of Hiroshima's neighbors. But the city had been miraculously preserved. Fantastic rumors abounded to explain this good fortune: President Truman's mother lived nearby; the Americans liked the city and wanted to visit it after the war; and more accurately, the city had been spared for some special punishment. The Americans themselves had encouraged the latter view by dropping 720,000 leaflets on Hiroshima telling the people that their city and others would be destroyed if Japan did not surrender.

But despite such warnings, in Hiroshima it was difficult to maintain a sense of danger. Even the air-raid warnings had become routine. On August 7 when local radar stations picked up a single B-29 approaching the city the subsequent alert was lightly regarded by the citizens. They rightly assumed that the craft, the weather plane that preceded the *Enola Gay*, was an observation plane. When the all clear sounded at eight o'clock, most people were already at work or school.

Some busied themselves on the city's defenses. Soldiers dug hillside shelters and talked of resisting the invader "life for life." Others worked at dismantling wood-framed, tile-roofed houses to clear fire lanes in case of incendiary attack. But even in the midst of such war-related activities an atmosphere of civilian tranquility hung over the city in moments that years later would seem eternally present to the survivors of Hiroshima.

On the morning of August 7 Dr. Michihiko Hachiya is relaxing at home after a sleepless night on duty at the Communications Hospital. He lies exhausted on his living room floor, clad in his undershorts. The morning is "still, warm, and beautiful" as he gazes contentedly through open doors at sunlight, "shimmering leaves," and shadows in his garden.

A few miles away Father John A. Siemes, S.J., is at work in his room at the Novitiate of the Society of Jesus. Throughout the war he and his colleagues have done missionary work first in Tokyo and then, with the bombing of that city, in Hiroshima. A sensitive man and a professor of modern philosophy, he enjoys the new location on a hillside above Hiroshima. From his window he can look down a broad valley to the edge of the city. He is pleased with the "bright, clear summer morning."

In the center of Hiroshima the eighth-grade students of the girls' school are preparing to help a demolition squad clear a fire lane. They meet in the school yard at 7:30 A.M., and happy in their mutual friendship, the novelty of their work, and the glorious weather, they walk to the worksite singing a cheerful song, "Blossoms and Buds of the Young Cherry Tree." Naoku Masuoka puts down her first-aid kit, which she always carries with her, and goes to work with her friend, Setsuko Sakamoto. The girls and their teacher begin to pass roof tiles from one to another, singing in unison as they work.

A few miles away from this activity the men on the *Enola Gay*, beginning their deadly approach, see a different Hiroshima. Six miles above the ground, traveling at better than three hundred miles an hour, they are unaware of Dr. Michihiko Hachiya and Father John Siemes and the students of the girls' school. Their delicate machinery allows them only to see a target, a large cluster of buildings and houses fixed at the center of a Norden bombsight.

Bombardier Ferebee is seated in front of Tibbets and Lewis, looking intently at Hiroshima. As the target comes nearer, Tibbets orders the crewmen to fix their goggles on their foreheads, ready for use. With ninety seconds till the drop, Ferebee takes control of the aircraft, and radio operator Richard Nelson sends a signal to the *Great Artiste*, a thousand yards to the rear, to coordinate the instrument drop. Ferebee sees the aiming point, the Aioi Bridge, and sends a warning signal through the plane. An automatic device takes control, gauging the release. The bomb bay doors swing open. There is a pause, then the plane jerks suddenly upward as the nine-thousand-pound missile tumbles away. Seeing it fall, Ferebee shouts, "It's clear!"

Tibbets wrenches the *Enola Gay* into a sharp turn to the left, and the plane screams through the sky away from the bomb. "Make sure those goggles are on," he shouts. Ferebee can still make out the bomb as it hurtles downward. Higher up, the three instrument packages drift under their parachutes. The men wait anxiously, knowing the missile will fall free for exactly forty-three seconds.

The bomb rushes down with the sound of a freight train. Then, two thousand feet over Hiroshima, a gun fires inside its metallic shell forcing a small mass of fissionable material through a metal tube into a second mass. The two collide, and in less than a millionth of a second the atoms fly apart, vaporizing the four-ton bomb casing, issuing forth in a huge fireball, a blast of heat, and a thunderous concussion.

Aboard the *Enola Gay* several miles away a blinding purple light searches the interior of the plane and creeps up beneath the men's goggles. A shock wave shakes the plane, followed by another, then another. Caron can see the waves spreading through the air like ripples through water. At first Ferebee and Tibbets think enemy flak is exploding around them.

As the men look back, they see a gigantic multicolored cloud of smoke erupting upward. At the center is a huge ball of red flame; it looks as if the sun has been knocked out of the sky and is now rising again from the earth. Ferebee thinks he sees parts of buildings hurtling upward. A bubbling mass of flame spreads like lava over the city and into the hills. Overhead the cloud rushes upward mile after mile into the sky.

"My God!" says Lewis.

Hiroshima is hidden in a cloud of dust and flame. But on the ground the blast is registered clearly on buildings, trees, and flesh. A wave of radiant heat, traveling at the speed of light, burns granite blocks, melts hard roof tiles, and incinerates grass, trees, and houses. A shock wave follows, traveling at the speed of sound, knocking down everything in its way, collapsing buildings, tossing cars and trains through the air. Then dozens of fires started by the wave of heat or kindled by charcoal from overturned cooking stoves spread through the ruins.

More than two hundred thousand people are in the middle of this inferno. Near the center thousands are burned to cinders instantly. Some leave their shadows seared onto walls and roadways as their bodies vanish without a trace. Farther from the blast some are horribly burned by the wave of heat; others, indoors at the time of the explosion, are tossed about in their houses in a tangle of flying wood and glass. Some are pinned under beams; others are cut and bruised.

Even after the great heat and the deadening blast many are still alive. In the tortured quiet that follows the explosion, they look at themselves and one another with bewilderment. A man sees red strips of burned flesh hanging from his arm. A woman struggles to free herself from under a fallen roofbeam. A child stumbles through a ruined house looking for her parents. Everywhere people stare at one another with horror. They see scorched, mangled faces; blood flowing from gaping wounds; naked bodies with odd burn patterns; people stumbling through the streets that are no longer streets, throwing themselves into the river seeking to quench the thirst that will not be quenched, to stop the pain that will not be stopped, moaning, vomiting, dying.

In such ways tens of thousands of people die quickly. But others struggle to live. In the Jesuit mission house, Father John Siemes seeks to escape from his room. He is conscious of having seen a "garish light" in the valley toward Hiroshima. The blast that followed shattered his window, cutting his face and hands. Now he pounds on his jammed door until it opens and he stumbles into the hall, finding it cluttered with broken glass and fallen books. Most of his colleagues have been cut, but none badly. They go outside and see that the explosion has blasted away all the doors and windows on the southeast side of the house and severely damaged the chapel.

Some minutes later they see people surging up the valley from Hiroshima, instinctively fleeing the devastation behind them. Some come to the house seeking first aid. The priests apply fat on their burns but soon run out. They use bandages and drugs for the more seriously wounded and run out of these, too. By noon the chapel and library are filled with the wounded, but still they come.

A few miles away Dr. Michihiko Hachiya is closer to the blast and is more seriously injured than the Jesuit priests. As he gazes at the garden, he sees a flash of light. Then the garden disappears in a cloud of dust and he is vaguely aware of a wood support column "leaning crazily" at the corner of the house. Picking his way over fallen rubble into the garden, he feels weak, sees that he is naked, and finds slivers of wood and glass in his body.

Suddenly he remembers his wife. "Yaeko-san," he calls, "where are you?" She emerges from the ruined house, clothes torn and bloodstained.

"Let's get out of here as fast as we can!" he says.

As they walk away, their house sways and collapses. The wind grows vicious and fires begin to spread. Disturbed by his nakedness, Dr. Hachiya wraps his wife's apron around his loins. They move past a dead man, crushed by a falling wall; people with burned arms held out to their sides like scarecrows; a naked woman with her child. A wound in the doctor's thigh begins to spurt blood; he stops it with his hand, feeling faint and thirsty, but struggles on to his hospital. Friends greet him with alarm, place him on a stretcher, and begin to treat his wounds. He recognizes many of the other patients crowded into rooms and halls. It seems that the whole city is there.

At the clearance project the students from the girls' school have been badly burned by the blast. Some are already dead. The rest look with horror upon each other, faces scorched beyond recognition, clothes torn to rags. Their teacher, her hair turned white, holds her students close to her "like a mother hen protecting her chicks." The bewildered girls, "like baby chicks paralyzed with terror," thrust their heads under her arms.

Setsuko Sakamoto attempts to stay near her teacher. Her friend, Naoku Masuoka, searches for her family. Her hands are burned black; a yellow liquid drops "like sweat" from the broken skin. She feels lonely and afraid. "Why must I suffer?" she asks herself. "I don't want to die." As she wanders through the broken city, she sees someone pinned under a concrete wall, calling for help. Everyone hurries past. She sees a woman covered with burns writhing in agony and a bloody horse tied to a telephone pole, plunging wildly.

Fortunately, Naoku is picked up by a rescue squad and taken to a hospital. Lying on a blanket over a straw mat, she longs to see her family. Nearby another child dies after calling for her mother. Naoku is forlorn. Perhaps she will never see her parents again. In this moment of despair she hears her father calling her name. Tears come to her eyes, and when he appears, her "strong father" is crying, too. He can hardly speak as he cradles his badly wounded but still living daughter. Holding her to him, he repeats again and again, "I'm so glad, I'm so glad."

A few miles away, in another world, the men of the *Enola Gay* have little conception of what they have done. They saw smoke but not burned flesh, flames but not families, movement but not pain. They were separated from their victims by the mind-numbing toxins of war.

Accordingly, their act was brave and useful. Like the millions of other men of every nationality who had killed in the past decade of war, the men of the *Enola Gay* lived in a world in which good men could cause horrible suffering in pursuit of patriotic goals.

After the explosion the men experienced three sensations. First there was elation. The bomb had gone off and destroyed the target; the mission was a success. Then there was relief; they could leave behind the dangers of flak, fighters, and atomic accident. Finally there was awe, an overwhelming recognition of the world-destroying power of the bomb.

The planes circled Hiroshima slowly, attempting to see the city through the clouds of smoke. The men had shouted their amazement at the size of the blast, but now they were silent, subdued by what they had seen. It was difficult to find appropriate words. Finally Tibbets announced to the crews of the three planes, "Well, boys, we've just dropped the first atomic bomb in history." He spoke slowly, seeming to labor over the words.

A few minutes after leaving Hiroshima, Tibbets and Parsons composed a concise report on the mission. It read: "Results clear-cut, successful in all respects. Visible effects greater than in any test. Conditions normal in airplane following delivery." With another six hours of flying ahead, the men ate C-ration sandwiches and drank coffee. Then, exhausted from the day and a half without sleep, they took turns napping. There was some small talk. Tibbets asked tail gunner Caron how he had felt during the sharp dive away from the bomb. Caron answered that it had been "better than the cyclone ride you pay a quarter for at Coney Island."

"Well, I'll collect a quarter from you when we land," said Tibbets.

But there was little of this banter. Aboard the *Great Artiste*, Abe Spitzer, his hands shaky and clammy as he watched the atomic explosion, heard one of his comrades say, "I wonder if maybe we're not monkeying around with things that are none of our business." Albert Denhart, a quiet, solitary Texan who was the *Great Artiste*'s tail gunner, was awestruck by the explosion. "I think I'd just as soon have missed it," he said. "Come to think of it, I won't be mentioning it to my grandchildren." Looking back, Denhart could see the smoke from Hiroshima for mile after mile. It was still visible when the planes had flown 250 miles.

At three o'clock in the afternoon of August 6 the three planes set down on the long runway at Tinian. They were greeted by a throng of high-ranking military personnel. Gen. Carl A. Spaatz, commander of the Strategic Air Forces, presented Tibbets with a Distinguished Service Cross. Tibbets apparently had not been expecting this ceremony; he put his pipe in a sleeve of his coveralls and received his award.

The men were then escorted to the officers' club, given lemonade well laced with bourbon, and questioned about the mission. It was not difficult to describe all that they had seen on the bomb run. Tibbets summarized it in four jaunty words: "Saw city, destroyed same." But the interrogators also asked a more complicated question: How had they felt? Even to the seasoned airmen and the men who had worked on the bomb, there was something disquieting about its power. One of the scientists remarked, "I'm not proud of myself right now." Abe Spitzer had difficulty with the question but replied, "It was hell, absolute hell." He answered the question more fully a few months later in a book. He wrote: "I felt that we were seeing a thing that man should never see, that was too big for the human mind really to understand and, moreover and more important, that even in a war, even in a war in which the enemy in the Pacific had been the most sadistic, most inhuman, most cruel, most hateful enemy in history, we had unleashed a force too great to be understood and properly feared. That we had, in short, learned how to kill too many thousands too quickly."

That night Abe Spitzer drank more heavily than he had ever done in his life. So too did many of his fellow airmen. They had passed through a psychological ordeal the like of which few men ever had to face. Wearied by long hours without sleep, they had flown a strange mission that might easily have resulted in their own deaths, then dropped a bomb whose force was unearthly. There were many ways to see the event. It was a scientific triumph; it was a milestone in warfare; it was the death of thousands of people; it was an omen of future cataclysm; it was a way to shorten the war. In their minds feelings of triumph and tragedy, achievement and destruction, pleasure and regret mingled uneasily.

Abe Spitzer had difficulty sleeping. He kept seeing Hiroshima as he had imagined it a moment before the blast: "the green grass, the tiny trees, the bridges and the houses." Then he would see "that giant multicolored mushroom and that black smoke that had covered the city."

What neither Spitzer nor any of the other men could see then was Hiroshima itself on the first night of its ordeal, an ordeal that made the discomfort of the bomber crews seem insignificant. Four square miles in the center of the city were completely destroyed. Within a half mile of the blast 95 percent of the people had been killed. The survivors huddled in parks and ruined buildings. In a city park hundreds lay in eerie silence under pines, laurels, and maples. Most were horribly injured, but none cried. In one hidden corner of the park a group of soldiers clustered together preserving a grotesque semblance of military order. Their faces were burned, and the fluid from their burned-out eye sockets lay encrusted on their cheeks.

In the Communications Hospital, Dr. Michihiko Hachiya was one of hundreds of patients. There were patients in every corner of the hospital, even in the toilets. Because most of Hiroshima's doctors and nurses had been killed or badly injured in the atomic blast, there were not enough trained personnel to care for the patients. Feces, urine, and vomit accumulated rapidly in beds and on floors.

In spite of all this human suffering, it was an animal that would impress many as the most grotesque symbol of their ordeal. For several days an injured horse—hairless, eyeless, and bloody—wandered through the rubble, bumping into walls and trees, apparently searching for a stable that was no more.

Surely no nation would continue to make war in the face of such a weapon. Such was the expectation of President Truman when he heard the news from Hiroshima. He was eating dinner with the crew aboard the *Augusta* in the mid-Atlantic on his way home from the Potsdam Conference. Jubilant, he told the sailors about the weapon that would end the war. They cheered as he made his way to the officers' mess with the news. "Keep your seats, gentlemen," he said, "I have an announcement to make to you. We have just dropped a bomb on Japan which has more power than 20,000 tons of T.N.T. It was an overwhelming success." He then issued a statement calling the atomic bomb "the greatest achievement of organized science in history."

On Long Island, Secretary of War Stimson released a longer, prepared statement describing the development of the bomb and calling on the Japanese to surrender. The communiqué reported that the atomic bomb derived its power from "a harnessing of the basic power of the universe. The force from which the sun draws its power." It claimed that Japan could have escaped if it had accepted the Potsdam Declaration. "Now," the statement continued, "if they do not accept our terms, they may expect a rain of ruin from the air, the like of which has never been seen on this earth." It was no idle threat.

Despite the awesome power of the bomb, Japan was not ready to surrender. The military chiefs were determined to fight to the end rather than capitulate, and so the official Japanese announcements on the bomb tended to minimize the danger from the weapon, even while characterizing the Americans as "inhuman" and "barbaric" for using it.

Two days after the destruction of Hiroshima the men who had seen the cataclysm and thought the war was over had to prepare for another deadly flight to Japan. This time the crew of the *Great Artiste*, commanded by Maj. Charles W. Sweeney, would drop a new kind of bomb, made of an artificial element, plutonium, rather than uranium derivative U-235, as in the first bomb. Nicknamed "Fat Boy," it was almost eleven feet long and five feet in diameter, somewhat larger and even more powerful than the "Little Boy" that had shattered Hiroshima.

Sweeney's crew was to switch planes and fly another B-29, *Bock's Car*, while the *Great Artiste* followed as an observer. At 3:49 A.M. on August 9 they took off from Tinian and headed north on the familiar pathway of destruction. The mission was plagued with difficulties from the start. The gasoline in one of the tanks aboard *Bock's Car* could not be used, and so her range was reduced. A third plane failed to join the other two at Iwo Jima. The primary target, Kokura, was hidden in clouds when they arrived. The planes circled three times, the pilots hoping for a break in the clouds, but none appeared, and the men were not allowed to bomb through cloud cover; *Bock's Car* flew on to another target. In the incredible fortunes of atomic warfare, Kokura had been saved by bad weather.

The two planes turned toward Nagasaki, a city built on hills overlooking a bay in the East China Sea. As they approached, it was hidden in the clouds, but when they were overhead the city came into view. Bombardier Kermit K. Beahan fixed his sight on a stadium beside the banks of the Urakami River, and at 11:01 A.M. an atomic bomb fell away toward Nagasaki. The plane sped off in the dive away from the holocaust. Again there was a bright light, followed by searing heat, jolting shocks, and the billowing cloud. Again tens of thousands of men, women, and children were killed or mortally wounded, and a city was destroyed.

On *Bock's Car* the men, who were seeing their second atomic blast in three days, were awestruck. This explosion seemed bigger than the last; it probed outward as if to swallow up everything in sight. "I've never seen anything like it," said Sweeney, with labored words, "and I hope I never do again." Ray Gallagher, the assistant flight engineer, was appalled as he looked at the huge fireball. Later he spoke the words that passed through his mind at that moment: "I thought maybe the world had come to an end, and we'd caused it." *Bock's Car* circled the remains of Nagasaki and then, perilously low on gasoline, headed for an emergency landing at Okinawa, where the crew ate and refueled. Flying to Tinian, they arrived home to a heroes' welcome. Most of the men were too exhausted to care.

In Tokyo it was evident to most that the end was near. Russia had declared war on Japan on the same day that the United States bombed Nagasaki. Reluctantly, the emperor instructed his cabinet to sue for peace. On August 14 Japan accepted an arrangement that would retain the emperor but place him under Allied rule. In an unprecedented action the emperor went on radio and announced that Japan had surrendered.

Eight days after the bombing of Hiroshima the war ended. For many of the citizens of Hiroshima and Nagasaki the ordeal of atomic warfare had just begun. The initial impact of the bombs had been like that of conventional bombs, killing and maiming by heat and blast. But a few days later effects of a new sort appeared. Radiation from the explosions caused hair to fall out and wounds to resist treatment. People became acutely sensitive to infection and died quickly or lingered on in a strangely weakened condition. Children were born with birth defects. Such injuries would persist for years, even for decades.

A war characterized by terror had ended in horror of a new kind. Soon the questions would arise: Had it been necessary? Was there no effective alternative to the use of the atomic bomb? Although the logic of violence was widely accepted in 1945, it would seem less understandable later to a world at peace. But it is impossible to separate Hiroshima and Nagasaki from the worldwide fabric of warfare that nourished the bomb's development and use. The ultimate tragedy of the atomic bomb was not that it was a careless aberration but that it was a "necessary" act according to the logic of that time. It was as necessary as Pearl Harbor or the German invasion of Russia or the D-Day landing in France. Total war justified surprise attacks on merchant vessels, torture of prisoners, and the bombing of civilian targets. It provided a rationale for unspeakable suffering and enabled men to kill seventy thousand people in a day's work. But the destruction was no less grotesque for being "necessary."

If, however, war blinded one person to another's suffering, it also created curious and unanticipated sympathies. In the chaotic crucible of atomic warfare there was sometimes a peculiar mingling of sensibilities by which the victim comprehended the oppressor and the oppressor sympathized with the victim. Among the Japanese at Hiroshima and Nagasaki, many regarded the bombing as a predictable act of war; some citizens even reflected that they were being punished for Pearl Harbor.

And among the crews of the atomic bombers there were those who recognized that the logic of warfare makes everyone a potential victim. This perception entered a troublesome dream that haunted Abe Spitzer soon after the two atomic blasts. In the dream he found himself in a briefing room with his fellow officers. The commander was a man whose shoulders were covered with honorific silver laurels. But he was a disquieting figure. Where his face should have been there were no eyes, ears, nose, or mouth—just blank space. All the other men in the room were also faceless except his fellow crewmen. The briefing officer showed slides of the target, a modern port city with skyscrapers. He explained that the new bomb would be "much more destructive" than the previous two and would drop at 12:01 P.M. when people would be going out to lunch. All the faceless men laughed.

In the dream Spitzer's throat was dry and he was nearly paralyzed with apprehension. The city with its modern buildings and docks was disturbingly familiar. He waved his hand frantically and finally caught the commander's attention.

"Where's the target?" he asked.

The man with no face replied smugly, "The target is the Bronx, New York."

This was Spitzer's home. He protested wildly.

"That's an order, Sergeant," he was told. Then he awoke.

The radio operator had been dreaming. But there was a bizarre rationality in his vision. The men of the 509th Bomb Group were at one and the same time brave and resourceful airmen and fearsome agents of destruction. They would, of course, bomb only real enemies. But the destructive power they carried and the logic of warfare that justified their missions would soon be available to faceless commanders with other targets to bomb.

In later years a mythology would grow up around the men of the 509th Composite Bomb Group. In an age of peace it seemed incredible that men could kill tens of thousands of human beings without suffering remorse. Many people believed that the commander of the *Enola Gay* went crazy with guilt, even that all the atomic crewmen suffered emotional breakdowns. Other legends hold that there were several planes with "atomic" bombs on each mission, one with the real bomb and two with dummies, so that no one knew who really destroyed the cities. The implication of each myth is the same: men could not knowingly drop an atomic bomb without experiencing unbearable feelings of guilt.

There is a small degree of truth in these myths. Many of the crewmen did feel sorrow in later years when they saw pictures of bomb victims. Some sought to warn other people about the terrors of atomic warfare. And one officer, Maj. Claude Eatherly, commander of the weather plane, who gave the go-ahead report on Hiroshima, did have a mental breakdown that he attributed to guilt about the bomb. His experience fed the myths about other men's mental suffering.

But the story of atomic warfare during World War II is fundamentally a story of cold resolve rather than of reluctant acquiescence. That spirit was apparent on the 509th's last bombing run. After the two atomic missions the group made a final flight over Japan to drop conventional bombs on Kokura. As Abe Spitzer surveyed the results, the planes appeared to be pelting the city with "bean shooters." For a moment the men were disappointed. They had grown accustomed to atomic warfare.

Bibliography

ALPEROVITZ, GAR. *Atomic Diplomacy* (1985). Argues that America's use of the bomb helped cause the cold war.

BOYER, PAUL S. *By the Bomb's Early Light* (1985). American responses to the news of the bomb.

CHANG, IRIS. *The Rape of Nanking: The Forgotten Holocaust of World War II* (1997). Graphic account of the Japanese devastation of a Chinese city.

DOWER, JOHN. *War Without Mercy: Race and Power in the Pacific War* (1986). Documents the brutality practiced by all sides in the Pacific War.

FEIS, HERBERT. *The Atomic Bomb and the End of World War II* (1966). On the diplomatic significance of the bomb.

FRANK, RICHARD B. *Downfall: The End of the Imperial Japanese Empire* (1999). Argues that the use of the atomic bomb was instrumental in ending the war and saving millions of lives.

HACHIYA, MICHIHIKO. *Hiroshima Diary* (1955). A doctor's memories of the atomic bomb and its aftermath.

HERSEY, JOHN. *Hiroshima* (1949). Classic account of what it was like to be in Hiroshima in August 1945.

LINDEE, M. SUSAN. *Suffering Made Real: American Science and the Survivors at Hiroshima* (1994). Studies of the medical effects of Hiroshima on the survivors.

NEWMAN, ROBERT P. *Enola Gay and the Court of History* (2004). How our views on the bombing of Hiroshima have evolved since 1945.

OSADA, ARATA, COMPILER. *Children of the A-Bomb* (1963). Children's memories of the bomb.

RHODES, RICHARD. *The Making of the Atomic Bomb* (1988). How the bomb was built.

ROSS, BILL D. *Iwo Jima* (1985). Account of one island battle that helps explain American reluctance to invade Japan.

SANGER, S. L. *Working on the Bomb* (1995). Oral history based on interviews with Hanford workers who helped build the atomic bomb.

SCHELL, JONATHAN. *The Fate of the Earth* (1982). Discusses the dangers of modern nuclear warfare.

SIEMES, JOHN A., S. J. "Hiroshima: Eyewitness." *Saturday Review*, May 11, 1946. A Jesuit priest's memories of the bombing.

SPITZER, ABE. *We Dropped the A-Bomb* (1946). Radio operator's account.

THOMAS, GORDON, AND MAX MORGAN WITTS. *Enola Gay* (1977). Well-researched account of the bombing.

TIBBETS, PAUL W., JR., ET AL. "15 Years Later: The Men Who Bombed Hiroshima." *Coronet Magazine*, August 1960. Interview with the crewmen of the *Enola Gay*.

TOLAND, JOHN. *The Rising Sun* (1970). Good overview of the Japanese empire from 1936 to 1945.

WYDEN, PETER. *Day One: Before Hiroshima and After* (1984). The story of those who made the atomic bomb—and were themselves surprised by its power.

Study Guide

Summary

This essay describes the most deadly single act of warfare ever carried out by human beings. The Hiroshima bombing was not as destructive as earlier mass bombings of Tokyo and Dresden, nor did it match in brutality the work of German gas chambers. But the leveling of Hiroshima by a single plane armed with a single bomb occupies a unique position in the annals of war. This essay centers on Hiroshima as an event: the *Enola Gay*'s flight, life in the city before the bombing, the moment of destruction, and the aftermath among the Japanese and the Americans. The essay seeks to show what the event meant in human terms to those most closely involved. It suggests that the most remarkable thing about Hiroshima is not that the bombing was an extraordinary act, but that the course of total war to that point had made the use of the atomic bomb seem a logical, even an inevitable, extension of previous policies.

Identification Topics

Tinian, *Enola Gay*, Paul W. Tibbets Jr., Albert Einstein, Manhattan Project, Alamogordo, Harry S Truman, Abe Spitzer, 509th Composite Bomb Group,

Robert Oppenheimer, Iwo Jima, Dresden, Potsdam Declaration, Hiroshima, Nagasaki, John A. Siemes, Naoku Masuoka

Study Questions

1. Describe the role of the following in the preparation for the bombing of Hiroshima: nuclear scientists, the Manhattan Project, Alamogordo, Wendover.
2. What role did the American experience at places like Iwo Jima have in the decision to use the atomic bomb? Would other nations have used atomic bombs in World War II if they had possessed them?
3. Was the bombing of Hiroshima comparable to the bombing of Dresden? Or was it a different kind of war act because it involved only one bomb?
4. Why did the United States decide to use the atomic bomb against Japan? What other options were there? What was "the logic of violence"?
5. Would the United States have used the atomic bomb against Germany if it had been available before Germany surrendered?
6. What did the atomic bomb do to Hiroshima? How were people killed and injured? What did they think had happened?
7. How would you characterize the men who bombed Hiroshima and Nagasaki? Were they ordinary Americans? Did they care about the people they killed? How did they react to taking part in the bombing?
8. Why did people believe that some of the atomic crewmen went mad?
9. Why did Japan not surrender after the bombing of Hiroshima? Why did Japan surrender after the bombing of Nagasaki? Could it have been defeated by other means without great loss of American lives?
10. The author argues that in a state of total war acts of terrible violence become "reasonable." How does this transmutation happen?

Research Topics

1. Study the history of other major acts of violence in the war, such as the bombing of Dresden or the extermination of the Jews. Did all of the war's participants have the same reasons for mass killings? Was there a qualitative difference between these acts?
2. Explore the Japanese conduct of the war in China and the Pacific. What role did the Rape of Nanking and the Bataan Death March have in shaping American policy?
3. Study the decision-making process that led up to the dropping of the atomic bomb. Were the alternatives carefully considered? Should other policies have been followed? Were the Japanese sufficiently warned? In the long run, were lives actually saved by the dropping of the bomb?
4. To what extent did domestic or international politics play a role in the use of the bomb? Would the Democratic party have suffered at the polls if the war had gone on? Did the United States want to impress the Soviet Union with its power?
5. Explore the history of the bombing of Nagasaki.
6. Investigate the Manhattan Project and the scientific effort required to build the bomb.

CHAPTER 11

The Cold War at Home

Joseph McCarthy and Anticommunism

The fundamental rules of American life were written into the Constitution and the Bill of Rights two centuries ago. But those rules have continually been reevaluated in response to new circumstances. After World War II the superpowers, the Soviet Union and the United States, became engaged in a bitter rivalry that came to be known as the cold war. The confrontation appeared so threatening that many Americans were willing to abandon the Bill of Rights in hunting Communist "subversives" in the United States. Joseph McCarthy's career reveals the urgency behind the anti-Communist crusade but also suggests the enduring American commitment to free expression.

The United States was at war in 1954. No troops were in the field and no ships were fighting at sea, but the country nonetheless was locked in a deadly struggle throughout the world against an "international Communist conspiracy." And in 1954 many Americans thought the Communists were winning. Communism had spread from Russia to China and Eastern Europe. It was winning in Vietnam. And worse still, Communist agents were active in the United States itself. In 1952 Senator William Jenner of Indiana charged that "this country today is in the hands of a secret inner coterie which is directed by agents of the Soviet Union." Senator Joseph McCarthy of Wisconsin declared that the United States had experienced "twenty years of treason" under Democratic presidents Franklin D. Roosevelt and Harry S Truman.

McCarthy believed that Communists had infiltrated every corner of American life. Schools, libraries, newspapers, and movies all showed their influence. In 1954 he was on the trail of Communists who had infiltrated the last bulwark of American freedom, the U.S. Army. That April the Senate began a public hearing on the Army–McCarthy controversy and opened the council chamber to a new medium, television. Day after day for seven weeks millions of Americans would watch the nation's preeminent anti-Communist at work. The hearing, which McCarthy promoted as a lesson about the Communist conspiracy, became more than that: a lesson about American democracy in the modern world.

American anticommunism began in the nineteenth century, before the world had its first Communist nation. After Karl Marx published the *Communist Manifesto* in Germany in 1848, his ideas circulated rapidly in Europe and the United States. Marx's claim that the laborers of the world were cheated out of their fair share of industrial profits inspired a socialist movement in the United States during the latter part of the nineteenth century. The movement grew into several parties, diverse in program but alike in holding that the instruments of industrial production, distribution, and exchange should be owned by the people as a whole and managed cooperatively for the benefit of all rather than competitively for the benefit of a few. They looked at men like Andrew Carnegie as greedy oppressors: Why should Carnegie earn $25 million a year, when his workers earned less than a thousand?

The socialists advocated radical restructuring of American society. They ran several impressive presidential campaigns beginning in 1910, polling nearly a million votes for their candidate, Eugene V. Debs. But neither the socialists nor the Communist party, which was formed later, could make much headway against a deep American antipathy toward what they regarded as foreign ideologies. Naturally the "captains of industry" were unfriendly to any doctrine that would deprive them of their wealth; most believed that business success was a reward from God for hard work. By 1900 they were already using the term "Communist" to condemn those who favored an income tax. And American workers, who might have supported socialism, were so imbued with the ideal of success through individual initiative that most regarded socialism and communism as exotic foreign doctrines, designed for people who were lazy and subversive, and not for American farmers and factory workers.

When the Russian Revolution in 1917 brought into being the first Communist state, most Americans were appalled. The United States actually stationed soldiers in Siberia between 1918 and 1920 to assist White Russians in an unsuccessful attempt to overthrow the Bolsheviks. During the same period the Communist party was founded in the United States under the direction of the "Russian International." Sporadic acts of violence by American radicals gave Attorney General A. Mitchell Palmer an excuse for attempting to root out Communists. The "Palmer raids" resulted in more than 4,000 arrests and deportation of 556 supposed radicals.

American hostility toward communism softened somewhat during the depression. Terrible economic conditions in the 1930s persuaded many Americans that unfettered capitalism could not provide for the economic well-being of all the people. Many American intellectuals and laborers joined the Communist party as an alternative to the individualistic ideals that seemed to have brought about industrial chaos. Roosevelt's own program, though far from communistic, involved many reforms that shifted power from individuals to the government. New Deal legislation enabled the government to provide jobs, housing, public works, and old age pensions. Most Americans regarded these measures as repairs to the political structure, not as a radical departure from traditional American values. But some feared "creeping socialism" and even accused Roosevelt himself of Communist leanings.

During Roosevelt's administration events in Europe encouraged a closer relationship with the Soviet Union. When Hitler came to power in 1933, Roosevelt granted diplomatic recognition to the Soviets, and eight years later the United States and the Soviet Union were allies in World War II. The two nations fought in the same cause, plotted strategy together, met in Allied conferences, and cooperated in creating the United Nations. Joseph Stalin, dictatorial ruler of the Soviet Union, was known to American politicians and soldiers as "Uncle Joe."

Mutual enemies brought cooperation between the Soviet Union and the United States during the war, but with the defeat of Germany and Japan in 1945, suspicions soon resurfaced. The Soviets suffered far more casualties in the war than any other Allied nation: about eighteen million Soviets lost their lives, compared to three hundred thousand American deaths—a 60 to 1 ratio. The Soviet Union's contribution to the war with Germany also was apparent in that three out of four German deaths in the war came in battles with Soviets. For several years Stalin had tried in vain to persuade the Allies to open up a "second front" in Western Europe to take some of the burden off Russia, and he suspected that the D-Day landings in Normandy were delayed until 1944 because the Allies wanted Germany to weaken the Soviet Union.

Having fought two costly wars with Germany during the previous three decades, the Soviets decided to protect themselves from further aggression by occupying not only the eastern sector of Germany, but also all the countries between Germany and the Soviet Union. Soviet occupation of East Germany was by joint agreement with France, England, and the United States, who occupied the western sector. The Communists extended their influence into Poland, Hungary, Czechoslovakia, Romania, and Bulgaria through force and guile. These acts, which the Soviets sought to justify as necessary defensive measures after a costly war, appeared in a different light in the West. In 1946 Winston Churchill composed a memorable description of Soviet advances. Speaking at Westminster College in Fulton, Missouri, Britain's wartime prime minister declared: "From Stettin in the Baltic to Trieste in the Adriatic an iron curtain has descended across the continent."

"Iron curtain" soon became a household phrase throughout the Western world. With Communist expansion in Eastern Europe the image of Soviets as friendly comrades-in-arms paled before the new Soviet specter as brutal and aggressive. Other signs of Communist activity abounded. After Communist Mao Tse-tung consolidated his power in China with a victory over Nationalist forces at Nanking in 1949, there were two Chinas; the Communists controlled the whole mainland, and the Nationalists were left with the island of Taiwan. In Southeast Asia Communist Ho Chi Minh was waging war against colonial control by France. In Greece and Turkey Communist guerrillas were active.

Americans believed that communism was monolithic, that each of these movements was sponsored by the Soviet Union. Moreover, the tentacles of Communist power seemed to extend to the United States itself and to its allies. In 1949, just four years after America had achieved a miracle in exploding the first atomic bomb, the Soviet Union exploded an atomic bomb. How had the Soviets been able to develop a bomb so quickly? How, indeed, without help from the United States? In 1946 several Soviet spy rings were exposed in Canada. In 1950 Americans learned that a British scientist, Dr. Klaus Fuchs, had delivered atomic secrets to the Communists and that he had worked with an American, Harry Gold. During the same year a spy ring including Americans Julius and Ethel Rosenberg, David Greenglass, and Morton Sobell was exposed.

Shortly after the end of World War II Americans began to talk about a "cold war," a struggle with the Soviet Union that was waged by spying and subversion. The intense hostility toward communism that pervaded postwar America was stimulated by objective facts: real Soviet expansion in Eastern Europe, real Communist gains in other nations, and real Soviet spies in England, Canada, and the United States. The anti-Communist movement also grew out of partisan reactions to the alleged "creeping socialism" of the New Deal. Many conservatives believed that the social programs and economic regulations of the Roosevelt administration had undermined American values and traditions. The American traitors were not merely those who had access to atomic secrets and sold them to the Communists, but also those who worked within the system to promote un-American programs and ideas.

President Harry S. Truman did not embrace the conspiracy theory: he approved of the New Deal, and he doubted that America was as riddled with traitors as some anti-Communists contended. But he did adopt numerous policies designed to resist expansion of communism. He favored the Marshall Plan, under which the United States spent billions of dollars to strengthen economies in Western Europe. He announced the Truman Doctrine in 1947, which became the basic statement of America's position in the cold war. There are "two ways of life," Truman declared, one free and one totalitarian. The United States should help "free people to maintain their free institutions and their national integrity against aggressive movements that seek to impose upon them totalitarian regimes." In particular Truman persuaded Congress to provide funds to support the governments of Greece and Turkey in their struggles against Communist insurrections. Moreover, in 1949 the United States joined Canada and ten European nations in creating the North Atlantic Treaty Organization (NATO) as a bulwark against Soviet expansion in Europe.

Truman also supported measures aimed at thwarting Communist activities in the United States. In 1947 he established the Loyalty Review Board to investigate government employees. During the next four years the government evaluated 3 million employees, dismissing 212 and forcing another 2,000 to resign under suspicion. In 1949 the government used the Smith Act, a 1940 law against advocating the violent overthrow of the government, as a basis for sending Communist leaders to jail. President Truman approved of these activities but opposed more extreme measures, such as the McCarran Internal Security Act, which made it unlawful "to combine, conspire or agree with any other person to perform any act that would substantially contribute to the establishment . . . of a totalitarian dictatorship." Under the act, passed by Congress in 1950, "Communist-front organizations" were required to register with the attorney general. Members of such organizations could neither work in defense plants nor travel abroad.

Although Truman had been active in ferreting out Communists, he felt that the McCarran Act went too far. Truman vetoed the bill, declaring that it "put the government in the business of thought control." But by 1950 few congressmen shared the president's scruples; the bill gained a two-thirds majority, enough to override the president's veto.

In the following year the U.S. Supreme Court endorsed the anti-Communist movement in the case of *Dennis et al. v. United States* (1951). Three decades before, in *Schenck v. United States* (1919), the Court had ruled that political expression could be limited only under rare wartime circumstances in which there was a "clear and present danger" of damage to the United States. In the *Dennis* case the Court reviewed the convictions of the eleven Communists jailed under the Smith Act. Justice Hugo Black argued that the Smith Act violated the First Amendment, and Justice William O. Douglas said the Smith Act failed to distinguish between a "conspiracy to overthrow the government" and the simple teaching of "Marxist-Leninist doctrine." Black and Douglas were in the minority, however; the Court endorsed the Smith Act and so the convictions held.

Every branch of the government was thus active in the anti-Communist movement, but some politicians questioned whether part of the problem might not be the government itself. These Red hunters favored a more rigorous effort to root out subversives within the government and charged that Truman himself was "soft on communism." He had opposed the McCarran Act, and he was clearly identified with the New Deal programs that had limited free enterprise in the name of communal welfare.

During the postwar years anticommunism was so powerful that the failure to be an ardent Red baiter could, in itself, be regarded as evidence of pro-Communist sentiments. A young naval lieutenant, Richard Milhous Nixon, returned home to California after the war and at thirty-three ran for Congress against H. Jerry Voorhis, a veteran politician. In platform debates Nixon charged that Voorhis was supported by Communists. The charges were unsubstantiated, but Nixon won the election. In Congress he helped write the anti-union Taft-Hartley Act, and he served on the House Un-American Activities Committee, which was created in 1938 as an anticommunism watchdog. Nixon prepared the House investigation of Alger Hiss, president of the Carnegie Endowment for International Peace and a former State Department official. In 1948 Hiss was accused by Whittaker Chambers, a former Communist, of having copied secret documents for the Russians. The evidence was flimsy, and President Truman called the case against him "a red herring." But Nixon insisted on pursuing the matter, and in 1950 Hiss was sentenced to five years in prison for lying about his involvement in the episode. In 1950 Nixon ran for the Senate against Helen Gahagan Douglas. As in his campaign against Jerry Voorhis, he launched an impassioned but unsupported attack on his opponent's loyalty, and again he won.

By 1950 many American politicians had learned the value of anticommunism. Fear of Communist expansion abroad and subversion at home led voters to admire any candidate who appeared to hate communism. In that year a young senator from Wisconsin, Joseph Raymond McCarthy, became the most outspoken anti-Communist in the Senate. In Wheeling, West Virginia, he delivered a shocking speech to the Women's Republican Club. "The reason we find ourselves in a position of impotency," he said, "is not because our only powerful potential enemy has sent men to invade our shores, but rather because of the traitorous actions of those who have been treated so well by this nation." Among the "traitors" known to McCarthy the most insidious were those who "infested" the State Department. Holding out his fist to the startled audience, he declared, "I have here in my hand a list of 205—a list of names that were known to the Secretary of State as being members of the Communist party and who nevertheless are *still working and shaping . . . policy*." McCarthy was speaking from notes, and accounts vary as to his actual claim as to the number of Communists. At other times he spoke of 57 and 81 "card-carrying Communists" in the State Department. But whether 57 or 205, his claim and his pretense to authority—he had the list right in his hand—electrified not only the Women's Republican Club, but people all over the country. Within a few weeks Joseph McCarthy was hailed by many Americans as the bravest and best of the anti-Communist warriors.

Joseph Raymond McCarthy was a natural figure to champion traditional American values against treason. He was born in a simple clapboard farmhouse at Grand Chute, Wisconsin, in 1908. His grandfather, who pioneered in Wisconsin, had left Ireland in 1848 during the potato famine. Working as a farmhand in New York, he saved enough money to buy a half section of land—320 acres—in Wisconsin. He arrived at his farm in 1858 driving a wagon pulled by a team of oxen. Within a few years he had cleared the land, built a log cabin, and started a dairy farm. He and his wife had ten children, including Timothy McCarthy, who bought a nearby farm and married a tall, heavyset woman, Bridget Tierney.

The Timothy McCarthys, Joseph's parents, lived on a 142-acre farm in the "Irish settlement" near grandfather McCarthy's farm. They raised corn, hay, barley, oats, and cabbage along with some cows, pigs, and horses. They had seven children, of whom Joseph, or "Joe," was the fourth. They were apparently a close, hardworking, and religious family. They rode to nearby Appleton for mass every week, whatever the weather. The McCarthy children generally finished eighth grade in the local one-room schoolhouse and then left and went to work.

Joe McCarthy was fourteen when he quit school. He was good looking, with black hair, blue eyes, and light skin, and he spoke with a slight Irish brogue. Joe was different from his six brothers and sisters in his enormous energy. He could get by on a few hours of sleep a night; he loved boxing, wrestling, and baseball; when an older brother brought home a motorcycle, Joe, age thirteen, had to ride it. A neighboring farmer remembered him as "always driving, always driving."

After quitting school Joe did farm chores for a time, but soon got bored and used $65 he had saved to build a chicken shed and stock it with chickens. He tended his poultry carefully, and by the time he was seventeen he owned two thousand laying hens and ten thousand broilers. But three years later his profitable business was ruined when a disease killed most of the chickens. Joe moved to Appleton and became manager of a grocery store. His was the smallest store in a chain of twenty-four, but it was soon the most profitable. Joe won customers by walking the country roads and introducing himself to farmers, inviting them to the store. At work he flattered old ladies, joked with teenagers, and made his shop into a kind of community center. He was gifted with an extraordinary memory and could recall hundreds—and later thousands—of names. Anyone who came more than once to the store was an old friend.

Joe McCarthy next turned to completing high school. At Appleton's Little Wolf High School, which he entered as a freshman, he was allowed to work on his own in the school study hall, taking examinations whenever he completed a subject. He completed first-year algebra in six weeks, was a sophomore by Thanksgiving, a junior at midterm, and a senior by Easter. He graduated that spring, with honors. While doing schoolwork for twelve hours a day, McCarthy also played basketball, taught boxing, and completed an extension course for the University of Wisconsin.

That fall he entered Marquette University. He intended at first to be an engineer but decided law was more interesting. He supported himself by working as a janitor, salesman, and short-order cook. At the end of his second year at Marquette he was managing two service stations. He spent much of his time working and enjoying life in a fraternity house, where he was an outstanding poker player. In just five years McCarthy earned a B.A. and a law degree. McCarthy's work was impressive, but in many areas his knowledge was superficial. He tended to get by with hasty memorization and other shortcuts that left him with only a hazy perspective on history and philosophy.

After a brief spell on his own, McCarthy took a job in a law office in Shawano, Wisconsin. He was so poor when he arrived that he had to sell his typewriter to set himself up in a boarding house. At Shawano he joined the Young Democratic Club and was soon president for his district. Although his boss was a Republican, Joe McCarthy supported Roosevelt's reelection in 1936 and distributed Roosevelt-for-President buttons. McCarthy proved himself an adequate attorney, and in 1937 he became a partner in his firm, but his real talent seemed to lie in his personal relationships. In 1938 he decided to run for the position of judge in Wisconsin's Tenth Circuit against an able incumbent, Edgar V. Werner.

Circuit judges were usually senior attorneys, but McCarthy believed that through hard work and personal contacts he could win the election. The district encompassed three rural counties, and McCarthy set out to meet every farmer in the region. During his visits he would swap stories, discuss farm problems, and even, occasionally, milk a cow. After each stop he would record notes on a dictating machine in his car while driving to the next farm. Using this information he sent each family a personal postcard before the election. Because he needed to send out thousands of cards, he left the writing to friends—he had many—so that each card was handwritten and appeared to come from the candidate himself. When the vote was tallied on April 5, 1939, Werner's total exceeded McCarthy's in Appleton, but McCarthy swept the rural areas, winning overall with 15,160 votes to Werner's 11,154. Only ten years after beginning high school McCarthy was the youngest circuit court judge in Wisconsin's history.

Judge McCarthy showed the same frenetic energy on the bench that had won him the election. He took office with a backlog of 250 cases. Holding that "justice delayed is justice denied," he held open his court twelve hours a day to work through the cases. He was a popular judge, liked for his even-handed running of the court and his good sense of humor. McCarthy might have spent his life on the bench, but he soon grew restless for other challenges. By 1941 he had decided that he wanted to be senator. He began exchanging circuits with other judges, in part for variety, in part to make political contacts throughout the state.

After Pearl Harbor, McCarthy considered joining the armed forces. His judicial position gave him an automatic deferment, but patriotism, a sense of adventure, and the obvious political advantages of a good service record all drove him to enlist. After finding that he could take a leave from his judgeship, he joined the marines. He took his political instincts with him. Reporters asked Judge McCarthy whether he expected to be made an officer, and he told them he was "more interested in a gun than a commission." Just before leaving for active duty he presided over a Milwaukee courtroom in his marine uniform.

McCarthy spent sixteen months in the South Pacific, most of it as an intelligence officer for a dive-bomber squadron. His work kept him at a desk most of the time, but he was able to go on a dozen missions as a photographer and tail gunner. The muscular Irish-American was popular with his fellow marines. He got around a liquor ban by filling three trunks with bottles and labeling them "office supplies." And he was an outrageous poker player. "He'd sit in a game," one friend recalled, "and suddenly, for no reason at all, bet $101.50, or $97.90. Not only would the bet knock other players off balance, but they'd have the problem of counting out the exact sum. Most times, they'd let him have the pot just to get on to the next game."

*"**Tail Gunner Joe.**"* McCarthy served with the marines during World War II. His service was honorable; later, in his own telling, it became heroic.

McCarthy's military career was honorable, but like his inflated poker bets, his hand in the war was subject to exaggeration. He slipped off a ladder and fractured his leg. The leg was further injured when an orderly mistook a caustic acid for a fluid used to soften the cast for cutting and, pouring the fluid on McCarthy's leg, gave him a severe burn. In different tellings this injury became a war injury and a battle injury. Similarly, the story of McCarthy's missions grew with the telling. He parlayed his twelve flights into thirty-two, and on that basis he received a Distinguished Flying Cross. That was in 1952, when few people were willing to challenge anything McCarthy said.

At the war's end "Tail Gunner Joe" was again "Judge McCarthy." But he was already planning his run for the Senate. His political views, however, had not yet crystallized. He would soon be considered a conservative Republican, but in recent years he had been a New Deal Democrat and an advocate for the United Nations. "There ought to be machinery to back such an international tribunal with force," he said. "As a circuit judge, my judgments would not have been worth the paper they consumed without the authoritative presence of the sheriff's department on another floor of the courthouse." A liberal Democrat could hardly have spoken more clearly in favor of a strong United Nations.

McCarthy's conservatism was a product of the postwar years, and he decided to become a Republican when he had assessed the political leanings of the voters in Wisconsin. He had won election to the bench in a nonpartisan race. To switch parties all he needed to do was register as a Republican. That much was easy. Winning recognition in a statewide election was much more difficult. While continuing his work as a judge, McCarthy stumped the state speaking tirelessly wherever he could find an audience. Voters were worried about Russian advances in Eastern Europe and about a rash of strikes in American factories, so McCarthy bemoaned the "loss" of Eastern Europe and warned about the corrosive influence of Communists in the labor unions. He was on the conservative side on issues that troubled many Americans, but his greatest asset was his personal appeal. If any political figure in the decade following World War II filled the role of "all-American boy," it was Joe McCarthy. He was a strong, handsome war veteran. And he was the incarnation of hard work and imagination: in one year he fought his way through high school, and when he was only thirty he won a position on the bench. His mother had taught her children, "Man was born to do something." In his campaign speech he echoed her words. "I don't claim to be more brilliant than the next man," he announced, "but I have always claimed that I worked harder. I am going to work harder. That's a promise."

McCarthy had to face two opponents in the Senate race. First he must beat Robert M. La Follette Jr., the popular incumbent senator, in the Republican primary; then he would face the Democratic nominee. During the campaign season McCarthy drove eighty thousand miles, visiting as many as twenty-eight towns in four days—all while continuing his work on the bench. He engineered another postcard blitz, paying people half a cent per card to send a "personal" message to each of the hundreds of thousands of voters in Wisconsin. The other side of the card was a smiling picture of Judge "Tail Gunner Joe" McCarthy. La Follette ran a lackluster campaign; assuming that he would easily defeat the upstart McCarthy, he appeared in Wisconsin for only ten days. The vote was close—207,935 to 202,557—but McCarthy managed one of the biggest upsets in Senate history.

Ironically, La Follette was on many issues a more ardent conservative than McCarthy in 1946. He opposed the United Nations and was critical of Stalin; after the election he claimed that Communists in the labor unions had contributed to his defeat. In the postwar era anticommunism was virtually a national credo. The question was not so much whether a politician was anti-Communist as how far that politician would go to demonstrate loyalty.

McCarthy still had to face the Democratic nominee, Howard McMurray, but by now the momentum was behind his campaign. He knew how to make the most out of his agrarian roots: "I'm just a farm-boy, not a professor," he told a pleased audience. Upon hearing that Henry Wallace, the liberal former vice president, was going to speak in Wisconsin on behalf of his opponent, McCarthy declared, "The people of Wisconsin completely understand only one language—the American language, and Mr. Wallace does not speak that language." McCarthy claimed that Communists, who surely did not understand the "American language," had moved into positions of power in business, labor, and the government. Pro-McCarthy newspapers joined the crusade. McMurray, said one, is "in favor of the enemies of our country." When the votes were tallied in November McCarthy had won by 250,000 votes.

A few weeks later Senator Joe McCarthy went to Washington. At thirty-eight he was the youngest member of the Senate, but he was neither awed by his success nor humbled by the company of his seniors on Capitol Hill. He held a press conference shortly after his arrival, ducked a prickly question about why a junior senator would do such a thing, and declared that coal miners, then on strike, should be drafted into the army. McCarthy insisted on being called "Joe" by everyone, not only fellow senators, but office workers and laborers, too. He invited eight Senate newswomen to dinner and cooked fried chicken. Friends remembered him chatting with black workers at a construction site and befriending the woman who made sandwiches in the Senate cafeteria. He was a popular figure in his neighborhood, too, where he shared an apartment with friends and played on the street with the local children. Joe McCarthy's personal tastes in Washington kept alive his man-of-the-people image. He wore inexpensive suits until they were shiny with age; at bedtime he read western pulp novels.

In an age of anticommunism McCarthy soon established himself as one of the leading opponents of communism in the Senate. He opposed the appointment of David E. Lilienthal as chairman of the Atomic Energy Commission because Lilienthal, while director of the Tennessee Valley Authority, had appointed men of dubious loyalty to positions of power. The stain of disloyalty was thin: one appointee was married to a woman with allegedly left-wing connections and another had a brother who was possibly a member of the Communist party. But this hint was enough for McCarthy. "I'd much rather run the risk of discarding a competent man than run the risk of being stuck with a dangerous man," he said. Lilienthal's appointment received a Senate vote of 51 to 30, enough to win confirmation, but far from a unanimous endorsement. A few weeks later the Taft-Hartley Bill, limiting the power of labor unions, came before the Senate. McCarthy approved of the bill wholeheartedly but wanted to add an amendment encouraging labor unions and employers to get rid of workers who were Communists. The proposal was poorly written and was probably unconstitutional. Senator Robert Taft, a conservative and an anti-Communist, felt that it would add nothing to his bill. Senator Millard Tydings of Maryland warned that it would encourage a "witch hunt." The proposal was rejected.

Although McCarthy met defeat on both the Lilienthal and the Taft-Hartley issues, he had added to his credentials as an anti-Communist. In July 1947 he was interviewed on *Meet the Press*. "We are at war," he said, "We've been at war with Russia for some time now. . . . Everyone is painfully aware of the fact that we are at war—and that we're losing it."

Despite these early signs of anticommunism, however, McCarthy's Senate career had not yet taken a clear direction. One of his biggest projects as a freshman senator was to conduct hearings on public housing. Although he felt that building should be left mainly to private enterprise, he wanted the government to help disabled veterans find suitable housing, and he fought corrupt business practices that influenced building costs. After the war "gray marketeers" hoarded scarce materials and sold them to contractors for inflated prices. McCarthy grilled a New York attorney, Isidore Ginsburg, one of the most active hoarders. Ginsburg responded, "We deal in nothing but free enterprise and take a reasonable profit, and nothing more." McCarthy snapped back, "Your enterprise is just too damn free, Ginsburg." The attorney claimed that "only in Russia" could his business be curtailed, and a newspaper claimed that McCarthy's attack on the gray marketeers could put America "in the straightjacket of Russia." Charges of Communist leanings came easily in the 1940s; anyone with a sympathetic word for government regulation or a harsh criticism of private enterprise could be labeled a Red, anyone including "Tail Gunner Joe."

McCarthy's most dramatic cause in his early years in the Senate was the investigation of alleged army brutality in the treatment of Nazi soldiers accused of massacring American troops at Malmédy, Belgium, in 1944. McCarthy read a report that American guards had placed hoods over prisoners' faces and beaten them with brass knuckles to extract confessions detailing their involvement in the massacre. Friends warned him that it would be political suicide to investigate the army for its activities at Malmédy. But McCarthy insisted that every suspect has a right to a fair trial. "We have been accused by the Russians," he said, "of using force, physical violence, and have accused them of using mock trials in cells in the dark of night, and now we have an army report that comes out and says we have done all the things that the Russians were ever accused of doing, but they are all right because it created the right psychological effect to get the necessary confessions."

In the Malmédy hearings McCarthy showed his willingness to adopt an unpopular cause when a matter of principle was involved, and he showed an attorney's regard for the importance of fair judicial proceedings. But his conduct in the hearings revealed a less attractive aspect of his character. The investigation was conducted by a Senate committee of which McCarthy was not a member, but an observer. Soon, however, he established himself as the most outspoken senator in the room, badgering the witnesses and the committee members with incessant questions, making wild charges, and accusing the committee chairman of a whitewash. He also claimed that he had seen damaging evidence that he could not produce and had, in fact, never seen. The Malmédy charges against the army proved mostly groundless, but McCarthy was so obsessed with his own view of the situation that he lost the ability to react intelligently to the evidence. The more the facts refuted his preconceptions, the more he insisted that he saw a coverup.

In the Malmédy proceedings McCarthy showed a tendency to combine genuine personal conviction (that all people, even ex-Nazi soldiers, deserve a fair trial) with a pathological compulsion to be right (blustering, intimidating, and lying to make his points). His fellow senators had difficulty evaluating their colleague from Wisconsin. Off the Senate floor he was friendly, thoughtful, and buoyant. But at work he was rude and obsessive. His behavior alienated many of the senior senators, who controlled committee appointments, and McCarthy soon found himself relegated to obscure committees on which he could have little influence on important public policy.

In 1949 Senator McCarthy finally tied himself to the cause that would win him lasting fame—and infamy. He had flirted with anticommunism in the past, but so too had many other congressmen. McCarthy's involvement became more intense in 1949 when he began a campaign to discredit the *Capital Times*, a Wisconsin newspaper that accused him of poor conduct in running for office while a judge and in failing to file proper tax returns. McCarthy claimed that the *Capital Times* was "the Red mouthpiece for the Communist party in Wisconsin." To substantiate his charge he claimed that the best way to evaluate whether someone was a Communist was to see whether they followed the "Communist party-line." "If a fowl looks like a duck, walks like a duck, swims like a duck, and quacks like a duck, then we can safely assume it is a duck."

As evidence that the *Capital Times* did indeed swim like a Communist duck, McCarthy found instances in which articles in the *Times* were printed shortly after similar articles in the *Communist Daily Worker*. He also pointed out that the paper complained about a double standard of justice in the United States, one for the rich and one for the poor—another sign of Communist leanings. The charges were totally unfounded. In fact, the *Capital Times* had a long history of anti-Communist articles and editorials. But McCarthy's charges were given favorable publicity throughout Wisconsin.

In McCarthy's account of his evolution as a crusader against communism he stresses a trip he made to rural Arizona, where he met "real

Americans without any synthetic sheen." Among them, he says, he laid plans for "the one great fight" he would make as a senator. In 1950 McCarthy agreed with Republican party leaders to deliver five Lincoln Day speeches to Republican gatherings across the country. This type of tour was standard fare in senatorial politics, but the consequences of McCarthy's efforts were explosive. Some time before leaving he decided that he would claim to have a list of known Communists in the State Department. No such list existed, but McCarthy assumed he could persuade willing listeners that he had the information. As in a good poker bluff he would bid high on an empty hand. In Wheeling, West Virginia, on February 9, he first claimed to have the names of Communists in the State Department. He repeated his claim at stops in Colorado and Nevada; by the time he reached Huron, South Dakota, his charges were headline news across the country.

McCarthy was evasive, of course, when reporters asked to see the list. He told one reporter he had left the list in a suit that had been lost on an airplane. After drinking late at night with two other journalists, he claimed they had stolen the list. One of the newsmen reported cynically, "He lost his list between his eighth and ninth bourbons." The *Washington Post* accused McCarthy of "sewer politics" and Communist tactics. "Rarely has a man in public life crawled and squirmed so abjectly," they declared. Such papers demanded facts, and McCarthy had no facts to give them. But scores of papers reported McCarthy's accusations uncritically, and millions of Americans needed little convincing. Like McCarthy they knew something was wrong with the country, and the more he was criticized the more they believed his charges were true. He was a brave patriot, they reasoned, and so naturally the Communists would attack him. After he spoke in Huron, South Dakota, the local paper ran a characteristically sympathetic letter by someone who had heard the senator speak. "He left us feeling proud we were Republicans. . . . McCarthy is a thinking, acting leader, not just a politician. There is a tremendous difference."

Soon afterward the senator from Wisconsin delivered a five-hour speech in Congress repeating his charges about the State Department and giving vague details about some of the alleged Communists. The public outcry following McCarthy's allegations was so great that the Senate decided to hold hearings to evaluate his evidence. McCarthy still had no evidence of Communists, but his assertions forced other anti-Communists to come to his assistance. J. Edgar Hoover, a friend of McCarthy's, was angered by his premature allegations, though he worried that if the senator was discredited the FBI's own investigations would be damaged. Hoover therefore tried to help McCarthy find evidence to support his claims. Richard Nixon urged McCarthy to be more cautious in his accusations, but he favored McCarthy's cause and helped the senator gain access to documents accumulated by the House Un-American Activities

Committee. Dozens of conservative politicians came to McCarthy's assistance because they realized that if he were discredited, their own anti-Communist efforts would be hampered. Veterans of the conservative movement were often surprised at how little McCarthy actually knew about the history and theory of the Communist movement. He had placed himself at the center of anticommunism through a monumental bluff.

McCarthy's initial test came a few months later. A Senate committee headed by Senator Millard Tydings of Maryland met to explore McCarthy's allegations. In highly publicized hearings the Tydings Committee heard a patchwork of charges put together by McCarthy and his supporters. The senator defined communism so broadly that any American who had supported a liberal cause during the previous twenty years was suspect.

McCarthy's first name was typical of his list as a whole. Dorothy Kenyon was a sixty-two-year-old New York attorney who had served on the United Nations Commission on the Status of Women from 1947 to 1949. The case for her Communist leanings was based on her association with various organizations that McCarthy and others described as "subversive." One was the "Abraham Lincoln Brigade"—Americans who had fought as volunteers against the fascist dictator, Francisco Franco, during the Spanish Civil War. Another was the League of Women Shoppers, a consumer rights organization. Others whom McCarthy mentioned include Philip C. Jessup, the State Department's ambassador-at-large, and Owen Lattimore, an adviser on China policy. In none of these cases did McCarthy prove membership in the Communist party, to say nothing of treasonous conduct. Eleanor Roosevelt, the president's widow, might have said of all the accused what she said of the first: "If all the honorable senator's 'subversives' are as subversive as Miss Kenyon, I think the State Department is entirely safe and the nation will continue on an even keel." Margaret Chase Smith, a Republican senator from Maine and a strong supporter of the House Un-American Activities Committee, accused McCarthy of trying "to ride the Republican party to victory through the selfish political exploitation of fear, bigotry, ignorance, and intolerance." Senator Tydings summed up his view of the hearings by calling McCarthy's charges "a hoax."

The charges were flimsy, but the press often printed them without comment, and millions of Americans were ready to believe whatever McCarthy said. Despite the unfavorable response of the Tydings Committee, the senator's popularity continued to grow. His influence now spread to the film community, where he numbered John Wayne among his good friends. In the fall elections of 1950 McCarthy spoke on behalf of sympathetic candidates across the country, reserving his best efforts for John Marshall Butler, a Maryland attorney who ran for the Senate against McCarthy's foe Millard Tydings. The senator from

Wisconsin assigned his whole staff to take part in a campaign to slander the incumbent, and helped Butler upset Tydings. The political lesson was clear: those who opposed McCarthy risked their own political futures.

McCarthy's self-assurance was so strong that by 1951 he could launch an attack on one of the most popular men in America, George C. Marshall, the secretary of defense. The address, delivered on June 14, 1951, lasted almost three hours and is the classic expression of McCarthy's anti-Communist rhetoric. Marshall had been Army Chief of Staff during World War II and proposed the postwar European recovery program that bears his name. But his position as foreign policy adviser to President Truman tainted him, in McCarthy's estimation. Having alerted reporters in advance, McCarthy delivered his attack to packed galleries. Men like Marshall, he said, were responsible for every recent failure in American foreign policy, especially the "loss" of China. Marshall was engaged in "a conspiracy on a scale so immense as to dwarf any previous such venture in the history of man. A conspiracy of infamy so black that, when it is finally exposed, its principals shall be forever deserving of the maledictions of all honest men."

Collier's magazine declared that McCarthy's speech "set a new high for irresponsibility." But McCarthy's supporters were uncritically appreciative. Senator Henry Jackson of Washington would later declare, "Throughout this whole period the major thread was fear." The rapid spread of communism through Eastern Europe and China nourished the fear that the "Red menace" was close to worldwide domination. The Russian development of the atomic bomb raised the specter of a nuclear holocaust—a danger so believable that thousands of Americans built concrete bomb shelters in their backyards and stocked them with food and water. Fear also dominated many Americans' thinking about their fellow citizens. A Wisconsin farmer summed up the way millions of Americans felt: "Yes," he said, "I guess almost everybody in this part of the country is for McCarthy. He's against communism—and we're against communism. Besides, if he wasn't telling the truth they'd 'a hung him long ago. He's one of the greatest Americans we've ever had."

And what of Joe McCarthy, himself? How did his meteoric rise to power affect his own life? Somehow he had to forget who he had been just a few years before—a Democrat supporting Roosevelt and the New Deal. And he had forgotten also the principles underlying his declaration in the Malmédy hearings that one of "the basic principles of American justice" was "the rights of the innocent." There were no innocent men or women in McCarthy's hunt for Communists, only insidious conspirators in a massive plot that he alone understood. In the early stages of McCarthy's political career his commitment to causes was balanced by an engaging ability to laugh at himself. Even when he began to number the State Department Communists, he confided to reporters that his figures were a bluff—he just wanted to see what he could find out. But as his career unfolded he became more and more of a true believer in his own anti-Communist crusade. Ambition and paranoia led him to believe that he represented the forces of light, and his enemies the forces of darkness—period.

At the same time, however, he was learning that there was simply no evidence of Communists in high places. Despite all the help he received from J. Edgar Hoover, Richard Nixon, and other public figures, he could not identify a single Communist in government. The men and women he singled out for his attacks were, in fact, persons whose ideas differed from his, but who were as fundamentally loyal as McCarthy himself. In his true believer's mind, however, the lack of evidence was itself evidence of the insidiousness of the plot—the traitors were so clever that you could not pin them down. Some writers have accused McCarthy of cynically manipulating events to his political advantage. But it is more likely that he was swept by events and by his own personality into a deeper and more obsessive commitment to his crusade. He had staked his political future on the existence of a massive Communist conspiracy in government. His friends agreed with him.

International events fed the American fear of communism and encouraged McCarthy's rise to power. On June 25, 1950, Communist North Korea invaded South Korea. The United Nations Security Council adopted a resolution urging member states to assist South Korea, and during the summer a UN force consisting mainly of American soldiers landed in Korea. After being forced south to a tiny foothold of land near Pusan on the tip of the peninsula, they pushed the North Koreans back to the Chinese border. Then on November 25, 1950, China entered the war and forced the South Koreans and their allies back to the 38th parallel, roughly at the center of Korea. During the next three years the two sides traded deadly assaults, gaining and losing ground in the neighborhood of the 38th parallel. McCarthy and his followers were discouraged by the indecisiveness of the war. The enemy was, of course, a formidable opponent, and bombing raids into China—favored by some Americans— might have resulted in a wider war with both China and Russia. But McCarthyites blamed the stalemate on American treason. The failure to whip the Chinese and North Koreans was looked on as yet another sign of the corrosive power of the Communist conspiracy.

McCarthy believed the conduct of the Democrats at their presidential convention in 1952 was a good example of their disregard for Korea. He remarked that on a day when they all sang "Happy Days Are Here Again," the Democratic theme song, 208 Americans had died in Korea. McCarthy was a leading figure at his own party's presidential convention, where he delivered a well-received speech about the Communist conspiracy.

His power was evident. Even Gen. Dwight D. Eisenhower, the American commander in Europe during World War II and now the Republican candidate for president, was reluctant to offend him.

Eisenhower would never forgive McCarthy for his attack on General Marshall, Eisenhower's comrade-in-arms during the war. He knew Marshall's loyalty was unassailable, and he despised the senator from Wisconsin for his unwarranted attack. But politics makes strange bedfellows. The general could not avoid a campaign swing by train through Wisconsin. Eisenhower was barely civil to the senator, who accompanied him. He would not mention him by name in his speeches, and he planned to deliver a rousing defense of Marshall at a political rally in Milwaukee. His advisers, however, urged him to remove the remarks, arguing that he needed the McCarthyite vote to win the election. Eisenhower was "purple with rage," according to one observer, but he agreed to expunge the offending remarks.

Although Eisenhower realized that the Red scare was a hoax as it touched on his friend Marshall, he tended otherwise to accept uncritically the views of the anti-Communists. In Milwaukee he claimed that Communists had penetrated American schools, newspapers, labor unions, and the government itself, and thus they had "poisoned two whole decades of our national life." The enemy, he said, had infiltrated "our most secret councils."

Learning that Eisenhower had abandoned his friend Marshall, Adlai Stevenson, the Democratic presidential nominee, charged that his Republican opponent was "grasping" for votes and had mortgaged "every principle he once held." Stevenson refused to join the Red-scare bandwagon. He shared the antipathy of most Americans to Communist expansion, and he was as opposed as any to domestic subversion, but he distinguished between actual and imaginary threats of subversion. In the atmosphere of the Red scare many men and women were unwilling or unable to make that distinction.

Eisenhower easily defeated Stevenson in 1952. The election was not simply a referendum on anticommunism. Many voters turned to Eisenhower because of his war record or because they felt that it was "time for a change" after five terms of Democratic presidents. But millions of voters were impressed by McCarthy's charge that the Democrats were responsible for "twenty years of treason." McCarthy himself was reelected in 1952 along with many other outspoken anti-Communists, all of whom redoubled their efforts to find subversives.

The Senate Internal Security Subcommittee, under William Jenner of Indiana, investigated allegations of communism in education. The House Un-American Activities Subcommittee, chaired by Harold R. Velde of Illinois, explored charges of communism in Hollywood. And Joe McCarthy continued to probe for Communists in government. As chair of the Senate Permanent Investigating Subcommittee of the Government Operations Committee he investigated between 1953 and 1954 the *Voice of America*, which produced pro-American radio programs for broadcast around the world, the State Department, and other organizations and individuals. One observer remarked that the Senate caucus room where the McCarthy Subcommittee met "stank with the odor of fear and monstrous silliness."

By now an increasing number of Americans were beginning to ask whether the crackdown on supposed Communists was going too far. In 1953 President Eisenhower denounced "the book burners" and insisted that everyone has a right to meet his or her accuser "face to face." McCarthy's campaign, however, knew no limits, and a year after Eisenhower took office the senator claimed that the United States had now experienced "twenty-one years of treason." He would try to prove his point by demonstrating that the army itself was full of Communists.

He focused his attack on alleged subversion in the Signal Corps Engineering Laboratories at Fort Monmouth, New Jersey, where he discovered that an army reserve dentist, Irving Peress, had been promoted and given an honorable discharge despite his refusal to sign a loyalty oath. Peress was never proven a Communist, but he had attended Communist meetings some ten years before. Refusal to sign the loyalty oath would normally have been grounds for a less-than-honorable discharge from the army, but here the system processing information about soldiers had broken down. Sensing a plot, McCarthy had demanded to know "Who Promoted Peress?" The question became a rallying cry, a kind of anti-Communist slogan. The Peress promotion was a clue McCarthy thought he could follow to the heart of the foul conspiracy he imagined to be at work in the army.

In the meantime, the army had its own grievance against McCarthy. One of his assistants, G. David Schine, had recently entered the military. McCarthy and his staff bombarded the army with requests for special treatment for the young private. Congressmen often sent polite letters to the army on behalf of favored constituents, but McCarthy's badgering was unprecedented. The conflict between the army and McCarthy was so heated that the Senate finally decided in spring 1954 to hold special hearings to evaluate both sides of the quarrel.

The Army–McCarthy hearings began on the morning of April 22, 1954. Eager to watch one of the most heralded debates in congressional history, hundreds of spectators and reporters crowded into an ornate caucus room on the third floor of the Senate Office Building. At the front of the room glaring television lights illuminated a twenty-six-foot mahogany table where McCarthy's Permanent Investigating Subcommittee sat without McCarthy. The Wisconsin senator had stepped down temporarily to preserve the neutrality of the body and had appointed another senator to take his place. The committee consisted of four Republicans and three Democrats, with Senator Karl Mundt as chairman. At one side of the room sat representatives of the army, led by Robert T. Stevens. Opposite him sat McCarthy and his staff.

As the trial developed, the two figures who captured the public imagination were McCarthy and army counsel Joseph Nye Welch, a short, balding Boston lawyer with twinkling eyes. Like McCarthy, he was born on a farm. His parents were Iowa pioneers who raised seven children near the little town of Primghar. Joe Welch, born in 1890, was the youngest of the seven. Like McCarthy, Welch worked hard as a young man, traveling by foot, buggy, and bicycle from door to door throughout the Midwest and in Pennsylvania and New York, selling state maps for $1.95 apiece. He later remarked that it was "hateful, hard work," but it helped him understand people. "It ranks above, or with, my law school training in value," he said.

Welch worked his way through Grinnell College in Iowa and then won a scholarship to Harvard Law School. The mental distance he would travel from his parents' home was apparent in a conversation he had with his father on the night before his departure.

> "Josie," the elder Welch said, "You're going off to Harvard?"
> "That's right."
> "That's a long way, ain't it?"
> "Yes, it's a long way."
> "Somewhere's in Michigan?"
> "No it's near Boston—or maybe in Boston . . . "
> "It'll take a heap of money, won't it?"
> "Yes. You know that little gray box up on the shelf? Well, you go and get it."

Welch did, and his father dumped the contents into his hands. "There was $19," Welch recalled, "all he had, his savings of 14 years, and he gave it all to me."

Welch went on to become a successful attorney with a respected Boston law firm. He put some of his wealth into a wardrobe that included eighteen suits and more than 150 bow ties. But he retained a simplicity and charm that suggested his Iowa farm background. Joe Welch, like Joe McCarthy, believed in hard work and scorned communism. But unlike McCarthy he was aware that anticommunism can itself become a threat to American values. During the eight weeks of the Army–McCarthy hearings the interchanges between these two midwestern farmboys-become-lawyers furnished revealing moments of high drama and helped the American public evaluate the various forms of anticommunism.

The army began by charging McCarthy with improper behavior in seeking privileges for his former assistant, Private Schine. Before the hearing was half an hour old McCarthy interrupted, shouting "Point of order, Mr. Chairman!" and complaining about the way the army was presenting its case. This procedure, which McCarthy repeated again and again, allowed him to dominate the hearings, even though he was a party in the dispute. During the next two months he would raise more "points of order" than all the other participants combined.

McCarthy's behavior in the hearings was like his conduct in previous Senate committee meetings. He was loud, rude, deceitful, and at times, vicious. On the first day he cross-examined Maj. Gen. Miles Reber, a thirty-five-year veteran and winner of a Distinguished Service Medal. Reber testified about the times that McCarthy's assistant, Roy Cohn, had pressured him on behalf of Private Schine. Unable to refute the facts in Reber's testimony, McCarthy announced that Reber's brother had resigned from the State Department because he was "a bad security risk." The charge was irrelevant to the case, but it was typical of McCarthy's tendency to smear everyone who crossed his path. Committee member Henry Jackson, senator from Washington, complained that "we may be trying members of everybody's family involved before we get through." But by now McCarthy was so accustomed to assigning guilt by association that Jackson's warning had no effect.

As the hearing dragged on day after day Senator McCarthy worked feverishly to establish his case that the army, and not he, had acted improperly in their exchanges. He spent the evening working with staff members and then stayed the night in his office, where he would work over papers, fortifying himself with glasses of bourbon and five-minute naps. An assistant would often stay until six in the morning and leave the senator still at work. Then would come the hearing and McCarthy would enter the fray like a boxer, issuing "points of order" and ripping at his opponents with volleys of words. At the two-hour lunch break he would confer with his staff, his jacket on a chair, his shirt soaked with sweat. Then he would go back to the hearing and more charges and countercharges.

In the past only a few spectators at a time had witnessed the frenzy of a McCarthy hearing. But now two television networks carried live broadcasts of the hearings nationwide. Television was still a new medium and relatively few families had sets, but friends gathered around them across the nation to watch the famous senator from Wisconsin at work. In all, ten million Americans saw the hearings on television. Millions more saw newsreels, heard radio broadcasts, or read newspaper accounts. In hundreds of schools, saloons, and theaters one could hear amateur and professional comics intoning the words, "Mr. Chairman, point of order . . . "

Among the millions who watched the army hearings was a young French student named Madeleine Biskey. Newly arrived in America, she was attending Columbia University, where she learned about the McCarthy hearings from fellow students. On a trip to Washington she talked to a soldier from Wisconsin who told her that McCarthy was the greatest man alive and that there were Communists everywhere. Curious about American ways, she attended the Senate hearings. "It was

McCarthy's show," she later recalled. And a strange show it was, led by a bloated McCarthy and his intense assistants, David Schine and Roy Cohn. From the vantage point of her own culture, the frenzy of anticommunism seemed strange to Mademoiselle Biskey. At home the French Communists had been active in the resistance to Hitler, and the great war hero, Charles de Gaulle, accepted them into his postwar government. Why were Americans so frightened of people who in France were simply members of another political faction? As the trial progressed and McCarthy's personality was revealed to millions of Americans, others came to ask the same question: What was the country afraid of?

The actual issues of the trial were less important than the exposure given to the character and tactics of Joe McCarthy as the nation's foremost Red hunter. McCarthy presented a carbon copy of an alleged FBI document: the document proved to be a forgery. It was, said army counsel Welch, a carbon copy of nothing at all. With each new performance by the senator, Welch's face showed bemusement and indignation. That face appeared on millions of television screens, and many viewers saw in it the echo of their own astonishment at McCarthy's behavior.

The hostility between the two men erupted on June 9 when Welch was examining McCarthy's assistant, Roy Cohn. The testimony was going badly for Cohn, and so McCarthy began to attack Fred Fisher, a young law associate in Welch's firm. Fisher had once belonged to the Lawyers' Guild, a legal organization that was associated with the Communist party. He was never a Communist and had quit the Guild some time before, but McCarthy had found a weakness in Welch's law family and went on the attack.

Roy Cohn was horrified at his boss's tactic. They had agreed in advance that McCarthy would not mention Fisher, and that Welch, in turn, would not mention that Cohn had flunked the physical test for admission to West Point. He scribbled a hasty note to McCarthy: "This is the subject which I have committed to Welch we would not go into. Please respect our agreement as an agreement, because this is not going to do any good."

McCarthy, however, had lost all sense of discretion and attacked Fisher before the committee and millions of television viewers who had no way of evaluating the charges, or even knowing why they mattered. Before those millions of witnesses the quiet lawyer from Iowa, trembling with emotion, addressed McCarthy. "Until this moment, Senator," he said, "I think I never really gauged your cruelty and your recklessness."

Welch explained that Fred Fisher was a young man starting "what looks to be a brilliant career" with Welch's law firm. He had accompanied Welch and his chief assistant, Jim St. Clair, to Washington for the hearings. Welch asked both men if there was anything in their backgrounds that might cause embarrassment at the hearings, and Fisher volunteered that while in law school he had belonged to the Lawyers'

Guild, as McCarthy alleged. Welch thought that the former connection was harmless, but decided not to use Fisher on his staff in Washington, explaining to him, "If I do, one of these days that will come out and go over national television, and it will just hurt like the dickens."

"So, Senator," continued Welch, "I asked him to go back to Boston. Little did I dream you could be so reckless and cruel as to do an injury to that lad. It is true he is still with Hale & Dorr. It is true that he will continue to be with Hale & Dorr. It is, I regret to say, equally true that I fear he shall always bear a scar needlessly inflicted by you. If it [is] in my power to forgive you for your reckless cruelty, I will do so. I like to think I am a gentleman, but your forgiveness will have to come from someone other than me."

McCarthy tried to resume his attack, but Welch interrupted:

"Senator, may we not drop this? We know he belonged to the Lawyers' Guild, and Mr. Cohn nods his head at me. . . .

"Let us not assassinate this lad further, Senator. You have done enough. Have you no sense of decency, sir, at long last? Have you no sense of decency?"

McCarthy tried one last time to attack Fisher. Welch cut him off: "Mr. McCarthy, I will not discuss this with you further. You have sat within six feet of me and could have asked me about Fred Fisher. You have brought it out. If there is a God in heaven, it will do neither you nor your cause any good. I will not discuss it further. I will not ask Mr. Cohn any more questions. You, Mr. Chairman, may, if you will, call the next witness."

The audience in the Senate caucus room had listened in stunned silence. When Welch finished, their applause thundered through the room, engulfing a tearful Welch and a stunned McCarthy. The hearings went on for a few more days, but for most observers the encounter over Fred Fisher was the climax of the proceedings. Never had McCarthy's anticommunism seemed more petty, malicious, and stupid, and never had an opponent of the senator's called more effectively for understanding, charity, and wisdom in the difficult task of distinguishing between patriots and traitors.

A few months later the committee issued a report criticizing both the army and McCarthy for misconduct. More important, during fall 1954 the Senate as a whole considered a motion to censure McCarthy. He had made many enemies by riding roughshod over fellow senators as well as by attacking hundreds of other loyal Americans. Additionally, questions about his campaign funds had arisen that McCarthy failed to answer satisfactorily. On December 2, 1954, all of the Senate Democrats and half the Republicans joined in adopting a resolution "condemning" McCarthy's actions.

Neither his humiliation at the army hearings nor the Senate condemnation removed McCarthy from the political scene. In November 1954, fifteen hundred supporters attended a birthday dinner at Milwaukee's Pfister Hotel. Huge banners with the slogan "WHO PROMOTED PERESS?" decorated the banquet hall, and the band played a song declaring "Nobody's for McCarthy but the people." Most of the people, however, no longer admired the senator. His popularity rating in Gallup polls dropped from a solid majority to a distinct minority. He was excluded from the White House invitations that went to other congressmen; journalists and politicians failed to take him seriously. Humbled and isolated, the senator became increasingly alcoholic, gulping down whole glasses of liquor before breakfast. His liver began to fail him, and in spring 1957, at age forty-seven, Joe McCarthy died.

The fear of communism did not disappear with McCarthy's death. Real spies would still be discovered from time to time in the United States. Moreover, international events laid the seeds for more anti-Communist activities abroad. During the Army–McCarthy hearings, Dien Bien Phu, a French stronghold in Vietnam, fell to the Communist insurgents under the leadership of Ho Chi Minh. A reporter asked Richard Nixon, now vice president of the United States, what the country would do if France were forced to withdraw from Vietnam. Nixon replied that if there were no other recourse, the administration would have to send troops.

But the events of 1954 discouraged the more repressive expressions of anticommunism. Soon it was apparent that thousands of innocent Americans had been slandered—and often lost their jobs—in the atmosphere of hysteria surrounding the anti-Communist crusade. Ironically, McCarthy, who had been the champion of anticommunism, became the symbol of its abuse. "McCarthyism" entered the dictionary as a word to describe harmful and irresponsible charges of disloyalty. The senator's tumultuous career thus encouraged Americans to distinguish between treason, the conscious effort to betray the country to an enemy, and freedom of expression, one of the strengths of American public life.

Bibliography

CAUTE, DAVID. *The Great Fear* (1978). Surveys anti-Communist activities during the presidencies of Truman and Eisenhower.

COHN, ROY. *McCarthy* (1968). Written by one of McCarthy's chief assistants.

DEAN, ROBERT D. *The Imperial Brotherhood: Gender and the Making of Cold War Foreign Policy* (2001). How ideas of masculinity helped shape American foreign policy and led to a purge of suspected homosexuals in the State Department during the McCarthy Era.

DMYTRYK, EDWARD. *Odd Man Out: A Memoir of the Hollywood Ten* (1996). Account of the persecution of alleged Communists in Hollywood by one of the accused who later became an informer.

DOHERTY, THOMAS. *Cold War, Cool Medium: Television, McCarthyism, and American Culture (2003).* Explores the simultaneous rise of television and McCarthyism, with the new medium facilitating both the rise and fall of McCarthy.

GOODMAN, WALTER. *The Committee* (1968). History of the House Un-American Activities Committee.

HOFSTADTER, RICHARD. *The Paranoid Style in American Politics* (1952, 1963). Classic examination of the tendency of some Americans to see conspiracies where none exist.

LATTIMORE, OWEN. *Ordeal by Slander* (1950). Personal account by a man accused by McCarthy of Communist leanings.

MACDONALD, CALLUM A. *Korea: The War Before Vietnam* (1986). Lucid account of the Korean conflict.

MCCARTHY, JOSEPH R. *America's Fall from Grace: The Story of George Catlett Marshall* (1951). Based on McCarthy's vituperative attack on Marshall in the Senate.

PHILBRICK, HERBERT A. *I Led Three Lives* (1952). Autobiographical account by an American counterespionage agent.

REEVES, THOMAS C. *The Life and Times of Joe McCarthy* (1982). Superbly researched and carefully balanced account of McCarthy's life.

ROVERE, RICHARD H. *Senator Joe McCarthy* (1959). A journalist's damning account of McCarthy's career.

SCHRECKER, ELLEN. *Many Are the Crimes: McCarthyism in America* (1998). Explores communism and anticommunism in America from 1919 to the 1950s.

Study Guide

Summary

The career of Joseph McCarthy displays anticommunism as a force in American history, particularly in the decade following World War II. The essay traces the growth of anticommunism in American life from its origins late in the nineteenth century to the 1950s and explores the tensions in American life that made the movement particularly popular after the war. It portrays Joseph McCarthy as an "all-American boy" whose career both shaped and was shaped by the anti-Communist movement. In describing McCarthy's downfall it suggests that although freedom of speech is sometimes curtailed in the United States, these attacks tend to create their own reactions in favor of freedom, as in the time of the Alien and Sedition Acts.

Identification Topics

Karl Marx, Eugene Debs, Palmer raids, creeping socialism, Uncle Joe, Second Front, iron curtain, McCarran Internal Security Act, Korean War, Roy Cohn, Richard Nixon, H. Jerry Voorhis, House Un-American Activities Committee, Alger Hiss, Dorothy Kenyon, Robert M. La Follette Jr., Millard Tydings, George C. Marshall, G. David Schine, Joseph Welch

Study Questions

1. Apart from McCarthy's efforts, in what ways did the American government attack communism at home and abroad? Mention specifically the activities of the president, Congress, and the Supreme Court.

2. In what ways did President Truman fight against domestic and international communism? What limits did he place on anti-Communist activity?
3. What were the objective reasons for American anticommunism in the post-war era? In what sense was the United States at war in 1950?
4. How did Russia use its experience in World War II to justify the creation of Communist satellites in Eastern Europe?
5. During the decade following World War II nearly everyone in American public life, including Presidents Truman and Eisenhower, and McCarthy himself, was accused of Communist leanings. Cite instances of these accusations and explain why they occurred.
6. Why was Eisenhower unwilling to criticize McCarthy during the 1952 presidential campaign?
7. In what ways did some anti-Communists confuse the ideas and actions of loyal Americans with treason?
8. What elements in Joe McCarthy's character and background made him an appealing national figure?
9. Assess McCarthy's anti-Communist crusade. Why did many Americans admire his efforts? In what ways were his investigations fair or unfair?
10. Evaluate Joseph McCarthy as a person. Are there attractive elements in his personality and his career? Why did he go "off the deep end" with anticommunism?
11. How did the army hearings discredit McCarthy? Examine especially the role of Joseph Welch.
12. What was the political legacy of McCarthy's career?

Research Topics

1. Explore the history of McCarthyism in Hollywood, college campuses, and other segments of American society.
2. Compare McCarthyism with the Red scare following World War I.
3. Read Richard Hofstadter's *The Paranoid Style in American Politics*. How well does Hofstadter's concept of the "paranoid style" apply to McCarthyism?

CHAPTER 12

The Civil Rights Movement

Martin Luther King Jr.

and the Road to Birmingham

The civil rights movement of the 1950s and 1960s is often called the "Second Reconstruction." It changed the lives of African Americans more significantly than any other event since emancipation. Although freed from slavery, blacks had been imprisoned in a circle of discrimination that restricted most to menial jobs and inferior public facilities. During the civil rights movement, many formal barriers to black equality were removed by tactics of nonviolent confrontation that exposed racial injustice and won public support for remedial legislation. The movement's success would encourage women, Native Americans, Mexican Americans, and other minorities to claim for themselves the birthright of equality.

In the last years of his life Martin Luther King Jr. liked to tell the story of Birmingham. He regarded the great struggle of 1963 in that city as a turning point in the civil rights movement. Not only did it result in reforms in Birmingham, but it also helped persuade Congress and the president to give their full support to civil rights legislation. When King described the episode in lectures and sermons, he depicted a cosmic struggle between justice and injustice, the forces of light and the forces of darkness. The leader of the opposition to integration in Birmingham, Eugene ("Bull") Connor, who directed the police attacks on civil rights demonstrators, was in King's view not merely a bigot but the very embodiment of injustice. The civil rights demonstrators, on the other hand, by resisting injustice without being tainted by violence, symbolized the moral superiority of an oppressed people and thereby won worldwide support for their cause.

As King told an audience at the Mount Zion Baptist Church in Cincinnati: "Bull Connor was always happy when some of the spectators on the sidelines would begin to throw rocks and throw bottles. He was very happy when he saw Negroes doing that. Now he was happy because he's an expert in violence and in dealing with violence." But when demonstrators protested peacefully Connor was confused. He "didn't understand this. He didn't know how to handle this. Because of this, that community, which said that it would never integrate its lunch counters and many of its facilities, has to face integration at its lunch counters today and in many other facilities. There's power in this method."

King's method consisted of nonviolent resistance to oppression. He regarded the civil rights movement as a great moral struggle between the oppressor and the oppressed; the villain was the person who lived by injustice, and the hero was the person who resisted tyranny without being degraded by it. Cowards ran from injustice; knaves became corrupted in fighting it. But the virtuous won the struggle by forcing the oppressors to reveal their cruelty to the world; for when the cruelty of segregation was fully exposed, no right-thinking person would accept its continuation. At Birmingham, King believed, the mindless villainy of segregation had been revealed in all its tawdry colors, and the heroic persistence of integration had won a great moral and political victory.

King's efforts to end segregation through nonviolent confrontation made him at once the most loved and most hated man in America. But Birmingham was more than simply the test of one man or one idea. It was the culmination, rather, of two forces that had been active in the country for almost a century: the effort to segregate blacks from the mainstream of American society and the movement to resist segregation.

The issue in Birmingham was whether whites could exclude blacks from a wide range of facilities, including the ballot box, schools, parks, public transportation, housing, restaurants, hotels, restrooms, and drinking fountains. Such restrictions were so familiar in many areas that they seemed inevitable. Segregation had begun long before emancipation, as Frederick Douglass learned after he escaped from slavery in Maryland. Even in the North he was a second-class citizen and had to ride on segregated jim crow railroad cars. In the antebellum period most northern states denied blacks the ballot, and some of the western territories passed laws declaring that nonwhites could not live within their borders.

The freeing of the slaves did nothing to end the racial prejudice that had contributed, in the first place, to black enslavement. They soon faced limitations on their social, economic, and political freedom that reminded them of their inferior status. This system of racial separation was widely accepted throughout the first half of the twentieth century. In the 1940s black athletes played on segregated teams. Baseball players who were as skilled as any contemporary white athletes were restricted to the Negro leagues. One player recollected traveling from game to game in an old bus; denied the use of segregated service-station restroom facilities, he and his teammates frequently had to urinate at the side of the road. During World War II thousands of African Americans gave their lives without achieving equality for themselves. In the army blacks were barred from white social facilities. At a typical training camp in Arizona there was only a white swimming pool; when a group of blacks sneaked in during the night to use it, the base commander punished them, then drained and refilled the pool, thus isolating his white troops—who were about to fight the race supremacist Hitler—from contamination by their nonwhite fellow soldiers.

During the war African American soldiers who conducted German prisoners by railroad between camps in the United States had to go unfed while the Nazi captives ate in white-only restaurants. As late as 1949 blacks were not admitted to theaters in downtown Washington, D.C., even to hear such celebrated black performers as Marian Anderson. The examples of segregation in the land of the free were unending. The policy of separation was not as restrictive as slavery, but like slavery it put strict limits on black enterprise. It meant that blacks were, as a matter of course, denied jobs, schooling, political power, and cultural and recreational opportunities.

From the earliest years of segregation some African Americans had resisted these restrictions. When they began to realize in the late nineteenth and early twentieth centuries that segregation was a fact of life, they offered many responses to the situation. The most famous was Booker T. Washington's proposal in 1895 that his people work their way to equality by developing their own skills so highly that all whites would recognize the mutual dependence of the races. Although not endorsing segregation, Washington argued that even without social equality blacks had "a man's chance" to succeed if they worked hard. Washington was considered the foremost black leader of his time by blacks and whites alike. His belief that the path to black progress lay through hard work, rather than in tearing down the barriers to white society, was reflected in the U.S. Supreme Court's 1896 *Plessy v. Ferguson* decision, which endorsed the segregationist concept of "separate but equal."

There were, however, those who criticized the ever-tightening hold of segregation on the nation's political and economic institutions. W. E. B. Du Bois, a Harvard graduate, approved of Washington's emphasis on hard work but felt that he overlooked "the emasculating effects of caste distinctions." In 1905 Du Bois met with a small group of black intellectuals and professional men at Niagara Falls to discuss the race question. This was the beginning of the Niagara movement. In the following year the participants met at Harpers Ferry and demanded an end to discrimination in public accommodations, education, and politics. "We are men!" they said. "We will be treated as men. And we shall win!"

After several more annual meetings most of the supporters of the Niagara Movement joined forces with a new organization, the National Association for the Advancement of Colored People (NAACP). The NAACP was formed by discontented blacks and by antisegregation whites, such as the socialist journalist William English Walling, who opposed racial injustice and wanted to revive "the spirit of the abolitionists." The NAACP charter of 1910 declared that the organization would seek "to advance the interests of colored citizens; to secure for them impartial suffrage; and to increase their opportunities for securing justice in the courts, education for their children, employment according to their ability, and complete equality before the law."

The NAACP soon embarked on an ambitious program of fighting segregation and racial injustice through publicity, politics, and the courts. When rioters in east Saint Louis killed thirty-two blacks in 1917, the NAACP organized a protest parade in New York City. After more than a thousand blacks had been lynched throughout the nation between 1900 and 1920, the NAACP campaigned for a federal antilynching bill. When blacks were convicted of crimes on flimsy evidence, the organization appealed their convictions to higher courts.

Although the NAACP enjoyed considerable support from both whites and blacks, it could only chip away at the great national edifice of racial injustice. Segregation, disfranchisement, and lynchings continued. In response, some blacks concluded that white America was hopelessly bigoted and that the only refuge for the oppressed was in Africa.

The foremost exponent of the back-to-Africa movement was Marcus Garvey, a Jamaican black who immigrated to the United States and in 1917 founded the Universal Negro Improvement Association in Harlem. Garvey publicized the idea of the fraternity of blacks throughout the world and advocated the creation of an independent black nation in Africa. In 1921 a Garvey convention in New York attracted twenty-five thousand participants, who immediately formed a provisional government for the proposed state and elected Garvey as president general. Although the movement declined after 1925 when Garvey was imprisoned for mail fraud, it had revealed the profound discontent that many blacks felt. Black nationalism found another prophet in the 1930s in the person of Wallace Fard, a young Detroit black who declared that the true African American religion was Islam. Christianity currently ruled the world, but soon, he said, members of his Black Muslim faith could overthrow white supremacy. Fard built up a strong following in the Detroit ghetto but relinquished leadership to Elijah Poole, soon to be known as Elijah Muhammad, who recruited more than one hundred thousand members of the new faith and established fifty temples across the United States. Although the Muslims did not advocate integration, they did share with other reformers a belief that the race problem was, in part, an economic problem. Thus, they encouraged blacks to establish independent department stores, restaurants, grocery stores, and other businesses. While other leaders saw such enterprises as a route to equality and integration, however, Elijah Muhammad favored business activity as a means of increasing the independent power of his people.

One of the most important civil rights initiatives in the 1930s was the Jobs for Negroes movement, which began in Detroit in 1933. The program organized boycotts to force white employers to hire blacks. Among its leaders was the Reverend Mr. Adam Clayton Powell, who later became a U.S. congressman. Through his influence blacks began to get jobs in stores, public utilities, and transportation.

Reform continued in a piecemeal fashion in the 1940s. African Americans were particularly successful in winning concessions from the nation's defense industries, in part because of their need for employees, and in part through federal action. When blacks found that most war contractors refused to hire them, they threatened to organize a massive march on Washington in summer 1941. President Franklin D. Roosevelt wanted to avoid the embarrassment of this demonstration at a time when war with Germany seemed imminent, and so he met with the parade leaders and agreed to issue an executive order prohibiting discrimination in war industries. His Executive Order 8802—perhaps the most beneficial document for blacks since the Emancipation Proclamation—established the Fair Employment Practices Commission. Although the new agency did not completely end discrimination in defense production, it did force many employers to hire blacks.

At the war's end discrimination still prevailed in schooling, politics, employment, and public services. But whereas in 1890 all the signs pointed to the elimination of black rights, in 1945 the system of segregation seemed to be weakening. In sports Joe Louis was in the eighth year of his reign as heavyweight champion of the world. In the ring, at least, a black man could stand up to a white man without fear of being lynched.

When Louis had won the crown from James J. Braddock in 1937, a black boy named Malcolm Little remembered that in Lansing, Michigan, his people "went wildly happy with the greatest celebration of race pride our generation had ever known."

Throughout the United States young blacks took up boxing as a means of moving up in the world. But there could be only one champion at a time, and most ended up like Malcolm Little—whose second and last fight lasted only ten seconds—seeking other forms of selfexpression. For the great mass of African Americans the less dramatic court victories of the postwar decade were more important than boxing victories.

The NAACP now focused most of its energies on legal challenges to segregation and disfranchisement. In 1944 the Supreme Court declared in *Smith v. Albright* that states could not prevent blacks from voting in political primaries, thereby eliminating—by law, at least—one of the most popular southern tactics for destroying the electoral influence of blacks. Equally important, the Court made a series of decisions that upheld the idea of equal access to public institutions of higher education.

But the most significant change of all came in 1954 with the Supreme Court's decision in *Brown v. Board of Education*. The case involved a young girl in Topeka, Kansas, who had been denied admittance to an all-white school. The NAACP, representing the plaintiff, argued that the old separate-but-equal doctrine was specious: the mere fact of separation put the black in a demeaning and discouraging position. The NAACP counsel, Thurgood Marshall, cited sociological and psychological evidence to show that segregation damaged black children. "The policy of separating the races," he said, "is usually interpreted as denoting the inferiority of the Negro group. A sense of inferiority affects the motivation of the child to learn." The Court decided unanimously in favor of the plaintiff. Separate educational facilities were inherently unequal and contrary to the equal protection clause of the Fourteenth Amendment.

The *Brown* decision was greeted as the death knell of segregation. But like the earlier decisions against segregation in higher education and discrimination in political primaries, the decision reflected a de jure, not a de facto condition. In 1954 segregation was still the reality in the South.

That reality was represented in a state of near perfection in the bus system of Montgomery, Alabama. Throughout the South blacks were required to ride at the back of the bus. But in Montgomery blacks were not merely prevented from riding in the preferred white section. Local law required blacks to board the bus at the front, pay their fares, then disembark, walk along the street to the rear, and reboard the bus. Thus, blacks were forbidden even to pass in the midst of the superior race. A further regulation set aside a middle section of the bus as a neutral area. If no whites needed its seats, blacks could occupy them. But if one white wanted to sit in the middle area, all the blacks seated there must get up and stand at the back of the bus.

These laws were inherently demeaning. But there were other indignities. Although the majority of the city's transit passengers were black, all the drivers were white. Some were polite enough to the blacks; but others lorded it over them, calling them "niggers," "black cows," and "black apes." They sometimes allowed black passengers to pay at the front and then drove off while they were walking outside to the back. There were stories, too, of passengers injured when the doors caught them halfway in—a blind man hurt when he was dragged along the ground, another man killed.

For the most part, the Montgomery blacks accepted the situation, for they had never known anything better. When the buses rolled past the state capitol the passengers could look up and see a Confederate flag flying in all its glory—above the American flag. Occasionally a black would become disgusted with the system and refuse to occupy the designated seats. The driver could then summon the police, and punishment would be inevitable. Until 1955 any such resistance was isolated and futile. But on December 1 a black seamstress named Rosa Parks refused to give up her seat and inaugurated a new era in the civil rights movement.

Mrs. Parks had spent the day working downtown at the Montgomery Fair Department Store. When she left, her shoulders and neck ached from leaning over the fabric press. Wanting a comfortable ride home, she did not board the first bus that passed her on Cleveland Street because it had passengers standing in the aisles. The next bus was less crowded; she paid the driver, walked along the street to the rear entrance, and found a seat with three other blacks in the middle section. The bus began to move, and Rosa Parks relaxed.

But after three stops whites had filled all their designated seats, and one white man was left standing. The driver turned and said that he would need "those seats." The four blacks would have to stand so that the one white man could sit.

For a moment no one moved. Then the driver said, "You all better make it light on yourselves and let me have those seats."

Three blacks left their seats, but Rosa Parks refused to move. She was a proud, handsome woman with strong features and an expression that revealed both intelligence and toil.

"Are you going to get up?" the driver asked her.

"No," she said.

"If you don't stand up, I'm going to have you arrested," said the driver.

Rosa Parks didn't move. The driver left the bus to find a policeman. The other passengers remained calm, but some of them began to leave the bus. The driver came back with a police officer and pointed out the troublemaker.

"Why didn't you stand up?" asked the officer.

Rosa Parks. Tired after a hard day's work, she refused to give up her seat on a bus to a white passenger. With her arrest, the modern civil rights movement began.

"Why do you push us around?" she answered.

"I don't know, but the law is the law, and you are under arrest," he said.

With that, Rosa Parks picked up her purse and shopping bag and went to the waiting police car. Within a few minutes she was booked at city hall and put in jail. "I felt very much annoyed and inconvenienced," she recalled, "because I had hoped to go home and get my dinner, and do whatever else I had to do for the evening. But now here I was sitting in jail and couldn't get home."

It is hard to imagine a more prosaic beginning to a revolution than Rosa Parks's refusal to give up her seat on the Cleveland Street bus. Vehicles in Montgomery and hundreds of other cities had carried millions of blacks from place to place in segregated seats. The affront to Rosa Parks was no worse than she and others had borne for many decades. But she had said no, and soon the whole system of segregation would be affected.

It weakened, however, not only because of the quiet stand of one woman, but also because of blows already delivered by the Supreme Court and because of the activities of Montgomery's African American community. The word of Rosa Parks's arrest soon spread through the city. The news reached many black leaders in Montgomery who were prepared to turn her random act into a well-organized protest.

There was Jo Ann Robinson, president of the local Women's Political Council, a black equivalent of the segregated League of Women Voters; E. D. Nixon, a member of the Brotherhood of Sleeping Car Porters and leader of Montgomery's black community; and Ralph Abernathy, pastor of the First Baptist Church. They all had deep roots in Montgomery, but the man who was destined to lead the protest had been in the city for only one year. He was the pastor of the Dexter Avenue Baptist Church, Martin Luther King Jr.

King was twenty-six years old at the time. His background linked him both to the strong Christian traditions of the black South and the intellectual formulations of modern theology. He had grown up in Atlanta, Georgia, where his father was pastor of the Ebenezer Baptist Church. He graduated from Morehouse College when he was nineteen, then went to Crozer Theological Seminary in Chester, Pennsylvania, and to Boston University, where he received a Ph.D. in systematic theology in 1955. In the meantime, he had begun work as a pastor in Montgomery.

King saw the problems of the South through the perspective of his training in philosophy and religion. He believed with many modern theologians that "sin is separation" and applied this concept to the separation of the races. He was impressed with Henry David Thoreau's argument in the "Essay on Civil Disobedience" that people could not accept injustice without being corrupted by it, and he was impressed with Mahatma Gandhi's belief that people can change history by nonviolent protest.

During his career as a civil rights leader, King often reminded blacks that they could never attain full equality without working to improve themselves. "We must set out to do a good job," he liked to say, "and do that job so well that the living, the dead, and unborn couldn't do it any better. So if it falls your lot to be a street sweeper, go on out and sweep streets like Michelangelo painted pictures, sweep streets like Beethoven composed music, sweep streets like Shakespeare wrote poetry, sweep streets so well that all the hosts of heaven and earth will have to pause and say, 'Here lived a great street sweeper, who swept his job well.'"

These words show that the legacy of Booker T. Washington, with its emphasis on honest toil, affected even Martin Luther King Jr. But unlike the sage of Tuskegee, King did not believe that black Americans could greatly improve their condition without the elimination of racial injustice. Blacks, he said, "live within two concentric circles of segregation. One imprisons them on the basis of color, while the other confines them within a separate culture of poverty. His struggle to escape his circumstances is hindered by color discrimination. He is deprived of normal education and normal social and economic opportunities. When he seeks opportunity, he is told, in effect, to lift himself by his own bootstraps, advice which does not take into account the fact that he is barefoot." True progress could come only with the removal of barriers to racial equality.

King had thought to spend his life as a minister. His wife, Coretta, believed that her husband could have been perfectly happy as a country pastor, living close to his congregation. But Rosa Parks's refusal to leave her seat changed King's life. He had already established himself as an effective preacher and an opponent of segregation. When Montgomery's black community wanted a leader for their protest against segregation, King was a natural choice.

The protest began with a one-day boycott of the city's buses. Sermons and leaflets proclaimed that segregation in busing must end and that the bus company must hire black drivers. On the first day almost the whole black community abandoned the buses. Some walked to work; others rode in black taxis at a reduced fare. The black leaders decided to continue the boycott until their demands were met and created the Montgomery Improvement Association to coordinate boycott activities.

They were highly conscious of their public image. They chose Rosa Parks as the focal point for their protest because she was well respected by her community. With the same regard to the dignity of their movement, they were attracted to King in part because he had received a prestigious degree from a northern university.

King became president of the Montgomery Improvement Association and spoke at its first public meeting held on the night after the opening day of the boycott. He addressed an enthusiastic audience of five thousand in a manner that would become familiar in the future years of the civil rights movement.

"You know, my friends," he said, "there comes a time when people get tired of being trampled over by the iron feet of oppression. There comes a time, my friends, when people get tired of being flung across the abyss of humiliation where they experience the bleakness of nagging despair. There comes a time when people get tired of being pushed out of the glittering sunlight of life's July, and left standing amidst the piercing chill of an Alpine November. We are here this evening because we are tired now."

It was oratory such as this that projected Martin Luther King Jr. into national prominence as a statesman for his race. He knew how to find the right words to express the sorrow and longings of his people. He could take a phrase like "people get tired" and weave it into melodic cadences that beat upon the heart. He could take images like "the abyss of humiliation" and "the piercing chill of an Alpine November" and form them into sounds that pulled at the emotions.

It was a rhetoric that grew out of his own southern black Christian heritage, from religious meetings at which people sang old spirituals, clapped their hands, and punctuated the minister's sermon with shouts of "Yes, Lord!" and "Tell it, Brother!" King was short and stocky; his hair and mustache were close clipped; his face was heavy and muscular; in the pulpit or behind the lectern his eyes seemed riveted on some eternal truth.

When he spoke, he usually began slowly, a preacher "opening" a biblical text. As he got into his subject, his voice became powerful and melodious, building to a thundering evocation of righteousness.

The circumstances might change, but King's fundamental ideas and his mode of expression remained the same. That night in Montgomery he made two points that he would repeat again and again throughout the civil rights movement. First, men and women must not accept injustice. Second, they must resist nonviolently in order to win the contest with a display of loving forbearance.

King's address was well received. The Montgomery bus boycott went on from day to day, week to week. The black people of Montgomery walked through the winter of 1955–1956, when the cold winds blew; through the spring, when the rains fell over the city; through the summer, with its sweltering heat; and into the autumn, when the leaves began to fall alongside the road. They negotiated with city officials; they spoke encouragement to one another. They refused to be provoked into violence. One night an angry segregationist threw a bomb onto Dr. King's front porch; it exploded, destroying the front of the house but luckily injuring no one; a crowd of three hundred angry blacks gathered, eager to retaliate; King spoke to them about nonviolence.

The Supreme Court finally decided the segregation issue at Montgomery. On December 13, 1956, it declared that Alabama's state law requiring racial segregation on public buses was unconstitutional. The bus company agreed to integrate and hire black drivers. For several months recalcitrant whites periodically attacked the buses, but the change took hold. Blacks had shown that they could break down the walls of segregation by refusing to accept an inferior status.

The victory at Montgomery enlivened the civil rights movement throughout the United States. It was not actually the first American victory for nonviolent protest. The Congress of Racial Equality, founded in 1942, had been engaged in "non-violent direct action" in the North for many years. In 1943 they had forced a Chicago restaurant to serve black customers, and they had engaged in many other local protests after that date.

But never before had a protest been organized on the scale of the Montgomery bus boycott. The boycott demonstrated the value of effective organization and strong leadership. It raised King to national prominence as a civil rights leader. And it showed how an effective demonstration could win sympathetic press coverage: the lines of determined black citizens walking to work furnished good photographs for the news journals and film for the newly available television news shows.

Even without systematic organization the idea of nonviolent protest would have proved infectious. The civil rights movement was like a great body of water pressing at cracks in a weakening dam. In 1956 a twenty-six-year-old black woman, Autherine Lucy, decided she wanted to attend the University of Alabama to study library science. She was unsuccessful, but in the next year nine black students integrated allwhite Little Rock High School. When they were initially barred by Governor Orval Faubus and the National Guard, President Dwight Eisenhower sent a thousand paratroopers into Little Rock to keep order and protect the students. Five years later an air force veteran, James Meredith, became the first black to enter the University of Mississippi. Governor Ross Barnett tried to bar him from the school, and campus riots after his arrival resulted in two deaths. But he gained admission with the help of federal marshals, a detachment of army troops, and the federalized Mississippi National Guard.

In such episodes three forces were joined: blacks who demanded their legal rights; federal courts that overturned segregation laws; and presidents who enforced integration edicts. The effectiveness of all three was ensured by the national public response to each issue. When Americans outside the South saw pictures of young schoolchildren in Little Rock marching between lines of angry whites or James Meredith seeking a college education on a riot-torn campus, their support went to the African Americans. In each case the white segregationists seemed violent, irrational, and cruel while the black students seemed calm, deliberate, and patient.

Efforts to desegregate public accommodations followed the same pattern. In 1960 four black college students in Greensboro, North Carolina, tried to buy food at a local Woolworth's lunch counter. They were denied service but refused to leave their seats. For three months they and their fellow students conducted a sit-in, finally forcing Woolworth's to integrate its lunch counter. The technique caught on throughout the South in the early 1960s. Groups of blacks, joined by sympathetic whites, would take seats at lunch counters and demand to be served. Hostile whites abused the demonstrators—pouring sugar or catsup over them, cursing them as "niggers" and "nigger lovers," and sometimes attacking them with fists or clubs. The demonstrators, trained in nonviolence, usually endured the taunts silently. Again they won national sympathy. Within two years, hundreds of restaurants, theaters, hotels, and other facilities had been integrated.

Martin Luther King Jr. was often at the center of such protests. After the Montgomery bus boycott he and other black leaders created the Southern Christian Leadership Conference (SCLC), whose aim was desegregation of all public facilities in the United States. Under King's direction the SCLC became the most powerful organization in the civil rights movement, raising funds, planning demonstrations, publicizing black grievances. Through private contributions and benefit concerts featuring such entertainers as Dick Gregory, Harry Belafonte, and Sammy Davis Jr., the SCLC was able to create an organization and a treasury capable of supporting large demonstrations in target cities.

In the years immediately following the Montgomery bus boycott, King devoted himself to many local activities, joining lunch counter sit-ins and preaching about civil rights. In 1957 alone he gave more than two hundred lectures throughout the country. In the half decade following Montgomery, he was arrested more than a dozen times. In 1961 he became a spokesman for the Congress of Racial Equality's (CORE) Freedom Rides. These were busloads of black and white volunteers who set out from Washington, D.C., to drive through the South on interstate highways in order to challenge segregation of public facilities. In several cities the volunteers were badly beaten and their buses were burned or pelted with rocks. But they won their point. On September 22, 1961, through Attorney General Robert Kennedy's intervention, the Interstate Commerce Commission ruled that passengers in interstate commerce must be seated without regard to color and that terminals must be desegregated.

Such victories were numerous in the five years after Montgomery. But King did not personally organize a single major protest movement during this time. His contribution had been primarily supportive. During the Freedom Rides, however, several hundred blacks were arrested in Albany, Georgia, for civil rights activities. King decided then to use Albany as the focal point for a new kind of demonstration aimed at abolishing discrimination in all public facilities. Hitherto, reform had been incremental—a school or a lunch counter in one place, a bus company or a theater in another.

The SCLC joined with the NAACP and CORE in Albany to mobilize the black community. During 1962, 6 percent of the blacks in the city were arrested for protest activities. Despite the willingness of many local residents to go to jail, however, little was achieved in that year. The black leaders had made few plans and could not agree on strategy; and the Albany police were discreet, avoiding dramatic incidents that would win sympathy for the demonstrators. At the end of the year there was little public interest in the confrontation; people were beginning to suggest that the era of King's leadership was at an end.

It was even possible that the public might have grown apathetic about civil rights. Television shows and newspapers had publicized many black victories in the past few years. It was easy to forget that most southern blacks still attended segregated schools, could not vote, had inferior jobs, and had access only to second-class public facilities. Within the past few years blacks who had attempted to register to vote in Fayette County, Tennessee, had been evicted from their homes. A man who photographed a "WHITE ONLY" sign on a Coke machine in Jackson, Tennessee, was arrested and fined for disorderly conduct. In Montgomery, Alabama, the average black earned only half as much as the average white, and fewer than 50 percent of the black families had indoor toilets. In many respects, the condition of black Americans had changed little in the previous decade.

Birmingham, Alabama, typified the persistence of the old racial barriers. King once called it "the most segregated city in America." A steel town with a population of three hundred thousand, it was proud of its ability to keep blacks "in their place." Of the ninety thousand registered voters in Birmingham only ten thousand were black. The NAACP had not gained a foothold in the city because it was outlawed by Alabama law as a "foreign corporation." Efforts to change the racial situation in the city were often met with violence. Between 1957 and 1963 alone there were seventeen unsolved bombings of black churches and homes in Birmingham. In 1961 a mob had beaten a group of freedom riders in the local bus station. The city government was as diligent as its citizens in enforcing segregation. When it became evident that the city's sixty-eight parks, thirty-eight playgrounds, six pools, and four golf courses would have to desegregate to comply with federal law, the city fathers closed them. The city's tough attitude toward black unrest was ably represented by Eugene ("Bull") Connor, one of Birmingham's three commissioners of public safety. Connor was a popular ex-baseball announcer who ran one of the toughest police forces in the South.

Many of Birmingham's black leaders were reluctant to attack segregation in the city head-on, but in 1962 the Reverend Mr. Fred L. Shuttleworth, leader of the Alabama Christian Movement for Human Rights, organized a boycott of Birmingham businesses that discriminated against blacks. After studying the situation, the Southern Christian Leadership Conference, under King's direction, decided to join Shuttleworth in attacking segregation in Birmingham. If they could win in Birmingham, they concluded, they could win anywhere.

The SCLC began planning for demonstrations in Birmingham in winter 1962–1963. They wanted to avoid the error they had made in Albany of beginning without extensive preparation. King and other leaders became acquainted with the local black community and began to teach them the philosophy and method of nonviolent resistance to segregation. Andrew Young, then vice president of the SCLC, remembered that in Birmingham this was a hard lesson to convey. Many of the city's tough young blacks believed that in a confrontation they would have to "kill or be killed."

The civil rights leaders established three major goals: removal of racial restrictions in stores, including segregated lunch counters, dressing rooms, drinking fountains, and restrooms; adoption of nondiscriminatory hiring practices; and creation of a biracial city commission to negotiate further desegregation. They made prospective demonstration participants sign a pledge of nonviolence. The signers agreed to "Remember always that the non-violent movement in Birmingham seeks justice and reconciliation, not victory"; to "Observe with both friend and foe the ordinary rules of courtesy"; and to "Refrain from the violence of fist, tongue, or heart." These rules and others like them were not mere window dressing. They were at the heart of the civil rights movement as King and others understood it. King carefully explained this Gandhian creed of peaceful protest at dozens of meetings of Birmingham blacks.

At the scores of organizational meetings that were held before and during the demonstrations King, Ralph Abernathy, Fred Shuttleworth, and other leaders also taught their people the "freedom songs." These were adaptations of old slave songs to modern times. King believed that both the words and the music of the songs reinforced the patient resolve that was essential to the movement. "Woke Up This Morning with My Mind Stayed on Freedom," he said, "is a sentence that needs no music to make its point." Another song, "Ain't Gonna Let Nobody Turn Me 'Round," taught persistence. "It is not just a song," wrote King. "It's a resolve."

The civil rights organizers set April 3 as C day in Birmingham—C for confrontation, for the great demonstration against segregation. The predominantly white electorate of Birmingham had just voted in favor of a new type of city government and had chosen a moderate segregationist for mayor over Bull Connor. But the election did not appear to signal an end of racial discrimination, and Connor was still in office at the time anyway. And so the demonstrations began.

On the first few days the organizers sent small groups of blacks downtown to sit in at department store lunch counters. They wanted to build up to the full force of confrontation slowly. On April 6 a crowd of demonstrators marched on city hall. The police ordered them to disperse but approached them cautiously. Connor had been persuaded that he should not allow himself to appear brutal, because the demonstrations were receiving national press coverage.

On April 12, Good Friday, King led a march toward city hall. The authorities had obtained a court injunction against the march, but King decided that he would disobey it. As he later wrote: "Any law that uplifts human personality is just. Any law that degrades human personality is unjust." As the marchers moved along the street singing "We Shall Overcome," the police moved in and arrested King along with fifty other demonstrators.

In prison King found himself in solitary confinement. He was not allowed to make calls or receive visitors. On Saturday morning shafts of sunlight coming through a high window barely illuminated his dismal cell. Then the beams of sunlight were gone. The day had ended, and he still had not been allowed to communicate with anyone outside the prison. He later wrote: "Those were the longest, most frustrating and bewildering hours I have lived." On Sunday his attorneys were finally allowed to visit him. The next day King learned that singer Harry Belafonte had raised $50,000 in bail for the prisoners. King was deeply relieved. After he was alone again, he contemplated his feelings of the last two days. He was stunned by "a profound sense of awe. I was aware," he wrote, "of a feeling that had been present all along below the surface of consciousness, pressed down under the weight of concern for the movement: I had never been truly in solitary confinement; God's companionship does not stop at the door of a jail cell."

King is so well known as a political figure that we easily forget the deep current of piety that influenced his life. But his sense of the reality of God infused his oratory and leadership with its prophetic tone. It was the minister in him that told his followers to "Refrain from the violence of fist, tongue, or heart."

While he was in prison, Martin Luther King Jr. read in the newspaper that eight white ministers in Birmingham had criticized the demonstrations as "untimely." King decided to reply. Not being allowed any writing paper, he began his composition on the margins of the newspaper, then continued on a legal pad obtained from his attorneys. The result was the "Letter from Birmingham Jail," the most important document of the civil rights movement.

The eight clergymen asked why King had come to Birmingham. King answered that his Southern Christian Leadership Conference had branches throughout the South and that he had been invited by a local affiliate to come to the city. "But more basically," he said, "I am in Birmingham because injustice is here." Segregation in Birmingham was not merely a local matter, he argued. "Injustice anywhere is a threat to justice everywhere. We are caught in an inescapable network of mutuality, tied in a single garment of destiny."

King's critics chided him for leading demonstrations. He replied that they should be equally concerned about "the conditions that brought about the demonstrations." They said that the demonstrators should seek change through negotiation. King replied that the city had never acted in good faith through negotiations. "We know through painful experience," he said, "that freedom is never voluntarily given by the oppressor; it must be demanded by the oppressed."

The eight ministers questioned whether the demonstrations were "well timed." King replied that blacks had waited 340 years "for our constitutional and God-given rights," and that was long enough. In the most eloquent passage in the long letter he described just what it meant to "wait" in a condition of inferiority:

> When you have seen vicious mobs lynch your mothers and fathers at will and drown your sisters and brothers at whim; when you have seen hate-filled policemen curse, kick, and even kill your black brothers and sisters; when you see the vast majority of your twenty million Negro brothers smothering in an airtight cage of poverty in the midst of an affluent society; when you suddenly find your tongue twisted and your speech stammering as you seek to explain to your six-year-old

daughter why she can't go to the public amusement park that has just been advertised on television, and see tears welling up in her eyes when she is told that Funtown is closed to colored children, and see ominous clouds of inferiority beginning to form in her little mental sky, and see her beginning to distort her personality by developing an unconscious bitterness toward white people; when you have to concoct an answer for a five-year-old son who is asking: "Daddy, why do white people treat colored people so mean?"; when you take a crosscountry drive and find it necessary to sleep night after night in the uncomfortable corners of your automobile because no motel will accept you; when you are humiliated day in and day out by nagging signs reading "white" and "colored"; when your first name becomes "nigger," your middle name becomes "boy" (however old you are) and your last name becomes "John," and your wife and mother are never given the respected title "Mrs."; when you are harried by day and haunted by night by the fact that you are a Negro, living constantly at tiptoe stance, never quite knowing what to expect next, and are plagued with inner fears and outer resentments; when you are forever fighting a degenerating sense of "nobodiness"—then you will understand why we find it difficult to wait. There comes a time when the cup of endurance runs over, and men are no longer willing to be plunged into the abyss of despair. I hope, sirs, you can understand our legitimate and unavoidable impatience.

This was what segregation was really like. This was what it did to its victims. The rest of King's letter explained the philosophy of nonviolent resistance to injustice. One could break an unjust law, he said, if one did so "openly, lovingly, and with a willingness to accept the penalty." He cited early Christian and American Revolutionary precedents for civil disobedience and argued that such acts were often the path to human progress.

He had been called an extremist. But he was really a moderate, King asserted, standing between those blacks who were afraid to act at all and those who tended toward violence in the face of oppression. Or if he was an extremist, he acted in the tradition of Jesus, Paul, and Luther, who were extremists for love. "Perhaps," he said, "the South, the nation and the world are in dire need of creative extremists."

In contrast, too many southern ministers were cautious men who could go to church without ever troubling themselves about racial injustice. He had once hoped that southern white churchmen would rally around the civil rights movement. But he had been disappointed by their indifference or hostility. He now called upon the church as a whole to "meet the challenge of this decisive hour."

Lastly, King's critics had praised the Birmingham police department for doing its job well. King conceded that they had not engaged in any acts of overt violence. But the very system they were supporting was wrong; they were using "the moral means of nonviolence to maintain the immoral end of racial injustice." They were not the heroes of the South.

Yet the South did have its heroes, men and women who stood up for justice. "One day," King said, "the South will recognize its real heroes." Those were people like James Meredith, who went alone to integrate the University of Mississippi. They were people like the seventy-two-year-old black woman in Montgomery, Alabama, who joined her neighbors in refusing to ride the segregated buses. Asked whether she was tired, she replied, "My feets is tired, but my soul is at rest."

The "Letter from Birmingham Jail" was a celebration of such people and of the aspirations and achievements of the civil rights movement. King concluded on a note of optimism for the future: "Let us all hope that the dark clouds of racial prejudice will soon pass away and the deep fog of misunderstanding will be lifted from our fear-drenched communities, and in some not too distant tomorrow the radiant stars of love and brotherhood will shine over our great nation with all their scintillating beauty."

Such were the thoughts that Martin Luther King Jr. committed to paper in his narrow cell. Eight days after his arrest he was released on bail and rejoined the civil rights workers in Birmingham. He revised the letter and released it to a sympathetic world. The rhetoric of King's letter was made all the more compelling by the events of the next four weeks.

Day after day large groups of well-organized demonstrators walked to downtown Birmingham. On May 2 a thousand young people marched. The civil rights leaders were criticized for exploiting children. In reply, King asked where these critics had been when the children had been forced to enter segregated schools and were barred from downtown lunch counters. With the passage of time the tensions in Birmingham mounted, and Bull Connor became frustrated with the failure of his restrained police work to end the demonstrations. So he began using police dogs and firehoses.

There were now more than a hundred reporters in Birmingham who sent out pictures of Connor's men at work: five policemen pinning a middle-aged black woman to the ground; demonstrators thrown against a wall by streams of water powerful enough to strip the bark off trees; police dogs sinking their teeth into unresisting blacks. Bull Connor did nothing to dispel the image of brutality. When the local demonstration leader, Fred Shuttleworth, was injured by a hard blast of water and carried away in an ambulance, Connor told reporters that he wished "they'd carried him away in a hearse."

After several weeks of pictures and comments like these, there was strong nationwide support for the Birmingham demonstrators. President John F. Kennedy, who had been following the confrontation closely and sensed the surge of public sympathy for the demonstrators, remarked, "The civil rights movement owes Bull Connor as much as it owes Abraham Lincoln."

The leaders attempted to keep their moral edge over the opposition by demanding that their followers keep to the tactics of nonviolence. On May 10 their followers broke ranks briefly after bombs exploded at the A. G. Gaston Motel, the demonstration headquarters, and in front of the home of King's younger brother. For three hours blacks rioted, burning stores and vehicles. King and Ralph Abernathy responded by conducting a "pool hall pilgrimage" urging tough young blacks to practice nonviolence.

By late spring 1963 the Birmingham demonstrations were beginning to achieve results. The city government and downtown merchants in Birmingham finally agreed to desegregate public facilities and to hire blacks. President Kennedy began to advocate strong civil rights legislation. He had initially been reluctant to offer King more than token support, telling him that his narrow electoral margin of barely one hundred thousand votes in the 1960 presidential contest against Richard Nixon did not justify an aggressive integration policy. But during the Birmingham crisis both he and his brother, Attorney General Robert Kennedy, had been in frequent contact with the demonstration leaders in Birmingham. On June 19, 1963, John F. Kennedy delivered a speech endorsing strong civil rights legislation. No one had ever barred black Americans from fighting and dying for their country, he said. It was time that they be fully accepted in other areas of American life.

In the next two years the favorable current of public opinion created by the Birmingham demonstrations carried the civil rights movement to its greatest triumphs. In fall 1963 King and other leaders spoke to a crowd of 250,000 supporters in Washington, D.C. King delivered there his famous "I Have a Dream" speech, calling for Congress and the people to "let freedom ring" for African Americans throughout the United States.

The movement lost one of its supporters with the assassination of President Kennedy on November 22, 1963. But his successor, President Lyndon Johnson, persuaded Congress to pass the Civil Rights Act in 1964 and the Voting Rights Act in 1965, the most significant legislation for blacks since Reconstruction.

King, too, went from victory to victory. He won a Nobel Peace Prize in 1964—becoming the youngest person to win the award—largely on the strength of his leadership in Birmingham and his letter from the city's jail. In the next year he led demonstrations at Selma, Alabama, to dramatize the continuing disfranchisement of blacks.

Despite these triumphs, however, King's position would become increasingly difficult in the last five years of his life. Between 1963 and 1968, when he was assassinated in Memphis, Tennessee, it became more and more difficult to rally blacks and whites around the clear-cut distinctions between segregation and integration. New black leaders began to assert that blacks could achieve more with fists and guns than with nonviolence. They and other new leaders were often less interested in integration than in black nationalism. Some of their young protégés in American colleges and universities even demanded separate dormitories and dining tables to preserve black identity. At the same time, the problem of providing equal access to jobs resulted in affirmative action, which sometimes replaced favoritism for whites with favoritism for blacks. Then, too, the nation discovered that de facto segregation in the North was almost as extensive as de jure segregation in the South.

All these new cross-currents of opinion, fact, and policy would complicate issues that King had so ably expressed in words like justice and injustice, light and darkness. The civil rights movement of the 1950s and early 1960s had exposed the most glaring examples of racial injustice in America. It had succeeded, quite simply, because the racial bars—disfranchisement and segregated public facilities—were so blatantly inconsistent with American ideals of human dignity and equality. Civil rights leaders revealed those inconsistencies and moved African Americans a stride toward the just society that Martin Luther King envisioned.

Bibliography

ANSBRO, JOHN J. *Martin Luther King, Jr.: The Making of a Mind* (1982). Explores the philosophical basis of King's nonviolence.

BASS, JACK. *Unlikely Heroes* (1991). Account of the role of federal judges in implementing desegregation in the South.

BASS, JONATHAN S. *Blessed Are the Peacemakers* (2001). Study of King's writing of the "Letter from Birmingham Jail" and of the eight white clergymen toward whom it was directed.

BRANCH, TAYLOR. *Parting the Waters* (1988). A history of America during the King years, 1954–1963. His *Pillar of Fire* (1998) takes the story to 1965; and *At Canaan's Edge* (2006) continues to 1968.

BRAUER, CARL M. *John F. Kennedy and the Second Reconstruction* (1977). Kennedy's role in the civil rights movement.

CARSON, CLAYBORNE. *In Struggle: SNCC and the Black Awakening of the 1960s* (1981). History of the Student Nonviolent Coordinating Committee.

ESKEW, GLENN T. *But for Birmingham: The Local and National Movements in the Civil Rights Struggle* (1997). A study of the local and national forces at work in Birmingham—both in defending and attacking segregation.

GARROW, DAVID J. *The FBI and Martin Luther King, Jr.* (1981). Describes surveillance of King, whom the FBI considered a threat to the social order.

KING, MARTIN LUTHER, JR. *Stride Toward Freedom* (1958). King's account of the Montgomery bus boycott.

———. *Why We Can't Wait* (1963). King's account of Birmingham with his "Letter from Birmingham Jail."

LANDSBERG, BRIAN K. *Enforcing Civil Rights: Race Discrimination and the Department of Justice* (1997). Account of the activities of the Civil Rights Division by a former attorney for the Department of Justice.

LAWSON, STEVEN F. *Black Ballots: Voting Rights in the South, 1944–1969* (1976). A study of the expansion of voting rights in the South.

LEWIS, DAVID LEVERING. *Martin Luther King* (1978). Definitive King biography.

MALCOLM X. *Autobiography* (1966). Life story of the foremost black nationalist of his time.

MEIER, AUGUST, AND ELLIOTT RUDWICK. *CORE: A Study in the Civil Rights Movement* (1973). Close examination of one of the most influential civil rights organizations.

MORGAN, CHARLES, JR. *A Time to Speak* (1964). Account of Birmingham by a white citizen who spoke out against segregation and violence—and was forced to leave.

NUNNELLEY, WILLIAM A. *Bull Connor* (1991). Biography of the police commissioner who opposed King at Birmingham.

Study Guide

Summary

We begin this essay by surveying early civil rights activities including the formation of the NAACP. We then focus on events in Montgomery that placed the modern civil rights movement on the national stage and the demonstrations at Birmingham that tipped the balance of public support toward a civil rights bill. We follow Martin Luther King Jr.'s course through these episodes and read his classic statement about the evils of segregation in the "Letter from Birmingham Jail." The essay suggests that in the years ahead the civil rights movement would be complicated by new issues and forces, such as affirmative action and black nationalism, and concludes that some of the most blatant inequities in the treatment of African Americans were effectively attacked in the Civil Rights Act and the Voting Rights Act.

Identification Topics

Martin Luther King Jr., Eugene "Bull" Connor, Booker T. Washington, *Plessy v. Ferguson*, W. E. B. Du Bois, NAACP, Marcus Garvey, Muslims, Executive Order 8802, *Brown v. Board of Education*, Rosa Parks, Montgomery Improvement Association, Southern Christian Leadership Conference, Freedom Rides, "Letter from Birmingham Jail," "I Have a Dream," Civil Rights Act of 1964, Voting Rights Act of 1965

Study Questions

1. In what ways were African Americans discriminated against in the 1940s and 1950s? Why was segregation harmful to blacks? How was it harmful to American society as a whole?

2. In what ways did these individuals, organizations, and events anticipate the civil rights movement: W. E. B. Du Bois, the NAACP, Marcus Garvey, Jobs for Negroes, Executive Order 8802, Joe Louis, *Smith v. Albright*, and *Brown v. Board of Education*?

3. Why did blacks decide to boycott buses in Montgomery? What tactics were used in Montgomery that were significant for the later civil rights movement? What role did Rosa Parks play?

4. Why was Martin Luther King Jr.'s brand of nonviolent protest so effective in the years 1954–1964? Would he have succeeded two decades earlier?

5. Martin Luther King Jr. was the most articulate spokesman for the civil rights movement. Explain the significance of these King statements: (a) "Sweep streets like Beethoven composed music"; (b) blacks "live within two concentric circles of segregation"; (c) "God's companionship does not stop at the door of a jail cell"; (d) "Freedom is never given voluntarily by the oppressor"; (e) "We find it difficult to wait"; (f) "One day the South will recognize its real heroes."

6. What role did these play in the civil rights movement: nonviolence, civil disobedience, sit-ins, Freedom Rides, the media, the Southern Christian Leadership Conference, the Congress of Racial Equality, civil rights songs, Bull Connor?

7. Why was Birmingham chosen as a target for civil rights action, and why was victory there so important to Martin Luther King Jr.?

8. In what ways did segregationists try to resist the civil rights movement? How did their resistance affect the movement?

9. Why did John F. Kennedy decide to take a stand for civil rights legislation?

10. In what ways did new currents in racial relations in the late 1960s complicate the struggle for racial equality?

11. In what ways did the civil rights movement of the 1950s and 1960s improve conditions for blacks? In what respects were blacks still disadvantaged in relationship to other Americans?

12. Why did so many African Americans abandon King's ideals of nonviolence and racial harmony after 1965?

Research Topics

1. Study more fully the life of Martin Luther King Jr.

2. Investigate the lives of other black leaders in modern America. Compare King's ideas with those of Malcolm X and other African Americans.

3. Explore the activities of other civil rights organizations, such as CORE.

4. Research the *Bakke* Supreme Court decision. How does it affect earlier rulings on civil rights?

5. Read through newspapers and magazines at the time of the Montgomery bus boycott, the Birmingham demonstrations, and other civil rights episodes. Compare publications for their attitudes toward blacks, the South, and civil rights.

6. Explore why it was so important to many white southerners to uphold segregation.

7. Investigate how important the media was to the civil rights movement. In what ways did the media help the movement gain support?

8. Consider to what extent has the position of African Americans changed since Martin Luther King's death in 1968. Are blacks "better off" today?

CHAPTER **13**

Turmoil on the Campuses

Berkeley in the Sixties

The University of California at Berkeley had a long tradition of fostering radical movements and offbeat behavior. It was often compared to the Left Bank in Paris and Greenwich Village in New York. In 1964 the campus gave birth to a student revolt that would set the stage for nationwide protests and antiwar demonstrations during the remainder of the decade. The movement began with an orderly discussion of free speech, developed into acts of mass protest and disobedience, and led eventually to clashes with police and national guardsmen. During the 1960s, confrontations at Berkeley and at other campuses across the nation were the most dramatic expressions of a multifaceted movement. Students protested injustice and war, examined educational policies, and carried out a cultural revolution that affected clothing, sex, hairstyles, music, and the universities themselves.

The day was May 20, 1969, and the United States was in the fifth year of the Vietnam War. On a sunny afternoon, a helicopter swept in low over its target: several hundred men and women running for cover. Earlier that day, these people had taken part in a funeral procession for a man who died in battle a few days before. As the crowd scattered, the helicopter unloaded its cargo of CS gas—the most powerful tear gas in the army's arsenal. The chemical floated downward, a dry powder that stung the skin of its victims. According to an army training manual, the normal effects of the gas also included "extreme burning of the eyes, accompanied by copious flow of tears, coughing, difficulty in breathing and chest tightness."

This episode might have occurred in the jungles of Vietnam; instead it took place on the picturesque campus of the University of California, Berkeley. The tear gas attack was one of many confrontations between 1964 and 1970. The revolution at Berkeley began in 1964 with the free speech movement in which students sought to establish their right to listen to any speaker they chose to invite to the campus.

Ironically, the first person to win attention during the sixties for defending free speech at Berkeley was not a student rebel, but rather the president of the university system, Clark Kerr—a liberal who would later be regarded by activists as an archenemy of their movement. Kerr lived in a ranch house in the Berkeley hills overlooking San Francisco Bay. The local campus was only one of several institutions in the state university system, but Berkeley was especially important as the oldest, largest, and most prestigious school. Kerr was widely respected for his intellect, his energy, and his negotiating skills. He was said to be able to stand in a reception line greeting two thousand students and pick out those who went through twice. "It's nice to see you again," he would say. He invariably wore a blue suit, white shirt, and wire-frame glasses; his face was oval and he was bald except for a fringe of hair that made him look like a tonsured monk. His reputation extended across the country, and he was regarded as one of the most effective labor-management negotiators in the nation.

During the early fifties, Clark Kerr led the fight against the loyalty oath at Berkeley. This was a document that university faculty members were required to sign declaring they were not members of subversive organizations. Most professors considered the measure repressive and demeaning. But at the height of the McCarthy era, American politicians sought to outdo one another in proving their loyalty, and the measure became state law. Most professors signed the oath reluctantly, but a few refused to sign and lost their jobs. Attempting to placate the faculty, the regents—the governing board of the university system—appointed an opponent of the oath, Clark Kerr, as head of the Berkeley campus in 1952; six years later they made him president of the university system as a whole.

In 1959 Kerr enraged California right-wingers by granting an honorary degree to Edward C. Tolman, a professor who had lost his position for refusing to sign the loyalty oath. Kerr even persuaded the regents to honor Tolman further by naming a campus building in his honor. In 1960, when Berkeley students were arrested for disrupting a House Un-American Activities Committee hearing in San Francisco, Kerr refused to heed demands that he suspend or expel the students.

During the height of the McCarthy era, the university regents had banned Communist speakers from the campus. But in 1961 Clark Kerr, along with Governor Edmund G. Brown, defended the right of Frank Wilkinson, an alleged Communist, to speak at Berkeley. A group of students had issued the invitation, and some three hundred conservative Californians urged Governor Brown to block Wilkinson's appearance on campus. The governor responded, "Let the people say anything they want to. If they do anything criminal while they're speaking or after they're speaking, then they can be prosecuted."

President Kerr was determined to defend the university as an "open marketplace," and he also supported Wilkinson's appearance. In response, the American Legion castigated him for defying their request to bar Communist speakers. California's Senate Committee on Un-American Activities entered the fray by accusing Kerr of opening the campus to anyone "who cares to utilize the university property as a brawling ground for political controversy." At a Charter Day ceremony, Clark Kerr answered such charges with a resounding defense of free speech. "Those of little faith," he said, "are disposed to see in one episode, or in one speech, the end of all they hold dear. But America is stronger than that."

The following year, a familiar figure in California's anti-Communist movement, Richard Nixon, sought to exploit the speech issue in his campaign to replace Edmund Brown as governor of California. Sixteen years before, he had won a seat in Congress after claiming that his opponent, H. Jerry Voorhis, was supported by Communists. The situation at Berkeley provided Nixon the opportunity to renew his anti-Communist crusade. He promised that if he were elected governor, he would bar not only Communists from Berkeley, but also anyone who had invoked the Fifth Amendment while appearing before government investigators.

During the campaign the incumbent, Edmund Brown, retreated from the high ground of his earlier defense of free speech on college campuses, saying that he agreed with Nixon in principle. But he warned that Nixon's proposed changes would undermine the constitutional authority of the university regents. Brown won reelection, and on June 21, 1963, the University of California Regents voted fifteen to two to lift the longstanding ban on Communist speakers on university campuses. In defense of their action, the regents declared that they had "confidence in students of the university and in their judgment in properly evaluating any and all beliefs and ideologies that may be expressed in University campuses by off-campus speakers." With this measure, the regents embraced the Jeffersonian position that the best way to defeat an unsound idea is to allow it—and the arguments against it—to circulate freely. A few days later, the *New York Times* praised the California regents, noting that universities are designed to sharpen the "critical faculties" of their students. Ideally, students will be exposed to "clashing viewpoints under circumstances that will help them make reasoned evaluations of what is sound and what is false in each." The editorial was headlined "Freedom Unlimited."

In a widely publicized speech titled "The Idea of a University," Clark Kerr declared, "Members of the university community, faculty members and students alike, deserve the same right to freedom of thought and expression which every citizen enjoys outside the campus boundaries. The university is not engaged in making ideas safe for students. It is engaged in making students safe for ideas. Thus it permits the freest expression of views before students, trusting to their good sense in passing judgment on these views." In 1964 Clark Kerr received an award from the American Association of University Professors for his contributions to academic freedom.

The issue of free speech at Berkeley had apparently been resolved on grounds that would satisfy the inquisitive students as well as the cautious regents of the university. Within a little more than a year, however, the carefully crafted arrangement would fall apart, and Berkeley would become the scene for a student movement unimagined by Clark Kerr, Edmund Brown, and even the students themselves. Having warded off attacks from the right for more than a decade, Kerr would soon be attacked by the left for alleged insensitivity to student rights.

The person who led the charge was Mario Savio, a twenty-one-year-old New Yorker who was enrolled at the university. He had been top in his class of twelve hundred students at Martin Van Buren High School in New York; he attended Manhattan College, then Queens College, before coming to Berkeley. Savio spent the summer of 1964 working for the civil rights movement in Mississippi, in a world where "clashing viewpoints" were seldom resolved with reasoned discourse. He and two other men once had to flee from club-wielding thugs. Savio outran them, but one of his friends did not. That summer in Mississippi the bodies of three murdered civil rights workers were found beneath an earthen dam.

Back in Berkeley that fall, Savio discovered that the regents' new policy on speech was not as liberal as it first appeared. Students could be disciplined for advocating illegal acts on campus or for taking part in illegal acts off campus. Since civil rights activists often broke the law—as when they held sit-ins at segregated lunch counters in the South—the regents' ruling could be used to discourage campus recruiting for such activities.

Additionally, Berkeley had customarily allowed students to set up tables on the edge of the campus, where they would engage in political recruitment and funds solicitation. These activities were restricted to a narrow strip of land, twenty-five by sixty feet, at the corner of Bancroft and Telegraph Avenues, on the south side of the campus. From those tables on the "Bancroft Strip," students had recently been organized to stage a sleep-in at the Sheraton Palace Hotel in San Francisco to protest discrimination against blacks. Mario Savio had been one of many protesters arrested in that demonstration. During the summer of 1964 students ventured forth from Berkeley to demonstrate against conservative presidential candidate Barry Goldwater at the Republican National Convention in San Francisco. They also campaigned against a state constitutional amendment repealing California's Fair Housing Act.

Then the regents ruled that the strip could no longer be used for advocacy. Since such activities were already prohibited elsewhere on campus, the ruling eliminated all soliciting for off-campus political activity. Mario Savio was angered by the new policy. He was president of the Berkeley chapter of Friends of the Student Nonviolent Coordinating Committee (SNCC—pronounced "snick"), the organization he had worked for in Mississippi during the previous summer. The university ruling on advocacy would limit his ability to recruit students for more SNCC activities.

The ban went into effect on September 21, and in response Savio and other students organized what came to be known as the Berkeley free speech movement. Tall, slender, sandy-haired, and cloaked in a trademark fleece-lined sheepherder's jacket, Savio was a colorful figure, and he set the standard for forceful student oratory. The *New York Times* noted that his "occasionally hip, occasionally gamey turn of phrase recalled Mort Sahl, the comedian." Day after day, Savio and other students spoke to large audiences in the university's Sproul Hall Plaza, encouraging students to oppose restrictions on speech and advocacy. The original members of the movement included representatives of the campus Young Republicans and supporters of Barry Goldwater, as well as members of the Young People's Socialist League, the Young Socialist Alliance, and a Maoist organization, the Progressive Labor Party. In their early meetings, it was the civil rights veterans—like Mario Savio—who led the way. "We've often had to radicalize the socialists," he said.

On September 28 student protesters interrupted a university meeting where Chancellor Edward W. Strong, the head of the Berkeley campus, was speaking. (In California, the chancellor is the leader of the local campus, while the president—in 1964, Clark Kerr—is the head of the university system as a whole.) The next day students occupied Sproul Hall, the university administration building, and spent the night camped out in its corridors. Administrators circulated among them, taking names, and soon afterward Chancellor Strong announced that eight of the students had been suspended.

On October 1, 1964, tables appeared again on Bancroft Avenue, in defiance of the ban on recruitment and funds solicitation. The university called in the police, who arrested one of the recruiters, Jack Weinberg, a member of the Congress of Racial Equality (CORE), for trespassing. At about noon, officers drove into the main plaza of the campus and parked in front of Sproul Hall. Weinberg was led to the back seat, but as the car was about to leave, a student sat down in its path; then others followed. Several thousand students spent the afternoon milling around in the plaza and blocking the police car. They let the air out of the tires, carried a microphone to the roof, and used the police cruiser as a speaker's platform. Mario Savio was the most notable of the speakers. At nightfall the students were still there.

The bizarre standoff continued through the night and into the next day. Several hundred police officers were sent to the campus to liberate the squad car, but they took no action. Finally, at about seven o'clock the next evening, Jack Weinberg was released, having spent thirty-two hours in the back seat of a police car. The university agreed not to press charges against Weinberg and promised to address the underlying problem of campus advocacy by creating an eighteen-member committee consisting of students, faculty, and administrators.

During the following week the committee met several times, but when demonstrations resumed on November 7 the university retaliated by abolishing the study committee. In the meantime, a faculty group examined the matter of the eight student suspensions and declared that the measures were improper. Admittedly, students had violated university regulations during the Sproul Hall sit-in, the committee reported, but they had been motivated by valid principles.

Later that month, on November 20, the board of regents met on the Berkeley campus and reevaluated the ban on political advocacy. While the regents were deliberating, some five thousand students gathered nearby, listening to a concert by folksinger Joan Baez and waiting for a report from the university policymakers. Eventually a report from the meeting reached the crowd: the regents agreed to change the rules; students would be allowed to set up tables to recruit participants for civil rights demonstrations. Additionally, the regents lifted the suspensions of the eight students who had been disciplined for the Sproul Hall sit-in. This was precisely what Mario Savio, Jack Weinberg, and other activists had advocated.

A few days later, however, Savio and three other students received an unwelcome letter from the university. They were to be disciplined for inciting students to resist the police during the Jack Weinberg incident. This action fueled a growing suspicion among students that even while the university proclaimed its support for free speech, it was determined to crush political activity at Berkeley. The administrators had just lifted the discipline against one set of protesters; now they were going after others.

On December 2 thousands of students gathered in Sproul Hall Plaza. Joan Baez sang songs from the civil rights movement, including "We Shall Overcome." Then Mario Savio's voice boomed through the microphone. He described the failed negotiations between students and Berkeley and then gave a soon-to-be famous call for action: "There is a time when the operation of the machine becomes so odious, makes you so sick at heart, that you can't take part; you can't even passively take part, and you've got to put your bodies upon the gears and upon the wheels, upon the levers, upon all the apparatus, and you've got to make it stop. And you've got to indicate to the people who run it, to the people who own it, that unless you're free, the machine will be prevented from working at all!"

Savio urged the students to occupy Sproul Hall and "stay until the police remove us." Charles Powell, the elected president of the student body, tried to stop the demonstrators. "Do not do this thing," he pleaded. But Joan Baez told the crowd, "have love as you do this thing, and it will succeed."

Hundreds of students heeded the call to occupy the administration building. They walked through the big front doors overlooking the plaza and fanned out through the corridors. At seven o'clock—the usual scheduled time—campus officials locked the doors of Sproul Hall. During the night a few students who wanted to leave were allowed out the doors, but about eight hundred spent the night in the building. Walking through the halls, one could sense among the demonstrators that night not only a revolution in student activism, but also a revolution in student culture. According to Wallace Turner, reporting for the *New York Times*, there was "an air of festivity" at the sit-in. In an age when most men shaved their beards and wore their hair short, long hair and full beards were common among the students in Sproul Hall. Many carried guitars, and much to the surprise of the *Times* reporter, "at least one young man came in barefoot."

Within a few years a barefoot student would hardly raise an eyebrow at Berkeley. But at the onset of the free speech movement, campus life was formal and sedate in comparison to the years to come. Men wore coats and ties, and women wore dresses. Dorms were strictly segregated by sex; men could not visit women's rooms; and women were required to be in the dorm at fixed times, called "parietal hours," that would meet the approval of the most doting parents.

The young men and women who spent the night of December 2, 1964, in the corridors of Sproul Hall seemed to have rejected not only a university policy on political activity but also current expectations about student life. They mingled together comfortably, sang songs to the strumming of guitars, and waited for something to happen. At 3:10 in the morning of December 3, Chancellor Edward Strong entered the building and read a statement to the students, urging them to leave. A few did, but most stayed. Then scores of policemen moved into the building.

The students were concentrated on the second, third, and fourth floors of Sproul Hall, having barricaded the stairway up from the first floor. The police took an elevator to the top and began booking and removing the demonstrators one by one. Each demonstrator was told, "You are under arrest for trespass and unlawful assembly." They were informed that if they walked out of the building, there would be no further charges. But if they had to be dragged or carried away, they would be charged with resisting arrest.

Most of the students refused to walk. Women were lifted by the arms, pulled to a booking desk, fingerprinted, and searched by sheriff's department matrons. Then they were placed in an elevator, taken to the basement, loaded into police vans, and driven to the county jail. Men were denied the luxury of the elevator. They were grabbed by the arms and dragged down several flights of stairs. One of the deputies remarked, "There'll be some sore rumps in jail tonight." Students shouted "good luck" to their friends as they were carried away.

During the night, leaders of the free speech movement (FSM)— identified by armbands—had circulated through the corridors. The next day, as they were removed from the building, they knew that they had succeeded in using the classic tactic of the civil rights movement— provoking their adversaries to use force. On his way out of Sproul Hall, Mario Savio shouted, "This is wonderful—wonderful. We'll bring the university to our terms." As he was being led away by the police, another student leader shouted, "Good! The kids have learned more about democracy here than they could in forty years of classes."

When the police finished clearing out Sproul Hall, roughly eight hundred students had been arrested. The discussion of free speech that had begun with Governor Brown, President Kerr, and the Berkeley students sharing a common ground had disintegrated into a standoff between opposing camps. At a noon rally, one of the few free speech leaders not in jail told a crowd of five thousand in the plaza that Clark Kerr should be removed as president of the university. Kerr, in turn, issued a statement accusing the FSM of intolerance, lying, irrationality, and indecency. Governor Edmund Brown, who had recently defended the right of Berkeley students to hear controversial speakers, was appalled by the Sproul Hall sit-in. "We're not going to have anarchy in the state of California while I'm governor," he said, "and that's anarchy."

The campus turmoil continued in the wake of the sit-in. The protesters were freed from jail after posting bail totaling $86,000. Back on campus, they mounted a strike against university classes, demanding amnesty for the protesters and the removal from office of Clark Kerr and Edward Strong. Many students supported the strike; others wanted to get on with their courses. Fights broke out along the picket lines. At one rally some students carried signs saying, "Law Not Anarchy" and "Throw the Bums Out." But Mario Savio was adamant. "We have promised that this university shall not run," he said, "and we shall keep that promise."

A few days later, the university tried to allay student unrest by hosting a meeting of reconciliation in the Hearst Greek Amphitheater, an open-air facility in the Berkeley hills above the campus. President Kerr announced to a crowd of thirteen thousand students and faculty that he favored a compromise. When he finished he was applauded loudly, and it appeared that the crisis had been defused. But then in a moment, the atmosphere of trust collapsed.

From the side of the stage, Mario Savio approached the microphone, intending to announce a rally on campus later that day. As he placed his hands on the podium, a policeman threw his arm around Savio's throat and forced his head back. Another helped drag the student leader from the stage. The audience gasped; students rushed the stage and grabbed Savio by the legs. The jumble of humanity moved off out of sight with Savio in the middle; students and police officers exchanged blows. A roar of shouts and boos came from the crowd.

Clark Kerr had already left the stage and was confused, himself, as to what was happening. Robert Beloof, a member of the speech department, came up to Kerr with Art Goldberg, one of the leaders of the free speech movement (FSM). "You have to let him speak," Beloof shouted, "He must be allowed to speak." Goldberg tried to say something, and Beloof, whose patience with the student activists was wearing thin, exploded. "For once in your life," he said, "shut up!"

Kerr explained to Beloof that Robert Scalapino, as chairman of the meeting, would have to make the decision. Savio had approached Scalapino earlier asking for the opportunity to speak, and he had been told that the convocation was "a structured meeting" with no provision for student speakers. In the midst of the melee, however, with the police and students pummeling each other backstage, thousands of spectators filling the air with their shouts, and the president himself confused as to what was happening, the meeting could no longer be called "structured." Mario Savio was allowed to speak. With his clothes still ruffled from his encounter with the police, he approached the microphone for a second time. He simply announced that there was a rally scheduled for later that day; then he left the stage—unassisted.

Savio later commented that if he had been allowed to speak in the first place, "We would have been dead." Instead, because of his encounter with the police, the FSM won a huge public relations victory. Civil rights activity in the South had taught Savio and other student leaders that political activism can be a real-life theater with men and women such as Rosa Parks and Bull Connor as heroes and villains. When Berkeley students saw Mario Savio dragged from the microphone, they had no trouble getting the point. So did students elsewhere in the United States. In Boston several hundred students and professors from Harvard, Radcliffe, Brandeis, Tufts, and Simmons staged a rally in support of the demonstrators at Berkeley.

A few days later the faculty senate at Berkeley met in a large auditorium in Wheeler Hall and debated a resolution calling for freedom of speech and faculty control of disciplinary policy. One professor remarked, "We need to let people say what's on their minds." The discussion was carried over loudspeakers to a large crowd gathered outside of the building. After a long debate the proposal passed by a vote of 824 to 115, and the crowd cheered so loudly that their shouts could be heard inside the auditorium. Mario Savio commented, "They've given us what we've been after for months."

Other Californians were less enthusiastic about the measure, believing that the faculty had caved in to student fanatics. State Senator Hugh M. Burns commented that the regents "must decide whether to run the university or turn it over to a group of malcontents, silly kids, [and] addle-headed teachers egged on by Communist stooges." On December 18 the board of regents rejected the faculty measure, reaffirming their authority to determine standards for student behavior. Mario Savio called the regents' action "a horrendous decision." But the board's position was less confrontational than it first appeared. Having satisfied their honor, so to speak, by retaining the authority that was theirs by law, they went on to endorse the principle that the students should enjoy the same freedom of speech on campus as every citizen was guaranteed under the First and Fourteenth Amendments. That declaration was considered a student victory.

The FSM at Berkeley had focused on a single issue, the use of a narrow strip of brick walkway at the entrance to the campus. Mario Savio cared enough about the issue to jeopardize a promising career as a professor. In addition to facing the possibility of expulsion from the university, he fared poorly in his classes during the fall of 1964, having spent most of his time as a protest leader. "My grades have suffered," he remarked, "from my political interests."

Savio explained those interests. Speech was important, but it was a means to an end, a tool to be used in exposing the nation's ills. One of those ills was racism, and the movement to eradicate racism had been the proving ground for the FSM leaders. As Savio remarked, "I spent the summer in Mississippi. I witnessed tyranny. I saw groups of men in the minority working their wills over the majority. Then I came back here and found the university preventing us from collecting money for use there and even stopping us from getting people to go to Mississippi to help."

A. H. Raskin, a writer who had been a student activist during the 1930s, visited Berkeley during the winter of 1965 to write an appraisal of the FSM. He met with Mario Savio and other FSM leaders at the headquarters of the Graduate Coordinating Committee, a key unit in the FSM. The office was a garret room above the university's drama workshop, accessible by a set of wooden stairs outside the building. The room was without furniture except for a dingy green sofa "with sags where the springs should be." The students sat on camp chairs. In one corner there was a table with a telephone.

Raskin noted that the ultimate goals of the student activists seemed unclear, but their sense of alienation from the university and contemporary society was palpable. They were so suspicious of all adult institutions that they seemed reluctant to embrace any ideology. Raskin quoted another observer who said of the FSM, "All the old labels are out: if there were any orthodox Communists here, they would be a moderating influence." Savio and other students discussed goals with Raskin that went far beyond the free speech demands of the fall. They told him they wanted to create a "loving community" and to lead fuller lives: "It is ours to demand meaning: we must insist upon meaning!" They complained that the professors at Berkeley were separated from the undergraduates by "five hundred feet of lecture hall" and an army of teaching assistants. Savio noted that the Pentagon, oil companies, and farm interests considered the university a kind of "public utility."

Ironically, President Clark Kerr had foreseen just such complaints almost two years before the advent of the FSM. While speaking at Harvard University, Kerr lamented the emergence of a new kind of institution of higher learning, such as Berkeley, which he called the "multiversity." It was too big, too diverse, and too powerful to provide a cohesive academic community. Kerr predicted that in such an atmosphere students would feel neglected and depersonalized. According to Raskin, "everything Kerr warned of then is embodied now in the FSM lament that the student is being downgraded to the status of an IBM punchcard in a computerized multiversity."

Asked what the FSM had achieved, one of the students told A. H. Raskin, "There has been a great strengthening of democratic institutions on the campus. . . . We have won, though how much is not clear." Mario Savio said simply, "We committed the unpardonable sin of being moral and being successful." When Raskin left his meeting with Savio and other activists, after three hours of intense discussion, he reflected on the future of the FSM. He noted that some of the leaders seemed to be anticipating a period of inactivity. They had won their major points; they needed to get back to their studies. But Raskin also sensed that there were deeper forces at work. The activists had developed "a vested interest in finding things to fight about." Activism for its own sake was a powerful antidote to the ennui of modern life. Some of the students even seemed to want conditions to deteriorate: "The worse things get, the easier it will be to generate mass resistance." Raskin noted that the students appeared to be willing to use civil disobedience with "reckless prodigality."

Savio and other student protesters had focused their efforts on the issue of free speech, but they were buffeted by other currents of unrest, some of which even they themselves probably did not fully understand. Asked what the campus turmoil meant to him, Savio answered cryptically, "Woe to him who would try to pour oil on the waters when God has brewed them into a gale." During the next few years, Berkeley would become more tumultuous rather than less. Savio's remark foreshadowed the comment a student made at a Berkeley party several years later; high on liquor or drugs, he said, "I like apocalyptic things." During the sixties, there was a sense of an apocalyptic presence at Berkeley, a feeling of disorder and change larger than any single political issue.

Across the bay in San Francisco, the Haight-Ashbury district had become the mecca of counterculture America. The flower children, or hippies, had taken a leap beyond the conventional mores of contemporary society, embracing free love, casual dress, experimental drugs, and communal living. Telegraph Avenue, near the Berkeley campus, became a kind of outpost of Haight-Ashbury, a place to find tie-dyed shirts, drugs, and friendship with other young men and women who had "dropped out."

Some Berkeley students left the university for the communal life off campus; others stayed in class but shared the values of the hippies and took part in the counterculture. Like students elsewhere, men and women at Berkeley saw themselves in several of the films of the time. *The Graduate* portrayed the sense of dislocation of a young college graduate whose only advice from the adult world was the single word "plastics." The film's moving ballad, "Sounds of Silence," was a haunting expression of the questioning of a generation cut off from its moorings. Another popular film, *Easy Rider*, told the story of two long-haired men crossing the country to New Orleans on a motorcycle with a stash of drugs concealed in their gas tank. As they traveled through the South, they passed through towns where the women loved them and the men hated them. At the end of the film, they were shot dead by a redneck on a back-country road; the audiences in Berkeley reacted as if personal friends had been killed.

During the sixties the student movement at Berkeley became increasingly an expression of counterculture values. Jack Weinberg, who had spent thirty-two hours in the back seat of the police cruiser in Sproul Hall Plaza, coined a popular slogan for the movement: "Don't trust anyone over thirty." Counterculture leaders Abbie Hoffman and Jerry Rubin appeared often in Berkeley. The student leaders who demanded and won the right to free speech on campus went to the microphones again and again, challenging American values and campus rules. The first major issue following the FSM fall was an abortive "filthy speech movement" in early 1965, where students tested their freedom by featuring four-letter words in their speeches and on placards in Sproul Hall Plaza. That movement died of its own silliness: most students who cared about the speech issue thought it was being trivialized. But many other issues won broad support.

Almost every day at noon there was a kind of teach-in at the plaza on the subject of American institutions. The enemy was called "the power structure" or "the establishment." One by one, the alleged evils of society were exposed. Sitting on steps of Sproul Hall while eating a sack lunch in the warm sun, one could hear speakers quoting Dwight D. Eisenhower's warnings about a "military industrial complex." Supporters of a farm workers' strike in California's Central Valley, including their leader, Cesar Chavez, came to Berkeley to denounce the capitalists who were mistreating migrant laborers.

Chavez was born in 1927, the son of Mexican American parents, and spent his childhood on his family's farm near Yuma, Arizona. In 1938 in the midst of the Depression the family lost their farm and became migrant workers following the crops in California. This mobile labor force numbered about three hundred thousand at the time, lived in dingy shacks without plumbing or electricity, and had no union to help them secure better wages and working conditions. Because of their mobility, the migrant children were often unable to attend school. Cesar Chavez attended dozens of elementary schools and never advanced beyond eighth grade. Chavez recalled that his people were "one of the strikingest families in California." At the first shout of "*Huelga!*" (strike), they would leave the fields. But none of these sporadic work stoppages was effective.

While laboring in the fields, Chavez became interested in improving the lot of farm laborers. In 1952 he began working for the Community Service Organization, an agency engaged in improving the lot of migrant workers. He took part in schooling projects and helped instruct the laborers in their rights, including in the case of Mexican immigrants, the path to citizenship. Chavez hoped to start a union, but most laborers rightly feared that they would lose their jobs if they bucked the system. In 1962 he turned to full-time labor organizing, and within six months he had three hundred recruits for the National Farm Workers Association. At a meeting in Fresno, California, they adopted a flag with a black eagle in a circle against a red background. The movement came to be known as *LaCausa*, the Cause. In 1966 the organization merged with another to form the United Farm Workers.

In the meantime Cesar Chavez and his wife, Helen, had moved to a small house in Delano, California, in a poor neighborhood known as *Sal Si Puedes*—Flee if You Can. His wife went to work in the fields to support the family, and Cesar traveled from town to town recruiting members for the new union. In a phrase strikingly similar to Mario Savio's famous words on fighting a corrupt "machine," Cesar Chavez said: "If you're outraged at conditions, then you can't possibly be free or happy until you devote all your time to changing them and do nothing but that. But you can't change anything if you want to hold onto a good job, a good way of life and avoid sacrifice."

In 1965 some farm workers went out on strike, leaving grapes rotting on the vine, but the growers quickly found strike-breakers to work in the fields. Chavez continued organizing and led a five-year program of boycotting grapes and striking against the growers. In 1968 he won worldwide publicity for *La Causa* by conducting a twenty-five day hunger strike. Senator Robert Kennedy came to Delano to be with Chavez on the last day of the strike and called the labor leader "One of the heroic figures of our time."

Proximity to Berkeley made the cause of the farm workers all the more compelling on campus. A few miles away luscious grapes were growing, but to buy them was the moral equivalent of helping to starve the children of migrant workers or taking the part of growers who had hired armies of thugs to intimidate strikers. In Sproul Hall Plaza in 1968 speakers provided constant updates on Cesar Chavez's fast, and the image of this principled man growing thinner by the day felt as real and as close as Sproul Hall itself.

During the 1960s activists at Berkeley searched out every imaginable area of injustice on campus and in the nation as a whole. Speakers criticized the university itself for doing research on behalf of the military, and they announced that the university's stock portfolio included companies like Crown Zellerback that did business in South Africa. They also accused the university of supporting racism because there were few African Americans at Berkeley and almost no black studies courses. And there were also gestures of support for the young men and women who began to pay fines or go to jail in 1967 for their part in the big Sproul Hall sit-in. When Mario Savio went off to serve his two-hundred-day prison sentence, fellow students presented him with a chocolate cake with a hacksaw in the middle. Savio never used the blade, but he did get out of jail early, after 120 days, because of "good behavior."

Often the campus gatherings were peaceful; sometimes they were not. In 1968 students tried to arrange a course to be taught by Eldridge Cleaver, whose *Soul on Ice* told of his transition from jailed rapist to black power leader. Cleaver, who was the minister of information for the Black Panther party, was slated to teach a course that would be called "Dehumanization and Regeneration in the American Social Order." The board of regents blocked the class, and several hundred students staged a sit-in in Moses Hall, with the inevitable police intervention and arrests. A strike followed with students shouting, "On strike, shut it down," and

"Ashes to ashes, dust to dust, we hate to close it, but we must, we must." Eventually Cleaver was allowed to give a lecture on campus. He spoke calmly about the causes of racism and remarked later that he had "enjoyed himself very much." After he left the lecture hall, he made a wry allusion to the furor over his appearance on campus. "The building is still standing," he noted, "and the sun is still shining."

A few months later the Third World Liberation Front, a loose alliance of African Americans, Asians, and Hispanics, mounted a campus strike, demanding the formation of a College of Ethnic Studies. Students and nonstudents from the surrounding community blocked the gates to the university, threw rocks and bottles at the police, and marched down Telegraph Avenue smashing windows.

At the time, the governor of California was a former movie actor, Ronald Reagan, who had come to office in 1966 with the promise to do something about Berkeley. During his campaign Reagan opposed the readmission of Mario Savio to the university. After winning the election he promised that he would remove the microphone and loudspeakers from the steps of Sproul Hall. Once in office Reagan immediately tried to cut the university budget and raise student fees. With each new crisis on campus, he strengthened his following among California voters with attacks on "the mess at Berkeley." During the Third World Liberation Front protest, Reagan declared that Berkeley faced an "extreme emergency" and insisted that the university find a way to end the "guerrilla warfare" on campus.

Immediately following the ethnic studies disruptions came a dispute over the use of a university-owned vacant lot located near Telegraph Avenue, a few blocks south of the campus. Students and other residents had decided to take over the unused land and make it into a park. They planted flowers and built a playground. Then during the night, the university built a chain-link fence around the ground. Thousands gathered on campus for a mass rally at noon the next day, and many marched off after being urged by one speaker to retake the ground they called "People's Park."

This time the police were armed with shotguns. They were told to fire birdshot at the demonstrators—which would have been intimidating but not lethal—and because the supply of birdshot was limited, they were also given buckshot. For several hours, Telegraph Avenue was a battle zone. Protesters turned over a police car and set it on fire. The police officers used up their birdshot and then loaded their guns with buckshot. At the end of the day, thirty-five protesters and bystanders had been shot; one was blinded and one killed. The National Guard was ordered to Berkeley and posted around the campus with fixed bayonets. Students walked up to the guardsmen and placed flowers in the rifle barrels.

During the 1960s the student protest movement which began at Berkeley gained adherents throughout the United States. Shortly after he was dragged off the stage at the Hearst Greek Amphitheater in 1964, Mario Savio and three other student leaders traveled across the country to speak at the University of Michigan, Queens College, and Columbia University. Drawing a moral from the FSM, Savio declared, "For the first time, students used civil disobedience to get their own rights." Savio blamed right-wing businessmen and politicians for the pressure that led to the curtailment of advocacy rights at Berkeley. "What happened at Berkeley," he said, "is merely a taste of what may happen in the future if other university administrations fail to stand firm against them."

Savio was a persuasive speaker, and undoubtedly many of the five hundred students who gathered in December 1964 around a campus Christmas tree at Columbia University to hear him speak were impressed with his biting attack on universities that served "the military industrial complex." But the students at Columbia had not seen eight hundred of their classmates hustled off to jail or watched with thirteen thousand other spectators as a student leader was throttled by the police. Few American college students in 1964 thought there was anything fundamentally wrong with their country or their campuses. It would take an episode of political violence on a global scale to radicalize America's college students as a whole.

As it turned out, just such an event occurred.

On February 7, 1965, when students at Berkeley were emerging from the turmoil of the FSM, the United States began to bomb North Vietnam. American troops had been in Vietnam for years as advisors to the South Vietnamese, but the air raids over the North were the first of many steps in a process that came to be known as "escalation." When the United States finally withdrew from Vietnam in 1973, several million Americans had served in the nation's longest and most controversial war.

At Berkeley and other campuses, students and professors took part in teach-ins during the early stages of American involvement. The proponents of the war characterized it as an invasion from the North against a unified and pro-American South. The opponents studied maps of enemy locations in Vietnam—published in easily accessible places such as *Time* and *Newsweek*—and found that some of the greatest concentrations of pro-Communist sympathizers were in the Mekong Delta, south of Saigon and far from Hanoi. Many Americans came to believe that the war in Vietnam was a civil war and that the leaders in Saigon were corrupt. During the early stages of the war, the evening news broadcasts in the United States carried pictures of Buddhist monks burning themselves to death in defiance of Saigon—confirming for American war critics the idea that the government for which tens of thousands of Americans were to die did not enjoy the support of its own people.

Many years later, after the last American soldier left Saigon, the chief architect of the war, former Secretary of Defense Robert McNamara, published *In Retrospect: The Tragedy and Lessons of Vietnam*, a book declaring that the government had pursued the war under a false assumption about Vietnam. He would write, "We were wrong, terribly wrong." Had McNamara spoken those words in Sproul Hall Plaza during the 1960s, thousands of war protesters at Berkeley would have said, "Right on!" But at that time McNamara was presiding over the military buildup in Southeast Asia; he was so intimately involved in the action that it was often called "McNamara's War."

During the sixties the Vietnam War became the paramount issue in campus politics. Phrases like, "Hell no! We won't go!" and "Make love, not war!" became as popular as "No taxation without representation!" had been on the eve of the American Revolution. Many students at Berkeley who had been dubious about the wisdom of spending a night in Sproul Hall and were turned off by the abortive filthy speech movement were deeply troubled by the war. And they were repelled by televised reports depicting the results of weapons such as napalm, which clung burning to the skin of its victims. During the war thousands of students at Berkeley and millions of Americans nationwide boycotted products sold by Dow Chemical, the manufacturer of napalm.

The war entered student lives through intellectual debates and vivid images. It also entered their consciousness as a personal threat. During the Vietnam War every able-bodied male student in America realized that his own neck was at risk. In later years, there would emerge a stereotype of Vietnam protesters as men and women who hassled war-weary American troops as they returned from the front. For most student protesters, however, such tactics were repugnant. The soldiers were high school and college classmates, friends, and brothers. The protest movement was directed toward the war itself, not toward the soldiers.

A few months after the FSM at Berkeley had degenerated into the filthy speech movement, speakers at the university found a cause more appropriate to the principle of academic freedom. In 1965 Berkeley students formed the Vietnam Day Committee and mounted one of the nation's first antiwar marches. Fifteen thousand war protesters massed on the campus, listened to antiwar speeches and music, and at nightfall marched to the Oakland city line—where they were met by a police barricade and a crowd of jeering counterdemonstrators. The marchers turned back toward a Berkeley city park and settled in for more speeches and music.

During the following years this scene would be repeated again and again across the United States. As David Harris, a student leader at Stanford, remarked, "Berkeley was the torch. That was where we got our energy." If Berkeley was the torch, the Vietnam War was the fuel. The antiwar movement led to student activism across the country. In San Francisco, for example, Berkeley students would join a parade of five hundred thousand protesters who marched to Golden Gate Park for an antiwar rally.

Many speakers came to Berkeley and talked about the Vietnam War. Senator Wayne Morse was one such visitor; he was one of the two senators who had voted against the Tonkin Gulf Resolution of 1964 that gave President Lyndon Johnson a free hand in Vietnam. Senator Eugene McCarthy of Wisconsin drew loud cheers when he visited the campus during his antiwar presidential campaign of 1968. The most compelling speaker of all was Martin Luther King Jr., who stood on the Sproul Hall steps and denounced the war. Contrary to the advice of many of his friends, King had come out against American involvement in Vietnam. They told him that he would dilute his civil rights message if he entered the war debate; he answered that the war was undermining the civil rights movement, and added that, in any event, he would speak as his conscience dictated. At Berkeley the Nobel laureate condemned the war more passionately than any other public figure who visited the campus. Standing under the hot sun, with sweat forming on his face, he mesmerized thousands of listeners. King told the Berkeley activists something they already knew—that any struggle will involve many setbacks. Then in his strong voice, he quoted James Russell Lowell:

Truth forever on the scaffold

Wrong forever on the throne

Yet that scaffold sways the future

And behind the dim unknown

Standeth God within the shadow

Keeping watch above his own.

A few weeks later Martin Luther King Jr. was dead, killed by a sniper's bullet in Memphis. That news reached Berkeley in the late afternoon after most students had left for home. The next morning the plaza was crowded with thousands upon thousands of mourners. No one said a word. During the turmoil at Berkeley following the free speech fight, and during all the loud speeches that reverberated across Sproul Hall Plaza, no words had been more moving—none more suggestive of the idealism and the confusion and the questioning of those times—than the sound of silence that noon at Sproul Hall Plaza.

Millions of students, along with other Americans, lamented King's death in 1968. By then the multifaceted protest movement had spread across the country. Protests at Berkeley and elsewhere tended to follow a cycle determined by events in Southeast Asia. In 1970 President Richard Nixon announced that the United States had begun to bomb Cambodia in order to cut off supply lines from North Vietnam. Activists on campuses nationwide regarded this as a dangerous escalation of the war.

At Kent State University in Ohio, hundreds of students were lined up facing a troop of national guardsmen. The soldiers began to shoot, and four students were killed.

By the time of the Kent State deaths, the campus tumult that first appeared during the FSM had epicenters throughout the nation. The disposition to question all regulations and regulators—campus rules, business values, military spokesmen—was present on virtually every college and university campus in the land. But a few years later it was hard to tell whether college campuses had been changed significantly by the tumultuous sixties. The Vietnam War was over, and the largest political organization at Berkeley was the Young Republicans Club. In Sproul Hall Plaza in 1980 one would be more likely to hear a jazz concert than a political speech. Nationwide, the most widespread form of unconventional student behavior during the seventies was "streaking," an event in which one or more students removed their clothes and ran naked through a public space. In national politics, beginning in 1968, four out of five presidential elections were won by conservative politicians who had criticized student activism at Berkeley—Richard Nixon and Ronald Reagan.

By filling the board of regents with his appointees, Reagan had been able to undermine Clark Kerr as president of the university. Kerr was fired and never reached his goal of staying in office until 1968, the university's centennial year. He retained a professorship in industrial technology at Berkeley and presided over an important study of American universities conducted by the Carnegie Commission for Higher Education. Five years after the FSM, Kerr remarked, "What with all the worldwide attention Berkeley has commanded, the remarkable thing is not how much things have changed, but how little. I would challenge you to prove that there has really been a 1 percent change in anything basic." At about the time that Kerr made this remark, even Mario Savio seemed to have retreated into a more conventional life. Married, the father of two children, and less than three years away from becoming "older than thirty," he was eager to get on with his studies. "It's not so easy for myself to get busted at the drop of a hat," he said, "when I've got two children I'm responsible for."

The student revolution of the 1960s did not produce results as dramatic as, say, the American Revolution or the New Deal. And yet changes were abundant at Berkeley and other American campuses. Many universities committed themselves to minority hiring and adopted ethnic studies courses during the sixties. College housing programs that formerly divided men and women into separate facilities now allowed coeducational housing. Men let their hair grow long and left their ties in the closet; men and women on campus wore blue jeans to class. Students became members of campus administrative committees. Most importantly, the sixties fostered a new sense of who college students are.

Bibliography

CAPUTO, PHILIP. *13 Seconds: A Look Back at the Kent State Shootings* (2005). Compelling account of the Kent State massacre, focusing on students injured and killed, written by a Pulitzer-prize-winning journalist who was on the scene soon after the event.

DICKSTEIN, MORRIS. *Gates of Eden: American Culture in the Sixties* (1977). Explores the multifaceted connections between culture and politics during the 1960s.

DRAPER, HAL. *Berkeley: The New Student Revolt* (1965). A contemporary history of the free speech movement with statements by Mario Savio, Jack Weinberg, and other participants.

GOINES, DAVID LANCE. *The Free Speech Movement* (1993). Colorful examination of the events of 1964, including some two hundred photographs and the Free Speech Songbook.

HEIRICH, MAX. *The Spiral of Conflict: Berkeley 1964* (1971). A careful analysis of the free speech movement based on contemporary research and interviews.

KAISER, CHARLES. *1968 in America: Music, Politics, Chaos, Counterculture and the Shaping of a Generation* (1997). An exploration of the Americans who, in 1968, believed that fundamental change was possible in America.

LIPSET, SEYMOUR MARTIN, AND SHELDON S. WOLIN. *The Berkeley Student Revolt: Facts and Interpretations* (1965). A documentary history including excerpts from Clark Kerr's *The Uses of the University*.

MATTHIESSEN, PETER. *Sal Si Puedes (Flee If You Can)* (2000). Well-written account of Cesar Chavez and the United Farm Workers, focusing on a three-year period (1968–1971) when Matthiessen worked with Chavez.

RASKIN, A. H. "The Berkeley Affair: Mr. Kerr vs. Mr. Savio & Co." *New York Times*, February 14, 1965, 24–25, 88–91. Illuminating interviews with Clark Kerr, Mario Savio, and other student leaders in the wake of the free speech movement.

RORABAUGH, W. J. *Berkeley at War: The 1960s* (1989). An exceptionally well-researched and comprehensive treatment of the many facets of the turmoil at Berkeley.

Study Guide

Summary

Arguably the most tumultuous time in the history of American higher education began with the free speech movement at Berkeley in 1964. This essay shows that University of California administrators such as Clark Kerr at first embraced free speech at Berkeley, then shows how the student movement adopted educational, social, and political doctrines far more extreme than Kerr and other liberals had anticipated. The free speech movement merged with a cultural revolution and an antiwar movement that ultimately spread across the United States.

Identification Topics

Clark Kerr, Richard Nixon, Mario Savio, Edward W. Strong, Jack Weinberg, Hearst Greek Amphitheater, counterculture, Eldridge Cleaver, Third World Liberation Front, Robert McNamara, Edmund G. Brown, Frank Wilkinson, free speech movement, Sproul Hall, Joan Baez, Haight-Ashbury, filthy speech movement, Ronald Reagan, People's Park, Kent State

Study Questions

1. What evidence do you see in this essay that McCarthyism was still a force in California during the years leading up to the free speech movement?
2. In what ways was Clark Kerr an advocate for academic freedom during his tenure as president of the University of California?
3. During the early 1960s, Edmund Brown, Clark Kerr, and the board of regents embraced freedom of speech, but they had a different idea than campus activists of how political discourse should take place. What was their view? How did the reality of student activism on campus vary from their expectations?
4. Schooled in the tactics of the civil rights movement, the leaders of the free speech movement realized that every time the University of California adopted restrictive measures, the free speech movement would gain new supporters. What were the "oppressive" acts that built support for the movement during 1964?
5. What was the connection between the free speech movement and the civil rights movement—in personnel and in tactics?
6. In addition to the speech issue, what were the other political and cultural ingredients in the campus turmoil of the 1960s? What was the counterculture? How did its values contribute to the turmoil at Berkeley?
7. How did the following persons or movements contribute to unrest at Berkeley: the proposed Eldridge Cleaver course, the Third World Liberation Front, People's Park, and Kent State?
8. How and why did the Vietnam War contribute to student unrest during the 1960s?
9. How were Richard Nixon and Ronald Reagan able to win support from some California voters for their positions on the situation at Berkeley?
10. How did the sixties change Berkeley and other college campuses?

Research Topics

1. What happened at Kent State? Explore this question, looking at both the national guard and the student protestors' points of view.
2. Mario Savio and other Berkeley activists had taken part in the Student Nonviolent Coordinating Committee (SNCC) in the South. What was SNCC and what role did Savio and other students play in its activities?
3. Study the student movement on another college campus during the 1960s—possibly your own campus.
4. What was the "counterculture" of the 1960s? How did it influence our own times?

CHAPTER 14

America and the Cold War

Colin Powell's Military Career
from Vietnam to the Persian Gulf

During the four decades following World War II, the principal goal of American foreign policy was the containment of communism. Alliances were formed, coups were arranged, and wars were fought in the name of this design. The two biggest American wars during the second half of the twentieth century, Korean and Vietnam, were waged in the name of stopping communism. Neither resulted in complete victory. The Korean War ended in a stalemate, and the Vietnam War ended in defeat for the South Vietnamese, America's ally. But in the cold war as a whole, the United States was triumphant. During the 1980s, without firing a shot, America won the struggle against its foremost communist opponent, the Soviet Union. As a career soldier, Colin Powell was a witness to many of these events. Additionally, he was a witness to the emergence of new threats and responses as the United States shifted its attention from communism to terrorism. While observing and taking part in American foreign and military affairs, Colin Powell was leading a life that was, in itself, exceptional. An African American, born to poor Jamaican immigrants, he rose to the highest position in the American armed forces, indicating the changes in the U.S. Army and America as a whole that followed in the wake of the civil rights movement.

On a February afternoon in 1992, Colin Powell, the top military officer in the United States, and his wife Alma were traveling in a Jeep caravan on a dirt road into the interior of Jamaica. When the primitive road ended in a path, the Powells got out of their vehicle and walked down "a rutted trail" to a place called Top Hill. Suddenly "something quite magical happened," Powell recalled. Villagers approached from every direction: "young and old, some colorfully dressed, some in tatters, some with shoes, some bare-foot." A band of youngsters in black uniforms appeared, playing "The Star-Spangled Banner." Then the crowd parted and a smaller group of men and women came forward. Colin Powell was "choked with emotion" as he realized that these were his Jamaican relatives, many of whom he had never met. They escorted him to a tiny house, with walls of rough stucco and a roof of sheet metal. In this house, in 1898, the father of Colin Powell— later to become the Secretary of State—had been born.

That afternoon Powell and his wife boarded a Black Hawk heli-copter and flew over Westmoreland, Jamaica, the birthplace of his mother. Colin Powell thought about his parents' journey to America: "I wondered if they could have imagined how much this act of courage and hope would shape the destiny of their son." America was a place where "life, liberty, and the pursuit of happiness" meant something.

Luther Powell, Colin's father, had left Jamaica in his early twenties. "He literally came to America on a banana boat"—a United Fruit Company steamer. Luther Powell settled in Harlem and while living in an apartment with other Jamaican immigrants, he met Arie McCoy. They married and in 1937 she gave birth to a son, whom they named Colin. Both Arie and Luther Powell worked in the garment industry.

When Colin was six, the Powells moved to an apartment in a four-story tenement building on Kelly Street in the South Bronx. The section was known as "Banana Kelly" due to a curve in the street near their house. The neighborhood was rough: burglaries and street fights were common. But in contrast to later times, when drugs devastated the region, the South Bronx during the 1940s and 1950s was relatively stable. A "rough-edged" tolerance prevailed among the residents of African, Irish, Polish, Italian, Hispanic, Jewish, and Chinese descent.

Reading Colin Powell's account of his childhood in his autobiography, *My American Journey*, one finds almost no hint of his later success. Young Colin had difficulty in school: "I was a happy-go-lucky kid, amenable, amiable, and aimless." He was thrown out of a church camp for buying beer and hiding it in a toilet tank to cool. And his father once caught him in an illegal game of poker—"with off-duty cops, no less." He fared poorly in sports. Even in romance he was "unprecocious and unaccomplished."

"All the guys carried condoms in their wallets," he writes, but "mine [was] yellow and brittle with age."

Years later, remembering his boyhood, Powell credited his family with strengthening him: "I was a contented kid, growing up in the warmth and security of the concentric circles my family formed." Those circles extended from his parents to a large number of aunts and uncles and cousins: "Family members looked out for, prodded, and propped up each other."

America entered World War II when Powell was only four, but he was fascinated. He built model planes of balsa wood and tissue paper and waged battles with lead soldiers on the living-room rug. He and his friends stood on the rooftops of their apartment buildings searching for German planes on bombing runs over the Bronx. A few years later the United States was at war again, in Korea. "Warfare held a certain fascination for me," Powell recalled, "as it often does for boys who have not yet seen it up close." That phrase is important, suggesting the perspective of the mature, battle-tested Colin Powell, a warrior who had learned firsthand that war "up close" is not all glory and adventure.

Powell finished high school with a C average, just good enough to get into the City University of New York. Like hundreds of his classmates, he joined the Reserve Officers Training Corps (ROTC). The Korean War was winding down, but the draft was still in effect, and common wisdom held that if you had to go into the army, best go in as an officer. Powell was also drawn to the army by movies about the two recent wars: *Thirty Seconds over Tokyo, Guadalcanal Diary, Pork Chop Hill*, and *The Bridges at Toko-Ri*. On campus he joined the "Pershing Rifles," the ROTC equivalent of a fraternity. Powell found a model and a mentor in fellow cadet Ronald Brooks, who "could drill men so they moved like parts of a watch." He enjoyed the discipline and camaraderie of his unit: It reminded him of "the caring atmosphere within my family." For Powell ROTC was partly a game, as when he led a drill team to victory in a city-wide competition. But ROTC was also about preparation for battle. Powell remembered a tough sergeant who told the cadets: "Gentlemen this is a Browning Automatic Rifle. I am going to teach youse how to disassemble and assemble the BAR. Listen to me, cuz if youse don't youse could die in combat. Any questions so far?"

Colin Powell graduated from City University with solid marks in geology, his major, a distinguished record in ROTC, and mediocre grades in other subjects. At graduation he took an oath "to defend the Constitution of the United States against all enemies foreign and domestic." Powell was deeply moved by the ceremony. "We live in a more cynical age today," he wrote in his autobiography, published in 1995. "We are embarrassed by expressions of patriotism. But when I said those words almost four decades ago, they sent a shiver down my spine. They still do."

Army life began with intense training in the South. He and his fellow soldiers learned the "Australian rappel," where they ran forward down a

150-foot cliff, supported by a rope. They practiced parachute jumps from 250-foot towers and later from planes, conducted patrols in knee-deep water, and followed a five-mile compass route through a forest in the dead of night. Reflecting on that lesson some forty years later, after Vietnam, and after the Persian Gulf War, Powell added a crucial note: "We were taught at Fort Benning, however, that American soldiers must know the reason for their sacrifices. Our GIs are not vassals or mercenaries. They are the nation's sons and daughters. We put their lives at risk only for worthy objectives. If the duty of the soldier is to risk his life, the responsibility of his leaders is not to spend that life in vain."

During his training in the South, Colin Powell discovered another, deeply troubling, lesson. He learned about being regarded as an inferior because of his color. The lesson did not come, however, from within the army. In 1948 President Harry Truman had issued Executive Order 9981 ending segregation in the armed forces. There were already seasoned black officers moving up through the ranks, and Powell came to regard the army—with good reason—as the most integrated profession in America. But life off the bases in the South was another matter. Powell received his first taste of segregation while still a cadet in ROTC. Driving home from summer training at Fort Bragg, North Carolina, he and two white cadets stopped at gas stations that featured three restrooms: men, women, and colored. Powell later quipped, "we were apparently ahead of our time, already unisex."

After basic training, Powell—now Lieutenant Powell—was assigned to the Third Armored Division in West Germany. This was the era of the cold war. Powell recalls, with a touch of irony, "I was excited to be going to the front line, with our godless communist adversary deployed just across the Iron Curtain." Later he and other Americans might question the assumption that Communism was monolithic, organized from some central command post, and that all communists were evil. But by the 1950s the ideological lines had been drawn, and Colin Powell was posted near Frankfurt, Germany, only a few miles from one of those lines, the one marking the border with Soviet-occupied East Germany. If the Russians invaded, the Americans were expected to "fight like the devil," then fall back and "watch the nuclear cataclysm begin." Under the presidency of Dwight D. Eisenhower, this approach for beating the Russians was known as "massive retaliation."

Back in the United States Lieutenant Powell was assigned to post duty at Camp Devens in Massachusetts. While there he went on a blind date with a woman named Alma Johnson. They were soon "inseparable." Remembering their courtship years later, Powell wrote that she was "beautiful, intelligent, refined, and fun to be with, and, all too rare in a romance, she was my friend." Her parents were the principals of the two black high schools in Birmingham, Alabama.

The wedding took place without a hitch, but the young couple soon faced the inconveniences of black life in the South. Colin Powell was transferred to Fort Bragg, North Carolina, and on the drive to the post they were barred from public restrooms and had to park beside the road and go into the woods to relieve themselves. Once at Fort Bragg they discovered that the only housing available for blacks was in squalid neighborhoods outside the base. A white couple with a large house on the base urged them to move in with them—and they did. When several neighbors complained about the African American couple in the neighborhood, their hostess, as tough as she was principled, "told these people what they could do with their prejudices."

Powell was enrolled in the Unconventional Warfare Center where he studied the history of Vietnam and learned Vietnamese phrases. Communists in South Vietnam, supported from North Vietnam, were attempting to take over the country. The United States was beefing up its army of "advisors" in South Vietnam to a total of 11,000 in 1962. Powell was taught that "By God, a worldwide communist conspiracy was out there, and we had to stop it wherever it raised its ugly head." Later he came to question this assumption, but "it all had a compelling neatness and simplicity in 1962."

Before Powell was shipped overseas, Colin and Alma spent a few days together in Birmingham. She was four months pregnant and moved in with her family to a house in a reputedly "safe" neighborhood. While Colin was in Vietnam, Alma would be in another battle zone. Alabama governor George Wallace had recently declared that he supported "segregation forever." And in Birmingham police chief Eugene "Bull" Connor planned to enforce that policy against a growing protest movement, soon to be led by Martin Luther King Jr. By then Colin Powell was thousands of miles away in Southeast Asia.

On January 17, 1963, he was looking down on the Vietnamese jungle north of Saigon from a marine helicopter. His fellow passengers were soldiers of the Army of the Republic of Vietnam (ARVN). Bags of rice and live pigs and chickens completed the cargo. They landed in a remote region of mountains and jungles near the Laotian border, at an outpost known as A Shau. From here they were expected to harass traffic on the Ho Chi Minh Trail, the main supply route from North Vietnam to the south. Powell was surprised to note that the camp lay in the shadow of a mountain from which it could easily be attacked. "Why is the camp there," he asked the Vietnamese commander.

"Very important outpost," he was told. "Outpost is here to protect airfield."

"What's the airfield here for?" Powell asked.

"Airfield here to resupply outpost."

Powell would remember that conversation long afterward; it provided a haunting foreshadowing of the entire Vietnam War: "We're here because we're here, because we're. . . ."

But in January of 1963 Colin Powell was a young American lieutenant, excited by the immediate prospect of helping the ARVN soldiers become effective fighters. Soon after his arrival they went on long marches, camping in the jungle by night. "A force of armed men moving into the unknown has a certain power," Powell writes, "even a touch of majesty, although the squealing pigs and cackling chickens accompanying us in wicker baskets detracted somewhat from the martial aura." They climbed hills, forded streams, and walked through clouds of insects.

On the sixth day, slogging down a muddy path, Powell heard the sound of gunfire at the head of the column. He ran forward and saw a medic attending a wounded man. Another man lay crouched in a fetal position, dead. The Viet Cong—South Vietnamese opponents of the American-supported regime in South Vietnam—had attacked, then vanished. Powell writes: "The lark was over. The exhilaration of a cocky twenty-five-year-old American had evaporated in a single burst of gunfire. Somebody got killed today. Somebody was liable to get killed tomorrow, and the day after. This was not war movies on a Saturday afternoon; it was real, and it was ugly."

During his first two months on patrol Powell saw the results of more ambushes, but never saw the enemy. The ARVN soldiers contented themselves with torching straw houses in little mountain hamlets and cutting down cornfields with their bayonets. "As a young officer," Powell writes, "I had been conditioned to believe in the wisdom of my superiors, and to obey." Destroy the crops and starve the Viet Cong, thus thwarting North Vietnam, thus thwarting Communist China and Russia who were "our mortal enemies in the global struggle between freedom and communism."

"It all made sense in those days," he later wrote, with a touch of irony.

During the weeks on patrol Powell worked on gaining the confidence of his men and became their commander "in all but name." He remembered fondly a night when they listened to the song "El Paso" on the radio and sang it together. "Every verse ended with an aye-aye-aye that the Vietnamese loved." Lieutenant Powell's time in the field came suddenly to an end when he was himself wounded—not by bullet or grenade, but by a weapon as old as the bow and arrow, a punji stake. As he was walking along a trail, his right foot dropped suddenly into a hidden hole onto a sharp object. Powell tried to continue walking but the pain became "excruciating." The punji stake, which had penetrated several inches into his foot, had been dipped in dung—a primitive agent of biological warfare—and the poison was spreading.

Back at camp the medic cut away Powell's boot, looked at his purple foot, and called in a helicopter to evacuate him. He left his comrades "with more than a tinge of regret."

Returning to Birmingham, Colin Powell returned also to the realities of segregation—which made no exceptions for veterans. While he was away there had been eighteen terrorist bombings in Birmingham, plotted by segregationists to intimidate civil rights activists. Martin Luther King had already led demonstrations in the city, was jailed, and wrote his "Letter from Birmingham Jail." But segregation still prevailed in much of the South. At a hamburger joint near Fort Benning, Georgia, a waitress refused to seat Lieutenant Powell, offering instead to pass him a burger through a window at the rear of the building. He refused and went away hungry. A year later conditions began to improve. President Lyndon Johnson signed the Civil Rights Act, and Colin Powell returned to the same cafe and was served.

In the meantime the war in Vietnam had begun to "escalate"—a phrase designed to make the buildup to 500,000 Americans in Vietnam seem innocuous, as if this were only a small increase from the 10,000 "advisors" who were the entirety of the American presence during Powell's first tour. At Fort Benning the change was marked by the frequent arrival on the base of yellow cabs, a recurring event depicted vividly years later in the film *A Soldier's Story.* Powell writes, when a taxi "pulled up to a house and the driver got out, you knew he was delivering a telegram from the Defense Department and Benning had another widow and a new family of fatherless children." As the death toll mounted, close friends of Colin Powell were among the dead.

During the early years of "escalation," Powell stayed in the states and was moved from post to post for advanced training. At Fort Leavenworth, Kansas, he was enrolled in the army's Command and General Staff College. While he was there, the Viet Cong mounted the Tet Offensive in South Vietnam. Like millions of other Americans, Powell learned about the attacks when he turned on his TV on the morning of February 1, 1968. Enemy soldiers were fighting in Saigon on the very grounds of the American embassy and beside the presidential palace; throughout Vietnam they attacked more than 100 towns. Although the Viet Cong were driven out of every place they attacked, hundreds of Americans died during the offensive, and the blow to American morale was decisive. Powell writes: "The images beamed into American living rooms of a once faceless enemy suddenly popping up in the middle of South Vietnam's capital had a profound effect on American opinion. Tet marked a turning point, raising doubts in the minds of moderate Americans." The antiwar movement gained strength. Peace parades around the country drew as many as 500,000 marchers.

The year of the Tet Offensive was tumultuous in America as well as Vietnam. Black radicals were challenging Martin Luther King's leadership of the civil rights movement. "Burn, baby, burn," a phrase coined by H. Rap Brown, became the slogan of the new militants. And then the great good voice of King himself was snuffed out in Memphis by an assassin's bullet.

By now Colin Powell had found his home professionally in the army. Martin Luther King had said, "I have a dream that my four children will one day live in a nation where they will not be judged by the color of their skin but by the content of their character." Powell found that tolerant place in the U.S. Army. He had reservations about the Vietnam War, but in 1968 the direction of that war was in other hands. "Politicians start wars," he later wrote, "soldiers fight and die in them. We do not have the luxury of waiting for a better war."

Powell was shipped back to Vietnam during the summer of 1968. Before leaving, he took Alma to dinner in one of the best restaurants in Birmingham—now open to blacks as well as whites. At the table he gave her an envelope with instructions in case he failed to return. If he were to die in Vietnam, he hoped to be buried in Arlington National Cemetery.

Soon afterward Powell, now Major Powell, was in Vietnam at a place called Duc Pho, where he served as executive officer of a battalion within the Americal Division. Powell's work ranged from filing reports to visiting the battlefields. One day he rode out with a helicopter to a firebase where nine American soldiers had just been killed. The helo landed toward nightfall, took on the dead, and lifted off quickly. On the ride back Major Powell stared at "nine recently healthy young American boys, now stacked like cordwood." Back at the field hospital the bodies were taken to a tent to be confirmed dead. One by one the ponchos were unrolled and the bodies examined. "People in combat develop a protective numbness that allows them to go on," Powell observed. But then he heard a gasp as a nurse discovered a familiar face beneath one of the ponchos: "Oh my God, it's. . . ."

This casualty was a medic who had gone out to the firebase the previous day and been caught in the fight: "Nurses and medics started crying."

When Powell remembered that episode years later, he reflected that the men in Vietnam were as brave and dedicated as in any other war in American history. But the war was less illustrious. At home the administration was having trouble selling the cause to the American people. In Vietnam 100,000 ARVN troops were deserting every year. Nguyen Cao Ky, the South Vietnamese head of state, had come to symbolize what was wrong with the country that Americans were dying to defend. A flamboyant young pilot and playboy, he dressed in a silk flying suit, and proclaimed that Adolf Hitler was his hero: "This was the man for whose regime three, four, even five hundred Americans were dying every week in 1968. They were dying with the same finality as in Valley Forge or Normandy, but with little of the nobility of purpose."

Thus far in his military career, Colin Powell had been one of thousands of junior officers, working their way up through the ranks of the military. He suddenly entered a higher profile position when the general commanding the division saw an article in the *Army Times*, indicating that Powell had been second in his graduating class from Command and General Staff College at Fort Leavenworth. The general felt that a man with such a background belonged at headquarters, and he placed Powell in charge of "operations and planning."

Later Colin Powell wrote of the division: "Its reputation would be forever tarnished by one of the darker chapters in American military history at a place called My Lai." Shortly after Powell's departure from Vietnam, news broke in the United States that a platoon led by First Lieut. William Calley of the American Division had rounded up 347 Vietnamese men, women, and children and killed them in cold blood.

Powell notes that while in Vietnam he seldom thought beyond the immediate tasks at hand, but "as time passed another part of my brain began examining the experience more penetratingly." He came to deplore the use of the "body count" as a measure of progress in the war. The system encouraged inflated figures and even needless killing: "dark episodes like My Lai resulted, in part, because of the military's obsession with . . . that grizzly yardstick." In various other ways, Powell charges, the military created a false overlay of heroism and success to cloak sordid realities. Military honors were awarded at an accelerated pace, and these wholesale awards diminished the achievements of the real heroes.

For Powell the tragedy of misinformation and misunderstanding in Vietnam came down to the fact that lives were lost in a cause that could not be satisfactorily explained. This revelation was not simply a logical deduction based on the analysis from afar. It was, instead, as immediate and deeply felt as Powell's memory of a GI who stepped on a mine near Duc Pho: "One leg hung by a shred, and his chest had been punctured." Powell sat beside him on the evacuation helicopter on the flight back to the field hospital: "He was just a kid, and I can never forget the expression on his face, a mixture of astonishment, fear, curiosity, and, most of all, incomprehension. He kept trying to speak, but the words would not come out. His eyes seemed to be saying, why? I did not have an answer, then or now. He died in my arms before we could reach Duc Pho."

Here was the tragedy of Vietnam summed up in a single death: there was no good answer to the question, why?

No answer, "then or now."

Once he completed his second one-year tour in Vietnam, Powell returned to the United States and entered the government and business administration program at George Washington University. This educational interlude was part of a standard career path: The army needed higher-ranking officers with administrative skills. The army next encouraged Powell to apply to be a White House Fellow, a position that would enable him to study the American government. The competition was stiff, but Powell was chosen, and spent a year in a program that included tours of China and Russia.

After several years in Washington, Powell was eager to go back among soldiers. In 1973 he was transferred to Korea. Powell, now a colonel, was stationed at Camp Casey near the demilitarized zone (DMZ) separating North and South Korea. His immediate superior was a general known as "Gunfighter" Emerson. General Emerson would speak to the troops with "a modest premise, mounting fervor, and an apoplectic windup." Powell first saw Gunfighter in action when he lined up the whole division on the parade ground at Camp Casey, gave the troops a brief overview of the armistice ending the Korean War, and explained that their job was to help the South Koreans if the North broke the armistice. As the commander warmed to the subject, he grew more animated. Powell heard one of the sergeants whisper, "Here he goes," and then the commander began to shout:

"And if these North Korean sons of bitches ever cross that DMZ, we're gonna kick their asses!"

The commander's "eyes were flashing and the veins throbbed on his neck."

"And if the Chinese throw a million troops across the border, we're gonna kick their asses too!"

Excited, the soldiers began shouting, "Go, Gunfighter, go."

The officers during Powell's assignment in Korea faced two challenges: training their troops to the highest levels of efficiency, and working on the morale issues that could weaken a unit. At Camp Casey, the morale problem was a race problem. One flash point was the balance of music in local bars between soul, favored by the black soldiers, and country and western favored by whites. The soldiers marked out their own DMZ between black and white bars. Gunfighter Emerson said, in effect, no way. In Powell's words, "No vigilante code superseded the authority of the army." To encourage racial harmony, Emerson showed the film *Brian's Song* repeatedly at the post theater. It tells the story of Chicago Bears football teammates Gale Sayers, black, and Brian Piccolo, white. Divided by race at first, they became close friends. A discussion always followed the film. What had divided these men? What brought them together? What were the lessons for Camp Casey? Colin Powell saw the film and led discussions at least six times.

Back in the United States, Colin Powell next undertook a series of assignments that shifted him between Washington, D.C., and various posts around the country—Fort Campbell, Kentucky; Fort Carson, Colorado; and Fort Leavenworth, Kansas. In 1983 he was back in

Washington as military assistant to Caspar Weinberger, the Secretary of Defense. His assignments in Washington brought him into contact with a sequence of events that slowly shifted the focus of American foreign policy from the cold war to international terrorism. Shortly after going to work at the Pentagon, Powell learned that a suicide bomber had driven a truck, loaded with explosives, into the Marine barracks at the airport in Beirut, Lebanon. With each new report, the body count rose higher, reaching a final total of 241 dead Marines.

What were the Marines doing anyway in an exposed position in Lebanon? Colin Powell asks this question in his autobiography and concludes that the reasoning had been "fuzzy." The Lebanese army was fighting Shiite Muslims lodged in the mountains near Beirut. The marines had been sent in to provide a peace-keeping "presence" between the contending forces. Secretary of Defense Weinberger opposed this deployment, but lost the policy debate. In Powell's view the U.S. forces had been placed between two "powder kegs."

Soon after the American deployment in Beirut, Muslims had shelled the base killing several Marines. President Reagan ordered the battleship *New Jersey*, offshore in the Mediterranean, to lob shells into the Shiite positions in the mountains—"as if we were softening up the beaches on some Pacific atoll prior to an invasion." Since the Shiites could not reach the battleship, they found "a more vulnerable target," the marines at the airport. "What I saw from my perch in the Pentagon," Powell writes, "was America sticking its hand into a thousand-year-old hornet's nest with the expectation that our mere presence might pacify the hornets."

In 1986 General Powell was back in Germany as head of the Fifth Corps, 75,000 soldiers in all. Powell had assumed one of the foremost American commands in Europe. With the possibility of the Soviets attacking West Germany declining more with each passing year, he had to be wary of another kind of threat—one that would play a larger role in the world during the years ahead. A few years before, at the Munich Olympics, terrorists had killed eleven members of the Israeli team. That was only the most dramatic of a series of terrorist incidents that made Americans nervous. The Frankfurt PX, on the base where Powell would be stationed, had recently been bombed. Their house near the base was surrounded by barbed wire, and soldiers manned a guardhouse at the gate twenty-four hours a day. One of the bathrooms has been converted into "an armor-plated sanctuary in which we were to lock ourselves until rescued in case of a terrorist attack."

On his return to Washington, Colin Powell took part in a series of epochal meetings with the Soviets during these final years of the cold war. In 1987 he became National Security Advisor, a position in which he would work directly with President Reagan as well as with the secretaries of state and defense. Given that until recently the position of ambassador to Liberia had been the highest post open to African Americans, Powell experienced his own rise to prominence in Washington as "dizzying."

Most of the White House servants were African Americans and were grateful for their positions as workers in the foremost residence in the land. But for a fellow black to be not simply a servant in the White House but one of the leaders of the land, was something special. At one reception in the East Room an usher said to Powell, "Sir, I was a private in the army in World War II, the old segregated army. I never thought I would see the day when a black general would be in this house. I just want you to know how proud we all are."

Under the Reagan administration, the U.S. government embarked on a deliberate policy of outspending the Soviets in weapons development. The cold war had become a war of economies, and the American economy had proved the more robust, despite huge budget deficits accumulated during the Reagan years, 1981 to 1989. Mikhail Gorbachev, the new leader of the Soviet Union, had embarked on a policy of *perestroika* and *glasnost*—restructuring and openness—within his country, and he was eager to negotiate treaties with the United States to bring a halt to the costly arms race. As Colin Powell took up his new position, the Soviets and Americans were engaged in negotiations about intermediate-range nuclear force (INF) missiles.

During a preliminary meeting in Geneva in 1988, Powell met a "tough-looking" Soviet soldier named Marshal Sergei Akhromeyev. He was a veteran of World War II, still in the army more than 40 years after the end of the war. He told Powell, "I am the last of the Mohicans." Powell learned that this erstwhile cold war foe was a fan of James Fenimore Cooper, Jack London, and Mark Twain, "all your best writers." Powell reflected on the changing times. A year before he had been commanding an American corps in Germany, "whose sole mission was to hurl back Akhromeyev's armies."

In December 1988 Gorbachev came to Washington for INF missile negotiations. Meeting in the cabinet room, Colin Powell was impressed. Not only was Gorbachev in command of the technical details about nuclear missiles but he was also in command of surprising intelligence about the American arsenal. He not only knew, for example, that the United States was getting ready to produce new chemical weapons at a facility in Pine Bluff, Arkansas but also the kinds of artillery shells that would carry the chemical payloads.

President Reagan seemed unprepared and awkward at the initial meeting. His first remark was a joke in such poor taste that "the Americans wanted to disappear under the table, while Gorbachev stared ahead, expressionless." The American staff spent most of the night developing a better reply for the President, and the next day the discussions were on a more even footing. In these and subsequent meetings the two superpowers agreed on the terms of the INF treaty, limiting nuclear weaponry. In the meantime East Germany, Poland, and the other Soviet satellites were gaining their independence. In 1989 the Berlin Wall, the foremost symbol of cold war divisions, came down. Seeing the future, Mikhail Gorbachev remarked to Colin Powell at one of their meetings, "What are you going to do now that you've lost your best enemy?"

Little did either of them know that the decade ahead would bring the United States into a number of smaller wars, independent of the cold war. In 1989 George Bush was inaugurated president and appointed Colin Powell as Chairman of the Joint Chiefs of Staff. Powell had only recently received his fourth star and was appointed over the heads of a number of more senior officers. But he soon won the respect of his fellow chiefs, the commanders of the army, navy, air force, and marines. At that time he was the youngest man, the first African American, and the only ROTC graduate ever to serve as Chairman of the Joint Chiefs.

Soon after his appointment Powell's attention was directed to Panama and General Manuel Noriega. Powell had met Noriega during a trip to Panama in 1983 and remembered him as a man with "beady, darting eyes." Powell had the "crawling sense that I was in the presence of evil." Noriega was on the payroll of the CIA and also took money from Libya, and allowed Soviet intelligence to operate in Panama. "You could not buy Manuel Noriega," Powell writes, "but you could rent him." Noriega was even welcomed on one occasion at the Pentagon. Powell remarks: "Cold war politics sometimes made for creepy bedfellows."

Noriega's corruption and arrogance finally led to his downfall. He dealt in drugs and laundered Columbian drug money, which in the tortured logic of the cold war was not entirely despicable as long as some of the money went to the Contras, forces fighting against a socialist regime in Nicaragua. But in 1988 grand juries in Miami and Tampa indicted him for drug dealings. Panamanians went to the streets, hoping that the United States would topple Noriega. But this did not happen. Powell explains: "Though it may surprise some people, the military is not necessarily eager to apply force to achieve political ends, except as a last resort. . . . In the end, it is the armed forces that bring back the body bags and have to explain why to parents." Moreover, Ronald Reagan declared that the United States would seem like a bully if the country "invaded Panama just because we did not like the way the Panamanians handled their internal affairs."

In 1989, however, the situation in Panama grew worse. When an opponent appeared to be winning a presidential election, Noriega simply called off the election. Adding to the regime's reputation as a gang of thugs, the general's henchmen beat up the opposition party's vice presidential candidate in view of American TV cameras. The situation came to a head soon afterward when Panamanian soldiers killed an American marine at a roadblock, interrogated a navy officer who had seen the shooting, and abused his wife. President George Bush convened a White House meeting of key advisors including Colin Powell and Secretary of Defense Dick Cheney. After reviewing plans for a surprise attack by night, President Bush said, "Okay, let's do it. The hell with it."

Plans for a possible invasion of Panama had used the code name "Blue Spoon." With a real invasion imminent, the name was changed to the more ennobling phrase, "Just Cause." On December 19, 1989, the United States arranged for Guillermo Endara, the duly elected president of Panama, to be sworn into office. Then in the predawn hours of the next day American forces swept out of the American-controlled Canal Zone in coordination with soldiers from bases in the United States—a joint force of about 22,000—and fought their way to Noriega's headquarters in Panama City. The fighting was over in four days, and the elusive Manuel Noriega surrendered ten days later. Twenty-four Americans died in the fighting along with about 500 Panamanian soldiers and civilians. As a percentage of total population, the Panamanian losses were large, almost as high as the United States suffered during the entire eight years of the Vietnam War. But despite these losses, polls showed Panamanians, by great majorities, grateful for the invasion—one measure of Manuel Noriega's unpopularity. In 1992 the former dictator was tried in Florida and convicted of cocaine smuggling.

The Panama Invasion, as it came to be known, was the first military action in years that Colin Powell considered a complete success. Shortly after the American victory, Colin Powell went to Panama and visited the troops. In an unguarded moment, with a TV camera rolling, he told the soldiers, "Goddam, you guys did a good job!" Letters soon flooded the mailroom scolding the chairman for taking the Lord's name in vain. But his rhetoric reflected his mood; this was a characteristic Colin Powell moment, the highest ranking soldier in America pumped at being among his troops. Just Cause had confirmed Powell's views about what makes a successful military operation: "Have a clear political objective and stick to it. Use all the force necessary, and do not apologize for going in big if that is what it takes. Decisive force ends wars quickly and in the long run saves lives."

The Panama Invasion occurred just shortly after the fall of the Berlin Wall. Panama was the first of four military actions undertaken during the four years Powell would serve as chair of the joint chiefs. The other three—in Haiti, Somalia, and Kuwait—each grew out of unique circumstances. But they all share at least two common threads, the idea of going to the aid of an oppressed people and the ambition of securing "stability" in one part of the world or another. The largest of these operations was the Persian Gulf War, fought with Iraq in 1990 and 1991.

The relationship between the United States and Saddam Hussein had been guarded but not hostile during the 1980s. The United States provided loans and aid to Iraq, largely because Saddam Hussein—while known for brutality toward his own people and for the use of chemical weapons in the current war with Iran—was considered a useful player in achieving a balance of power in the Middle East. He was a secular leader in contrast to his neighbor in Tehran, the Ayatollah Khomeini. In the desperate, final years of the war between Iran and Iraq, both sides took to lobbing chemical weapons at each other. But apart from restrained criticism from outside countries, some of whom had supplied the ingredients for those very weapons, the world paid little heed to the use of poison gas in the Middle East.

Then, in March 1988, reports came out of Iraq of a horrible new use of chemical weapons. Wave after wave of Iraqi aircraft had flown over the Kurdish town of Halabja raining a deadly storm of mustard gas and nerve gas on the people. Journalists arrived on the scene—a green valley between snow-capped peaks—soon after the attack. The carcasses of sheep, cattle, cats, and dogs lay in the streets along side the bodies of men, women, and children. Their faces were waxen. One reporter encountered "four small girls in traditional dress lying like discarded dolls by a trickling stream." An old man in a turban lay "clutching a baby on a doorstep." In all roughly 5,000 Kurds were killed in the attack, and the State Department issued a statement condemning Saddam's use of chemical weapons.

This was, however, little more than a mild slap on the wrist, for the United States continued supporting the Iraqi regime. Years later in 2001 when George W. Bush gave reasons for invading Iraq, one of his rationales was Saddam Hussein's cruelty in having used poison gas during the 1980s. But ironically, back then, when American outrage might have been effective in stopping the use of what came to be known as "weapons of mass destruction," the country accepted Halabja as the price of maintaining stability in American–Iraqi relations. In a prophetic article on the aftermath of Halabja, H. D. S. Greenway, writing in the *Boston Globe*, argued that the pictures of the victims and the failure of the world to act, might be seen as making chemical weapons "if not respectable at least permissible." The genie of chemical warfare was out of the bottle: "By the end of the century, it may prove a greater threat to stability and peace than the atomic bomb."

When the Iran–Iraq War ended in a stalemate in 1988, Saddam Hussein was saddled with a huge war debt. Having failed to conquer Iran, a more populous country than Iraq, he turned his attention to Kuwait, a smaller, oil-rich neighbor. At the time the United States was still seeking closer ties with Iraq. Early in 1990 Assistant Secretary of State John H. Kelly told Congress that Saddam Hussein was "a force of moderation" in the Middle East. And in April 1990 a delegation of five U.S. senators, led by Bob Dole of Kansas, met with Saddam and told him they were eager to keep open the Iraqi market for American grains. Moreover, Dole carried a message from President Bush to the effect that the United States wanted "better relations with Iraq"—again, despite his recent use of chemical weapons. On July 24 as Saddam's forces were massing on the Kuwait border, April Glaspie, the U.S. ambassador to Iraq, told Saddam that the United States had no "opinion on inter-Arab disputes such as your border dispute with Kuwait." In fact, President Bush wanted to "broaden and deepen" American relations with Iraq. She reminded Saddam that the President had written him on Iraq's national day, expressing his desire for friendship. Glaspie reported to Washington that Saddam told her he had been "touched by those messages."

On advice from Egypt, Jordan, Saudi Arabia and other Arab countries that Iraq was only bluffing on Kuwait, President Bush sent a mild note on July 28 urging restraint: Saddam should avoid military action in the spirit of Iraqi–American "friendship." This was hardly a firm declaration, and George Bush was criticized later for not being tougher at that moment with Iraq. But at the time, Iraq was not regarded as a rogue state or an enemy of the United States. Saddam may have reasoned that since the United States had supported him in his war with Iran, even despite his use of chemical weapons, what could be the problem with occupying Kuwait? He continued massing soldiers and tanks near the border.

Colin Powell watched these developments closely, noting that the Iraqis were moving artillery to the front, laying down communications, and stockpiling fuel and ammunition. These were clear signs of an impending attack. Gen. Norman Schwarzkopf, in charge of the armed forces in the Middle East, provided briefings to government officials on likely Iraqi moves and possible responses. Then on August 2, 1990, Iraq crossed the border into Kuwait with 140,000 soldiers and 1800 tanks. Citing old territorial claims, Saddam annexed Kuwait, calling it the nineteenth province of Iraq.

Faced with the actuality of an Iraqi occupation of Kuwait, the Bush administration responded promptly, warning Iraq against invading neighboring Saudi Arabia and preparing for war. Through painstaking diplomatic efforts, including globe-trotting by key American officials, the United States organized a coalition of forty-three nations to liberate Kuwait—thirty of these eventually sent military or medical assistance. The alliance involved most of the members of the North Atlantic Treaty Organization (NATO) including Britain and France, the Soviet Union, and several Arab states, notably Egypt and Syria. Bush personally lobbied members of the United Nations Security Council, urging them to take a tough stand on Iraq. Soon the UN passed resolutions demanding that Saddam withdraw from Kuwait and imposing economic sanctions. In the meantime, the United States sent an initial 200,000 troops to the Gulf to protect Saudi Arabia. This maneuver came to be known as "Desert Shield." By November the American force had grown to 500,000, augmented by another 175,000 troops from other countries.

As Chairman of the Joint Chiefs, Colin Powell was the liaison between the White House and the armed forces. Shortly after the American troop deployment in Saudi Arabia, Powell visited the encampments in Saudi Arabia. "At this early stage," he writes, "morale among our troops was high, but the desert was a bleak, forbidding world, hedged in by Muslim moral strictures uncongenial to GIs from the Western world." One of those strictures was "No Bibles." Powell discussed this rule with Prince Bandur, the Saudi ambassador to Washington. "Are you kidding?" Powell said. "The Arabs will take our sons, but not their Bibles." Bandur explained that the rule was that Saudi customs officials were required to confiscate Bibles. Finally it was agreed that Bibles could be shipped in large numbers directly to the American air bases, then distributed to the troops. The arrangements to accommodate American Jewish soldiers were even more difficult. Bandur explained that no Jewish services could be conducted on Arab soil. "They can die defending your country, but they can't pray in it?" Powell asked. The Saudi restriction held, and Jewish troops were to be taken by helicopter to American ships off shore for their services.

During the fall and early winter of 1990–1991, the United States and allied forces assembled in Saudi Arabia, preparing for an attack. The United Nations Security Council adopted Resolution 678 giving Iraq until January 15, 1991, to withdraw from Kuwait. The vote was 12–2 in favor of the resolution, with only Cuba and Yemen opposing.

Just before the deadline, the Bush administration took a request to Congress for authority to use force under UN auspices. The debate was heated. Senator George Mitchell summed up the arguments against war: "An unknown number of casualties and deaths, billions of dollars spent, a greatly disrupted oil supply and oil price increases, a war possibly widened to Israel, Turkey, or other allies, the possible long-term American occupation of Iraq, increased instability in the Persian Gulf region, long-lasting Arab enmity against the United States, a possible return to isolationism at home."

After four days of debates, Congress by a narrow margin gave the president authority for military action under United Nations auspices in Iraq. In the meantime Saddam's refusal to budge was impressive. He declared that he would fight the "mother of all battles" against anyone who tried to remove him from Kuwait. "I was amazed," writes Powell, "given the forces and power now arrayed against Saddam Hussein, unmatched since D-Day, that he still had not blinked."

The sun set on January 15, 1991, the day established by the United Nations for withdrawal with Iraqi forces still occupying Kuwait. Two days later the allied campaign began with the aerial bombardment of Saddam's positions in Iraq and Kuwait. After five weeks of constant bombing the allied ground forces, under the leadership of Gen. Norman Schwarzkopf, crossed into Iraq and Kuwait on February 24 in an operation known as "Desert Storm." The Iraqis fled down what came to be known as the "Highway of Death," falling by the thousands under heavy aerial attack. But they managed to set fire to some 800 oil wells on the way out of Kuwait.

By February 28 the allied forces were in clear command of Kuwait and the Iraqi army, having suffered tens of thousands of casualties, was in full retreat. Seemingly the United States could have swept right into Baghdad, but the reasons for restraint were abundant. For one, UN Resolution 678 authorized the liberation of Kuwait but not the conquest of Iraq. In Powell's words: "We were heading an *international* coalition carrying out a clearly defined UN mission." Then there was the strategic argument. Conventional wisdom held that a unified Iraq helped achieve a regional balance of power. If, say, Iraq was defeated and fragmented into Kurd control in the North, Suni in the center, and Shia in the South, Iraq would not be able to keep Syria and Iran in check. "The only way to have avoided this outcome," Powell writes, "was to have undertaken a largely U.S. conquest and occupation of a remote nation of twenty million people. I don't think that is what the American people signed up for." Nor could the United States count on the Iraqis themselves to establish a strong democratic regime. Had Saddam fallen, Powell later observed, there was little likelihood that he would be replaced by "a Jeffersonian in some sort of desert democracy where people read *The Federalist Papers* along with the Koran. Quite possibly, we would have wound up with a Saddam by another name."

These arguments—voiced by Powell and others, including Norman Schwarzkopf and George Bush—won the day, and after only 100 hours, the ground war came to a halt. In the Gulf War the United States lost 148 soldiers killed in battle, some by friendly fire, and another 145 killed in noncombat accidents. The total number of coalition forces killed was 240. Iraqi deaths totaled more than 25,000. The statistics are one indication of a remarkable victory, but they are incomplete. In addition to 467 wounded Americans listed in standard accounts of the war, there were at least 100,000 Americans injured by a mysterious affliction known as "Gulf War Syndrome." The symptoms include pain, fatigue, irritability, and nausea, and they affect many veterans of the Gulf War in France, Britain, the United States, and other coalition countries. In many cases these problems are more debilitating than, say the loss of an arm or a leg to enemy fire. While a specific cause for the syndrome has not been discovered, the epidemiological evidence is clear: Veterans who served in the Gulf War suffer these symptoms far more frequently than other veterans. Thus thousands of soldiers were "wounded" in the gulf without even being aware initially of their injuries.

Medical researchers and others are exploring a variety of leads, including reaction to the immunization "cocktail" received by soldiers in the Gulf, residues from destroyed chemical warfare depots in Iraq, and even contamination in over-heated cans of cola. The explanation that has received the most attention is that residues from depleted uranium, used in the hundreds of thousands of shells fired by the allies in the Gulf War, may be the culprit. Whatever the cause of Gulf War Syndrome, it is a reminder that human costs of war sometimes go far beyond the wounds and deaths occurring on the battlefield.

During the course of the Gulf War, Colin Powell gave regular briefings to the media. He won the respect of millions of television viewers for his calm and deliberate reports on the war and emerged along with "Stormin' Norman" Schwarzkopf as a national hero. The two military men along with other administration officials were feted with victory parades in Chicago, Washington, and New York. "After the stalemate in Korea and the long agony in Southeast Asia," Powell writes, "the country was hungry for victory." Assessing the Gulf War in his autobiography, Powell noted the beneficial results in the Middle East from the Gulf War. American prisoners were freed in Lebanon, Israel appeared to be on the way to better relations with Arab neighbors, and "Iraq remains weak and isolated, kept in check by UN inspectors. Not a bad bottom line."

Colin Powell stayed on as Chairman of the Joint Chiefs through George Bush's presidency and into the first year of Bill Clinton's presidency. Shortly after the end of the Gulf War, the United States became involved in Operation Restore Hope in Somalia. The object there was to support a UN relief effort to provide food in a region ravaged by war and starvation. The relief program went well, but then came the problem of what to do next. As soon as the United States and other nations withdrew, the rival warlords would likely return to fighting and the hunger would begin all over again. The troops stayed on into 1993. Shortly before retiring, Colin Powell warned President Clinton that the United States should withdraw from Somalia: "We could not substitute our version of democracy for hundreds of years of tribalism."

A few days after Powell's retirement, American soldiers were sent into Mogadishu to capture several warlords. In the battle that followed eighteen Americans were killed, along with hundreds, perhaps thousands, of Somalis. The film *Black Hawk Down* tells the story of the American soldiers trapped in hostile territory. It is a compelling account of American bravery, but when the film was shown in Mogadishu, the Somalis were disappointed: Their own people were stereotyped and the enormity of their losses was ignored.

While Colin Powell still chaired the joint chiefs, the Clinton administration considered using air strikes to support Bosnians fighting against Serbs near Sarajevo. Powell warned against becoming involved in the fight without a clear political objective. The air strikes would not necessarily deter the Serbs and the United States would likely need to send in ground forces. In one of the administration discussions of Croatian policy, Madeleine Albright, U.S. Ambassador to the United Nations, asked Powell why brag about the American forces and not use them. Powell recalls: "I thought I would have an aneurysm. American GIs were not toy soldiers to be moved around on some sort of global game board."

Colin Powell's caution in committing forces—for which he received the nickname "The Reluctant Warrior"—was part of a wider set of strategies. Enter any conflict cautiously, he argued, make certain that the objectives are clear, have the support of the American people, go to battle with sufficient power to win quickly, and have a good "exit strategy" for ending the conflict. This cluster of ideas came to be known as the Powell Doctrine.

On September 20, 1993, Colin Powell's second and final term as chairman of the joint chiefs—as well as his army career—came to an end. In a ceremony hosted by President Bill Clinton, he retired from the chairmanship and from the army. The army band played ("for the first and maybe the last time," Powell notes) a piece composed for the occasion, "Eye of the Storm: The General Colin L. Powell March." Bill Clinton hung the Presidential Medal of Freedom around the general's neck. "He clearly has the warrior spirit," Clinton remarked, "and the judgment to know when it should be applied in the nation's behalf." In reply Powell told the crowd that he would have "had to be sour-dead not to marvel at the trajectory my life had followed."

Colin Powell's story does indeed follow a remarkable trajectory. It is a "rags to riches" story on several levels. From a humble immigrant background he rose to a position where he gave advice to presidents. Without benefit of an education in one of the elite military academies he became the top officer in the armed forces. And although he was denigrated early in life by some Americans as a member of an inferior race, he became one of the most respected leaders in the nation. Among his many honors in retirement Colin Powell was given the key to a southern city where a few years before he had not even been allowed to use the key to a restroom.

On his first morning in retirement, Alma Powell told Colin that the sink was stopped up and leaking on the floor. His first instinct was to tell his wife to call the post engineer. Then he realized that his former staff of ninety had shrunk to none: "I spent my first civilian morning crouched under a dripping sink." Powell was fifty six at the time and, counting his time in ROTC, he had served almost four decades in the army.

With the fame he acquired during the Gulf War, Colin Powell was in demand as a public speaker, received job offers in industry, and was asked about his availability as a presidential candidate. While indicating that he might one day consider a political career, he preferred to devote his attention to writing his autobiography, giving speeches on American life and values, and engaging in a variety of public service events.

Looking at the world changing around him—including a peace process underway in Northern Ireland, the ending of apartheid in South

Africa, more humane regimes coming to power in Cambodia, El Salvador, and Angola—Powell was optimistic about the course of history. In his autobiography, completed in 1995, he wrote: "I am heartened by the reconciliations taking place around the globe, by a fundamental shift from chronic conflict to negotiated settlements." Conflicts once thought "intractable" were "resolving themselves through the exhaustion of the protagonists and diplomatic intervention, especially on the part of the United Nations."

A few years later in 2002 Colin Powell was Secretary of State when President George W. Bush alleged that Saddam Hussein's Iraq was saturated with weapons of mass destruction. Powell urged the president to work with the United Nations in finding the weapons and avoiding a war. But in a cruel twist of fate, Powell was delegated to present a flawed case for war that failed to win UN support and included "evidence" that proved later to be faulty. Additionally, the very arguments Powell made during the 1990s for avoiding the occupation of Iraq or Somalia were ignored by the President, Congress, and even Powell himself in 2002 when the United States went to war. The story of the Iraq War is still unfolding at this writing.

Bibliography

BINKIN, MARTIN. *Who Will Fight the Next War?* (1993). The author focuses on "the changing face of the American military" through the Gulf War, including the place of women and African Americans in the armed forces.

JENTLESON, BRUCE W. *With Friends Like These* (1996). Details the ways that Presidents Reagan and Bush supported Saddam Hussein as a counterweight to Muslim fundamentalist regimes in the Middle East.

LANE, CHARLES. "The Legend of Colin Powell," *New Republic*, April 17, 1995. Brings to light some of the criticisms of Powell's career—many of which strike me, however, as overstated or unfounded.

LEOGRANDE, WILLIAM M. *Our Own Backyard: The United States in Central America, 1977–1992* (1998). History of U.S. support—often secret—of counterinsurgency in Nicaragua and El Salvador during the final years of the cold war.

MOSKOS, CHARLES C., ET AL., EDITORS. *The Postmodern Military: Armed Forces After the Cold War* (2000). Essays on the evolution of the military in twelve Western democracies during the past decade.

PELLETIERE, STEPHEN C. "War Crime or an Act of War." *New York Times*, January 31, 2003, section A, page 29. Pelletiere, who was the Central Intelligence Agency's senior political analyst on Iraq during the Iran–Iraq war, makes the argument that Iran and Iraq share the responsibility for the civilian deaths at Halabja in March 1988.

POWELL, COLIN. *My American Journey* (1995). Powell's book is one of the best-written and most informative autobiographies by any American public figure.

PRUDEN, CAROLINE. *Conditional Partners: Eisenhower, the United Nations, and the Search for a Permanent Peace* (1988). Americans in 2003 were following closely the relationship between the United States and the United Nations over Iraq. This book describes the early history of cooperation and tension between the United States and the United Nations, focusing on such matters as Korea, Indochina, and Guatemala.

PYTHIAN, MARK. *Arming Iraq: How the U.S. and Britain Secretly Built Saddam's War Machine* (1996). The role of the United States and Great Britain in arming Iraq during the Iran–Iraq War of 1980–1988.

WOODWARD, BOB. *The Commanders* (1991). Colorful contemporary account of the Gulf War and its leaders.

———. *Bush at War* (2002). The first year of the George W. Bush presidency, including the war in Afghanistan and the role of Colin Powell in placing the Iraq question before the United Nations.

Study Guide

Summary

The story of Colin Powell provides a window on several important threads in recent American history. As an officer in the United States Army, both in the field and in Washington, Powell witnessed crucial episodes in American military history, including events in Vietnam, Korea, Germany, Panama, and Iraq. Through his military career we see the transformation of a country focused on the expansion of communism to a nation preoccupied with the threat of terrorism. His career also shows the transforming power of the civil rights movement in providing new fields of opportunity for minorities: "In retirement Colin Powell was given the key to a southern city where a few years before he had not even been allowed to use the key to a restroom."

Identification Topics

Jamaican roots, Luther Powell and Arie McCoy, "Banana Kelly," *My American Journey*, Executive Order 9981, Fort Benning, Fort Bragg, Birmingham, A Shau, ARVN, the punji stake, the Tet Offensive, My Lai, Camp Casey, Beirut, Ronald Reagan, Mikhail Gorbachev, Manuel Noriega, Operation Just Cause, Halabja, Kuwait, Desert Shield, Desert Storm, Norman Schwarzkopf, UN Resolution 678, Gulf War Syndrome, Operation Restore Hope, Somalia, the Powell Doctrine

Study Questions

1. Colin Powell did not experience discrimination during his early years. Why was his youth free of prejudice? In what ways did he experience bigotry later in life? What was his approach to situations in which he experienced discrimination? And what was the special appeal of the army to Powell and other African Americans?

2. What did Colin Powell mean by this statement: "If the duty of the soldier is to risk his life, the responsibility of his leaders is not to spend that life in

vain." How did he apply it in different circumstances in deciding that particular American military actions were justified—or unjustified?

3. The cold war influenced much of America's foreign policy during Colin Powell's career as a soldier. Based on his experience, what do you learn about the cold war in Vietnam, Korea, and Germany?

4. At several points in this narrative we see Colin Powell encountering the sobering reality of war. Give examples of these encounters and explain how they shaped his emergence as a "reluctant warrior."

5. Despite his successes in Washington, Colin Powell's wife, Alma, noticed that he seemed happiest in the field among other soldiers. What are some examples of his pleasure and fulfillment in army life?

6. Why did Colin Powell come to believe that the Vietnam War had been a mistake?

7. With the end of the cold war, the United States has been involved in a number of military conflicts around the world, most notably in the Persian Gulf region. What is the underlying pattern in these events? Do they reflect a consistent set of strategic goals?

8. Why did the United States decide against expanding the war to Baghdad in 1991?

Research Topics

1. Read Colin Powell's autobiography, *My American Journey*, and expand on a theme developed in this essay—for example, his experiences in Korea or his observations on the winding down of the cold war.

2. Study the experiences of African American soldiers in the armed services since World War II. Was Colin Powell's rise through the ranks unusual or did other black soldiers also rise to positions of influence?

3. Read Bernard Fall's *Street Without Joy*. Powell said of this "perceptive book" that if Kennedy or Johnson had read it, they would have extricated the United States from "the quicksand of Vietnam." What does Powell mean by this statement?

4. What were the major arguments at the time for and against the United States becoming involved in the Gulf War? What was the role of the United Nations in that war?

5. The causalities among the Americans, French, English, and other coalition forces in the Gulf War were much higher than originally reported. This is because the debilitating Gulf War Syndrome, experienced by many of the soldiers, did not become apparent until long after the end of the war. But as many as one hundred soldiers may have been "wounded" with this affliction for every one soldier reported as wounded in combat. Explore current research on the mysterious syndrome. What are the symptoms and the possible causes?

6. In 2001 Colin Powell returned to Washington in a civilian capacity as secretary of state. His reputation has suffered since then because of his role in the Iraq War. Study Colin Powell's career as secretary of state. Were the policies that he supported between 2001 and 2005 in relationship to Iraq consistent with his statements about occupying countries such as Iraq a decade earlier?

CHAPTER 15

The New Age of Technology

Steve Jobs and Apple Computer

The computer industry is the fastest growing business in the world. In 1960 there were roughly ten thousand data-processing computers in operation and the number reached one hundred million by 1990. By 2000 the computer industry was second only to agriculture in revenue. While falling behind in areas such as automobile manufacture, the United States has led the world at almost every stage in the development of the modern computer and computer software. The role of Steve Jobs in establishing Apple and the personal computer as a major force in modern technology illustrates the inventiveness and entrepreneurship that made possible the creation of a new industry and its continuing growth in the twenty-first century.

On June 12, 2005, the commencement address at Stanford University was delivered by Steve Jobs, cofounder of Apple Computers, famous for his many presentations about Apple products and more recently his pitches for iPod music players. This speech, however, was not about a product, but about a philosophy. Although at the height of his fame, Jobs would speak as much about disappointment as about success. Looking out over a crowd of more twenty thousand, Jobs admitted that he had never before attended a college graduation, nor even completed a college education.

"Today," he said, "I want to tell you three stories from my life. That's it. No big deal. Just three stories." The stories would cover these topics: connecting the dots, love and loss, and finally, death.

Jobs told his Stanford audience that he had begun life in 1955 as the son of an unmarried graduate student who put him up for adoption. His birth mother instructed the adoption agency that she wanted her child placed with parents who were college graduates, and so a well-educated lawyer and his wife were expecting to be the adoptive parents. But "when I popped out," Jobs related, "they decided at the last minute they really wanted a girl." So the agency contacted another couple who agreed to take the baby boy. This arrangement nearly fell apart when the birth mother learned that neither prospective parent had a college degree. But the couple promised that the boy would go to college, and the adoption went forward.

Compressing his account of childhood into a few sentences, Steve Jobs carried the graduation audience forward to when he was seventeen and enrolled at Reed College in Oregon. After only a few months he decided to drop out, doubting the value of the required courses he was taking. He was troubled about college costs and "spending all of the money my parents had saved their entire life." Jobs stayed on at Reed for another eighteen months, sleeping on the floor in friends' rooms and auditing the courses he really wanted to take. He made some money by collecting soft drink bottles and returning them to merchants for a five-cent deposit refund. Every Sunday he walked seven miles to the local Hare Krishna temple for a free meal. In the meantime he was taking the classes he wanted and, he recalled, many of the courses he "stumbled into by following my curiosity and intuition turned out to be priceless later on."

As an example, Jobs mentioned a calligraphy class. Reed College had an exceptional program in penmanship, and on campus even the event posters were works of art. He doubted the practical value of this information, but enjoyed seeing the visual appeal of different typefaces and spacing. Later, when Jobs and others were designing the first Macintosh computer, his calligraphy training came back, and the development team designed "multiple typefaces" into the computer. The Macintosh was "the first computer with beautiful typography," Jobs noted. And "since Windows just copied the Mac," all computers today have "the wonderful typography that they do."

The Stanford audience laughed and applauded Jobs' allusion to Apple's archrival, Microsoft, which modeled its Windows operating system on the Mac operating system. The richness of typefaces was possible, Jobs noted, because a young student dropped out of college and studied calligraphy. This led to one of the lessons he made in the commencement address: "You can't connect the dots looking forward; you can only connect them looking backwards. So you have to trust that the dots will somehow connect in your future. You have to trust in something—your gut, destiny, life, karma, whatever. This approach has never let me down, and it has made all the difference in my life."

In a sense, the computer revolution as a whole—a revolution in which Steve Jobs continues to play an important role—can be described as a long historical process of "connecting the dots" over hundreds, even thousands of years. The early story of computers begins with the Greeks, who used pebbles to make calculations. In about 500 B.C. Babylonians strung counters on wires, mounted on a frame. This invention, the abacus, was popular in Egypt, India, and China into the twentieth century.

The nineteenth-century British inventor Charles Babbage first envisioned the modern computer. He called his device an "analytical engine." Babbage proposed a machine with fifty thousand moving parts—thousands of wheels, levers, and belts, working together in perfect unison. Babbage worked on the idea for forty years and built a simple model, but the craftsmen of his time were unable to make the parts required for the analytical engine. The device would have been the size of a football field and would have required six steam engines for power. Babbage's machine was forgotten until 1937, when his writings were rediscovered. Today he is considered the first person to have envisioned a programmable computer.

The first actual computer was built by an American, Herman Hollerith, who developed a calculating machine during the 1880s. The U.S. government, fearing that it would take a decade to tabulate the 1890 census, sponsored a competition to develop a machine to help. Hollerith won. His machines used cards with holes punched to indicate data on topics such as age, sex, marital status, race, and occupation. The machines substantially reduced the time required to analyze the census.

Hollerith founded the Tabulating Machine Company in 1896. During the next few years, it went through several mergers and was finally absorbed into a company that in 1924 adopted the name International Business Machines Corporation (IBM). IBM's punch-card machines, the successors to Hollerith's computers, were the dominant business information system until the 1960s. In comparison to modern computers these machines were painfully slow.

A much more promising technology began during the 1930s with the application of the binary numbering system to computing. A nineteenth-century British mathematician, George Boole, had devised "Boolean algebra," a system of mathematics based on 0 and 1 with no other numbers. In this system, 2 is represented by 10. Three is 11, 4 is 100, 5 is 101, 6 is 110, 7 is 111, and 8 is 1000. Boolean algebra was simply an exotic branch of mathematics until two American physicists, John V. Atanasoff and Clifford Berry, noted that the binary system could be represented in electrical circuits, switched either on or off, representing 0 or 1. The modern computer term "bit," for one on-off switch, comes from the binary system. A bit is a binary digit. In early computers, bits were shuttled around within the computer eight at a time. Clusters of eight bits came to be known as "bytes."

Bits and bytes are the building blocks of software programs. Each byte is a cluster of eight switches each of which can be either on or off. All together there are 256 possible permutations, or arrangements, of the eight switches. In word processing, these 256 possibilities are used to represent characters, including lowercase and uppercase letters from A to Z, accented letters, spaces, and tabs. The standard binary code for the letter A, for example, is 01000001.

These possibilities grow out of numerous combinations of switches that are either on or off. In sufficient quantity, switches can also represent other information, such as digital drawings. To present a simple image, switches are used to tell dots on a screen whether they should be black or white, or, with the development of larger storage devices and better screens, what *color* they should represent. Huge numbers of switches, working together, allow computers to store and play digital music, images, and films. About 8,000,000 "switches," or 1 megabyte ("meg") can provide enough information to store two 250-page books. Roughly 3 megabytes (24,000,000 switches) are needed to contain the information required to present 1 *second* of a digital movie in a computer program such as Apple's iMovie. Thus, storing 1 second of film takes as much digital space as 6 books. An hour of film in a program like iMovie takes as much space as digital versions of about 20,000 books. A 250 gigabyte hard drive can hold roughly 10 2-hour films in this format, or about 500,000 digitized books, the capacity of a medium-sized college library. The sort of storage, taken for granted in the twenty-first century, was unimaginable several decades ago. The first computers—even the most sophisticated—could not begin to represent complex images or films. They were vast in size but with minuscule processing power compared to modern computers.

The march toward modern computing was slow. During World War II, scientists in Germany, England, and the United States began devising computers using the binary system. Howard Aiken, a Harvard mathematician, worked with IBM engineers to develop the Harvard-IBM Automatic Sequence Controlled Calculator, later called the Mark I. Using

3304 on-off switches (about 400 bytes), it worked up ballistic tables used for naval artillery. The British developed a computer using vacuum tubes instead of switches and used it to decode German messages.

After the war, two Americans, John W. Mauchly and J. Presper Eckert Jr., created the first general-purpose computer, known as the Electronic Numerical Integrator and Calculator (ENIAC). Its capacity was about 2000 bytes, or 2 megabytes of information—enough to hold one digitized book or less than one second of an iMovie file. The ENIAC occupied 1500 square feet of surface area and was housed at the University of Pennsylvania. Its vacuum tubes were an improvement over earlier computers using electromechanical switches, but ENIAC was temperamental, functioning only in short bursts. When it worked, it could perform 5000 simple calculations per second. This was a thousand times faster than the Mark I, but much slower than today's most basic personal computers or calculators.

In order to undertake new operations, ENIAC had to be rewired by hand, like the wire and plug connections used on old telephone switchboards, a process that took several days. One day ENIAC refused to function; finally someone found a moth caught in one of the tube sockets— the historic basis for the computer term "bug."

A new stage in computer sophistication came with the UNIVAC I, which beat out an IBM competitor for a Census Bureau contract in 1951. It became the world's first commercially distributed computer. In 1952 a UNIVAC I was used to tabulate the results of the American presidential election. The machine astonished the country by accurately predicting the overwhelming victory of Dwight D. Eisenhower only forty-five minutes after the polls had closed. In fact, the UNIVAC worked so fast, and its news of an Eisenhower landslide was so surprising, that the TV network using it suspected a flaw and fudged the figures, announcing a lesser margin of victory than the computer had predicted. But later election tabulations proved that the computer had been right.

Despite UNIVAC's vote-counting success, vacuum-tube computers often overheated and failed. The next step in computer evolution came with the introduction in 1947 of the transistor, developed by three scientists at Bell Labs. The transistor replaced the cumbersome switches and tubes used in earlier computers. Fortunately for the growth of the computer industry, transistors can be made from silicon, an inexpensive substance found in sand. Smaller than a vacuum tube, transistors are also much faster, cheaper, and more reliable. They revolutionized many branches of electronics besides computing, including radio and television.

During the late 1950s the invention of the integrated circuit allowed transistors to be connected on a silicon chip. Developed simultaneously by Jack Kilby of Texas Instruments and Robert Noyce of Fairchild Semiconductor, the microchip is the fundamental ingredient in the modern computer. Over time, engineers have been able to increase the number of electronic components on a chip. By 2000 they could manufacture chips with millions of transistors on one square inch of surface area.

Another essential element of the modern computer arrived in 1971 when the central processing unit (CPU) of the computer was put on a silicon chip. This device, the microprocessor, was invented by American engineer Ted Hoff. The first such chip was known as the Intel 4004. It and subsequent variations are the essential component in the computer. They can be programmed for a variety of tasks from running a watch to steering a spacecraft.

By the 1970s microchips and microprocessors reduced the cost of computing, but no one had yet built a computer for personal consumption. In 1974 Micro Instrumentation Telemetry Systems of Albuquerque, New Mexico, brought computers one step closer to the general public by introducing the first personal computer or "PC." This was the Altair 8080. The Altair has long since been superceded by a series of computer innovations unimaginable in 1974. But the Altair provided the inspiration for two sets of friends—Bill Gates and Paul Allen at Harvard University and Steve Jobs and Steve "Woz" Wozniak in Silicon Valley—to become leaders in the computer revolution.

Bill Gates's first contact with a computer came at Lakeside School in Seattle in 1968. At that time, computers were far too expensive for a high school to own, but Lakeside bought time on a PDP-10 computer, located in downtown Seattle. Manufactured by Digital Equipment Corporation, the PDP-10 was a "minicomputer," about the size of a refrigerator. It was linked to Lakeside by Teletype. At Lakeside, Gates befriended Paul Allen, his future partner in founding Microsoft. While other students were absorbed in dating and sports, Gates and Allen were obsessed with computers. "We were off in our own world," Gates remembered. "Nobody quite understood the thing but us. I wanted to figure out exactly what it could do."

In 1973 Bill Gates entered Harvard. During his freshman year, he worked on a computer baseball game. Like other leaders of the computer revolution, Bill Gates learned a lot about computers by writing and playing computer games. On a December morning in 1974 his friend Paul Allen was browsing through magazines in Harvard Square, when he caught sight of the current issue of *Popular Mechanics*. On the cover was a story about a computer kit called the Altair 8080, marketed by a small company in Albuquerque, New Mexico. Allen ran across campus to find Bill Gates. In one version of the conversation, Allen shouted to Gates, "Look, it's going to happen! I told you this was going to happen, and we're going to miss it!" Gates was nineteen at the time; Allen was twenty-one.

The father of the Altair, Ed Roberts, was typical of the hobbyists who sparked the computer revolution. In Albuquerque he founded a company called Micro Instrumentation Telemetry Systems (MITS), which he operated out of his garage. At first Roberts sold mail-order model rocket equipment and radio transmitters for model planes. When his fortunes looked bleak, Roberts made a momentous decision. He would build a personal computer and sell it for $397. In retrospect a few decades later, after millions of personal computers had been sold across the United States, Roberts's decision seems like a safe bet. But in 1974 the major computer manufacturers were building machines designed strictly for big business and government. Companies like IBM could no more imagine selling to American households than the Boeing Corporation today would envision building airplanes to fit in the family garage.

The brain in Roberts's machine was an Intel microprocessor, the 8080, which came on the market in early 1974. Normally the chip would sell for $350, but Roberts persuaded Intel to sell them to him for $75 apiece. Roberts's twelve-year-old daughter suggested the name "Altair" after a star visited by the *Enterprise* on *Star Trek*. Roberts himself coined the term that soon became a household word, "personal computing." He later recalled, "I was trying to convey a small machine you could afford to buy that didn't sound like a toy."

By the standards of a few years later, the Altair was a primitive machine. Buyers paid $397 for their computer, unassembled. After they put it together, they had to work the machine with switches rather than a keyboard. It had no permanent memory—no floppy disks or hard drive; so if the power went out, the user had to begin all over. The typical Altair had a random access memory (RAM) of about two thousand bytes, or 2K. That's the capacity built into the 1500 square-foot ENIAC of a few years before. But in contrast, personal computers manufactured in 2006 are much more powerful—for example, typically having, at least 256 megabytes of RAM, more than 100,000 times the capacity of the original Altair.

One of the Altair's limitations was that it came without software. Most fundamentally, it needed language software. A computer language provides a way for a user to instruct a machine to operate in a particular way—that is, to program it. Over the years many languages had been developed for computers. One of the most popular was Beginner's All-purpose Symbolic Instruction Code, or BASIC. It had proven useful to people working with large computers such as the PDP-10, but it was unclear whether BASIC could be adapted to a machine with such a small capacity as the Altair 8080.

In Cambridge, Massachusetts, Bill Gates and Paul Allen thought they could solve the puzzle, and called Ed Roberts at MITS to tell him so. It turned out that dozens of other callers had made the same claim. Roberts said he was willing to work with whoever could actually deliver the product. Gates and Allen went to work at Harvard's computer center, laboring day and night for eight weeks refining BASIC for the Altair.

Gates would fall asleep at the keyboard, wake up, and continue working. Or he would take a nap behind the PDP-10.

In February 1975 Gates and Allen flew to Albuquerque to meet Ed Roberts. Paul Allen had never seen an Altair before. He had no way of knowing for certain whether the program would work until he tested it in front of Ed Roberts. Allen fed the program into the computer, then anxiously entered the command, "print 2 + 2." The Altair answered, "4." "I was pretty stunned myself that it worked the first time," Allen later admitted. With that humble beginning, Paul Allen and Bill Gates were on their way to creating a billion-dollar software company.

Ed Roberts recalled: "I was dazzled. It was certainly impressive. The Altair was a complex system, and they had never seen it before." Using BASIC, Allen then ran a computer game, a lunar landing program. This was the first software ever run with what came to be known as Microsoft BASIC. When Allen returned to Boston, he and Gates, not yet old enough to drink legally, celebrated over ice cream and 7 Up.

For a few months the Altair was at the center of the personal computer revolution. It was a catalyst for meetings of computer fans across the country, and in many cities clubs were formed where enthusiasts could trade ideas. One of these was the Homebrew Club, founded in March 1975 in Menlo Park, California. Two of its members were Steve Wozniak and Steve Jobs. Like Bill Gates, Steve Jobs became a major player in the computer revolution shortly after the arrival of the Altair.

A few years before the birth of the Altair 8080, the Jobs family had moved to Los Altos, California, at the heart of Silicon Valley. At the time, at age sixteen, Steve Jobs was something of a hippy, with shoulder length hair, an interest in electronics, and a knack for business. He became friends with Steve Wozniak, five years his senior, an electronics genius. With other friends they discovered that they could make free long distance connections by imitating the sounds AT&T used for routing calls. One of the group acquired the nickname "Cap'n Crunch" after he discovered that the whistles included in the cereal boxes of that name could be used to produce the needed frequencies for free calls.

Wozniak and Jobs decided to produce an electronic version of the whistle. Of the two Steves, Wozniak was the more gifted in technology, Jobs in business. Jobs acquired the needed parts, Wozniak assembled the devices in his dorm room at Berkeley, and Jobs sold them. Given the dubious legality of the scheme, it lasted only briefly, but it began a business connection between Jobs and Wozniak that would blossom in the future.

After high school Steve Jobs went north to Reed College in Oregon. That was in 1972, and in addition to exploring calligraphy, he studied Eastern mysticism. Then two years before the release of the first Altair 8080s, Jobs moved back to his parents' home in California. A local company named Atari was manufacturing an electronic game called Pong.

A ball moved across a screen: strike it with an electronic paddle, hear a "pong" sound, score points. Several decades and thousands of computer games later, Pong would not raise an eyebrow today, but at the time it was a wonder. People lined up to play the coin-operated version, and Atari made millions. Steve Jobs read an Atari help wanted advertisement offering the chance to "Have fun and make money."

Al Alcorn, Atari's chief engineer, remembered Jobs coming to the office "dressed in rags basically, hippy stuff. . . . I don't know why I hired him, except that he was determined to have the job and there was some spark. I really saw the spark in that man, some inner energy, an attitude that he was going to get it done." Alcorn was one of the first to recognize Steve Jobs as a visionary: "He had these great ideas without much to back them up. Except that he believed in them."

After a short time at Atari, Jobs took a kind of furlough in 1974 to go to India, where he and a friend wandered the countryside seeking spiritual guidance. One day they hiked up a dry river bed finally reaching a cliff which they ascended by a stairway. At the top they met a yogi, but not unfortunately the spiritual guide the young men were seeking. Jobs recalled, "He was really into his wardrobe, changing his clothes all the time. And he was very flowery with his language too. All 'the essence of existence is so and so.' Which did not impress us one little bit." Steve Jobs returned to California and checked in at Atari, wearing a saffron robe and hoping the company would let him go back to work. Atari said yes.

Jobs soon became reacquainted with his friend Steve Wozniak who was working then at Hewlett Packard. Wozniak helped Jobs with engineering problems, and working at night at Atari, Jobs let Wozniak play Gran Trak, the first computer game to use a steering wheel. While Bill Gates and Paul Allen were developing software for the Altair, Steve Jobs and Steve Wozniak were exploring hardware and, in particular, the possibility of a simpler, but more advanced personal computer. Once again, Wozniak was the engineering genius and Jobs the business entrepreneur.

Wozniak credits the Homebrew Computer Club in Silicon Valley at that time with helping him develop his ideas: "It was in early 1975, and a lot of tech-type people would gather and trade integrated circuits back and forth." The group leader would begin every meeting by announcing the convening of the Homebrew Computer Club, which he said, "does not exist," and everyone would "applaud happily." Wozniak recalled that the "theme" of the club was "Give help to others." Meetings would begin with a "mapping period" where individuals would describe computer projects and ask questions. A "random access period" followed in which members would trade ideas and information.

In an interview in 2005, on the thirtieth anniversary of the founding of Homebrew, Steve Wozniak remembered these sessions as "the finest social event of my entire life." He described himself as shy, a guy who liked to sit in the back row, listening to others. Wozniak particularly recalled the idealism of the club members: "They combined their thoughts for humanity and for people getting along and some of the goodness of society along with the goodness of technology—how it's going to do good for us and how it's going to help us do good in other ways in our lives."

He and his colleagues felt that they were part of a revolution—a revolution that the big corporations could not even understand. Thanks to microprocessors, and in particular thanks to that first affordable chip, the Intel 8080, computers could now be available for the average consumer. The corporate executives of the world scoffed at the idea of personal computers while tiny company's like MITS and its Altair 8080 were leading the way to a new era.

The informality and idealism of the attendees at Homebrew and other similar technology clubs led one observer to declare that the personal computer owes "it all to the hippies." In an influential article published in *Time* magazine in 1995, Stewart Brand made that claim. His essay has the suggestive subtitle "Forget antiwar protests, Woodstock, even long hair. The real legacy of the sixties generation is the computer revolution." Brand, who created *The Whole Earth Catalog*, wrote, "Most of our generation scorned computers as the embodiment of centralized control. But a tiny contingent—later called 'hackers'—embraced computers and set about transforming them into tools of liberation. That turned out to be the true royal road to the future." Brand quoted some of the chief tenets of "The Hacker Ethic":

> Access to computers should be unlimited and total.
> Computers can change your life for the better.
> Mistrust authority—promote decentralization.
> You can create art and beauty on a computer.

Stewart Brand cited Steve Wozniak and Steve Jobs as examples of this idealism; they were "hard-core counterculture types" at the heart of the personal computer revolution. Brand described Jobs in the mid-seventies as "a Beatle-haired hippie." At the moment when the Altair 8080 was opening up new horizons for technology enthusiasts, Steve Jobs wore long hair and a "Fidel Castro" beard and often went barefoot. He explored facets of the counterculture lifestyle, including Zen Buddhism, which stresses meditation and a degree of withdrawal from the world. At the Los Altos Zen Center he studied under a master from Japan named Kobin Chino. Chino became influential in his life and years later Jobs invited him to perform his marriage ceremony. Jobs once considered a dramatic form of withdrawal himself—going to live in a Japanese monastery.

But Steve Jobs also liked enterprise, and the Stewart Brand article on hippies and technology helps provide an explanation of the link between the two realms, the world of business and the spiritual life. In the world of Steve Jobs, entrepreneurship offered a means of self-expression. His old friend Steve Wozniac would provide the engineering genius, while Jobs showed a gift for design and publicity. Together they could build something *new*.

The two friends began working together on a computer in the garage of the house owned by Jobs's parents. Their first product was a printed circuit board without a keyboard or monitor; it could be used for running BASIC and playing simple games. Wozniac had a gift for writing computer programs: to him, writing good code was an exciting challenge. He once said, "I'm into it for aesthetic purposes, and I like to consider myself clever. That's my puzzle, and I do designs that use one less chip than the last guy." Wozniac wanted to make the computers for the fun of showing them off at Homebrew meetings; Jobs persuaded him that they should start a business and market the computers.

What should they call the company? Jobs had worked in an apple orchard one summer in Oregon. The word *apple* suggested simplicity, and they wanted to create user-friendly products. Additionally, in the local phone books "Apple" would come before "Atari." For business capital they raised $1300, with Jobs selling his Volkswagen van to pay for his share and Wozniak selling his Hewlett Packard calculator. On April 1, 1976, at the Homebrew Club the partners introduced the computer they would call the Apple I. Within a few months they had sold 150 of them at $666 apiece for revenues of about $100,000. That amount appears insignificant today when Apple's revenue from its iTunes music store alone adds up to more than $1,000,000 every day. But it was a start, and their initial success helped Jobs and Wozniac raise the money for a far more ambitious project, the Apple II.

Earlier personal computers such as the Altair 8080 and the Apple I were sold in kits and lacked the most basic elements of the modern personal computer. They were relatively accessible in terms of cost, but to assemble and use them required a familiarity with technology far beyond skills of the average person. The Apple II would come with a keyboard, monitor, and memory. In addition, the computer would be designed to look attractive.

With the Apple II, Steve Jobs showed the interest in design that would become a hallmark of his influence on technology in the years ahead. The Altair and the Apple I looked like a technology project on a workbench, but not the Apple II. At the West Coast Computer Faire in 1977, one of America's first computer trade shows, Jobs and Wozniac waited eagerly for the new plastic cases to arrive to show off the Apple II. When the cases came the day before the show, Jobs hated the way they looked and set an Apple crew to work sanding and painting them late into the night, getting them ready just in time for the opening the next day. It was the hit of the show.

The Apple II sold for $1,350, and Apple quickly added new features: a disk drive in 1978 and a spreadsheet called VisiCalc in 1979. The Apple II quickly became the most popular personal computer in America. In 1980 revenues reached $117 million; three years later Apple sales totaled $985 million. Jobs developed a reputation for promotion: He sold computers, he sold a company, and he sold a *vision* of a world of easily accessible personal computing. In 1982 he was on the cover of *Time* magazine, featured as the personal embodiment of the computer revolution. By then the Apple II had widened the number of persons who used computers beyond the small coterie of technologically savvy individuals who were the first customers for the Altair and the Apple I. Today the Apple II is recognized as the first general-purpose personal computer.

During those early years, the computer industry was similar to the American automobile industry at its inception, when dozens of companies marketed automobiles then fell to the competition. Today we look back at the Pierce Arrow and the Stanley Steamer as elegant failures of the early automotive age. Similarly, many computer companies began and ended in the 1980s. In 1983, for example, a historian purchased a sleek machine called an Otrona. Weighing about twenty pounds, the Otrona was one of the first of a new breed of "portable" computers. The owner took it to the Roosevelt Library at Hyde Park on a research trip, and the librarians there were so impressed—it was the first PC ever used at Hyde Park—that they convened a special staff meeting to see how it worked. To their amazement the machine performed such marvels as cutting and pasting text.

The machine thus had its moment of glory, which was then followed by a pitiful decline. During the next two years, the Otrona went into the shop four times for major repairs, while its owner learned new terms like "motherboard"—usually in the context of sentences like "Your motherboard has failed." In the meantime the Otrona company also failed. The last time the computer went into the shop, no parts were available. Calling for a report on his machine, the owner was briefed by a lighthearted repair man:

> "Do you own a boat?" he said.
> "Why do you ask?"
> "Because you've got a new anchor."

The failure of Otrona, one of many companies that went under in the 1980s, was a process comparable to the "survival of the fittest" theories of the nineteenth century. During the 1980s, the hardware and software companies that did survive carried out one of the most important revolutions in the history of technology, manufacturing products that were hardly imaginable a few years before.

For several years the Apple II was the great success story in computer manufacture, but then in 1981 IBM introduced its own personal computer and quickly closed the gap. By 1983 IBM's market share was

30 percent to Apple's 21 percent, and it kept growing. Apple developed new computers, hoping to repeat the Apple II magic. The Lisa came first, but was too expensive at about $10,000 per machine. Then Apple released the Macintosh in 1984.

Andy Hertzfeld was a software engineer at Apple when work began on the Macintosh. In an interview conducted just before Apple's thirtieth birthday in 2006, Hertzfeld recalled the atmosphere in the Macintosh division. One afternoon Steve Jobs came by Hertzfeld's carrel at Apple, where he was busy programming. Jobs said, "Hey, I've got good news for you. You're on the Mac team now." Hertzfeld was pleased and asked for a day to finish up his current project. Jobs replied, "What's more important than working on the Macintosh," then unplugged Hertzfeld's Apple II, picked it up, and walked away. Hertzfeld followed as Jobs walked out to his car and dumped the computer in the trunk. They drove the three blocks to a "little building" where the Macintosh team was at work.

Hertzfeld was now a software engineer on the Macintosh project. Jobs, he remembered, talked constantly about the Mac: "It was the future of Apple. It was the next great thing. It was the reincarnation of the Apple II for the eighties. We were all really excited about it, but Steve was great about articulating how, you know, we were going to do the greatest thing ever." Jobs worked the development team hard, providing parties, medals, and bonuses. And he insisted on long days of work. T-shirts at the MacIntosh division read, "Working ninety hours a week and loving every minute of it." The development team was sworn to secrecy.

Andy Hertzfeld described the *atmosphere* surrounding the development of the Macintosh. The Apple II had taken the computer into the American household, but it was still austere compared to modern computers; its interface consisted of lines of text and it had no mouse and no images. "We had a chance to do something better," Hertzfeld recalled, "for the first time make the computer enjoyable to use—make it easy to use for an ordinary person, not a technical person. You know we were basically kicking down the doors that were stopping computers from improving the lives of millions of people. . . . We knew that it had the potential of changing the world if we did a good enough job. That's a lot of pressure, but it's also an incredible blast."

During the 1984 Super Bowl, Apple aired what many critics consider the most effective television commercial of all time. In a large auditorium a "Big Brother" figure (read "IBM") is delivering an on-screen pep talk, while hundreds of blank-faced drones listen passively. Suddenly a woman, built like an Olympic runner (read "Apple") rushes into the auditorium from the back, chased by heavily booted storm troopers. She swings a sledge hammer around and around, and in slow motion it flies off into space, whirling into the screen and shattering the menacing face.

Then a voice says: "On January 24, Apple Computer will introduce the MacIntosh, and you will see why '1984' will not be like '1984.'"

In the *1984* of George Orwell's novel, thought and behavior are tightly regimented. In the actual year 1984, Apple promised the MacIntosh would offer a different kind of computer experience than what was offered by IBM and a growing assortment of IBM clones, all of which used the Microsoft operating systems. In particular, Apple was the first company to offer a personal computer with a mouse and a graphical user interface, consisting of images on the desktop providing avenues for opening, saving, moving, and deleting files.

The graphic interface had been pioneered at a Palo Alto research facility called Xerox PARC. Jobs reportedly told a contact at Xerox, "I will let you invest a million dollars in Apple if you will sort of open the kimono at Xerox PARC." In exchange for the chance to buy into Apple before the public offering of the stock, Xerox allowed Steve Jobs and other Apple employees to visit their facility. Once inside Jobs quickly saw the importance of Xerox software. According to one account, he leaped into the air and shouted, "This is the greatest thing! This is revolutionary!" In an interview with *Wired* magazine in 1996, Jobs said, "Within ten minutes, it was obvious that every computer in the world would work this way someday."

Because the graphic interface quickly became a hallmark of Apple's own operating system, some critics have suggested that Apple "stole" the idea from Xerox. That would not account for the million-dollar investment deal that opened the door for Jobs to see what Xerox had accomplished. Eventually, Apple would hire some fifteen employees away from Xerox PARC, but the Apple operating system was not merely a duplicate of the Xerox interface. George Pake, director of Xerox PARC, noted the similarity between the development of Apple's graphic interface and the Russian development of the A-bomb, which had followed quickly on Hiroshima and Nagasaki. Russia did not need spies to explain how to build an atomic bomb. "They developed it very quickly once they realized it was doable." Similarly, once Steve Jobs and others at Apple saw a graphic interface, they knew it was "doable" and went to work doing it themselves. As Andy Hertzfeld put it, "We were the ones that took it across the threshold to the people."

Twenty years later Apple's own passion for secrecy was legendary. When in 2005 a student publication released information about a new Apple product in advance of the official announcement, Apple sued the publication to discover who was responsible for the leak. Some critics saw this as a mean-spirited attack on well-intentioned college students. But behind Apple's harsh approach to leaks and leakers is the Xerox PARC experience: The goal of entrepreneurship is not simply to have a good idea; additionally the entrepreneur must get that idea developed and marketed before anyone else can.

The Macintosh computer was the result of that secrecy and inventiveness. *Time* magazine said that it looked "like an offspring of E.T. and R2-D2 that might start walking." And walk the Mac did, right off the store shelves. Apple sold 250,000 Macintoshes during its first year, a record at that time. The Apple II also continued to sell well. But despite these accomplishments, IBM continued to increase its sales lead over Apple; in 1985, Apple's profits declined.

Two decades later at his Stanford commencement address, Steve Jobs described what happened next. "My second story," he said, "is about love and loss." He had been lucky, he said, finding "what I loved to do early in life." He and Steve Wozniak had built a two billion dollar company: "We had just released out finest creation—the Macintosh—a year earlier, and I had just turned thirty. And then I got fired. . . . So at thirty I was out. And very publicly out. What had been the focus of my entire adult life was gone."

Describing the episode in 2005, Steve Jobs asked "How can you get fired from a company you started?" He went on to describe his dispute with "someone" who had been hired to run the company. That person was John Sculley, whom Apple had hired away from Pepsi, where he was president. The courtship of Sculley had began in 1982 when Sculley was told that working in Silicon Valley was "the equivalent of being in Florence during the Renaissance." That did not persuade Sculley to leave Pepsi, and so Steve Jobs asked him, "Are you going to sell sugar water for the rest of your life when you could be doing something really important?" Sculley came to Apple and won the respect of the board of directors. But Jobs told the Stanford audience "our visions of the future began to diverge and eventually we had a falling out. When we did, our Board of Directors sided with him." Steve Wozniac had already resigned from Apple, and during the summer of 1985 Steve Jobs, losing influence in the company, was forced out.

Wozniac and Jobs each left Apple with more than $100 million in stocks, but for Steve Jobs the transition was "devastating." "I was a very public failure," he said in 2005, "and I even thought of running away from the valley." In 1985 Jobs's historic position as the foremost popularizer of the personal computer was secure, and at thirty he was one of the wealthiest men in America. But he was not ready to retire. He considered calling a press conference and attacking John Sculley and the Apple board, but he changed his mind. He went to Europe, bicycled in Italy, fumed about his loss. Then, as he explained in 2005, he discovered an important fact: "Something slowly began to dawn on me—I still loved what I did." Computers were his life, and with his substantial personal fortune, he could begin again.

Jobs turned his attention to a new project, hoping to build a high-end computer capable of digital imaging for academic and medical research.

He recruited some top people from Apple and founded a company called Next. Apple sued Jobs over the defections, claiming that he had concocted a "nefarious plot" to steal their technology. In an interview with *Newsweek* Jobs noted the disparity in the size of Apple and Next: where was the threat? "It is hard," he said, "to think that a $2 billion company with 4300-plus people couldn't compete with six people in blue jeans." According to one of the Next founders the lawsuit was valuable as a "bonding experience." No harm came from the case because Apple weighed the possibility of a public relations disaster and dropped its complaint.

The history of Next provided an outlet for Steve Jobs's continuing fascination with aesthetics. The designing of the new computer began with the logo—for which the company paid $100,000—and a stylish headquarters. Given Jobs's star status, Next had no trouble hiring top people. The press sought leads on what the new company would build, but had difficulty piercing the veil of secrecy surrounding the enterprise. Jobs himself had a poster near his desk with the famous World War II slogan, "Loose lips sink ships."

Next hoped to have its first computers available in 1987, but progress was slow, and company expenses began eating away at Jobs's personal fortune. He was reluctant to sell shares in the company, but then Ross Perot came calling. Perot was an oil billionaire and soon-to-be presidential candidate. He came to visit the Next factory in California, a cavernous building, full of promise, but light on progress. As Jobs was showing Perot around, he saw something out of place and began shouting at the offending employee. Jobs's temper was famous—an essential part of his management style or a debilitating flaw, depending on the perspective of the observer. Perot, an older man, had his own take on the situation. "I used to be like that . . . ," he said, "but then I learned you catch more flies with honey. Steve, leave him alone and let's get to work." Get to work, they did, and Perot bought 16 percent of Next for $20 million.

Perot enjoyed the connection. He told Jobs that they could present quite a publicity show. "You're a white monkey," he said, "and I'm a white monkey. Put the two of us in a cage and it's a real circus." A reporter who saw them together at a news conference was struck by how impressed the older, wealthier Perot seemed to be: "He was acting like a starstruck teenager. He was just totally blown away by Steve."

While working at Next, Steve Jobs took on a second project, sometimes described as his "hobby." George Lucas, creator of *Star Wars*, had employed the greatest computer graphics team in the world. But needing cash to settle a divorce, Lucas needed to sell part of his business, and Jobs managed to buy the graphics division for $10 million. Soon afterward he incorporated it as "Pixar." The heart of the business was a group of computer animation specialists whose goal was to replace the old pen and ink version of cartoon graphics with digital techniques. They had begun working together on developing new computers and software for animation at a time when processing power was limited. In 1979 they estimated it would cost about $1 billion to make a single film using existing technology. That was far beyond the budget of any studio, but they knew that each year computers would become more powerful and less expensive. They wanted to be ahead of the curve.

When George Lucas was working on *Star Wars* in 1979, he was facing a problem: He wanted to put entire armadas of space ships on the screen. At the time, spacecraft were represented in films by scale models on movie lots. Lucas sent a representative to talk to the computer animation group. "Can you make a space ship fly around on the screen?" he asked.

The answer: "Sure, we do it every day."

Lucas hired the team, and they created animations for his futuristic films. Additionally members of the group worked on developing better animation software and hardware. This team was the segment of Lucasfilm Steve Jobs had bought. The first product of Jobs's new company was the Pixar Image Computer, which at $135,000 was hardly priced for the average person. Pixar hoped to prove the value of the new computers by producing and showcasing the kind of films they could make. The company's first success was a short film, less than three minutes in length, called *Luxo, Jr.* John Lassater, the lead member of the Pixar production studio, took as his model a Luxo lamp on top of his desk. He visualized two such lamps interacting, like parent and child, with the smaller child jumping on a rubber ball. John Lassater led the team developing the story, models, and animation. Like so many other leading figures in the computer revolution, Lassater worked long hours, spending his nights in a sleeping bag under his desk—all to be able to produce 150 seconds of video.

The film premiered at Siggraph, the focal event of the computer graphics world, in the summer of 1986, and it was the hit of the show. While other exhibitors were displaying special effects, Pixar's *Luxo, Jr.* actually told an engaging story. Two years later Pixar produced a film called *Tin Toy*, which included a little baby, a particularly challenging subject for computer rendering. In April 1989 *Tin Toy* won the Oscar for best animated short film.

The problem at Pixar, like the problem at Next, was how to make money with the expensive new technologies. The "burn rate"—the speed at which companies use up venture capital—was hard on Steve Jobs's personal fortune. By 1991 he had spent most of his money from Apple. That year Next sold only twenty thousand computers. Within two years Next had laid off more than half of its work force. The press had once idolized Jobs while he was at Apple, and the press continued to laud him during his first years with Next and Pixar, but when neither enterprise managed to turn a profit, the coverage changed. An article in *Forbes* magazine declared, "Steve Jobs, whatever his greatness as a visionary, is not much of a manager." The *Wall Street Journal* reported that "the Next workstation seems destined to become a high-tech museum relic." In an article on "America's Toughest Bosses" *Fortune* magazine characterized Jobs as brilliant and charming but explosive and abusive." Jobs, the magazine declared, was a "snake-oil salesman."

In 1993 Steve Jobs's fortunes at Pixar looked equally gloomy despite a promising deal with Disney to cooperate in producing feature-length animated films. Disney would supply capital and some direction, while Pixar would make the films. The first was to be called *Toy Story*. The creative genius at Pixar, John Lassiter, had done short films, but was new to the challenge of piecing together a larger story with more complex characters and plot development. At first Woody, the hero of the movie and leader of the bedroom toys, was a stiff, unappealing character. Disney closed down the project while they sorted it out.

With both Next and Pixar struggling, Steve Jobs was close to failure. Then two animated characters in *Toy Story*, Woody and Buzz, gave him a new lease on life. With the plot and character issues resolved, Disney released *Toy Story* in 1995, and it was an immediate success. The film earned $29 million at the box office during its first weekend. Soon afterward Jobs took Pixar public and began to make money with the company.

Jobs began spending more time at Pixar headquarters. His experience there underscores his charismatic management style—not because his magnetism worked at Pixar, but because it was absent. Pixar had its own charismatic force in John Lassiter. Whenever Steve Jobs visited the headquarters north of Oakland, he was perceived there as something of an outsider, more of a banker than a filmmaker. An executive whom Jobs transferred to Pixar from Next was surprised at the different atmospheres: "At Next, Steve said 'Jump' and we said 'How high?' At Pixar, they say, 'Oh, it's Steve.'" Another person familiar with the two scenes observed, "Steve is not Steve at Pixar."

Although Pixar's success helped reverse the decline in Steve Jobs's fortune, it left him in a curious predicament. He had a peripheral role in a burgeoning movie studio and a central role in a failed computer company. But Jobs had done some of his best work with difficult situations. At Stanford in 2005, Steve Jobs said this about the years away from Apple: "I didn't see it then, but it turned out that getting fired from Apple was the best thing that could have ever happened to me. The heaviness of being successful was replaced by the lightness of being a beginner again, less sure about everything. It freed me to enter one of the most creative periods of my life."

The creativity at Next had apparently ended in failure; certainly the company had not produced any profits. But then in one of the more remarkable developments in American business history, Apple decided to buy Next and bring Steve Jobs back to the company. Apple was struggling at the time, during the 1990s. Microsoft had captured more than 90 percent of market share for operating systems, and companies such as Dell were surging ahead of Apple in hardware sales. Apple lost $1 billion in 1995. Perhaps Steve Jobs could revive the magic.

Gil Amelio, who presided over Apple at that time, anticipated that Next software would infuse new life into Apple's operating system. And he anticipated that bringing Jobs back to Apple would be a public relations coup. What he did not foresee was that Jobs would soon run Apple, rather than Apple employing Jobs. In 1997 Jobs and Amelio shared the stage at the Macworld event in January, the annual Apple ritual in San Francisco. Gil Amelio took the stage and spoke haphazardly for two hours, often losing his train of thought. Then Steve Jobs came forward and the audience stood and cheered.

During the first three months of 1997, Apple lost another $700 million under Gil Amelio's leadership. Looking at the company's decline at that time when his own Dell Computer company was thriving, Michael Dell remarked that if Apple were his, he would "shut it down and give the money back to the shareholders." In July 1997 the Apple board ousted Amelio, making Steve Jobs the de facto leader of the company. But for several years Jobs refused any title other than "Interim CEO." Perhaps this formula was for Jobs an expression of the self-effacement he admired in Buddhism. A decade later, despite being on every list of top executives in America, he was still taking from Apple a salary of only $1 per year and refusing the bonuses that the company paid other top employees.

Steve Jobs was on the brink of what one biography would describe as "the greatest second act in the history of business." Jobs had found once more "what he loved." At Stanford he said: "Your work is going to fill a large part of your life, and the only way to be truly satisfied is to do what you believe is great work. And the only way to do great work is to love what you do. If you haven't found it yet, keep looking. Don't settle. As with all matters of the heart, you'll know when you find it. And, like any great relationship, it just gets better and better as the years roll on. So keep looking until you find it. Don't settle."

For Jobs, not refusing to settle, meant reinventing the company he and Steve Wozniak had created. He hired the advertising agency that produced the famous "1984" television commercial, and the agency provided the slogan "Think Different." He hired Jonathan Ives, a British designer, who gave Apple products a look that other companies would soon envy and imitate, including the iMac line of computers. The first iMac design shattered the idea that a computer has to be shaped like a box; the second was a computer that looked somewhat like the Luxo lamp; and the third—and most elegant of all—put the machinery of the computer into the screen itself. Upgrades in the Mac operating system provided stylish and handy new ways to use the computer.

Apple's new business innovation took many forms. Like Starbucks, Apple built its own stores around the country. At each new opening hundreds of fans would gather hours in advance to be there at the opening. And Steve Jobs, always the consummate salesman, became like a performing artist in his announcements of new Apple products, dressed in black turtleneck, blue jeans, and sneakers, alone on the stage with his latest computers, software, and gadgets.

One of Apple's most arresting products was iLife, a combination of images and sound managing programs. With the advent of digital photographs and movies one of Steve Jobs earlier visions suddenly became a genuine possibility. At a graphics convention a few years earlier, he had seemed hopelessly out of place when he suggested that sometime in the future ordinary men and women would be able to create digital movies on home computers. At the time, when a Pixar work station cost more than $100,000 dollars and only a few specialists could operate one, Steve Jobs's democratic vision of digital image management seemed as fanciful as the original personal computers had seemed to the executives at IBM. But a few years later in 1999 iMovie became standard software with a Mac and provided just such a tool.

Any of these products suggest the innovative quality Steve Jobs brought to Apple; but another product solidified his position as the leading American business entrepreneur of the new century. If Apple still commanded a small fraction of computer sales in America in 2006, Apple's success with the iPod was another story. When the first models appeared in 2000, most portable music players held about ten songs. The first iPods could hold roughly a thousand. At that time a Wall Street analyst claimed that if Apple could sell 250,000 of its players, the company would hit a "home run." In retrospect that estimate seems naive: iPod sales soared, and in 2005 alone, Apple sold more than 250,000 per week. In 2004 a new model held pictures as well as sounds; and in 2005 Jobs introduced an iPod that plays movies—while coyly refusing to call it the "video iPod," raising speculation that yet another iPod would provide a larger platform for videos. Apple's iPod success was helped by its iTunes software for Macs and PCs and the online iTunes store that sold its one billionth song in 2006.

At this writing, with the approach of Apple's thirtieth birthday, journalists are offering multiple visions of Apple's future. Some note that the company still sells only a fraction of the world's computers and wonder where Apple would have been "if only" it had licensed its operating system to other computer manufacturers during the 1980s when Microsoft began its meteoric rise. Others praise Apple for doing just what it does today, staying innovative, releasing operating system upgrades far more quickly than Microsoft, and developing imaginative new hardware such as the iPod and a new line of Macs using Intel chips. Podcasting became tremendously popular in 2005, creating a new use for iPods and other media players.

In 2006 *Business Week*, having written off Steve Jobs a decade before, listed Apple Computer as number one on its list of the fifty "best corporate performers." With the world seemingly on the brink of a revolution in visual digital films, would Apple come to dominate household media, the way it dominated portable sound? More than a century ago Horatio Alger wrote stories about business success in America, stressing always the importance of "luck and pluck." Jobs has been noted for pluck for several decades; with the growing importance of digital media, the case for Jobs's luck grows. In 2006 not only did he own a substantial share of Pixar, but Disney decided to buy Pixar, making Jobs the largest shareholder in Disney, and a member of the board. This gives Jobs a unique position as computer technology and popular media move toward each other.

At Stanford, completing the overview of his career, Jobs told his third story, ending on a somber note, saying in essence to the graduating seniors, someday you will die: "Sorry to be so dramatic, but it is quite true." Only recently he had barely cheated death himself. At 7:30 one morning he was diagnosed with a tumor on his pancreas, one of the most deadly forms of cancer. "I didn't even know what the pancreas was," he said. But the doctors told him he should get his affairs in order, "which is doctor's code for prepare to die." That evening the doctors did a biopsy to examine the tumor more closely. He told the audience at Stanford what happened next: "I was sedated, but my wife, who was there, told me that when they viewed the cells under a microscope the doctors started crying because it turned out to be a very rare form of pancreatic cancer that is curable with surgery. I had the surgery and I'm fine now."

Steve Jobs continued his commencement address by drawing out a lesson from his own life, a lesson that can be seen also as a fundamental truth revealed also in many other lives described in *American Realities*. "Your time is limited," he said, "so don't waste it living someone else's life. Don't be trapped by dogma—which is living with the results of other people's thinking. Don't let the noise of others' opinions drown out your own inner voice. And most important, have the courage to follow your heart and intuition."

At one level this could be seen as old fashioned graduation rhetoric. But Steve Jobs's story like, say, that of Eleanor Roosevelt or John Muir, exhibits the value of living an authentic life. Twenty years before the commencement speech at Stanford, Stewart Brand had complimented entrepreneurs like Jobs as pioneers "who embraced computers and set about transforming them into tools of liberation." Now Steve Jobs returned the compliment, noting Brand's work on the *Whole Earth Catalog*:

> On the back cover of their final issue was a photograph of an early morning country road, the kind you might find yourself hitchhiking on if you were so adventurous. Beneath it were the words: "Stay

Hungry. Stay Foolish." It was their farewell message as they signed off. Stay Hungry. Stay Foolish. And I have always wished that for myself. And now, as you graduate to begin anew, I wish that for you.

"Stay Hungry. Stay Foolish."

Epilogue, 2006

THE THIRTIETH BIRTHDAY

By a fortunate convergence, I was finishing this essay during the week leading up to Apple's thirtieth birthday anniversary, which arrived on April 1, 2006. The events of that week (and the ways that I could access them as a writer) underscore the huge distance technology has taken us during the past few years. When I wrote the first edition of *American Realities* about twenty five years ago, most writers were still using typewriters. You did a rough draft, marked it up with a pen, cut and pasted with scissors and tape, and then took it to a professional who typed up the copy for the publisher. I still remember the day I went to my typist's house and picked up her copy of the essay on Hiroshima. She was in shock, deeply affected by the words she had been typing.

Writing is more solitary these days, without the companionship that comes with another person engaged in typing the manuscript. But during this past week, while completing this essay, I enjoyed another kind of company, unimaginable in 1980. The technology that this essay describes played a major role in helping with the essay. While hiking in a national wildlife refuge, a few miles from my campus a few days ago, I was not alone. Steve Wozniak came along and recounted his early years at Apple. Of course, Wozniak was not there in person, but his voice was there, playing through the earphones of my iPod. He had been interviewed a few days before at a diner in Silicon Valley for one in a series of Apple interviews produced by the San Francisco *Chronicle.* And now his voice fit neatly into my pocket. Wozniak described his lifelong attachment to computers:

I had such an early, early life, from elementary school on, working with computers, designing them, building better ones than there were, telling my dad at the end of high school or the first year at college, I wanted to own my own computer someday, and I'd live in an apartment instead of having a house, just so I could afford it. . . . There was a large mass of people that really wanted their own computers.

John Sculley's voice was in my pocket too on that hike, taking part in another *Chronicle* interview. In books you can read about Steve Jobs's famous "sugar water" pitch to Sculley. But hearing it, in detail, enriched this writer's sense of the visionary Steve Jobs in his mid-twenties. The businesslike board at Apple considered Jobs too young to run the company, but gave him the key role in picking out who would. Jobs liked John Sculley, the chief executive at Pepsi. The two men had many conversations, leading up to spending a day together in New York City. Sculley took Jobs to Metropolitan Museum and showed him sculptures from ancient Greece; Jobs then took Sculley to his favorite music store. At sunset they were on the terrace of an apartment Jobs was purchasing in Manhattan. Sculley remembered their conversation, and repeated it through my ear phones:

> I said, "You know, Steve, I'd like to help you in any way I can, but I want to stay at Pepsi; I'm not going to join Apple." And that's when Steve looked down at his running shoes—he was in his pretty classic blue jeans and black turtle neck, and he looked up at me with his really strong, piercing, dark eyes that Steve has, and he said, "Do you want to sell sugar water for the rest of your life, or do you want to come with me and change the world?" And it was a pretty powerful statement. I didn't change my mind at that moment, but within a week I had changed my mind, and I ended up joining Apple. . . . What I had learned about Steve was that he was a visionary who was able to motivate people to want to follow him and build great products. And I think I would have always wondered, you know, what was I missing if I didn't go with him.

Along with online interviews, modern technology furnished other useful ways to research Steve Jobs. I had heard about Jobs's Stanford graduation address soon after he delivered it. And so I went online and soon found a text version, an audio version, and a video version. For easy review, I have listened to it again and again through the tiny speakers on a Motorola iTunes phone, another innovation of the past year. Technology builds unexpected contacts and communities: I told my doctor last week that I was working on an essay about Steve Jobs, and not only did he know about the Stanford address, he quoted several of his favorite passages.

A few minutes ago as I reviewed my paragraph about *Tin Toy*, I wondered: What does the baby in that story really look like? So I went to the iTunes store and for about the price of a cup of coffee, I downloaded *Tin Toy*, and there on my computer screen I saw an appealing short story that gives a hint of the filmmaking genius of John Lassiter, a talent that would lead a few years later to such films as *Toy Story* and *Finding Nemo*.

Steve Jobs likes to say, "I want to stand at the intersection of technology and the humanities." The beauty of Apple and the other players in the technology revolution of the past three decades is that it allows the rest of us also to stand at that intersection.

Bibliography

BRANDS, H. W. *Masters of Enterprise* (1999). Focuses on the lives of twenty-five American entrepreneurs including J. P. Morgan and Bill Gates and explores the difference each made in the growth of American business.

CRINGELEY, ROBERT X. *Accidental Empires: How the Boys of Silicon Valley Make Their Millions* (1992). Makes the interesting argument that the founders of Microsoft, Apple, and other companies achieved their success largely by accident.

DEUTSCHMAN, ALAN. *The Second Coming of Steve Jobs* (2000). Account of Steve Jobs's career before the iPod; excellent account of the origins of Pixar.

KIDDER, TRACY. *The Soul of a New Machine* (1981). The prize-winning account of the efforts of computer "whiz kids" at Data General to build a new computer.

LAMMERS, SUSAN. *Programmers at Work: Interviews with 19 Programmers Who Shaped the Computer Industry* (1989). Personal recollections of Charles Simonyi, Bill Gates, and other software pioneers.

LEVY, STEVEN. *Hackers: Heroes of the Computer Revolution* (1984). Colorful account of the grassroots origins of the personal computer revolution.

LINZMAYER, OWEN W. *Apple Confidential 2.0* (2004). Well-researched, highly engaging history of Apple.

QUITTNER, JOSHUA, MICHELLE SLATALLA, AND JOSH QUITTNER. *Speeding the Net: The Inside Story of Netscape and How It Challenged Microsoft* (1998). The birth of the Internet as a widespread phenomenon, focusing on Netscape.

SLATER, ROBERT. *Portraits in Silicon* (1987). Biographical sketches of computer pioneers including Howard Aiken, H. Ross Perot, Ted Hoff, Steve Jobs, and Bill Gates.

YOUNG, JEFFREY S. AND WILLIAM L. SIMON. *iCon: Steve Jobs, the Second Greatest Second Act in the History of Business* (2005). A bit "over the top" on Steve Jobs's personal life, but abundant information about Jobs and Apple through the advent of the iPod.

Study Guide

Summary

This essay explores the growth of the U.S. computer industry, focusing on the genesis of the world's first major manufacturer of personal computers, Apple, and the career of the company's principal leader, Steve Jobs. The essay suggests that the entrepreneurial risk and courage we often associate with nineteenth-century America is still in evidence in the birth, development, and growth of the new computer industry. Moreover, the essay explores how one computer company had bridged the gap between technology and the humanities. The article demonstrates that even the computers we use to write history papers or books or process data are a part of history.

Identification Topics

Apple Computer, Steve Jobs, Steve Wozniak, Bill Gates, Paul Allen, Altair 8080, Herman Hollerith, ENIAC, UNIVAC, transistor, Ed Roberts, BASIC, computer hobbyists, Homebrew Club, Atari, Otrona, Stewart Brand, Xerox PARC, hackers, Apple II, Macintosh, "Working ninety hours a week," 1984 ad, Ross Perot, George Lucas, Pixar, Next, John Sculley, iPod, podcasting

Study Questions

1. In what ways did the computer revolution revive the business characteristics of the age of Thomas Edison and Andrew Carnegie?
2. What were the three major points in Steve Jobs's 2005 Stanford commencement address?
3. Explain the contribution of each of the following to the computer revolution: Herman Hollerith, John V. Atanasoff, ENIAC, UNIVAC I, transistors, Ted Hoff, the Altair 8080, Steve Wozniak and Steve Jobs, Xerox PARC.
4. Explain the role of the following in the growth of Apple: the Altair, the Homebrew Club, Apple I, Apple II, Macintosh, Next, iPod, iMovie.
5. During the nineteenth century people commonly spoke of "luck and pluck" as the fundamental ingredients in business success. How did each of these factors influence the success of Steve Jobs at Apple?
6. In what ways does digital imaging take the computer industry to a new frontier?

Research Topics

1. Explore the careers of the early pioneers of the computer industry, such as Herman Hollerith and Howard Aiken.
2. Study the careers of other leaders in the modern computer industry, such as the founders of Microsoft or Intel. Compare and contrast them to Steve Jobs.
3. The essay on Apple focuses on the computer industry, arguably the most successful section of American business in the 1980s and 1990s and the early twenty-first century. Study some other area of the economy that was less successful. Possibilities include the decline of the automobile industry, the savings and loan debacle, and the "junk bond" market.

Credits

Index

1984 (Orwell), 339–340

ABERNATHY, RALPH, 271
Abolitionism, 5–6
Abraham Lincoln Brigade, 244
Adams, John, 119
Addams, Jane, 79, 112
Africa, 9, 59, 204, 260
African Americans, 1–20, 78, 80,
    101, 108, 109, 111, 129, 153,
    198, 257–276, 303–322
Agassiz, Louis, 51, 55
Aguinaldo, Crispulo, 71
Aguinaldo, Emilio, 65
  youth, 70–72
  relations with the United States,
    13–74, 76, 81
  leads insurrection, 80–81
Akhromeyev, Sergei, 314
Alabama, 12, 13, 17, 262–268,
    306, 307
  University of, 267–268
Alamogordo, 206–207, 209, 210, 213
Alaska, 57
Albany, Ga., 269, 270
Albany, N.Y., 189
Albright, Madeleine, 322
Albuquerque, 206–207, 332, 334
Alcorn, Al, 335
Aldrich, Mildred, 124–126
Alhambra Valley, 57
Allegheny Bessemer Steel
    Company, 33
Allegheny College, 159
Allegheny River, 25
Allegheny Valley Railroad, 34

Allen, Paul, 332, 334
Altair 8080, 332, 334, 336, 338
Amalgamated Association of Iron,
    Steel, and Tin Workers, 36
Amazon River, 16, 54
Amelio, Gil, 345
Americal Division, 311
American Civil Liberties Union
    (ACLU), 154–155
American Expeditionary Force, 145
American Federation of Labor
    (AFL), 79
American Heritage, 114
American Revolution, 23, 34, 79,
    86, 107, 128, 137, 139, 273
American Woman Suffrage
    Association, 111
Anderson, Marian, 195, 259
Anderson, Thomas, 76
Angola, 322
Anthony, Susan B., 1109, 110,
    111, 114
Anticommunism, 229–253. *See
    also* Communism; McCarthy,
    Joseph
Antin, Mary
  youth in Russia, 88–91
  life in America, 94, 97
Anti-Semitism, 100
Apple I, 337–338
Apple II, 337–338
Apple Computer, 327–349
Appleton, Wis., 236
Aristide, Jean-Bertrand, 363
Arizona, 59, 113, 242–243,
    259, 293

Arlington National Cemetery, 310
Armstrong, Samuel Chapman, 8–9,
    11, 12, 13
Army-McCarthy Hearings,
    248–253. *See also* McCarthy,
    Joseph
Army of the Republic of Vietnam
    (ARVN), 307–308, 310
Army Times, 311
A Shau, 307
Atanasoff, John V., 330
Atari, 334–335
Atlanta, 2, 14, 17
Atlanta Constitution, 17
Atlanta Exposition, 2–3, 14–18
Atlantic Monthly, 59, 132
Atomic bomb, 203–224
Augusta, the, 221
Australia, 59
"Australian rappel," 305
Austria, 124
Avord, 131, 132, 135

BABBAGE, CHARLES, 329
Bacon Resolution, 80
Bad Vilbel, 313
Baez, Joan, 286–287
Baghdad, 320
Balsley, Clyde, 138–139
Baltimore, 111
"Banana Kelly," 304
Bandur, Bin Sultan, Prince, 319
Bar mitzvah, 99
Barnett, Ross, 268
Barton, Bruce, 152
BASIC, 333, 337
Beahan, Kermit K., 222
Beard, Charles, 115
Behomme, 138
Beirut, 313
Belafonte, Harry, 268, 271
Belgium, 125
Bell Labs, 331
Beloof, Robert, 289

Berlin Wall, 315, 316
Berry, Clifford, 330
Beser, Jacob, 208
Bessemer, Henry, 30
Bessemer converter, 32–33,
    39–40
Beveridge, Albert J., 78
Bhagavad Gita, 206–207
Bible, 6, 48, 153, 154, 157, 158,
    161, 162, 163, 164, 165, 166,
    170, 171, 172, 173–174, 175,
    176, 177, 319
"Big Brother," 339–340
Birmingham, Ala., 258, 269–275,
    306, 307, 309, 310
Biskey, Madeleine, 251
Black, Hugo, 233
Black Hawk Down, 321
Blackhawk helicopter, 304, 321
Black Panther party, 294
Blacks. *See* African Americans
Blatch, Harriot Stanton, 112
"Blue Spoon," 316
Bock's Car, 221–222
Bohr, Niels, 205
Bolsheviks, 231. *See also*
    Communism
Book of Martyrs (Foxe), 48
Boole, George, 330
"Boolean algebra," 330
Borroughs, James, 3, 5
Bosnians, 321
Boston, 7, 88, 90, 93, 95, 96
    University of, 111, 265
Boston Globe, 317
"Bottle of Death, the," 137
Braddock's Field, 30
Brand, Stewart, 336, 347
Brian's Song, 312
Bridges at Toko-Ri, the, 305
Britain. *See* England
Bronx, 304, 305
Brooklyn, 93
Brooklyn Bridge, 33

Brooks, Ronald, 305
Brown, Edmund G., 283, 288
Brown, H. Rap, 309–310
Brown v. Board of Education, 262
Browning Automatic Rifle, 305
Bryan, Mary, 175
Bryan, William Jennings, 79,
    152, 160
  career in politics, 155–157
  religious activities, 157–159
  compared to Clarence Darrow,
    163, 164–166, 176–177
  in the Scopes Trial, 165–175
Bryan, William Jennings, Jr., 163
Bryan University, 176
Buddhism, 336, 345
Bulgaria, 232
Bullard, Edward, 129
Bullock, Rufus Brown, 2, 15, 17
"Burn, baby, burn" 309–310
Burns, Harry, 118
Burns, Lucy, 114
Bush, George, 315, 316,
    318, 320
Business Week, 347
Butler Act, 154–155, 159
Butler, James Davie, 51
Butler, John Marshall, 244
Butler, John Washington, 154

CACHY, 140
California, 46–47, 54–57, 110, 111,
    113, 293
  University of, Berkeley,
    281–299
Calley, William, 311
Call It Sleep (Roth), 96
Cambodia, 322
Camp Casey, 312, 313
Camp Devins, 306
Canada, 52, 117, 232, 233
Capital Times, 242
"Cap'n Crunch," 334
Caribbean Sea, 77

Carnegie, Andrew, 23, 79, 230
  assessment of his career, 25–26,
    34–40
  childhood in Scotland, 25
  early years in Pittsburgh, 25–27
  begins his career, 27–30
  builds Carnegie Steel, 30–33
  philanthropy, 33, 37–38
Carnegie Corporation of
    New York, 38
Carnegie Endowment for
    International Peace, 234
Carnegie, Margaret, 25–26
Carnegie, McCandless and
    Company, 30
Carnegie Steel Company, 24, 30,
    33, 34, 38
Carnegie, Tom, 26
Carnegie, William, 25–26, 27–28
Caron, George, 203–204, 210,
    213–214, 216
Carr, Ezra Slocum, 51
Catholicism, 70, 78, 167–168
Catt, Carrie Chapman, 111,
    117–118, 119
Cavite, 68, 73, 74, 75
Central Intelligence Agency
    (CIA), 315
Century magazine, 58
Chambers, Whittaker, 234
Chapman, Victor, 137
Châteauroux, 132–133
Chattanooga, 161
Chattanooga News, 174
Chavez, Cesar, 293–294
Chavez, Helen, 293–294
Cheney, Dick, 316
Chicago, 155, 159, 160, 361
  University of, 160, 174, 206
China, 67, 69, 77, 86, 211, 232,
    246, 308, 312, 319
China Sea, 222
Chinese-Americans, 100–101
Chino, Kobin, 336

Christ, 54, 152, 164, 175
Christianity, 78, 87, 89, 94, 96,
    98–99, 151, 157, 159,
    162–163, 170, 172–174, 175.
    See also Fundamentalism;
    Modernism; Scopes Trial
Christmas, 60
Churchill, Winston, 114, 232
Cincinnati, 28
Civil Biology (Hunter), 166
Civil Rights Act of 1964, 275, 309
Civil Rights movement, 308, 309
    Birmingham demonstrations,
        258, 270–275
    early achievements, 260–262
    Montgomery demonstrations,
        263–267
    other demonstrations, 267–270
    and Colin Powell, 306, 343–344
Civil War, 4, 6, 10, 14, 23, 28, 29,
    31, 53, 66, 77, 109, 111,
    116, 127
Cleaver, Eldridge, 294–295
Cleveland, 93
Cleveland, Grover, 17
Clinton, Bill, 322
Cohn, Roy, 251–252
Cold War, 232–233, 354–355
Collier, Charles A., 3
Colliers magazine, 245
Colorado, 113, 243
Columbia University, 250, 296
Columbus, Christopher, 91, 132
Command and General Staff
    College, 309, 311
Commoner, The, 156
Communism, 230, 231, 232–233,
    306, 314. *See also*
    Anticommunism; McCarthy,
    Joseph
Communist Manifesto (Marx),
    198, 230
Community Service Organization,
    293

Conant, James B., 206
Congress of Racial Equality
    (CORE), 267–269
Congressional Union for Woman
    Suffrage, 114–115
Connollsville, 33
Connor, Eugene ("Bull"), 258, 270,
    274, 337
Contras, 315
Coolidge, Calvin, 152
Cooper, James Fenimore, 314
Corregidor, 69
Cotton States Exposition, 2. *See
    also* Atlanta Exposition
Croatia, 321–322
"Cross of Gold" speech (Bryan),
    155–156, 174–175
Crown Zellerback, 294
Crozer Theological Seminary, 265
Cuba, 54, 65, 66, 73, 78, 79, 319
Czechoslovakia, 232

DAILY WORKER (NEWSPAPER), 242
Daniels, Josephus, 145
Darjeeling, 59
Darrow, Amirus, 159
Darrow, Clarence, 152
    career in law, 159–160
    compared to William Jennings
        Bryan, 160–161, 164–165,
        176–177
    in the Scopes Trial, 163–177
Darwin, Charles, 35, 153–154,
    161–162
Darwinism, 153–154, 157–158,
    160–161
Davis, Sammy, Jr., 268
Dayton, Tenn., 151, 152, 154–155,
    161–162, 163–164, 169, 172,
    174–176, 177
D-Day, 223, 232, 319
Debs, Eugene, 159, 230
Deep South, the, 118
Dell, Michael, 345

Demilitarized Zone (DMZ), 312
Democratic Convention (1968). *See*
    Chicago Democratic
    Convention (1968)
Democratic party, 247
Denhart, Albert, 219
Dennis et al. v. United States, 234
Descent of Man (Darwin), 166
"Desert One," 316
"Desert Shield," 318
"Desert Storm," 319–320
Detroit, 93, 176
Dewey, George, 101
    background, 66–67
    blockades Manila, 67–69,
        73–77
    relations with Filipinos, 74, 77,
        81–82
Dexter Avenue Baptist Church, 265
Dickens, Charles, 26
Dien Bien Phu, 253
Disciples of Christ, 48, 49
Disfranchisement, 11, 18, 260
"Dixie," 3
Dole, Bob, 317–318
Do Not Touch Me (Rizal), 72
Douglas, Helen Gahagan, 234
Douglas, William O., 234
Douglass, Frederick, 259
Downer, William, 210
Dresden, 212–213
Du Bois, W. E. B., 18, 260
Duc Pho, 310, 311
Dunbar, 47–48
Dunbar Castle, 47–48
Dunfermline, 25, 37
Dunne, Finley Peter, 38
Duquesne Steel Works, 35–36
Dwellings, 93–94
    slave, 3, 6
    free black, 6, 9
    for laborers, 26
    John Muir's, 49–50
    in the Philippines, 70

    at Arthurdale, 194
    military, 313
"Dying Aviator, the," 140

EASY RIDER, 292
Eatherly, Claude, 224
Ebenezer Baptist Church, 265
Eckert, J. Presper, Jr., 331
Economics
    industrialization, 23–40
    and Philippine annexation,
        77–78
    Jewish difficulties and
        achievements, 86–88, 90,
        92–93, 94–97
    and woman suffrage, 107–108,
        114
    of discrimination against blacks,
        265–266, 272–273
    and the Cold War, 314
Edinburgh, 25
Edison, Thomas, 34, 52
Education
    of Booker T. Washington, 6–11
    ideas on and achievements in, by
        Booker T. Washington, 13–17
    of John Muir, 49–52
    of Emilio Aguinaldo, 71
    in the Philippines, 79–81
    among Jews, 88, 97–98
    and Darwinism, 154–155,
        161–177
    and civil rights, 267–268
    for children of migrant laborers,
        293
    of Colin Powell, 305, 309
Egypt, 318
Eighteenth Amendment, 117–118.
    See also Prohibition
Einstein, Albert, 205, 213
Eisenhower, Dwight David,
    247–248, 268, 293, 306, 331
Ellis Island, 86, 92, 93
"El Paso" (Song), 308

Emancipation Proclamation, 5, 9, 261

Emerson, "Gunfighter," 312

Emerson, Ralph Waldo, 51

Endara, Guillermo, 316

England, 30, 73, 75, 76, 112, 113, 114, 117, 124, 159, 232, 233, 318, 320, 330

ENIAC, 331

Enola Gay, the, 204, 205, 210, 211, 213, 216, 218–219, 224

Epstein, Jacob, 96

Escadrille N–124, 136–137

"Essay on Civil Disobedience" (Thoreau), 265

Europe, 59, 66, 85, 124. *See also* individual countries

Executive Order 8802, 261, 306

Ex-slaves, 5–7, 9–10, 14–15, 111

"Eye of the Storm: The General Colin Powell March," 322

FAIRBANKS, DOUGLAS, 98

Fairchild Semiconductor, 331

Fair Employment Practices Commission, 261

Falcons of France (Hall and Nordhoff), 143

Family
  of Booker T. Washington, 3–6
  of Andrew Carnegie, 25–28, 38
  of John Muir, 47–50, 53, 57–58
  of Emilio Aguinaldo, 70–71
  of Mary Antin, 88–91, 94–95
  and woman suffrage, 107–108, 111–112
  and discrimination against women, 108
  of Eleanor Roosevelt, 184–185
  effect of discrimination upon, 272–273
  of Colin Powell, 304–305, 306–307, 309, 322

Fard, Wallace, 261

"Farewell My Own True Love," 9

Farewell to Arms (Hemingway), 126

Farragut, David G., 66

Farrell, Thomas, 205, 206, 207

Faubus, Orval, 268

Federal Steel Company, 34

Federalist Papers, The, 320

Ferdinand, Archduke Franz, 124

Ferebee, Thomas W., 214, 216

Ferguson, Jane, 4–5

Fermi, Enrico, 205, 206

Filipinos, 66, 70, 74, 76, 79–80, 81–82

Film industry, 98

First Amendment, 163–164, 234, 290

Firth of Forth, 25

Fisher, Fred, 251–252

Fitzgerald, F. Scott, 153

509th Composite Bomb Group
  bombs Hiroshima, 203–220
  training, 208–211
  aftermath of bombing, 220–224

Florida, 54, 154, 157, 158, 163, 316

Forbes, 343–344

Ford, Henry, 52

Fort Benning, 306, 309

Fort Bragg, 306, 307

Fort Campbell, 312

Fort Carson, 312

Fort Leavenworth, 309, 311, 312

Fort Monmouth, 248

Fort San Antonio, 77

Fortune, 344

Fosdick, Harry Emerson, 157

Fountain Lake, 49

Fourteenth Amendment, 163–164, 262

Fox River, 49

France, 72, 75, 86, 124, 126, 129, 142, 159, 223, 232, 253, 318, 320

Franco, Francisco, 244
Frankfurt, Germany, 306
Franklin, Benjamin, 7, 27
Franks, Robert, 160
Freedman's Bureau, 6, 10
Freedom Rides, 269
Free speech movement, 282–292
French and Indian War, 30
French Flying Corps, 128, 129, 142
French Foreign Legion, 126
French Ministry of Foreign Affairs, 129
French Revolution, 143
Fresno, 293
Frick, Henry Clay, 33, 36–37
Fuchs, Klaus, 232
Fulton, Mo., 232
Fundamentalism, 154, 164, 168, 169, 179
Funstan, Frederick, 81

GALLAGHER, RAY, 222
Garland, Hamlin, 36
Garvey, Marcus, 260–261
Gates, Bill, 332, 334
Genet, Edmund, 143–145
George Washington University, 311–312
Georgia, 129, 269, 306, 309
German Jews, 87, 97
Germany, 72, 75–76, 86, 87, 91, 116, 124, 125, 142–143, 156, 159, 204, 205, 210, 212, 223, 231–232, 306, 313, 314, 315, 330
Ginsburg, Isidore, 241
Glanost, 314
Glasgow, 25, 48
Glaspie, April, 318
God, 47, 51, 53, 55, 58, 110, 153–154, 158, 161, 162, 166, 167, 168, 169, 171, 173, 175, 231, 272, 307, 310
Gold, Harry, 232

Gold, Sally, 119
Goldberg, Art, 289
Goldwater, Barry, 285
Goldwyn, Samuel, 98
Gompers, Samuel, 79, 80
Gone with the Wind, 18
Gorbachev, Mikhail, 314–315
"Gospel of Wealth" (Carnegie), 33
Government
    in Reconstruction, 10–11
    and civil rights, 18–19, 260, 262, 267–269, 274–275
    and conservation, 58–60
    of the Philippines under Spain, 70–73
    of the Philippines under the United States, 79, 81–82
    and woman suffrage, 105–120
    and Darwinism, 153–155, 176–177
Government Operations Committee, 247
Grand Chute, Wis., 235
Grant, Madison, 100
Great Artiste, the, 204, 207, 214, 219, 221
Great Britain, 86. *See also* England
Great Central Valley, the, 46, 54
Great Depression, the, 152, 192–195
Great Flood, the, 51, 171
Great Lakes, 33, 49
"Great Monkey Trial." *See* Scopes Trial
Great War, the (World War I), 124–147, 152, 168, 187
Greece, 87, 233
Greensboro, N.C., 268
Greenway, H. D. S., 317
Grinnell College, 249
Gros, Edmund L., 129
Groves, Leslie R., 206
Guadalcanal Diary, 305
Gulf of Mexico, 46, 53

Gulf War, 306, 316, 319–321, 322
"Gulf War Syndrome," 320–321

HACHIYA, MICHIHIKO, 216,
    217–218, 220
Hague, the, 38
Hale's Ford, 3
Hall, James Norman
    flight training, 130–136
    combat duty, 140–143
    shot down over Germany,
        142–143
Hampton Institute, 7–9
Hanford, Wash., 206, 209
Hare Krishna, 328
Harriman, Edward H., 60
Harvard University, 51, 57, 128,
    206, 249, 260, 291, 330, 332
Havana, 67
Hawaii, 209
Hay, John, 74
Hebrew Immigrant Aid Society
    (HIAS), 92
"He Kept Us Out of War," 116
Hemingway, Ernest, 126
Henry Street Settlement
    House, 117
Hester Street, 96, 101
Hetch Hetchy, 59–60
Hickok, Lorena, 189–193
Hicks, Sue K., 155, 163
High Adventure (Nordhoff),
    130, 141
"Highway of Death," 319–320
Himalayas, the, 59
Hiroshima, 203–224
Hertzfeld, Andy, 339, 340
Hewlett Packard, 335, 337
Hiss, Alger, 234
Hitler, Adolph, 205, 231, 251, 310
Hobart, Garret A., 80
Ho Chi Minh, 232, 255
Ho Chi Minh Trail, 307
Hoff, Ted, 332

Hoffman, Abbie, 292
Hollerith, Herman, 329
Hollywood, 101, 247
Homebrew Club, 334, 335
Homestead Works, 33, 36
Hong Kong, 67, 73, 74
Hoover, J. Edgar, 243, 246
Hopkins, Harry, 192
House Un-American Activities
    Committee, 234, 243–244,
    247, 283
Howell, Clark, 17
Howells, William Dean, 79, 86
Humboldt, Alexander von, 52
Hungary, 232
Hunter, George, 166
Huron, S.D., 243
Hussein, Saddam, 316–317, 318,
    319, 320
Hyde Park, 188

"I HAVE A DREAM" (KING), 275
Ickes, Harold, 194
Idaho, 113
Illinois, 108, 155, 157
Immigration, 14, 25
    of Russian Jews, 86–87,
        89–93, 95
    opposition to, 100–101, 153
Immigration Restriction League,
    100
Indiana, 46, 52, 53, 70
Indianapolis, 52
Indianapolis, the, 205, 211
*Influence of Sea Power upon
    History, The* (Mahan), 67
Intel, 332, 333, 336, 346
Intermediate-Range Nuclear Force
    Missiles (INF), 314, 315
International Business Machines
    Corporation (IBM), 329,
    338–339
Interstate Commerce Commission
    (ICC), 108, 269

Iowa, 111, 249
iPod, 346
Iran, 316, 317, 318, 320
Iraq, 316–321
Ireland, 86, 235
Irish-Americans, 100
"Iron Curtain," 232, 306
Islam, 167, 261, 319, 320
Israel, 319, 321
Isthmus of Panama, 54
Italy, 72, 86, 341
Iwo Jima, 211–212, 213, 221

JACKSON, ANDREW, 69
Jackson, Henry, 245, 250
Jamaica, 304
Japan, 66, 75, 204–205, 211–218,
    221–224, 231
Japanese-Americans, 100
J. Edgar Thomson Works, 30–31
Jay, John, 137
Jefferson, Thomas, 119, 156
Jenner, William, 230
Jeppson, Morris, 205, 207
Jessup, Philip C., 244
*Jewish Daily Forwar*d, 97
Jews, 85–101, 319. *See also*
    German Jews; Russian Jews
Jim crow laws, 2, 17, 78, 259
Jobs for Negroes, 261
Jobs, Steve, 332
    Stanford Commencement
        Address, 328–329, 341, 345,
        347–348
    youth, 328
    education, 328–329, 334
    early career and founding Apple,
        334–341
    working with Next and Pixar,
        341–345
    returns to Apple and introduces
        the iPod, 345–349
John Muir Trail, 47
Johnson, Lyndon B., 275, 309

Johnson, Robert Underwood, 58
Jones, "General" Rosalie, 106, 107
Jones, John, 9
Jones, William R., 31, 35–36
Jordan, 318
"Just Cause," 316

KAMIKAZIS, 212
Kanawah Valley, 6, 7, 11
Kansas, 81, 109, 113, 262, 309,
    312, 313, 317
Katipunan, the, 72
Kawit, 70, 71, 72
Keller, Helen, 107
Kelly, John H., 317
Kennedy, John F., 198, 274
Kennedy, John, Jr., 133
Kennedy, Robert, 269, 275, 294
Kent State University, 299
Kentucky, 53, 312
Kenyon, Dorothy, 244
Kerr, Clark
    liberalism of, 282–284, 299
    response to free speech
        movement, 288–289, 299
    warnings about the
        "multiversity," 291
Keystone Bridge Company, 29
Khomeini, Ayatollah, 317
Kilby, Jack, 331
King, Coretta, 266
King, Martin Luther, Jr., 198, 298,
    307, 309–310
    in Birmingham, 258, 270–275
    in Montgomery, 265–268
    in other civil rights activities,
        269
    writes "Letter from Birmingham
        Jail," 272–274
Kipling, Rudyard, 78
Kitty Hawk, N.C., 125
Kokura, 214, 221–222
Koran, 320
Korea, 305, 312, 321

Korean War, 246, 305
Ku Klux Klan (KKK), 153, 169
Kuwait, 316, 317, 318, 319–320
Ky, Nguyen Cao, 310

LA CAUSA, 293–294
La Havre, 128
Lafayette Escadrille
   formed, 128–129
   training on the ground, 129–130
   training flights, 131–136
   combat duty, 136–146
   legacy, 146–147
Lafayette Flying Corps, 137
Lafayette, Marquis de, 137
La Follette, Robert M., Jr., 239
Lake Erie, 33
"La Paloma," 75
Lapham, Increase A., 54
Lapu-Lapu, 52
Lassater, John, 343
Lattimore, Owen, 244
League of Women Shoppers, 244
League of Women Voters, 119, 265
Lebanon, 313, 321
LeMay, Curtis, 209–210
Leopold-Loeb case, 152, 160
Leopold, Nathan, 160
"Letter from Birmingham Jail"
    (King), 272–274
Lewis, Isaac N., 127
Lewis, Robert A., 207, 210, 216
Liberia, 314
Libya, 315
Lilienthal, David E., 240–241
Lincoln, Abraham, 4–5, 195, 274
Lincoln Memorial, 195
Lindbergh, Charles, 152, 169
Lippmann, Walter, 97
Lisa, 339
Lisitzky, Ephraim, 95–96
"Little Brown Brothers"
    (Kipling), 78
Little Rock, 268

Little Rock High School, 268
Lodge, Henry Cabot, 67, 77–78
Loeb, Richard, 160
Long, John D., 67
London, Jack, 314
Lord's Prayer, 99
Los Alamos, 206, 209
Los Angeles, 93, 115, 163
Louis, Joe, 261–262
Louisiana, 10
Lowe, Caroline A., 112–113
Lower East Side, 87, 93, 96, 97–98,
    100, 117
Loyalty Review Board, 233
Lucas, George, 342–343
Lucy, Autherine, 268
Lufbery, Raoul, 138, 145–146
Lusitania, the, 156
Luxeuil-les-Baines, 137
Luxo, Jr., 343
Luzon, 68, 74, 76, 81

MACINTOSH, 339–341, 345
Mackie, Mary F., 8
Macy's, 97
Madison, Wis., 50
Magellan, Ferdinand, 70
Mahan, Alfred Thayer, 66–67
Maine, the, 67
Malcolm X (Malcolm Little), 262
Malden, W. Va., 6, 10, 11
Malone, Dudley Field, 116, 163,
    167–170, 177
Managua, 350, 352
Manhattan Project, 206, 208, 213
Manila, 67, 68, 69, 70, 72, 73, 74,
    75, 76–77, 101
Manila Bay, 65
   Battle of, 67–70, 74–75
Man Nobody Knows, The (Barton),
    152
Mao Tse-tung, 232
Mark I, 330
Marne, Battle of the, 125–126

Marne River, 124, 127
Marquette University
    (Wis.), 236
Marshall, George C., 245–247
Marshall Plan, 233
Marshall, Thurgood, 262
Marx, Karl, 230
Maryland, 244
Massachusetts, 128, 306
Massachusetts Institute of
    Technology, 55
"Massive Retaliation," 306
Masuoka, Naoko, 215–216, 218
Mauchly, John W., 331
Mayer, Louis B., 98
McCargo, David, 34
McCarren International Security
    Act, 233–234
McCarthy, Eugene, 298
McCarthy, Joseph, 230
    childhood, 235–236
    education, 236
    early career in law, 236–237
    in the Marines, 237–238
    wins Senate seat, 240
    in the Senate, 240–253
    and the Malmédy hearings,
        241–242
    alleges communists in
        government, 242–248
    and the Korean War, 246
    and the elections of 1952, 247
    and the Army-McCarthy
        hearings, 248–252
    decline, 252–253
McCarthy, Timothy, 235
McCoy, Arie, 304
McEnery Resolution, 80
McKinley, William, 66, 76, 78–79
McMurray, Howard, 240
McNamara, Robert S., 296–297
Meadowbrook Country Club, 184
Meat Inspection Act of 1906, 108
Mediterranean Sea, 66, 313

Mekong Delta, 296
Mellon, Andrew, 34
Memphis, Tenn., 275, 310
Mencken, H. L., 162
Merced River, 54
Meredith, James, 268, 274
Merritt, Wesley, 76
Mesabi Range, 33
Methodists, 13, 78, 162, 164, 175
Mexican Americans, 293–294
Miami, 157
Michigan, 30, 52, 262
    University of, 159
Micro Instrumentation Telemetry
        Systems (MITS), 332, 336
Microsoft, 329
Middle East, 317, 318
Middle Passage, the, 3
Milholland, Inez, 106–107, 115
Mindanao, 70
Minnesota, 33, 86
Mississippi, 68, 112, 285
    University of, 268, 274
Mississippi River, 23, 29, 49,
        52, 68
Mississippi, the, 66
Missouri, 112, 234
Missouri River, 29
Mitchell, Billy, 146
Mitchell, George, 319
Modernism, 154, 161, 169. *See
        also* Scopes Trial
Mogadishu, Somalia, 321
Monongahela River, 25, 33
Montgomery, Ala., 262–267,
        268–269, 274
Montgomery Improvement
        Association, 266
Montojo, Admiral, 69, 75
Morehouse College, 265
Morgan, J. P., 33–34, 38
Morse, Wayne, 298
Moscow, 88, 90
Motion-picture industry, 98

Motorola, 349
Mount Rainier, 58
Muhammad, Elijah (Elijah Poole), 261
Muir, Ann, 50
Muir, Annie, 57
Muir, Daniel, 48–50, 53
Muir, Helen, 60
Muir, John, 45, 101
   assessment of his career, 46–47, 60–61
   boyhood of, 46–50
   at college, 50–52
   in business, 52–53, 57
   wilderness journeys of, 52–61
   marriage, 57
   conservation activities of, 58–60
Muir, Sarah, 49
Muir Woods, 47
Mundt, Karl, 248
Munich Olympics, 313
Muslims, 319
   Shiites, 313, 320
   Kurds, 317, 320
   Sunni, 320
Mussolini, Benito, 205
Mutiny on the Bounty (Nordhoff), 130
My American Journey (Powell), 304
My Lai, 311
Mystery of Life, The (Darrow), 176

NAGASAKI, 67, 214, 222–223
National American Woman Suffrage Association (NAWSA), 106, 111–112, 114–115, 117, 119
National Association for the Advancement of Colored People (NAACP), 18, 114, 260, 262, 269, 270
National Farm Workers Association, 293

National Forest Commission, 58
National Men's League for Woman Suffrage, 107
National Origins Act of 1924, 100
National Woman's Party, 115–116, 119
National Woman Suffrage Association, 109–111
Native Americans, 2, 46, 101
Naval Academy, 66
Nebraska, 155, 156, 158
Nelson, Richard, 208, 216
Neuilly, France, 143
New Bedford, Mass., 8
New Deal, 192, 194, 231, 233, 234, 299
New England, 112, 154
New Jersey, 156
New Jersey, the, 313
New Mexico, 206
New Orleans, 68, 69
New Republic, The, 115
New South, the, 2
New World, 85
New York, 49, 106, 113, 117, 119, 348–349
New York City, 25, 86, 87, 92–101, 113, 117, 119, 162, 188, 198, 260, 321
New York, City University of, 305
New York Times, 106, 124, 284, 286
Next, 342
Niagara Falls, 260
Niagara Movement, 18, 260
Nicaragua, 315
Nineteenth Amendment (Susan B. Anthony Amendment), 114, 116, 117, 122. *See also* Woman suffrage
Nixon, E. D., 265
Nixon, Richard, 234, 246, 283, 301
Nixon, Tom, 47

"Nobody Knows the Trouble I've Seen," 9
"No Irish Need Apply," 100
Nordhoff, Charles, 130, 143
Noriega, Manuel, 315–316
Normandy, 232, 310
Norris, J. Frank, 159
North Atlantic Treaty Organization (NATO), 233, 318
North Carolina, 125, 268, 306
North Sea, 126
North, the, 4, 13, 17, 259, 276
North Vietnam, *See* Vietnam
Noyce, Robert, 331
Number 91, the, 204, 214

OAKLAND, CALIFORNIA, 55–56, 297
Oak Ridge, 206, 209
Oates, William C., 17
Oberndorf-am-Neckar, 139
Ohio, 159, 299
Ohio River, 26, 30
Okinawa, 212, 222
Oklahoma, 154
Old Glory, 146
Oliver, Henry W., 34
Olympia, the, 67, 73
Omaha, 29, 79
103rd Aero Pursuit Squadron, 145
Ontario, 52
On the Origin of the Species, (Darwin), 35, 153
"Operation Restore Hope in Somalia," 321
Oppenheimer, J. Robert, 206, 207
Oregon, 6, 113, 337
O'Reilly Telegraph Company, 27
Osgood, Smith, and Company, 52
Otrona, 338
Our National Parks, (Muir), 59

PACHECO PASS, 54
Pacific Northwest, the, 57
Pacific Ocean, 67, 204, 209, 211

Page, Walter Hines, 59
Pake, George, 340
Pale of Settlement, 87–90
Palmer, A. Mitchell, 231
Panama, 315–316
Pankhurst, Emmeline, 113
Paris, 78, 124, 125, 132, 136
Parks, Rosa, 263–264, 266
Parsons, William S., 204–205, 207, 208, 210, 214, 219
Passing of the Great Race, The (Grant), 100
Paul, Alice, 113–114, 115, 116, 117, 119, 120
PDP-10, 332
Pearl Harbor, 203, 211, 223, 237
Penguins, 130, 131
Pennsylvania, 25, 86, 249
    University of, 113, 331
Pennsylvania Railroad, 28–29
Pentagon, 312, 313, 315
Perestroika, 314
"Pershing Rifles," 305
Perot, Ross, 342
Petrified Forest, 59
Philadelphia, 7, 29, 88
Philippines, 38, 67, 68, 70
    during Dewey's blockade of Manila, 69–77
    under Spanish rule, 70–76
    during American control, 76–77, 80–81
    debate over annexation, 77–80
Piccolo, Brian, 312
Pinchot, Gifford, 58–59
Pinkerton's National Detective Agency, 37
Pittsburgh, 25–27, 29, 30
Pixar, 342–343, 346
Platt, E. Spencer, 73
Plessy v. Ferguson, 260
"Plucky Class, The," 11
Pogroms, 89
Poland, 86, 87, 232, 315

Pong, 334
Popular Mechanics, 332
Pork Chop Hill, 305
Portage, Wis., 49, 50
Potsdam Conference, 213, 221
Powell, Adam Clayton, 261
Powell, Alma Johnson, 304, 306,
    307, 310, 313, 322
Powell, Colin
    family of, 304–305, 306, 307,
        310, 313, 322
    childhood, 304–305
    early military career, 305–307
    and Racial Prejudice, 306, 307,
        312, 314, 315
    in Vietnam, 307–311
    in Korea, 312
    and the Cold War, 313–315
    and Panama, 315–316
    and Iraq, 317–321
    retirement, 322
    as secretary of state, 323
Powell Doctrine, 322
Powell, Luther, 304
Prejudice. *See* Racial prejudice
Prendergast, Robert, 159
Presbyterianism, 157, 159, 162
Prince, Norman, 128, 129, 137,
    139–140
Princeton, 38, 129
Progressivism, 108, 112, 119
Prohibition, 79, 107–108, 153,
    157, 169
Promised Land, The (Antin),
    88, 97
Puerto Rico, 78, 79
Pullman boycott, 159
Pullman cars, 29
Punji stake, 308
Pure Food and Drug Act,
    The, 108
Puritans, 85, 86, 89, 96, 97, 151

Quakers, 109, 113

Racial Prejudice, 100–101
    against blacks, 2–3, 7–11, 16, 17,
        18–19, 112, 114, 195,
        258–276, 306, 307, 312,
        314, 315
    of Americans and Spaniards
        against Filipinos, 71–72, 76,
        79–80, 81
Rappelyea, George, 154, 155, 161
Raulston, John T., 161, 168, 170,
    171, 174
Reagan, Ronald, 313, 314, 316
Reber, Miles, 250
Reconstruction, 10, 12
Red scare, 247. *See also*
    Anticommunism; McCarthy,
    Joseph
Reed College, 328, 334
Religion. *See also* Christianity;
    Islam; Jews
    of Andrew Carnegie, 37–38
    and geology, 51
    of John Muir, 53–54, 57
    in the Philippines, 70, 71, 78
    Jewish beliefs and customs,
        87–88, 98–99
    and Darwinism, 156–177
    in the Civil Rights movement,
        265–267, 272, 273–274
Republican party, 239, 243, 244,
    247
Reserve Officers Training Corps
    (ROTC), 305, 306, 315, 322
Richmond, Va., 7, 86
Rickenbacker, Eddie, 146
Rizal Jóse, 72–73
Roaring Twenties, the, 152
Roberts, Ed, 332–333, 334
Robinson's drugstore, 154–155, 163
Rochambeau, the, 128
Rockefeller, John D., 34
Rockwell, Kiffin, 137–138, 143
Rocky Mountains, 57
Romania, 232

Romorantin, 132, 133, 134
Roosevelt, Cornelius, 184
Roosevelt, Eleanor
 and the Great Depression, 181,
  184–185, 191–195
 her compassion, 181, 183, 188,
  192–196, 198–199
 and Franklin, 182–183, 186–189,
  192, 196
 as a career woman, 183,
  188–189
 childhood, 184–185
 adolescence, 185–186
 as a young bride, 186–188
 and Lorena Hickok, 189–193
 as first lady, 189–196
 her later years, 196–199
Roosevelt, Elliot, 184–185
Roosevelt, Franklin Delano,
  182–183, 186–189,
  192, 205–206, 230, 231, 233,
  236, 261
Roosevelt, Sara, 187
Roosevelt, Theodore, 59, 67, 69,
  101, 108, 184–185
Rosario, Hilaria del, 71
Rosenberg, Julius and Ethel, 232
Roth, Henry, 96
Ruffner, Lewis, 7
Ruffner, Viola, 7
Russia, 86–90, 91, 93, 95, 117,
  124, 212, 222, 223, 231–232,
  239, 241, 306, 308, 312, 314,
  315, 318
Russian Jews, 85, 86
 in Russia, 87–91
 in America, 91–101
Ruth, Babe, 152

SABBATH, THE, 89, 94–95
Saigon, 307, 309
St. Louis, 29
Sakamoto, Setsuko, 216, 218
Sal Si Puedes, 293

San Francisco, 47, 54, 56, 60, 86,
  207, 283, 285, 292
Sarajevo, Serbia, 124, 321
Saudi Arabia, 318, 319
Savio, Mario
 background, 284
 leads free speech movement,
  285, 286–292
 describes Civil Rights
  background, 290
 goes to prison, 294
 Ronald Reagan opposes his
  readmission to Berkeley, 295
 travels across country for student
  rights, 296
 returns to his studies, 299
Schenck v. United States, 234
Schine, G. David, 248, 249,
  250, 251
Schwab, Charles M., 31, 33
Schwarzkopf, Norman, 319,
  320, 321
Scopes, John Thomas, 152,
  154–155, 162, 163, 166, 174
Scopes Trial, 154–179
 background, 152, 162–164
 significance, 152, 176–177
Scotland, 25, 26, 47–48
Scott's Run, W. Va., 192–194
Scott, Thomas, 28, 29
Scripture, 48, 51, 95, 153. *See also*
  Bible, the
Sculley, John, 341, 341, 348–349
Sea Islands, 10
Sears, Roebuck, 97
Seeger, Alan, 126
Segregation, 258–260, 261–268,
  269–271, 272–273
Senate Internal Security
  Subcommittee, 247
Seneca Falls Convention, 109, 118
Sentinel Rock, 55
Sequoia National Park, 47
Serbs, 321

Shakespeare, William, 27, 35
Shanghai, 67
Shaw, Anna Howard, 106, 111
Shaw, Pauline Agassiz, 111–112
Shawano, Wis., 236
Sherman, William Tecumseh, 2, 6
Shuttleworth, Fred L., 270, 271
Siemes, John A., S. J., 215–216,
    217
Sierra Club, 58
Sierra Nevada, the, 47, 54, 55,
    57, 59
Signal Corps Engineering
    Laboratories, 248
Silicon Valley, 341
Singapore, 73
Sioux, the, 137
Slavery, 1, 3–6, 8–10, 14–15,
    109, 111
Smith Act, 233, 234
Smith, "Hell Roaring Jake," 81
Smith, Margaret Chase, 244
Smith v. Albright, 262
Sobell, Morton, 232
Social Darwinism, 35, 158
Socialism, 230–231
Soda (lion), 137
Soldier's Story, A, 309
Somalia, 321
Somme, Battle of the, 126
Somme River, 127, 140
South Africa, 322
South America, 54, 59
South Carolina, 10, 17
South Dakota, 243
Southern Christian Leadership
    Conference (SCLC), 268,
    269, 270, 272
South Pacific, 208, 237
South, the, 2, 5–6, 10–11, 13,
    14–16, 17, 19, 54, 112, 265,
    267–269, 274–276, 284, 306
Southwest, the, 206
South Vietnam. *See* Vietnam

Souvestre, Marie, 185–186
Soviet Union. *See* Russia
SPA-124, 140
Spaatz, Carl A., 219
SPADs, 140
Spain, 65, 66, 67, 71–73, 76–78,
    79, 80, 81
Spanish-American War, 66–69, 73,
    76–77. *See also* Philippines
Spanish Civil War, 244
Spencer, Herbert, 25, 35
Spitzer, Abe, 207, 210, 214,
    219–220, 223, 224
Sproul Hall, 285–288, 292–293,
    294, 297, 298, 299
Stalin, Joseph, 231–232, 239
Stanford University, 328,
    341, 347
Stanton, Elizabeth Cady, 109–110,
    111, 112, 114
"Star Spangled Banner, The," 3, 304
Star Wars, 342–343
State Department, 243, 244, 245
Statue of Liberty, 92
Stimson, Henry L., 206, 213, 221
Story of My Boyhood and Youth,
    The (Muir), 59
Strentzen, Louie, 57–58
Strong, Edward W., 285–286
Strong, Josiah, 66
Student Nonviolent Coordinating
    Committee (SNCC), 285
Subic Bay, 68, 75, 76
Susan B. Anthony Amendment, the
    (Nineteenth Amendment),
    114, 116, 117–118, 120. *See*
    also Woman suffrage
Sweeney, Charles W., 221–222

Tabulating Machine Company,
    329
Tacoma, 100
Taft-Hartley Act, 234, 240–241
Taft, Robert, 241

Taft, William Howard, 81, 108
Taiwan, 232
Teale, Edwin Way, 46
Tehran, 317
Television, 250–251, 309, 316
Teller amendment, 73, 77
Tennessee, 53, 118, 151, 152, 154, 155, 158, 168, 169, 175, 177, 206, 269, 275
 University of, 154
Tennessee Valley Authority (TVA), 240
Terrorism,
 in West Germany, 313
 in the Middle East, 316–319
Tet Offensive, 309
Texas Instruments, 331
Thalia, the, 98, 101
Thaw, William, 129
Thenault, Georges, 137, 139, 145
"Think Different," 345
Third World Liberation Front, 295
Thirty Seconds Over Tokyo, 305
Thomson, J. Edgar, 28–29. *See also* J. Edgar Thomson Works
Thoreau, Henry David, 28, 47, 65
Thousand-Mile Walk to the Gulf, A (Muir) 53
Tibbets, Paul W., Jr., 204–205, 206, 207, 208, 210, 213, 216, 219
Time, 336
Tinian, 204, 205, 207, 209, 219, 221, 222
Tokyo, 205, 215, 222
Tolman, Edward C., 283
Top Hill, 304
Towe, Joseph B., 9
Toy Story, 344, 349
Triumphant Democracy (Carnegie), 35
Truman, Harry S, 197, 210, 213, 221, 230, 233, 306
Turkey, 232, 319
Tuskegee, 12–13, 17, 19

Tuskegee Institute, 13–18, 38
Twain, Mark, 79, 314
Tydings, Millard, 241, 244–245

UNCONVENTIONAL WARFARE CENTER, 307
Unions, 36–37, 239, 240
United Farmworkers, 293–294
United Fruit Company, 304
United Nations (UN), 238, 318, 322
 UN Resolution, 678, 319, 320
United States Defense Intelligence Agency, 317
United States Steel Company, 31, 34
UNIVAC, 331
Universal Negro Improvement Association, 260
Utah, 113, 208–209

VALLEY FORGE, 310
Vanderbilt, Cornelius, 34
Van Kirk, Theodore, J., 208, 213
Vassar, 115, 196
Velde, Harold R., 247
Verdon, the Battle of, 140
Vermont, 7, 55, 74
Viet Cong, 308, 309
Vietnam, 253, 306, 307
Vietnam War, 282, 296, 307–308, 310–311
 protests against, 296–299
Virginia, 3, 7, 176
VisiCalc, 338
Vocations
 for blacks, 7, 8–9, 10, 13, 15–16, 261–262, 266
 linen manufacture, 25, 26, 27–28
 industrial labor, 25–27, 36
 entrepreneurship, 28, 34–35
 John Muir's choice of, 49–54, 57–60
 of Jews, 90, 92–93, 94–97
 of women, 109

Vocations (*cont.*)
  migrant laborers, 293–294
  Colin Powell's military career,
    312–316, 321–322
Voorhis, H. Jerry, 234
Voting Rights Act, 275

WALD, LILLIAN D., 117
Wallace, George, 307
Wallace, Henry, 240
Wall Street Journal, 344
Warfare. *See also* Vietnam War;
    World War I; World War II
  between Spain and the United
    States, 67–69
  between Spain and the Filipinos,
    72
  between the Filipinos and the
    United States, 80–81
  bombing of Hiroshima and
    Nagasaki, 204–224
Warner Brothers, 98
War of 1812, 66
Washington, Booker T., 45,
    259–260, 265
  and the Atlanta Exposition
    Address, 2–3, 14–17
  early life, 3–7
  education, 6–10
  as an educator, 11–14
Washington, D.C., 12, 67, 73, 76,
    106, 113, 114, 115, 117, 176,
    269, 275, 312, 313, 314, 318,
    319, 321
Washington, George, 143
Washington Monument, 33
Washington Post, 243
Washington (state), 6, 100, 113,
    206
Waverly Novels, 50
Wayne, John, 244
Webster Literary Club, 27
Weinberger, Casper, 313
Welch, Joseph Nye, 249, 251–252

Wendover, 208–209
Werner, Edgar V., 236–237
West Coast Computer Fair, 337
Westinghouse, George, 34
Westminster College, 232
Westmoreland, Jamaica, 304
West Virginia, 6, 7, 10, 11, 235,
    313
Whiskey (lion), 137
White House, 78, 116, 183, 189,
    192, 253, 312, 314, 316, 318
White House Fellow, 312
"White Man's Burden," 78
Whitney, Josiah D., 55
Whole Earth Catalogue, The, 336,
    347
Wilson, Woodrow, 106, 108, 115,
    116–117, 126, 143, 145,
    156, 187
Windows, 329
Winthrop, John, 96
Wired, 340
Wisconsin, 49, 50, 52, 53, 86,
    235–237, 239
  University of, 50–51, 52, 236
Wisconsin River, 49, 52
Woman's Declaration of
    Rights, 110
Woman suffrage
  parade in support of, 106–107
  reason for delay, 107–109
  early movement for, 109–113
  in the twentieth century, 112–120
Women's party. *See* National
    Woman's Party
Women's Political Council, 265
Women's Republican Club, 235
Woodward, Charlotte, 118
World War I, 90, 124–130,
    136–147, 152, 156, 159. *See
    also* Lafayette Escadrille
World War II, 81, 196, 204–224,
    231, 232, 239, 305, 314,
    330–331. *See also* Hiroshima

Woziak, Steve, 332, 335–337, 341, 345, 348
Wright, Orville, 125, 128
Wright, Wilbur, 125, 128
Wyoming, 110, 113

XEROX PARC, 340

YEMEN, 319
Yiddish, 88, 96, 98, 99

Yom Kippur, 99
Yosemite Falls, 46, 54, 60
Yosemite National Park, 58, 59, 101
Yosemite River, 46
Yosemite, The (Muir), 59, 60
Yosemite Valley, 46, 54–55, 59
Young, Andrew, 270
Yuma, 293

ZEPPELIN, 127